UNLOCKING THE FRONT DOOR

Leo L. Nussbaum

A Personal Memoir

From Depression Years on the Farm to College Presidency

KayT Publishing
Long Beach, CA

The cover depicts the author behind the horse team
drawn walking plow, one of the tedious farm tasks
In his youth

Cover illustration by Miriam Garay

ISBN 0-9716565-1-7

Manufactured in the

United States of America

Printed by
A&A Printing, Inc.
6103 Johns Rd., Suite 5-6
Tampa, FL 33634

To My Family

Foreword

Family life on the farm, where I spent my first twenty years, was so different from urban life of the twenty-first century that to our grandchildren it may seem to be medieval history. Possibly no part of the dramatic changes that have occurred during the twentieth century has been greater that what took place in the agricultural sector. Even farmers who lived through these decades have found farming very greatly transformed. For persons of any age who never lived on the farm, descriptions of what occurred in my lifetime may seem like life on another planet.

As our children, Felicity, Luther and Margaret, were growing up, I often told them about incidents that occurred in my childhood. Some were of interest to them, others were dismissed as having no relevance. Yet, over a period of years, the curiosity of each offspring was piqued as they learned about certain events, vignettes, or stories. Approaching middle age they, strongly supported by my wife, Jan, suggested that my boyhood and youth should be recorded for them and their children who would find my life on the farm very odd and perhaps unbelievable.

Beyond farm life itself, was the particular community of recent generation Swiss descendants, and largely of Amish and Mennonite religious extraction that in combination might make my early life seem to them incomprehensible and foreign. Many of my early experiences had caused me in mid-life to want to forget and not reopen some of the most emotionally painful events, such as the financial depression of the 1930s, my struggle for a high school and college education and the disintegration of the church of my youth. But with the urging of my family, and my recognizing that some parts of my earlier life might well be of great interest to them, I decided to begin the writing. Perhaps grandchildren and great-grandchildren in the future would indeed find my life story a curiosity like some pages from medieval history. This prospect was considerably accentuated when, as I undertook the task. I realized how little my parents and grandparents left

1

as records of their eras and generations. Despite some half-dozen sketchy family records that were published, we have very little about the human interest and intimate lives of our relatives and ancestors. Had our parents and grandparents written their autobiographies how historically fascinating, significant and valuable some of those memoirs would have been to our generation.

In the early stages of my writing, I found myself reluctant to want to expend so much time and energy looking backward, rather than looking ahead and planning for the future to which most of my life had been devoted. After digging into the past layer by layer, I began to realize the cathartic, if not therapeutic, value of recalling and looking back into distant times and places I had once experienced.

I was the oldest of seven sons, no daughters, followed in sequence by Elmer, Alvin, Milo, Reuben, Victor and Carl spaced between 1918 and 1930. In the spring of 1920 my parents and I moved from my father's family home to the farm four miles north of Berne, Indiana, a move of two and a half miles. This remained the family home for more than 30 years. Later, the farm was purchased by Reuben and his wife, Estella, for their family on which they reared six children. Recently Reuben and Estella sold 70 acres to their son, Denver and his wife, Jane, on which they built a family home, but retained five acres that contain the original buildings. Among the predominantly Swiss immigrants from the German sector family roots were deep. Beginning in about 1840 they moved to the community of Berne and surrounding area. All four of my grandparents and most aunts and uncles lived within a radius of four miles. A majority of the Swiss community was of the Mennonite, Amish or Reformed Church faith. People of my generation are largely third or fourth generation Americans.

Writing my memoirs took on added meaning when I contrasted my life with Jan's. When we were married in 1942, except for time in college, I had lived all but my first year and a half in one farm home near Berne, Indiana. She had lived in Idaho, where she was born, Washington, Montana, Nebraska, Iowa and Ohio, having moved more times than she can

2

confidently recall. In some states she lived in more than one location. Together, we lived in Virginia, Indiana, Illinois, Iowa, Texas, Florida and India. My life had deep roots and many connections in one community; Jan's roots were shallow and transitory. Such contrasts and their effects could be examined by future generations with astonishment and curiosity.

I was reared in a home that had several German Bibles and only a half dozen other books without access to a library. My religious upbringing was in a small rural church congregation that had split from the Old Order Amish and adopted the name Amish Christian. I graduated from the eighth grade at the Amish Christian Parochial School when that was the maximum education permitted. The Church disintegrated at a propitious point in my life that enabled me to continue my education. I dreamed then of becoming a teacher in grade school. Later in my life doors opened and I earned a Doctor of Philosophy degree at Northwestern University. On my retirement, I was named President Emeritus of Coe College, Cedar Rapids, Iowa.

I hope that readers will find these memoirs interesting and informative. Because so much of the early source material depended on my memory, I apologize for errors of fact or inaccuracies of interpretation. In retrospect, I wish I had kept more written accounts of events as they occurred. Hopefully, this will prompt some readers to do so.

Acknowledgments

In assembling a life history, I had to gather information from many sources including several layers of my memory. Several published family records were very helpful, particularly in determining when certain events occurred. To list them all would be very complicated. The one that served most often as a reference was authored by my mother's brother, D. D. Mazelin, *The Mazelins in America: 1840-1940*. Two other family histories served as frequent references: *A Short History and Records of the Nussbaum Family* compiled by Sylvan L. Nussbaum and *The Lengacher-Steury Family History* by Joseph Stoll. Other sources included family histories, catalogs and other publications by colleges with which I was identified, unpublished family records, and legal documents such as certificates of birth, marriage and death.

Two persons who devoted countless hours to this treatise stand out. First our daughter, Felicity A. Nussbaum, Professor of English and Women's Studies at the University of California at Los Angeles to whom I owe a huge debt for editing, professional counsel, and encouragement. The other person is Frank J. Corbett, former Professor of Social Work and Director of the Department of Urban Affairs at The State University of New York at Buffalo, who labored relentlessly on grammar, punctuation, capitalization, sentence structure and style.

I owe special thanks to our son, Luther J. Nussbaum, Chairman and CEO, First Consulting Group, Long Beach, California, for engaging an artist and providing the front and back covers. He read drafts and made helpful observations about events that occurred during his memory.

My loving wife, Jan, former teacher of English writing and literature, fervently encouraged me and regularly read draft pages adding many helpful comments and suggestions. Our other daughter, Margaret S. Cooley, read drafts and responded with observations concerning events that occurred within her memory. Credit for the title of the book goes to, Margaret's husband, Guy Cooley.

Numerous other persons provided perspectives, insights,

and comments. From my five brothers I received suggestions. I was also reminded how the three younger ones perceived the family as if they had grown up in a different household. Milo, a sounding board, found some errors that were corrected; Reuben, in zealous pursuit of authenticity, found legal documents that were essential and Carl offered occasional commentary.

Of special importance to me was a good friend, Heinz Gasser, with whom I have common Swiss roots. He assembled my new computer and patiently nurtured me in overcoming my aversion to its uncompromising character. In reading the draft chapters, we discovered intersecting early life experiences that for many months generated mutually rewarding conversations. To him I owe a large debt for his skilled services.

To many other persons who read drafts, some with helpful comments and corrections, I owe a word of thanks. If there are errors of fact or misinterpretations, I apologize. I alone have to assume responsibility.

Chapter 1: The Locked Front Door

Our farm home was a two-story square house with beveled white siding, a four-way shingled roof and a red brick chimney at the point where the angles of the roof were joined. When we moved there in the winter of 1920, its windows were all wood frames and sash with a large single pane up and a symmetrical single pane down each with a pair of sash cords and hidden iron weights. There were no built-in fly and mosquito screens and no storm windows to guard frigid wintry winds. The inside walls were made of wood lathe covered with plaster; under the out-siding was a thin layer of paper next to the shiplap boards with no insulation around the windows, in the walls between the studs, or in the attic.

The first floor consisted of a kitchen with a pantry, dining room, living room and our parents' bedroom without a closet. Their bedroom was crowded with their double bed, a dresser, a three-quarter-size double bed for two boys and when number three was born, also a baby bed. When child number four was born two oldest moved upstairs. Upstairs were four rooms, each with a closet. Yellow pine floors throughout the home, with some wear, yielded splinters when swept with a broom. Paint was too costly for the walls of these less used rooms so for years Mother used a broad brush to apply a mixture of lime and water. Annually, she washed the painted walls and ceilings and re-limed the non-washable rooms. There was no other permanent floor covering, no built-in cabinets or cupboards, no running water, hot or cold. Downstairs, walls and ceilings were painted with a semi-gloss paint. Upstairs rooms were assigned for boys' bedrooms as needed. The fourth room always served as storage for dried fruit and vegetables, beef and pork in various cuts sealed in lard contained in crocks of one, three or five gallon size. Each bedroom was furnished with double bed and dresser. In place of a mattress we slept on feather filled pillows and a cloth bag filled with dusty cornhusks supported by a flat spring. During my army days tests revealed that I was allergic to dust and feathers. Furthermore, dust of soybean hay and rust on oats

6

sheaves generated severe allergic reactions. I finally realized why I so often seemed to have a cold, no doubt another factor in my dislike of farming.

There was no indoor toilet or bathroom; seven boys and parents in turn took baths in a wooden wash tub on Saturday night to be clean for church on Sunday morning. We carried all necessary water into the house. Soft water for cooking, dishwashing and personal use came from the cistern adjacent to the house. We carried drinking water, called hard water, in buckets from the central well next to the barn several hundred feet away. Dishes were washed in a tin or aluminum dishpan. Enameled metal bowls served in lieu of lavatories for scrubbing hands and faces. On the kitchen cabinet stood two buckets of hard and soft water. Water was heated in teakettles and in the five-gallon tank at one end of the kitchen stove fired with wood or coal. Under the house a full cellar contained three rooms; one room held the coal or wood for cooking and heating; later a woodshed provided space for the fuel. One room was used for storage of potatoes, apples, cabbage, carrots, red beets and turnips. There was no refrigeration in the house; the coolest place was the cellar. The cellar stairway, with outside entrance halfway up, made a right turn to the kitchen. The cellar was also a place for occasional bare-bottom spankings by Dad with switches cut from fruit trees.

Cellar walls consisted of rows of concrete block; and a concrete floor with drain. The unfinished ceiling exposed two-by-ten inch wood beams. During heavy rains, the cellar occasionally flooded with inches of grime-laden water backed up from the drain with a malfunctioning trap. A one-cylinder gasoline engine separately powered the wood-tub washing machine and clothes ringer. Water boiled on the kitchen stove, was carried down the steps as were all the clothes for the family of nine persons who lived here (there was no clothes chute). In turn the clothes when washed and wrung were carried up the landing at the right angle turn in the stairs out the door. Clothes were hung with clothespins to dry on the outdoor clothesline on the opposite side of the house during all seasons. Add the ironing and patching to the routine three meals which comprised my mother's eighteen-hour Monday toil for her large family. On a rainy Monday, clothes were hung on wires in the cellar, on chair backs in the kitchen and dining room--a tedious, wearying job.

In this large basement room were stored canned cider, canned vegetables and fruit, wine bottles, jugs and kegs, eggs to be sorted, encased and sold weekly. Because the temperature there was the lowest in the house it served as the storage place for milk, butter and any leftover food to be saved for another meal. It also contained an old incubator which for several years was used to hatch chicks from fertilized eggs gathered in our own henhouse which contained perhaps 350 Leghorn hens and one rooster for every 12 chickens. As commercial hatcheries provided chicks this machine became obsolete; then it served for many years as a storage table for anything without another assigned space.

There was no electricity for some fifteen years of my life. We did all night work by kerosene lamps, or on occasion, when a brighter gasoline lamp could be made to function, in the all-purpose dining room. Lacking central heating, our home had one black stove in the dining room which served that room, some heat for the kitchen to supplement the kitchen stove and a little heat seeped through a register in the ceiling to the bedroom above. During the depression years, we often could not afford enough good quality coal to enable the stoves to function at their best, and good dry wood was not available on our farm with no wooded area. November through March we all wore long arm and leg wool and cotton combination underwear. In bed, we were covered with one or two blankets and heavy wool comforters. On the coldest nights 15 below zero, even the urine froze in the pots under the beds. Oh to be in school where steam furnace heat kept us warm!

The wood shingles on the roof were weathered and tinder-dry. On occasion embers from wood- stove fires among our neighbors' houses set a roof aflame. With no modern fire fighting equipment available, in a short time the home was totally destroyed. Such a frightful sight generated some youthful nightmares.

The front of the house facing the road had a long porch, at a level requiring four steps up. Three circular wooden pillars supported the porch roof. Here was the front door; however, this door was always locked and never used as an entrance or exit. The family, visitors and guests, all entered our home through the back door which faced the barn, silo and other outbuildings, chicken house, hog house, garage, (or earlier the buggy shed) granary, corn storage bins, and tool shed. The garden and lawn were enclosed with a gated four-foot wire fence. The path to the cistern for soft water also was on the path to the well for drinking water. Sidewalks led to two gates: one to the gravel driveway leading to the road in one direction and to the barn and outbuildings in the other direction. The gate on the opposite side opened to the two-person privy (a small wooden outhouse, two holes for sitting with an old Sears Roebuck catalog for toilet paper) which adjoined the garden, the orchard and the woodshed. The back door of our home had a smaller porch with two carved pillars and also had four steps. Although there was also an inside door between the back porch and the dining room, it was rarely opened and almost never used except for ventilation during hot summer days. The two back entrance doors had wooden screen doors but the front door had none.

Since the front door was always locked, during spring house-cleaning it was hard to open. Symbolically, the locked front door kept out the evils of the world, including layers of dust from the gravel road some forty feet away. We turned our backs to the world; there was no sidewalk to the front porch, no gate from the lawn to the road. The front offered neither entrance nor exit, not even a path worn on the grass. To communicate with the world was circuitous; a daily trip to the mailbox meant going out the back door, walking to the gravel drive leading to the road. The heavy or frequent pedestrian traffic was not to explore the world or to leave home. The heavy traffic was between the manual labor of the livestock, the fields, and the farmhouse to which one repaired for food and rest, eating, sleeping and for confirmation of simple truth and moral principles. The essence of living had to do with work, grinding, unending work seven days a week. Whatever escapes from work we found were not in commercial entertainment but in farm-invented recreation or in church. As a family, we never ate a meal in a restaurant; never attended a movie, theater, or orchestra, never took a trip, never attended an athletic contest, or sports event connected with school, never saw a circus, a zoo, or a carnival, and never took a vacation. The locked front door was symbolic; no one ever told me what it meant, but in retrospect all of life was turned to make the front door unnecessary. The front door's large glass pane was frosted, non-transparent, with an etched design; the back door pane was of clear glass. Even that contrast seems symbolic.

In these respects our home was perfectly typical of that Swiss-German community. We often visited the home of my mother's parent's two miles away. We always entered the house through the kitchen into the large dining room, which served as the casual visiting room. The large living room also served as the bedroom for my grandparents.

We had no guests in social terms. Social intercourse was part of the farm work with neighbors helping each other in threshing, silo-filling, butchering, cooking apple butter, harvesting corn, wheat, oats or soybeans. Or the visit was church-related such as summer catechism classes or a Sunday afternoon call on relatives. Mom and Dad were not socially inclined; there was neither time nor energy and socializing had a very low priority. They did not have close friends. There were no doorbells. One knocked with one's fingers or fist. Our back door was rarely locked; sometimes the only key we had was lost. On occasion we might replace the lost key with a skeleton key bought at the five and ten cent store. We trusted our neighbors; theft was almost unheard of. I cannot remember that we ever had anything stolen.

The closed front door, symbolic in itself, was an index to much broader exclusion from the world. When we moved there, we had no telephone, electrical power, or radio. Television was not yet invented. World news and advertising did not invade the home as now. The local newspaper contained very little advertising; it was delivered by U. S. mail three times a week from Berne, four miles away. It was titled the *Adams County Witness* or later, a competitor, *The Berne Review* and arrived the day after it was printed. It contained no world news. In later years we also intermittently subscribed either to the *Decatur Daily Democrat* or the *Fort Wayne Journal-Gazette*, but we could afford neither of these during the years of depression from 1931 on. Our only books were several copies of the *Bible*; the *Martyrs' Mirror* and the hymnal used in church, *Der Ausbund,* all in the German language. *The Prince of Peace*, (whose author I do not remember) and Paul Bunyan's *Pilgrim's Progress*, ironically, that I later studied in a literature class at Ball State University.

We had no library cards. Periodicals included no church publications since, according to the Bishop, all other denominations were not on the "true path." Intermittently, Dad subscribed to *The Farmers Guide* and *Successful Farming* that offered practical helps to the farmer.

The locked front door, a screen from the world, was also symptomatic of a fundamental exclusion from things regarded by the Bishop of the church as either evil or non-essential. Having separated from the Amish church in 1894 the Bishop led his group in a church reformation. Concerning Bible, theology and church history he knew only what he had learned and experienced in the Amish church with its total isolation from the rest of society. The Amish maintained relationships with congregations in other counties and states with whom they were in periodic communication and with whom, though there were differences in detail of faith and practice, there was occasional consultation. But this Bishop declared that there was no other church with which consultation, communication, or shared communion could be beneficial. He became the sole theocrat accountable only to God. His two minister associates were subordinate and rarely challenged him or asserted their differences with him on matters of faith and practice. Laymen had no advisory or governing role.

The Bishop also locked his people from the fresh air of learning, from other denominations or other perspectives concerning educational, social, political or economic information. The church supported its own school from about 1910 until the thirties. One of the associate ministers was the non-teaching principal until the Bishop's son, having taught grades six to eight, was named principal by his father. By 1925, the Bishop selected his own nephew to teach grades one through five; in 1928 as the number of pupils increased, requiring three teachers, the Bishop's granddaughter was appointed to teach grades one through three.

Until I began this writing, I had not realized the pervasive, metaphoric significance of the locked front doors. The residents entered their homes from the side of the house facing their work; their guests were similarly admitted through the kitchen. Undoubtedly, no one was concerned about the symbolic significance. All were practical people unschooled in the art of gracious living.

Chapter 2: My Early Years on the Farm

Some of the earliest memories reach back to the time when I was perhaps two years old. I remember after winter, which seemed endless, the urgent desire to go barefoot in the spring the first time the thermometer reached 70 degrees. Each day I would beg my mother to allow me to take off my shoes and socks to feel the gentle caress of the grass on my bare feet.

One of the early photos that I have is of me standing on the front porch wearing a straw hat, barefoot, the sun shining brightly. I was ready to run out on the warm sidewalk and then on to the grass after the long winter confinement of socks, shoes, overshoes, boots and long woolen underwear worn in the cold and snow.

I was the oldest of seven boys--no girls. Other boys had sisters. Why didn't I? In that culture women and girls did house and garden work; men and boys did no cooking, dish washing, laundry or house cleaning. They worked outdoors caring for animals and planting, cultivating and harvesting crops. Early we learned how different our family was in that our gender imbalance required boys to help Mother in the house.

As soon as my parents moved to their own farm in 1919, they planted peach and cherry trees in the lawn so that we would, in the early years, have some fruit. I remember the thrill of seeing the cherry blossoms in April, then green cherries, and after waiting what seemed a very long time, spying cheeks of red in the month of May looking toward June when they would ripen. We had both sweet and sour cherries, and it was a special thrill to climb the sweet cherry tree. As the birds, we ate cherries before they were fully ripe.

Later, my parents planted an acre of orchard which contained many varieties of apples, such as Yellow Transparent, Wealthy, Northern Spy, Bellflower and Jonathan, Grimes Golden, Red Delicious, Golden Delicious, Rambo and McIntosh, along with more cherries peaches, plums and pears. In the garden were grapevines, currant and gooseberry bushes, ground cherry plants and rhubarb, and each spring we enjoyed growing a wide variety of vegetables, peas, beans, corn, lettuce, carrots, radishes and turnips.

We were surrounded by nature's generous provision of food--when joined with our labor. We relied on farm produce for fruits and vegetables, as well as milk, eggs, pork, beef and chicken. The farm was our work, our living, our recreation, and our principal source of food.

I cannot clearly remember the arrival of my brother, Elmer, born on September 2, 1920, when I was about two years and two months old. When I asked Mom why I was named Leo, she said that she knew a man in the local hardware store named Leo Lehman and that she always liked the name. I was not named after the series of Roman Catholic popes by that name. I do not recall that she told me why she named Elmer. Later, I realized that there was also an Elmer Lehman, a brother to Leo, in the same hardware store.

After Elmer was born, I remember Mom telling us stories as she prepared supper while Dad was doing the farm chores. Stories were vignettes from her youth, stories about her father in pioneer days, her relationships, as the eldest of nine living brothers and sisters, assorted with Bible stories. Though somewhat vague in my memory it seems that even then she conveyed to me that school for her was an interesting and exciting place. As became more evident much later, her father was the key member of the family in her early life.

I remember when a brother was born Martha and Leona, her younger sisters, then late teenagers, helped with the weekly washing and mending. In early summer time they helped with weeding and cultivating of the garden; at harvest time they helped with picking and canning of vegetables and fruit.

Very early I remember asking Mom why Aunt Leona, her youngest sister and Uncle Dave, her second oldest brother, were not as agile as Martha or Mom. For Leona and Dave to climb stairs required a sturdy railing at our back porch. Bending over to pull weeds was difficult; for Uncle Dave to hand-crank the motor of the Ford car required special effort and strenuous exertion. (I will discuss Dave and Leona's muscular dystrophy in chapter 12.)

The kitchen stove was our central utility; it burned only

14

wood or coal, with which Mother did her water heating, cooking and baking. Soft water was rain from the roof of the house channeled through gutters and down spouting into the adjoining cistern where it was retrieved by a lift pump. We used an antiquated substitute bathroom. On Saturday nights we carried in water from the cistern, brought in wood, heated water in the stove tank and in kettles and pans on top. For bathing, each of us in turn used the same round wooden tub that Mother used in weekly family washing in the basement of our home.

The well next to the barn some 300 feet from the house provided water not only for family drinking, but also for watering dairy cattle, horses, pigs and chickens. The only water that didn't have to be carried was for the stock tank used by horses and cattle, located next to the well and pumped by a windmill. If the wind was calm we pumped the hundreds of gallons by hand.

The windmill was only forty feet tall; wind from the southwest was partly deflected by the adjacent barn roof. Dad had the windmill heightened by ten feet and installed a new oil-bathed Aermotor brand that not only turned with less wind. It was tall enough so that wind from all directions turned it. In April we welcomed the return of the migratory purple martins with their graceful gliding flight. They nested in a two-story birdhouse on the thirty-foot platform of the windmill.

Water for chickens, hogs, and for all flowering plants had to be carried in buckets. Water is a precious commodity on the farm and one comes to appreciate it even more when it cannot be had by turning on a faucet but by laboriously carrying many three to five-gallon buckets.

While water is essential during all seasons of the year, it is especially critical during the winter months. If water was not heated in the stock tank, in the hog house and the chicken house, it would freeze immediately. We either had to have appropriate coal, wood or kerosene heating devices or use the water promptly after it was pumped from the well. The stock tank was heated by a water-proof hard coal stove set in the middle of the stock watering tank, its smoke stack upright.

There was no refrigeration. Except in winter, we had no ice, and no electrical power; in hot weather there was no access to artificial cooling. There was no chilling of the milk produced by hand milking the cows every morning and evening seven days a week. The best we could do was to put the ten-gallon milk cans in the stock tank exposed to the summer sun; in winter it was also subject to freezing.

In those days work on the farm was never ending. Not only did the cows have to be milked twice daily -- fourteen times a week; all the farm animals, cattle, horses, pigs, chickens had to be fed on the same schedule. Eggs were gathered every evening.

How did the horses, cows, chickens, pigs, sheep, dogs, and cats fit into the animal constellation?

The order within the constellation on our farm was fairly typical of the general community. Horses, the basic motive power, were in many ways most important. Each horse and cow had a name that was the identification; if the animal was purebred the registration was by name and characteristics as shown in color drawing or photograph. Many horses and cows responded to the name. We had horses named Glen, Fan, Grace, Dick, Daisy, Barney, Pet or Nance. We never had more than four at one time. In the late twenties and early thirties blindness was rampant among horses, occasionally in only one eye but usually in both. Some blind horses could adapt and still be useful, but others could not. All blind horses were greatly diminished in value, for sale almost valueless but for farm work some could still be used. Each horse had a distinctive personality and some were very winsome. Each horse had its own assigned stall. Male workhorses were always gelded. Female workhorses, if of high quality and young, were often bred to raise colts. Children, especially, adored growing colts. We raised several colts.

Milk production of cows, both quantity and butterfat quality, was recorded by name. Each cow had its own stall for feeding, milking and sleeping. Our Holstein cows were mostly purebred and registered. Some of the names were Lucinda, Ellen, Bossie, Bess, Mercedes, and Beauty. Cows were less intelligent than horses and had a strong herd instinct. Some farmers were organized as the Adams County Dairy Herd Improvement Association. The association engaged a "tester" who once a month visited the farm at milking time, evening and morning, to test samples of milk from each cow for quantity and butterfat quality. Farmers culled the herds, retained and bred the best and sold or slaughtered those of lowest productivity. Cows were milked for nine or ten months; bred during that time and then dry, or not milked, during a rest period for two to three months. Production is highest right after a cow gives birth, freshens, and in the latter stages of the milking period production wanes. Female calves of the best cows were retained for later milk production. Female calves whose mother's had a record of low production and male calves were sold for veal. For several years I entered a calf in 4-H Club competition, once placed third in the Adams County fair.

Pigs or hogs were generally raised for market when they reached from 180 to 200 pounds in weight. Most families, depending on family size, butchered one or two hogs each winter. Hogs were generally nameless and rarely served as pets. A typical litter of pigs numbered from six to eight; male pigs were neutered at a few weeks of age. Lard was one of the most valuable pork products. The market wanted fat hogs for lard in contrast to current demands for lean pork with lard rarely used for cooking and baking.

Chickens were raised mostly for egg production; a laying chicken was valued depending on how many eggs it produced in a year. Chickens were usually sold or butchered (dressed) after two years and replaced with new stock. Unfertilized eggs were preferred in the market so roosters did not mingle with chickens but were sold young for the market.

Sheep were raised only in small numbers. They were rarely named and were grown mostly for wool when it was still used for domestic purposes. Raising sheep soon became a specialty; they were more economically raised in large flocks.

What was the place of dogs and cats? Most farm families had one or two dogs that served as watch dogs, helped herd cattle and hogs, for hunting game, as pets and some dogs served as rat catchers. Most family dogs had a name such as Sport, Shep, Nick, or Bob. Dogs were never allowed in the house; most had a doghouse near the family residence. Dogs were usually in the barn at milking time to claim their share. Cats were often not named, lived in the barn, served to reduce the mouse population and a large, strong male or female cat would be fatal to rats. Nearly every milking area had a dish from which the cats got their fill of milk. They were never house pets.

Each animal produced manure that had to be removed at regular intervals. All animals required oats and wheat straw bedding; in winter, straw was added daily for cattle and horses. Chickens slept sitting on elevated horizontal wood 2x2" railings mounted over a suspended solid floor. Manure was scraped weekly and hauled to the fields as fertilizer. The concrete chicken house floor also had a layer of straw that became mixed with daytime droppings. Manure in the cattle area was removed once or twice a day. Cattle manure was carted by wheelbarrow to the fenced yard behind the barn to be hauled away during the summer between other pressing chores. That was a very tedious task, extremely smelly and required a number of days to haul the accumulated manure from the fall and winter seasons. Manure from horses, chickens and, pigs was mixed with wheat or oats straw. Typically once a week or so it was spread on the land as fertilizer.

Not only was spring an exciting time for a barefoot boy walking in the grass; for the farmer it required a completely revised work schedule. He could turn out the livestock to pasture where the cattle and horses could forage some of their own feed, and drop their own manure. During the long late fall and winter all feed had to be brought to the animals. Without automated equipment feeding animals and removing manure were onerous tasks.

Although these tasks reduced the farmer's work in caring for farm animals, seasonal soil preparation and planting were fulltime work for several weeks. In sequence, plowing, disking, harrowing, fertilizing and planting demanded great time and energy from the horses and the farmer as well. This was often my work after school and on Saturdays. When the school year ended in mid-April, this was my full time work. In summer growing corn and other crops required cultivation to aerate the soil and to destroy weeds. Corn was cross-cultivated two or three times until it was some thirty inches tall. Each of these farm tasks also depended on friendly weather. There were no farm pesticides, fungicides or herbicides.

I was often given tasks to perform for which I was not old enough. Dad bought a corn cultivator with wood handle controls; the driver of the team of horses was seated in front. The other person walked behind and guided the cultivator with wood handles. Clarence Schrock, the next-door neighbor who was a year older than I, shared this operation with me when I was eleven years old. We rotated positions.

While working in the hot sun we dreamed of visiting his grandmother in southern Michigan. We had no money, so we put our inventive minds to work. He and I decided that when major summer crop work was finished we would collect worn out old cars, dismantle and sell them to the town junkman. We towed these clunkers home, stripped them and with the team and wagon hauled the salable parts to the junkman in Berne. By late August we had enough dollars to take the trip.

Incidentally, I remember that the Bishop had just approved white summer trousers for boys and men. Each of us rushed to buy white trousers as essential for the trip. As a twelve-year-old he drove his older brother's car. His grandmother received us well so we stayed three days. This was a momentous occasion! Mother was not as pleased to have to wash another pair of pants after each wearing.

Eagerly in spring, we welcomed the return of migratory birds: robins, red-winged blackbirds, meadow larks, killdeers, redheaded woodpeckers, cardinals, swallows, mourning doves and humming birds. They broke the monotony of the ubiquitous sparrows, pigeons, bobwhites and crows.

Hogs and chickens consumed family meal leftovers. No garbage was unused. Many items were bought in bulk, few packages to discard. Literally everything was recycled on the farm except pieces of metal or old machinery, which were sold to the local junk dealer. Everything was either consumed by humans or animals or otherwise tossed out to be returned to nature.

Across and parallel to the road in neighbor farmer's fields a ten-inch crude oil pipeline was buried several feet below the surface. Crude oil was pumped from the source in Ohio to a refinery west of us. At intersecting fence lines a white wooden post with a black top some three feet tall was planted to show the location of the line. The line would occasionally spring a leak and the oil would collect in the drainage ditch along that side of the road. If not repaired, oil would gradually collect at a low area in the farmer's field and seriously damage or destroy a growing crop. Pollution of the soil would last for several seasons.

To detect leaks as early as possible by smell, a man known as "line walker" twice a week followed the line. When he detected a leak he would stop at the next farmhouse to make a telephone call to company headquarters to summon repairmen. Damage to farmer's crops was reimbursed by the oil company. The line walker was a curiosity to children, whom he often befriended as he paused at a farm home for a drink of fresh water. As children, we thought that our road had something special which no other roads had. Farmers on the side of the road with the pipe line regarded it as a significant hazard.

What were our connections with nearby towns? What services did they offer? The closest town was Monroe with some 400 residents, two and a half miles distant, one-hour round trip by a team of horses and wagon. The town had a post office, two grain elevators, one filling station. A hand-operated gasoline pump stood in front of the single grocery store. On the main street there was a drug store with soda fountain, the post office, a chick hatchery, a dry goods store, harness shop combined with shoe repair, a barber shop, a furniture store and a small bank. Next to the railroad tracks the lumberyard also had a series of large coal bins. There were two churches, one Methodist, the other Friends. The Monroe school served grades one through twelve, eight grades for local residents and high school for the town and the surrounding community students who wanted to continue their education beyond the eight grades offered in the one-room country schools. Monroe served many of the rudimentary needs of the farming community.

The town of Berne, the center of the Swiss community, with perhaps 2,000 residents was four and a half miles in the opposite direction. Berne had each of the stores and facilities found in Monroe. In addition there were two hardware and implement stores, an ice cream factory and a milk condensery. Unusual for a town of this size, there were three furniture factories and a novelty factory that manufactured small cedar chests, including those with music movements. There were two newspapers, one Republican, *Adams County Witness,* the other Democrat, *The Berne Review*, a book store, a funeral director combined with a furniture store. Three automobile dealers, Ford, Chevrolet and Chrysler were actively competing. There was no Oldsmobile, Buick, Cadillac or Lincoln dealer; there is none today. A Whippet dealer continued until the manufacturer ceased. Before the financial depression there were two banks. After the bank holiday during the financial depression one never reopened. Two restaurants prevailed and one beer tavern. One bakery, quite complete, probably was most noted for its cookies and cinnamon rolls. One Rexall drugstore with ice cream and soft drink counter did a thriving business. There was no movie theater in town then and there has been none since. The junk dealer, who also bought and sold used farm implements, was the only known Jew. In addition, there was a clock and jewelry store. Four physicians, two dentists, one chiropractor, and two veterinarians served the community. There were several property and life insurance agents; liability insurance was not popular. Two ready-to-wear clothing for men and women and a general merchandise store also sold bolts of cloth by the yard. Sears, Roebuck & Co. and Montgomery, Ward & Co. mail order establishments were very popular in that community.

Berne had one of the largest Mennonite churches in North America that by any small town standard was architecturally ostentatious. There was a large Reformed church and several smaller churches of other Protestant denominations. There were no Lutheran or Roman Catholic churches and few, if any, residents of those faiths in either town, or in the surrounding community. No black residents lived in the towns or within the farming communities. We saw black persons only if we drove to Fort Wayne, some thirty miles away.

Both towns were served by the Grand Rapids and Indiana Railroad that later was purchased by the Pennsylvania Railroad.

The tracks ran less than half a mile from our farm; freight and passenger steam engine whistles, two long and two short were sounded before crossing any intersecting road, punctuated the days and nights. Today, with tracks and cross ties removed the railroad bed is used as a horse and buggy path, the only traffic artery unmolested by competing cars and trucks.

In my youth, none of the community roads were hard surfaced. On most secondary roads one lane was gravel, the other lane was dirt with weeds growing between the tracks. Automobiles used the gravel lane. When two cars met each driver moved to the right, one onto the edge of the gravel, the other onto part of the dirt lane, always a little lower than the gravel side. Horse drawn buggies and wagons used the dirt lane unless from recent rainfall it was too muddy. Dirt lanes were much easier on horse's hoofs; on gravel roads horseshoes protected the hoofs.

Every few months a county gravel truck dumped another thin layer of gravel to replace what had been ground to dust and blown away, flung into the gutter or pushed onto the ungraveled half. Every few weeks a road grader drawn by two teams of horses, in tandem, leveled the gravel-half of the road; one man drove the teams, another stood on the back to regulate the depth of the blade. On a typical day perhaps twenty cars and trucks and a similar number of horse drawn vehicles would pass the farm.

The town of Berne served nearly all the supportive services and supplemental needs for life on the farm. Self-sufficiency of a town was not only a principal goal but an economic necessity. Special needs might require an occasional trip to Decatur, the county seat. Monroe had no physician. Of the four family practice physicians in Berne some also did surgery and one prescribed eye-glasses. Decatur had surgeons and an Eye-Ear-Nose and Throat (EENT) specialist but no psychiatrist or ophthalmologist, or other medical specialists. Driving the distant thirty miles to Fort Wayne was a carefully planned day's undertaking, sometimes with neighbors sharing the ride. Compared with today, necessities were few; most luxuries, religiously and culturally, were not sustained.

What made life interesting? Some work was pleasure,

other work drudgery. Endless variety of tasks were mixed between dull monotony and challenges to more efficiency. There were fun tasks, many of them seasonal, such as picking cherries, apples, peaches. To children waiting for that season felt like a small eternity. Observing the development of a young calf or colt, shaping its own personality, the unveiling of a mystery. Currying horses in the spring as they shed their winter coats into fresh glistening shorter hair, despite allergies, was a seasonal regeneration. To watch the change of seasons, especially spring blossoms bursting forth after the long months of cloudy, dreary winter weather was truly exhilarating. To observe the daily weather changes shaped the farm work in response to our best home made weather forecasting. For much of the year correctly anticipating the weather was a tricky game. To predict correctly was its own reward; to lose could be frustrating and costly.

Driving a team for plowing, disking, harrowing in the spring amid the bursting vitality of nature, when one could think deeply has no urban counterparts. Watching the seedling plants of oats, wheat, checked rows of little corn grow into towering stalks, while observing, in detail, the summer clouds forming into a disturbing thunderstorm, that was farm life. To experience the fulfillment of a good harvest later in the summer cannot be matched in any other place. To see the crops damaged by the elements of nature such as windstorms, hail, floods, drought, chinch bugs, grasshoppers, weeds, was heart-rending, emotionally depressing, and financially disastrous. In the city, weather can spoil a picnic; on the farm it shapes your annual income. This was emotionally driven variety!

To drive the team and wagon with many bags of grain to be ground and mixed with McMillen feed supplement for chickens, cows and hogs at the town elevator in Berne or Monroe provided different perspectives, observing every farming neighbor and his fields of crops. Knowing most of them by name, mile after mile, offered its own kind of connections and relationships. One neighbor had a new car, young colts in the pasture. Another was painting his barn; a third had a huge washing hung on the clothes line to dry. Would I see friendly girls from school in the front yard?

The farm had its tragedies. A neighbor's barn burned, a neighbor's son died of typhoid fever. Many farm animals were members of the farm family; each cow and horse known by name. Finding a favorite cow or worse yet the best of four horses bloated from eating too much green corn dead despite the veterinarian's best efforts—and no money to replace her. We had to watch the health of every chicken, pig, cow and horse, each with a personality. Commingled with repetitive chores were dozens of tasks, each requiring its particular knowledge and understanding and a wide variety of challenges.

There was no TV and we had our first small radio when I was thirteen. By today's standards there was very little advertising; almost none of it entered into our home through any medium. A few highway signs fastened to farmers' fences as small as a kitchen bulletin board were the most impressive advertising signage that we saw. When we heard an occasional radio program the advertising was subdued and unobtrusive. We never thought of buying on the basis of advertising; when we bought an item, it was essential for our livelihood. National corporations did not yet advertise to stimulate people to buy what they did not need; basic needs could be scarcely met. There was no discretionary spending.

We did not expect anyone to entertain us; everyone was busy with chores. Whatever we did could not cost money. Books were limited to school texts; other reading was not an option. In today's commercially driven, urban society such a life with its limitations, values and motivations cannot be imagined, much less understood. We never thought that entertainment should be directly related to money. Money was so scarce that it was very valuable. There were no allowances for the seven boys; if on occasion we earned a few cents or dollars, the earnings were contributed to the general family fund. Parents needed to buy essentials, to pay interest on notes, or to make the semiannual mortgage payments. Poverty can be a very stern disciplinarian.

We never had a new toy. There were no shopping trips; there were no shopping malls or supermarkets. Groceries were shelved behind the counters available only to the clerks who walking up and down the aisle brought each separate item as recited from the shopper's brief list; prices were hand written on a sales pad and mentally added. The hand-cranked cash register showed only the total of the purchases and not the amount of change due.

Style, fashion, or gradations of taste were not factors to be considered. Practical, essential utility determined what we bought and what we did. Each of us had only one or two pairs of work pants and shirts and one dress suit for church or very special event elsewhere, such as a rare dinner with relatives. No family member went to a restaurant unless the meal was work related with carpentry in town.

The contrast with today's society is striking. Today's youth, our grandchildren, would find such conditions unimaginable, unreal, intolerable and overwhelmingly frustrating. Indeed, those days were another world.

Chapter 3: Food on the Farm

During the decades of the twenties and thirties, while I was growing up on the farm, most of our food was produced at home. We had eight to ten dairy cattle that produced milk. At times we sold whole milk; at other times, we used a cream separator, hand-cranked, to separate the cream from the milk. Cream was sold; skimmed milk was fed to hogs to speed their growth for market. We always had cream and milk for the family. At times we churned our own butter with a hand-cranked butter churn and rarely, mother made cottage cheese. Some farmers also made their own cheese, although there were no highly accomplished "cheese makers" in our community.

Meat was all produced on the farm, which included beef, pork, chicken and occasionally tame or hunted rabbit. Once, during the winter season, we would either buy a quarter of beef from grandparents, an aunt, or uncle who had slaughtered a cow. On occasion we slaughtered one of our own. Slaughtering a cow was a major undertaking, which involved several relatives who would share the meat. Lacking refrigeration, it was necessary to do the butchering during cold weather, ideally between 15 and 30 degrees Fahrenheit. Butchering a cow involved killing the animal, removing the hide, which was sold to a tanning company, and literally disposing of the whole carcass by the end of the day. Typically, we butchered a cow that produced below average milk, never a young heifer or steer.

Grandpa Nussbaum, who lived only two miles away, was the proud owner and user of a 32 caliber rifle. One of his specialties was killing the animal, cow or pig, with one bullet; if the bullet hit the brain, the animal would fall instantly. On the other hand, if the bullet did not hit the brain, the injured animal might start charging and could become very dangerous.

A quick knife to the main neck artery released the blood to drain into the earth. The carcass was suspended on a tripod made of sturdy hickory poles, tall enough that when hung by the rear legs, the head would be off the ground. Then the real work began. After removing the hide, the carcass was cut into parts. The bowels, heart, lungs, liver and external organs were

26

separated. This was no job for amateurs, but for experienced hands and heads. Meanwhile, 50-gallon iron and copper kettles full of water had been heated to boiling point for use throughout the day. Meat sorting and cutting directed by an experienced person such as Grandma Mazelin, my mother's mother, engaged people of all ages and talents. Numbers of well sharpened butcher knives were provided. Amateurs might also cut their fingers. Every part of the carcass, including brains, feet, ears, tailbone, nose, as well as the more choice parts, such as liver, lungs, flanks, loins, had to be cut into small pieces for cooking and canning or preserving in lard. Liver and sweetbreads were tasty, often nibbled as soon as cooked. There were no rib-eye, flank, sirloin, tenderloin, or other steaks cut for serving as is done in meat markets and restaurants. Interestingly, there was almost no meat ground into hamburger. On the rare occasions when we ate hamburgers they came from commercial sources.

Large temporary tables for meat cutting were set up out of doors if temperature was tolerable, as well as inside if the home or shops were large enough. everyone busy for ten to twelve hours to provide the beef or pork needed to feed several families, each of which had from six to ten persons, for a whole year. We never ate veal; female calves were raised as milk cows. Male calves were sold at a few weeks of age to be commercially slaughtered for veal. In the winter season on another day, one or two 250-300 lb. hogs were butchered to provide pork for one or two families. While a lesser undertaking than slaughtering a cow, it still required the help of two or more families because meat was immediately preserved. The hog was killed, the blood drained with a cut to the neck artery while the hog lay on the ground. Immediately, the carcass was put into a wooden tank half-filled with boiling water to loosen the hair, which was scraped with a sharpened disc tool with a short wooden handle. Pigs are not skinned the way cows were. When the hair had been removed, the carcass was hung on a smaller tripod, then the cutting began. With pigs the bowels were removed, the intestines cleaned and used as casing for sausage. Among farmers sausage was much more popular than hamburger. This required experienced talent; in scraping there was danger of cutting into the intestine. Any break in the intestine greatly reduced its value as sausage casing when later in the day the hand-cranked sausage-stuffing machine filled the ground sausage into the cleaned intestines. In preparation for stuffing, different uncooked meats were cut, ground together with a hand-cranked grinder and thoroughly mixed producing sausage. The sausage maker always thanked the cleaner of the intestines for long strands of perfect casing; each time that a break in the intestine occurred the end had to be tied then starting over. The sausage was sliced in serving lengths, 2 1/2 inches, before it was cooked.

After cooking it was either canned in glass jars of various sizes, or more often put into ceramic crocks of one, two or three gallon size. Melted lard, which had been rendered in large kettles, was then poured into the crocks filled to the brim. This was the preferred method of preserving pork for as long as a year. The cooled, hardened lard yielded results similar to that of freezing, which in those days was unavailable.

Hams of various sizes were frequently heavily salted then smoked for several days in the smokehouse found on nearly every farm. The smokehouse was perhaps four feet square, eight feet in height with smoke outlets just below the roof. Smoke produced by logs of green hickory wood was preferred. Other helping hands were cutting bacon from inside the skin of the hog that was then cooked or rendered into liquid in a large vat. Nothing was wasted, even pigs feet, the tail, the ears, the nose were used; some cuttings ended in sausage. Lard was a precious commodity on the farm used for cooking in place of vegetable or corn oils. Lard as liquid or solid is very greasy; at the end of a very long workday, every vessel, knife, tool and machine had to be thoroughly cleaned and scalded, itself a formidable task.

Chicken was frequently served at dinner or supper. More often, older chickens that had lost their value as egg producers were culled from the flock. These did not produce the choice breast of chicken in the supermarket and restaurant. Sometimes roosters were dressed in the season when fertilizing eggs was unnecessary. The chicken or rooster was beheaded, the body dipped into very hot water, and the feathers pulled out. When a dinner or supper guest came to the home, the family often had chicken as variation from pork or beef.

We always had plenty of eggs either fried at breakfast, sometimes boiled for dinner or supper and mixed with other foods. They were an important addition to lettuce salads. Children going to country school or a farm resident employed off the farm carried a lunch pail that contained fried egg, beef or pork sandwiches which formed an important part of the protein. On the farm the large noon meal was called dinner, the heavy evening meal was supper.

Income from the sale of eggs was significant. At times eggs were sold to the local grocer or traded for sugar, flour, spices, or other food items not produced on the farm. Candled eggs, to assure sterility, several cases sorted by size brought the highest prices when shipped via railway express to a wholesaler, Jelliffe, Wright & Co. in New York City. A case of eggs contained 36 dozens, was made of wood, eighteen dozen in each half, cushioned with dividers. Preparing the eggs for shipment was tedious; on occasion some eggs were broken in transit. That was our loss! At times Dad's enthusiasm waned; again we sold them locally, unsorted.

A neighboring farmer was an occasional fish peddler. He drove a small pick-up truck filled with crushed ice. He sold what he had either caught in the local river or bought fresh commercial catch at some distance. Fish were always very bony. Shrimp, scallops, clams, lobster, crab or other forms of seafood were never available. Following spring rains, mushrooms sprung up in the woods and pasture fields; we boys picked them by the bucketful. Mom had learned to sort the edible ones from the poisonous varieties. We never saw mushrooms in the grocery stores.

There were hunting seasons for rabbits, squirrels, pheasants, quail, possum and raccoons. Some families with members who enjoyed hunting for sport developed a taste for wild game, while others avoided all non-domesticated meats. Some boys and men were avid hunters or trappers; I never knew women or girls who hunted, carried a gun or set traps. I was not a very successful hunter, even a less effective trapper. On occasion I caught a wayward rat. Turtles were plentiful in warm seasons in the creeks and rivers. Turtle soup was a specialty for the few avid turtle hunters. Domesticated rabbits were sometimes raised for home consumption.

Turkeys were selectively grown. Wild turkeys were occasionally hunted, but domestic turkey was a specialty eaten only at Thanksgiving. Turkeys were grown only for that season. We always had a large vegetable garden about one-eighth of an acre. Many varieties of vegetables were grown in the garden. Carrots, lettuce, cabbage, turnips, peas, string and shelled beans, radishes, sweet corn, (although sweet corn was also grown in the field in special plots). Potatoes, in large quantities, were raised in a corner of a grain field. In the fall harvest, fifteen or twenty bushels were stored in a metal tank in the basement of the house. Potatoes were a staple served two or three meals a day. Most farmers, doing hard physical labor, did not have an adequate meal without potatoes. Sweet potatoes were raised either a substitute or supplement to the Irish potato, but grown in much smaller quantities. Some farmers had a small plot of horseradish. The roots were dug in early spring and prepared with a hand-grinder for seasoning, far hotter than the commercial variety. We grew asparagus only as a decorative lawn plan, never for vegetative consumption.

Peas, string beans and shell beans grown with sweet corn were canned every summer. Some farmers dried vegetables in a metal drying house. Dried vegetables could be stored indefinitely in an upstairs room or attic. Carrots were often left in the ground, covered with corn fodder and several inches of leaves then dug throughout the winter. Winter weather made them sweeter month by month. In the fall when cabbage was harvested, it was frequently sliced and salted, and put into crocks with a round one-inch thick wooden cover. As it matured it turned into sauerkraut. Turnips, first eaten fresh in the fall, were similarly preserved for winter use as sour turnips.

Fruit was available in copious quantities and varieties. Early and late apples, peaches, sour and sweet cherries, wild cherries, plums of many varieties, from the green to the blues and the dark browns, pears, and rhubarb. Some of these fruits along with gooseberries, currants, elderberries, blackberries, raspberries were canned as jams and jellies. Without refrigeration many of these fruits had a short shelf life. We ate fruit fresh between meals but rarely at mealtime. Fruits were cooked and canned in pints, quarts and half gallon Mason jars for meal consumption as desserts. Apples, peaches and plums were also dried. Varieties of apples supplied tastes for every palate -- Red Delicious, Golden Delicious, Wealthy, Jonathan, Northern Spy, Bell Flower, McIntosh, Greening, Grimes Golden, Rome Beauty, Yellow Transparent, Winesap, among others. We produced far more varieties than are typically available on the market today. In any season of the year, there was ample canned or dried fruit. In the Middle West, citrus fruits and juices were rarely purchased, bananas occasionally.

An interesting beverage variant was fresh cider, used as apple juice, and most desirable fresh from the cider mill. Cider was sometimes boiled for long term preservation, sealed in glass jars or in five to ten gallon ceramic jugs. A cork was sealed with a hot red or brownish sealing wax. Cider preserved in this way was almost equivalent to that of fresh cider. Some families let parts of the cider mature until it became "hard," turned into an alcoholic beverage.

Most farmers made apple butter, which is a mixture of sliced apples, cider with abundant sugar, continually stirred, boiled for hours in huge copper kettles. With butter, this was the most widely used bread spread. Bread was baked at home. In the latter twenties and thirties, some farmers would rarely buy bread. Generous bread spreads were essential for every meal. In addition to apple butter, there were many jellies and jams.

Many farmers raised sorghum cane from which they processed molasses for their own use or as a cash product. While standing, cane stalks were stripped of their leaves. Cane stalks were carted to the cane mill, typically located next to a cider mill. The juice was squeezed from the stalks and boiled with other elements added to produce molasses. Especially in winter, molasses was a favorite spread for pancakes or fried mush. Some farmers produced honey with a few hives of honeybees. These spreads were also widely used on pancakes or fried mush that served as typical or principal breakfast foods.

On the farm, beverages were extremely important. Drinking water was pumped from a well; all farmers had soft water usually drained into a cistern from the roof of the house. Farmers carried jugs of well water to the fields when they plowed, cultivated, sowed, or harvested. It was not possible to keep the water chilled; farms had neither refrigeration nor ice. Even when freshly pumped at the well into a one or two gallon jug, sealed with a cork, wrapped in wet burlap, and placed in the shade, by noontime water was lukewarm.

Some families made root beer. Many families made wine in season and had one, three, five-gallon jugs and thirty-gallon wood barrels stored in the cellar. My grandparents were more skilled and made much more and better wine than my parents. Wine was made from a great variety of fruits, such as dandelions, peaches, cherries, plums, rhubarb, wild cherries and sometimes from pears or elderberries but most often from grapes. Grapes were also used for fresh and canned juice, available the year round. Many farmers made their own alcoholic beer. Community mores emphatically limited alcoholic consumption. The very rare alcoholic was a social outcast. Drunkenness was regarded as uncouth and evil. Mennonite and Missionary churches opposed all alcoholic beverages and strongly opposed the one tavern located in Berne. The Amish and the local Reformed Church were more tolerant toward alcoholic beverages.

Fresh lemons were squeezed to make occasional lemonade, homemade root beer was prevalent. But Coca Cola or Nehi soda were a very rare treat in town only. Pepsi came later. Other commercial soft drinks were almost never served. In the thirties, a prominent soft drink was the Nehi brand, but became extinct in subsequent years. It was colorfully advertised showing a young woman's dress not reaching to the knee.

In 1920, the 19th amendment to the U. S. Constitution became effective; it prohibited the manufacture, sale or consumption of alcoholic beverages. This was totally ignored by many farmers in our community. In 1933 the 22nd Amendment to the Constitution countermanded the 19th again permitting the manufacture, sale, and consumption of alcoholic beverages. Only then did I realize that I, up to the age of fifteen, had been totally unaware of prohibition, because wine and beer had been an ordinary part of our families. Moderate drinking was enjoyed in the Amish Christian Church, with the prevailing political non-involvement by the church members. I do not remember that I ever heard this subject discussed, even in school. In our family and among close relatives I did not know of anyone who became drunk or used alcoholic beverages in excess. At the same time alcoholic beverages were not regularly served at social events; however, wine or beer were served to workers engaged in silo filling or corn fodder shredding. Wine and beer were always available for children as well as adults. Occasionally, some isolated bootlegged hard liquor was smuggled into the community, but I never knew of any produced there. In the larger community an occasional man--no woman that I can recall--was known for public drunkenness.

We went to town to buy salt, sugar, spices and flour, whether wheat, rye, corn or buckwheat. These grains were abundantly available but there were no flourmills nearby. Some farmers purchased butter and later the newly available white oleomargarine. In the dairy producing states, yellow margarine was illegal because it looked like butter. As an intermediary step, a bubble of yellowish coloring was available in a white margarine package that the purchaser had to mix tediously to make it look more like butter. Vegetable fats were rarely purchased for cooking, fats were nearly always butter and homemade lard.

In addition to bread, there were various other home baked goods. Noon and evening meals on the farm ended with one, two or even three so-called desserts, pie, cake or cookies along with canned fruit. Ice cream was a rare treat. Without refrigeration or freezer capacity, ice cream was homemade only on special occasions with a with a home mix in a hand-cranked home freezer. Ice came from the rare farm icehouse, cut into slabs from ponds or lakes and stored in buildings heavily lined with layers of sawdust in the walls and ceiling. This ice was neither clean nor sanitary; melted ice was not fit to drink. Only a few farmers, including my mother's parents, had icehouses. More often commercially produced ice was bought in burlap bags at the Berne ice cream factory.

Peanuts were a special treat bought at the grocery. However, hickory and walnut trees were abundant and in good season those were our nutmeats. Pecan, cashews, macadamia, pistachio-- never. Chocolate bars, rarely; a five-cent dish of ice cream at the drug store during the depression was a rare treat if not an extravagance.

It is evident that even during the worst of the depression years in the early thirties, farmers had enough food although not always in the variety that they would have preferred. But, no one of whom I knew was hungry on the farm

Food raised on the farm in the 1920s and 30s was mostly the equivalent of today's organic food. Although most farmers used commercial fertilizer, herbicides and pesticides were rarely available and almost never used. In those terms, they were "the good old days."

Chapter 4: Games Played on the Farm

The Church prohibited members from attending commercial entertainment such as public sporting events, the theater, and stage performances. In the early years such events as horse-pulling contests, the annual Adams county fair with its variety of entertainment were viewed with disfavor. Commercial entertainment in rural areas was very limited. It was available in larger cities such as Fort Wayne thirty miles away, too far by horse and buggy.

Farming was exceedingly demanding and time-consuming physical labor. Caring for the livestock, milking twice a day, feeding three times a day, was almost a full-time job for one person or a part-time job for several people. Recreation and time for home games were very limited. During warm weather we brothers would play in the evening or on Sunday afternoon. With seven of us, when all were of an age to play, sometimes Dad would join us in an outdoor game called scrub. The bases were placed in the same positions as in softball. The game needed two batters, a pitcher, a catcher, a man on each base and at least one fielder. When a batter was out, he went to the field and players rotated from bases to pitcher, to catcher then batter. The rules of the game called for a softball that was too costly. We substituted a sponge ball purchased at the five and dime store.

As growing boys, we enjoyed throwing rocks, hitting objects such as an apple on a fence post or a commercial advertising sign fastened to the fence, either a piece of metal, a piece of wood, or some other object. Practicing to hit the flag on the windmill was an object for trying one's arm. The barn had an unusual kind of roof made of flat concrete slabs. Each slab about one foot square was separately tied with wire around the wood strip sheathing. Rocks that landed on the roof cracked or broke slabs that caused leaks. Roof slabs had to inserted from the inside, a challenging and difficult task.. Commercial tile were expensive. Dad severely scolded us for throwing rocks that might land on the barn roof. But the admonition was never sufficient to keep us from trying to throw rocks successfully over the barn . When Dad was weary enough from replacing slabs, we could expect another spanking!

That reminds me of a game called Anthony Over, abbreviated as Andy-Over. The players chose sides and then would throw a small sponge ball over the roof. We couldn't play this game over the barn; the backside had a fenced in manure pile. We could use any building that had no fences to obstruct going around it. If the receiving side caught the ball thrown over the roof to them, they would run to tap the players on the throwing side, before they were aware that the ball had been caught. Any player tapped was a captive member of that team. The winning team was declared when all the players had been tapped and added to that side. It could be a very long game before one side finally won all the players.

Another popular game, both for boys and men, was pitching horseshoes. Horses were usually shod, old shoes which had been worn smooth when removed were used to pitch horseshoes. Worn out horseshoes were not the precision instruments used in today's regulation horseshoe games There was plenty of yard space for two steel or iron stakes driven into the ground at a specified distance and with four worn-out horseshoes we had a game. Games were played with competitive intensity, younger members were given encouragement--even concessions or handicaps.

An occasional family had one or two bicycles. Many families had none. To own a bicycle made one the envy of other boys. Our first bicycle came from the attic of the washhouse at Grandpa Nussbaum's place. One Sunday afternoon while visiting there, we boys were rummaging around and found an old rusty bicycle with flat tires. It had been stored when my uncles graduated to a family car. For a dollar and a half, we were able to take the bicycle home, restore it and learn to ride it. Neighbors, the Schrock family, had a bicycle. Occasionally, long daylight summer evenings after the chores were done, dinner dishes washed and dried, led to bicycle racing on the gravel road. That was a challenging and hazardous sport, rear wheel brakes locked, bikes skidded and fallen drivers removed gravel from skinned knees.

As automobiles came into general use, there were fewer riding horses. However, any horse on the farm, even a heavy draft horse, was a candidate for casual riding whether bareback, with a harness, or homemade saddle. I cannot remember in my youth that any of the nearby farmers had a commercial saddle. While informal horse racing occurred occasionally, horseback riding often served for travel or recreation. We had never seen a quality saddle or did we know about equestrian dress and equipment now used by some of our grandchildren.

Rope jumping was a cheap and popular game. With eight feet of thin rope, one could really develop one's skills while getting vigorous, exhausting exercise. There were two kinds of rope jumping: individual jumping and two persons twirling for one jumper between them.

Jumping appeals to boys. It was fairly simple to create from wood scraps one by two inch upright standards with spaced nails to support the wooden cross bar. Broad jumping was popular on any kind of grassy area, or if we were lucky enough to have a sandpit left over from a building project.

Hide and seek among young children was popular after dark on a summer evening. With farm buildings, trees and shrubbery, there was no limit to hiding places. Each player remained silent. One person was the seeker; the last one found became the seeker.

Swings suspended with a rope mounted on a branch of a large tree were a very important piece of play equipment. A piece of wood eight inches wide, 18 inches long, two inches thick with a hole drilled near each end and the rope pulled through provided the seat. Swings for adults could be of any height. Young children's swings were suspended no more than eight feet. The chinning bar, good to develop arm muscles, was popular.

Boys often engaged in wrestling. We brothers had many wrestling matches, both indoors and outdoors. Obviously the older boys had a great advantage, but as the younger ones grew and gained skill, competition became much keener.

One of the more unusual recreational events was building and walking on stilts. Stilts were made of two vertical pieces of wood, preferably a sturdy two by two, that had footrests fastened anywhere from a few inches to as high as three feet off the ground. The object was to learn to walk on two stilts, keep your balance to navigate with steps of different lengths, over uneven terrain and even to climb steps. That was a challenging game. Stilts were built for kids of all sizes and at all heights.

A winter sport was shinny, something like land hockey without uniforms or special equipment. Shinny sticks were made by cutting very small trees with a trunk 1 1/2 to 2 inches in diameter that had somewhat the shape of a golf club. Another source was a limb growing in that shape. A small sponge ball served as the puck. That game was played often in grade school. Free-swinging shinny players often suffered injuries to fingers and legs.

Another game was foot racing. Those sprints were for short distance of 50 to 150 yards. If a runner did not have a competitor, he could challenge himself by being timed.

The schoolyard included a dirt basketball court with a goal at each end. The game then was played very differently. Each goal counted two points. After each goal, the ball was returned to center for a jump. Almost no farms had basketball goals. A good basketball cost as much as a dollar and a half, too expensive for most youngsters.

What were some of the indoor games during winter evenings? Using a few sheets of scrap paper, we raced mathematical computation in addition, subtraction, multiplication and division. Dad, very adept with figures, though he completed only the seventh grade, challenged his sons. He frequently won. He had great facility with numbers, not only in mathematics, but especially with the carpenter's square as contractor and builder.

Checkers and Giveaway were popular games. Bridge decks were forbidden as too worldly. However, Rook cards were sometimes used and became more popular by the time I was in college.

To many people throwing darts was a fascinating game. The dart was homemade with a headless straight pin inserted in a split wooden matchstick and paper fins as the arrow. A homemade cork dartboard with appropriate markings hung on the wall.

Another outdoor game was rifle marksmanship. Today this would be regarded as too hazardous, especially with seven boys around the farm. We had a 22-caliber rifle from the time that I was about twelve years old; only the older boys were allowed to use it. We did some outdoor marksmanship though we used the rifle mostly to shoot sparrows and pigeons. Occasionally we hunted for squirrels, rabbits or clever crows that were regarded as a nuisance. We could not shoot the clever crows. We never had an accident though there were several times that the gun accidentally discharged. Standing on the concrete floor in the barn, rifle loaded, I was watching for sparrows when I accidentally fired the bullet on the floor within six inches of my foot. It was almost miraculous that we did not have a serious accident. Later on we also got a shotgun which is much more practical for most small game hunting. Dad rarely used a gun; during my years at home he did not own one. But Grandpa Nussbaum was a proud marksman who taught us the art.

With no commercial attractions, it is surprising how inventive farm kids were. They engaged in a great variety of activities individually or in occasional competition with the immediate neighbors but mostly with their own brothers and sister. Time was especially precious during the eight months of school (a short school year). There was almost no time left after school assignments following the farm work, completion of dinner and dishes. Games were limited mostly to holidays and weekends. That made game time more precious and boredom was unknown.

Chapter 5: The Impact of the Church at Home on the Farm

In the rural area near Berne, Indiana, where I was born and where my grandparents on both sides of the family lived, the social structure, neighborhood associations, shared farming tasks, as well as the religious community were centered in our Church. The solitary congregation (perhaps two hundred fifty persons including children by 1930) was formed when David Schwartz led a group of dissidents to break away from the Old Order Amish in 1894. My mother was two years old.

When the church was formed the homes were all rural. Families lived on farms with their devotion to the land. The Amish people had always been very productive farmers, they were stewards of the land and its conservation. The first generation of the Amish Christian Church, the dissident David Schwartz group, knew no other and held steadfastly to the farming tradition. However, by the third generation with the shift toward urban society, a small but growing number were attracted off the land. Some young men became carpenters or painters, a few young men and women were employed in nearby small town factories; the Bishop allowed a wider range of career choices than permitted by the Amish.

Their homes were very plain, sparsely furnished with simple decor. Barns, houses and outbuildings were functionally constructed without architectural awareness. Buildings were painted one color; no trimmings were permitted. Homes were unadorned, severe, and almost stark. There was nothing decorative either in the design of the furniture or the drapes; neither art nor patterned wallpaper was permitted. There were no commercial floor coverings, only occasional homemade rag carpets. Clothing was of solid colors; patterned striped or multi-colored clothing was prohibited. Windows characteristically had white transparent side curtains without draperies supplementing dark green rolled blinds. There were no large mirrors on walls or doors, small personal mirrors were usually kept in a drawer. Nothing was artistic and very little that showed cultivated awareness of color, design or aesthetic quality. Sense of beauty was found in nature, in trees, flowers and shrubs--God's gift to mankind. Families cultivated flowers as part of the vegetable garden, but there was little or no landscaping. Lawns were neatly trimmed and often bordered by flowers. Occasionally, attractive flowers were cut, placed in a vase in the dining room, but never on the table as a centerpiece. Flowers were seen as most attractive in their natural location.

Colorful foliage in the fall was extensive in that part of the country, especially the brilliant and dramatic color of maple and certain oak trees. That was part of God's gift in nature, but there was no exhibition of beauty for its own sake. Beauty per se was worldly and not to be exhibited with pride or ostentation.

People did not dress for attractiveness, the body was not to be an object or subject of decoration or admiration. It was the temple of the spirit. Conditions of arduous labor for every family member left little time or energy to defy this religious decree. Youthful deviants who did immediately became subjects of chastisement.

There was very little room for ideas. There was no participation in the political life of the community, no sharing in partisan politics. Voting at the polls was not permitted as testimony of "being in the world but not of it." It was another form of total disengagement, an historic tradition from the Amish. There was also an inclination to deal only in the practical. All things either had to have functional use at the moment or promised religious discipline leading to a reward in the next life. Conformity and control were pervasive. There was no latitude for people to think differently or to allow discussion of ideas that might lead them astray.

Further, about the home, tableware, tablecloths and towels were all one color, usually white, and totally plain. In dinnerware there was no sterling silver or silver plate. Water glasses were of the plainest sort; wineglasses were of one simple style.

Women were not permitted to cut their hair. Facial makeup and jewelry, necklaces, bracelets or rings were prohibited. Women did not wear engagement or wedding rings. My mother never had a wedding ring. (The Mennonite congregation that my parents later joined did permit wedding rings and modest jewelry.)

There was no socialization with persons outside that Church. No dating, social activities or marriage was permitted outside the congregation. So that in practice it was a totally closed community, even so far as shared farming activities were concerned. I will deal with this in another section.

It was assumed that any facial makeup, clothing in more than one color, patterns or stripes represented a haughty spirit. In the same way, to trim a house or barn with a different color was regarded as worldly. The simple, rural, unadorned life was considered a life of goodness. Evils attributed to the devil were found in complexity, especially in cities. Hard work represented spiritual discipline as well as economic and subsistence necessity. Conspicuous leisure activity was not permissible. Real sin was found in the urban and metropolitan locations, amid commercial and "worldly" pleasures that were to be avoided. Virtue was found in the rural setting among devout, plain, hard-working people. Until my later adolescence, German was the language of the Church and Sunday school. Conversation in the family and with neighbors was always in the Swiss-German dialect. English was the language of the "world."

The only books found in homes were Martin Luther's and other German translations of *The Bible, Martyr's Mirror* and hymnbooks. In some homes, there were other German translations of religious books authored by Menno Simons. In my home there was a book entitled, *The Prince of Peace* and another Bunyan's *Pilgrim's Progress* that my mother regarded as a kind of strangely bewildering volume. She was never certain that it had any meaning for her. We never had a dictionary at home; dictionaries were for schools.

Other reading material, all practical, included a three times weekly newspaper, the Adams County *Witness* was printed Monday, Wednesday and Friday. Before the Great Depression we received *The Fort Wayne Journal Gazette* by rural mail, the day after it was printed. A few practical magazines advised farmers such as, *Successful Farming, The Farm Journal, The Prairie Farmer* and *Farmer's Guide*. There were no other books in the home, and there was never a library card used by our family.

There was no musical instrument in the home until I was perhaps ten or eleven years of age when an old pump organ was permitted. About the time I went to college, we bought a piano in used condition that cost fifteen dollars. We boys had learned to read notes in school; Mom and Dad could not read music.

Radios were not permitted when they first became available. When I was perhaps twelve years of age, we did have a small table radio with access to three or four radio stations. That church restriction had been relaxed. Attending commercial movies was prohibited. Berne and Monroe, the closest towns had no movie theater. Decatur, eight miles away, had one. Dancing was evil, there were no social dances, folk or barn dances in the community. Other forms of leisure activity found in the urban setting, or in communities of different ethnic and denominational background, were forbidden. Frugality, honesty, simplicity, judiciousness, plainness and hard physical labor were all regarded as both necessary and forms of virtue. The Christian life was to be reflected in behavior, simplicity of dress, social exclusiveness helping to insulate one from worldliness. Education only through grade eight was to avoid being contaminated by the world of ideas. Members were prohibited from using the legal system to settle disagreements. To use the law to one's advantage or violating most laws was evil.

Ironically, during the years of prohibition, between 1919 and 1933, that community continually produced wine and beer that were regularly consumed in moderation. Some people occasionally purchased moonshine liquor. Open and continual defiance of the 18th Amendment was the practice. Also, there was an occasional marriage of first cousins, illegal in Indiana. I cannot recall that any member or youth of that Church was charged with violating the law, other than a rare traffic ticket.

Did members have a book of church order? These regulations were nowhere written; they were catalogued and interpreted in the mind of the Bishop who permitted no doubt as to their divine revelation.

Chapter 6: The Church of My Boyhood

My earliest memories, before we had an automobile, include riding in a storm buggy with windshield and glass-paneled wooden sliding doors on each side and a small oblong window in the back. The seat and back were thinly upholstered in black. There was a single footstep on each side; even for adults it took two steps from the ground to the buggy floor. The buggy was very narrow, so two adults almost filled the seat. The buggy had a small extension of the floor on the back, no more than two and a half feet by three feet and perhaps eight inches deep with leather lid, a kind of buggy trunk. The wheels had spokes and frames of wood with riveted steel rims.

. In summer heat we opened the windshield hinged at the top by pulling in the bottom fastening it inside to the roof. Side windows in the doors were sealed but in warm weather sliding side doors were left open. The small oblong window in the back was fixed. There were no side mirrors, no lights or reflectors for night driving. But there was a buggy-whip holder; the buggy whip served as the accelerator for the horse, brown Daisy. This was our only mode of transportation other than the farm wagon and a team of horses. We traveled only to visit both sets of grandparents, which was about two miles, to church each Sunday, and whatever business had to be carried on in towns, either Berne or Monroe

On Sunday mornings, Dad and Mom arose early; Dad fed the cows, horses and pigs, and did the milking. Mom fed the chickens, prepared breakfast, awakened and dressed us for church. Seated at the dining room table, Dad said grace in German. We ate breakfast of fried eggs, pancakes with molasses and hot chocolate. After the meal we knelt for a family prayer. Then Dad seated at the same table shaved with a straight razor, a small mirror on a stand, a cup of shaving soap, with shaving brush and water heated in the teakettle, poured into a wash bowl. Mom quickly washed and dried the dishes; both dressed in their plain Sunday best. We crowded into the buggy and Daisy trotted two miles to church. I was squeezed very tightly between Mom and Dad. I did not like the discomfort. When Elmer was born

Mom held him in her lap.

In cold weather, we used the horse-blanket to cover the family inside the buggy. On arrival Dad covered Daisy with the blanket and tied her to the metal hitching rack at one end of the cinder-covered church parking lot. Sometimes the church had evening services, during winter periods after dark. On one Sunday evening Daisy became restless, tied to the hitching rack, broke the bridle strap and walked home with the buggy. One of the uncles drove us home in his car. Most families already had cars, a few walked to church. Only four or five families came by buggy or by two-seater surrey.

When I was four years old, Alvin was born; then the buggy was too small to accommodate the family of five. Dad bought a thoroughly used Star brand sedan automobile with self-starter and floor gearshift. Mom was opposed, though I do not remember why. Perhaps it was because she was accustomed driving a horse and buggy, but never learned to drive a car. This was a little more upscale; many church families still had hand-cranked Ford touring cars, open sided, with attachable curtains. When I was nine years of age, Dad occasionally sent me on errands driving the Star to neighbors, but not to town. I was barely able to see the road from the low front seat. There were no odometer laws, no age limits for drivers and no drivers' licenses.

One Sunday morning when I was twelve, Dad stayed home to have a flock of roosters caponized.(unsexed) He told me to drive Mom and my brothers to church. At the crossroads one-half mile from the church, I failed to make the turn and crashed into the eighteen-inch thick concrete bridge railing, which was right in the intersection. Mom was sitting in the passenger seat holding Victor, perhaps eighteen months old. Autos had no seat belts and a windshield of window glass, Victor's head crashed into the windshield. He suffered a two-inch cut on the side of his head. A friend who came to the scene of the accident rushed Mom and Victor to Dr. Amos Reusser, the family physician, who closed the cut with a sharp clawed metal clamp.

We also missed church service. Mom interpreted the accident as God's punishment for Dad's putting business ahead of worship. Dad wasn't so sure. The Star was sold as junk. We got a scaled-down model T Ford with flimsy side curtains, hand-cranked. It soon was known for its erratic performance, particularly in cold weather.

The plain white, bevel sided church building had a wood shingle roof, clear glass windows. There was no sign to identify it. Inside it was equally plain. There was no designated communion table or altar. The walls and ceiling painted off white were devoid of any decoration except an eight-day Seth Thomas clock. There were no symbols, crosses, chandeliers, banners or stained glass windows. Pews of natural grained oak were coated with clear varnish, without cushions. A stand with slanted top served as a pulpit, rested on an eight-inch elevated platform. The concrete-walled and floored basement contained the steam furnace, coal bin and toilets, a luxury not found in many homes.

Our family shared a pew with Grandma Mazelin who was seated next to the center aisle. She declined to sit with the other ministerial wives in the pew behind their husbands. She always were a plain black scarf; I do not remember ever seeing her wear a hat. She often passed barbershop striped stick candy to help us keep quiet.

Except when ill, children and adults attended both Sunday school and worship services on alternate Sundays. Absolute quiet, no whispering, no color books were the order of the day. On arrival, church members practiced the Holy Kiss on arrival in the vestibule, in the aisles, or in walking toward one's seat in the forward part of the church. Members often paused at a pew. The member seated next to the aisle rose, shook hands and irrespective of gender kissed each other on the lips. Persons of the same or the opposite sex kissed each other. After the kiss, members often greeted each other with, "Der Herr segne dich (The Lord bless you.)"

Some hustling farm families arrived fifteen twenty-five minutes before the service. They visited about the events of the week, gossiped or read their Bibles. Bibles were not kept at the church but some members brought their own. Late comers were typically those who lived in Berne with no farm work.

Ministers were the Bishop, David Schwartz, assistant bishop, Jacob J. Schwartz (first cousins) and assistant, Daniel Mazelin, my grandfather. Their formal education was fewer than six grades and no theological preparation except self-study in the Amish tradition. Worship services opened at nine o'clock with a brief statement by one of the three ministers thanking God for the blessings of the week and keeping us in good health. There were no printed orders of service.

After the opening statement of three or four minutes, the minister of the morning announced the first hymn, although for some years the hymn composed by the Bishop was always sung first. Here is the part of the first stanza:

O Heere Gott, Du Seist gelobt
O, Lord God We Praise You
Benedeit und gepriesen
Blessed and Glorified
Geehret auch nicht aus Gebrauch
Honored not by custom
Sondern gib mir zu Siegen
Help Me to Be Victorious
Gib mir Übung und Verziehung
Give me practice, and pardon
Mit deinem Geist so reine
Through Your Pure Spirit

The Bishop's youngest son, Jacob D. R., (known as J.D.R.) who had some musical talent and a pitch pipe, served as song leader. A small choir of younger men and women, perhaps a dozen who stood in front led the congregation. For more than thirty years after the Amish Christian Church was established (1894) the Amish hymnal, *Ausbund*, was used. *Ausbund* was first published in 1564. Some hymns were added by the Bishop and church members in a special printing. Without musical scores, the congregation sang soprano. Four-part music and musical instruments were used on other occasions but not in worship at that time; they were regarded as marginally "worldly." Hymns had as many as forty verses. The minister announced each hymn with perhaps a total of twenty to twenty-five minutes of congregational singing. Some members and children did not sing; a few of the elderly might take a nap, others would stare into space.

Not according to any schedule the Bishop, claiming further revelation, made some changes. He authorized the use of a piano. His granddaughter, one of the few persons qualified, was named accompanist. In 1929, the song leader, the Bishop's son, persuaded his father that new modernized German hymnbooks with musical scales were needed. A new German hymnbook was developed unique to this congregation, complete with musical scores. No other hymnals were acceptable.

When singing ended, the minister who opened the service then called the congregation to prayer. Young and old who were physically able, turned around in their seats, knelt on the wooden pine floor. In prayer they either propped their heads up with their arms or put their heads down on folded arms on the seat for a long season of prayer by the minister. Prayer continued from ten to fifteen minutes covering a great variety of subjects. Persons were not named in the prayer--one of the many forms of de-personalization characteristic of this congregation. As a youngster, I remember thinking that the prayers were endless.

Once the season of prayer ended, this minister returned to his seat at the level of the congregation. The preacher of the morning then came to the simple pulpit to read the German scripture and preach the sermon in a mixture high German and Swiss dialect. The sermon sometimes was an unschooled exposition of scripture, Old or New Testament. Preaching was sometimes in the form of admonition with some effort at contextual biblical description but not related to current issues except to condemn the "world." The fearful nature of God was often dominant; love or tenderness was not feelingly included; on rare occasions the minister might exhibit some related emotion. The sermon typically was from thirty-five to fifty minutes long.

What did members and youth do during this time? Stern order was maintained. There was no whispering but often napping; for some this was a rest period to compensate for overworked farmers and craftsmen. A few might read their

48

Bibles intermittently. Preaching was seldom inspiring or emotional; there was no orating. When the preacher of the morning ended his sermon, the third minister offered a brief summary of the sermon or stressed some important points for five to ten minutes. Then, another hymn of several verses until about eleven o'clock. According to the season, there were various announcements. During the summer, the Bishop announced the catechism classes by number, the afternoon on which each class would meet and at a member's home. Some members, eager to remain in the good graces of the Bishop, extended open invitations to him, asking to have classes meet there more often than normal rotation. I attended these summer catechism classes for five summers. The Bishop, who had written his own 35-page catechism in German, taught each of three or four classes.

Weddings were an integral part of the church worship service; weddings pending were announced two weeks in advance. All couples were Amish Christian church members; no non-members were invited to attend. Bride and groom wore regular Sunday dress, no special attire. Weddings occurred only on worship service Sundays. After the sermon the minister asked the prospective bride and groom to stand in front of the congregation where vows, but no rings, were exchanged. The bride and groom did not kiss. No dinners or receptions followed the weddings. The newly-weds did not take any honeymoon trips.

Announcement time brought general admonition, at other times chastisement by name. If baptisms (only for mid-adolescents and young adults) were scheduled at a future date, their names were read. During the summer season special Sunday afternoon gatherings for spiritual conversations at some church member's home might be announced.

Finally, at 11:15 to 11:30 some Pauline variety or an Old Testament version of German benediction was offered: "The Lord Bless You and Keep You." (Numbers 6:24-26)

"Der Herr segne dich und behüte dich; der Herr lasse sein Angesicht leuchten über dir, und sei dir gnädig; der Herr hebe sein Angesicht über dich, und gebe dir Frieden. "(Martin Luther translation)

By tradition, the Lord's Supper (communion service) with foot washing was supposed to be observed twice a year on unspecified dates, but only at a time when the church was relatively peaceful, with no major unrest or discord. Rebellious members had been chastised and had confessed; members defying the church rules or besmirched with "worldly" behavior had either confessed and repented or been duly excommunicated. Weeks and months preceding the Lord's Supper were often stressful and anxious times, many members wondering whether the Bishop's allusions in sermons or post-sermon admonition might have referred to them and what the consequences might be. Women who wore high heels, short dresses, silk hose, faint rouge or facial power, lip stick, perfume or shaved their legs were particularly vulnerable prospects. Only pre-teen girls were permitted shorn hair. Teenagers and all women should part hair in the middle in an unstylish arrangement. Girls with shorn hair were not eligible for church membership. Men were ordered to cut hair moderately short (but no crew cuts), only inconspicuously parted, never combed backwards or tamed with hair lotions. Stiff collars were frowned on and all neckties or bow ties (until the latter 20s) were forbidden. Suspenders were much more decent than belts; hats were worn squarely on the head with no rakish tilts. No one attended movies, high school athletic contests, plays or musical concerts. During congregational dissension, the Lord's Supper was often postponed for weeks or months to avoid someone taking communion "unworthily", according to Paul's admonition.

On the designated Sunday, the Lord's Supper (abend Mahl, in German) followed by foot washing was observed exclusively by members of this congregation, each having been baptized as an adult and a member in good standing. No Christian baptized in any other church was qualified to share in the communion. In preparation on Saturday, Grandma Mazelin, wife of minister number three, usually baked four large loaves of bread. She selected a red wine in her wine cellar. Wine bottles and loaves were placed on a small table near the pulpit draped with a white cloth, which was used for this purpose. Hymns were sung for the usual twenty-five or thirty minutes, a sermon was preached, morning prayers followed. Then the Bishop announced the communion observance; he alone served communion elements to each member individually He took a loaf of bread, asked communing members to stand, beginning with the left of center section where ministers and other members were seated. Beginning at the front row, he broke a piece of bread, served each member who immediately was seated and ate it. Similarly, row by row to the right of the center aisle, from side and center aisles he served each member. As the loaf diminished, one of the other ministers brought a fresh loaf. After the serving with every member seated he asked that anyone who inadvertently had not been served make himself known.

To serve the wine, he followed the same order. He used a glass with a handle shaped similar to a measuring cup. He handed the cup to a member who took one swallow, returned the cup to the Bishop and was seated. With each member he followed the same procedure. Another minister followed with a bottle to replenish wine as needed until all were served.

Then he announced that all members by sections would retire to the basement for observance of foot washing. A white curtain was hung the length of the basement, women and men on separate sides. Benches with no back were set in rows with metal ten-quart buckets scattered about. Members paired themselves, one seated on the bench removed shoes and socks, and the other brought warm water in the bucket and ceremoniously washed his partner's feet. Then partners reversed roles and ended with the Holy Kiss. All returned to the sanctuary to conclude the worship service which ended after twelve o'clock .

.   On alternate Sundays, Sunday school was conducted all in the one room sanctuary. The congregation assembled as if it were worship, except young people not yet members sat in pews by classes organized by ages. The youngest class was six to eight years of age. Each pupil memorized a verse from the Psalms. The presiding minister of the day "taught" from the pulpit by calling on pupils to recite their memorized verses (in German from Martin Luther's translation) in sequence. Recited while standing in the pew, it nonetheless produced stage fright to youngsters. Some who had painful memory lapses or stuttered provoked the undisciplined amusement of the whole congregation.

I remember my entry into Sunday school. My first verse was Psalm 33, verse 1, "Freuet euch des Herrn, ihr Gerechten; die Frommen sollen ihn preisen (Rejoice in the Lord; the righteous shall sing his praises.)." I spent all week memorizing and petrified on Sunday morning, I succeeded. Each class of older students, in sequence read designated chapters of the assigned book of the Old Testament. When each student had read a verse the minister asked a few questions about the passage read, without contextual background, concerning the literal interpretation of the reading. Classes recited in order of age, beginning with the youngest; typically, there were four or five classes. The oldest class consisted of persons in mid to latter teens, rarely into the twenties.

Baptism constituted becoming a member of the congregation. No membership certificates were issued. With baptism, Sunday school participation ended. Rarely, youths postponed confession and baptism until their twenties. I was sixteen, almost seventeen, when I was baptized in April 1935. According the Bishop's record I was the last person baptized in that congregation. I participated in only one communion service. Very soon the church began to splinter and disintegrate; none of my brothers was baptized before it broke up. As others in their age category were baptized, those not baptized joined a new class of younger people. Persons older than eighteen or nineteen who were not yet baptized felt as if they failed the course, as they were reassigned to classes for persons several years younger

Alternate Sunday worship was carried forward from the Amish. On alternate Sundays, they visited family and friends. This congregation established Sunday school for non-members as more important than visitation.

There was no offering either at Worship or Sunday school services. On the last Sunday of each month one of the ministers, after the service, stood in the basement to receive checks or cash. Teachers at the parochial school, and church and school expenses were paid from these contributions. Ministers received no salary or expense reimbursement, so far as I know.

Custodians were some of the nearby members who contributed that service. For years this was done by the Mazelin family (my grandparents) who lived a thousand feet from the church building. Maintenance and renovations were funded by the Bishop's demands on some of the more prosperous members and other voluntary contributions of money or in-kind.

The carry-over from the Amish is very understandable because these ministers knew no other model.

Chapter 7: What Held the Community Together?

A group that broke away from the Adams County Old Order Amish in 1894 later chose the name Amish Christian Church. David Schwartz, eldest son of the Amish Bishop, in his early twenties had been elected a deacon. After two years, he was elevated to the position of full deacon that allowed him to fulfill the duties of the Bishop when the Bishop was not available. It seems that he had visions of becoming a reformer, based on claimed theological deficiencies in the Amish faith in contrast with his interpretation of scripture. After months of acrimonious sessions of the congregation, these differences led to a break with his father and the Old Order Amish Church. According to David, he was a reformer who saw the true light. He claimed that his father's part of the assembled congregation walked out. From the Amish perspective, this is a baffling claim because the father was upholding the traditional Amish faith. Literally, it was true that his father, the bishop, and his loyalists did walk out of the home where the final contentious meeting was held. From the Amish perspective, twenty-five-year-old David was the defiant young rebel who led his group away from the Amish; his father remained loyal to the Amish faith.

The Amish in all congregations continued to assert their "being in the world but not of it" --a total separation from other Christians--and with exclusive understanding and practice of the faith. Although their faith and practices are very different from other Christian denominations, many Amish feel no need to be judgmental about other groups who claim to be Christian. They point to the admonition of Jesus, "Do not judge, so that you may not be judged." (Matthew 7:1.)

Total separation, organizationally and without social intercourse, or intermarriage was and is the rule. Education among the Amish is limited to the eighth grade to shield them from intellectual pursuits. Hundreds of Amish congregations in various parts of the United States and Canada--though disagreeing in minutiae--commonly asserted the same or similar articles of faith and practice. Further, the members' conduct, dress, language, life-styles, modes of transportation, disengagement from political life and commercial entertainment, distinctive homesteads, different personal and social values, continues to be demonstrable testimony to their faith and practice.

It is helpful to recall that in the 1890s many of the present distinguishing manifestations then did not exist. There were no automobiles, motor cycles, electric lights, home appliances, telephones, radios, TVs, computers, farm tractors, airplanes or modern farm machinery. Electric lights and appliances were not available. Motive power was the horse. Clothing was homemade, homes were simple and sparsely furnished, in door plumbing was unknown in rural areas. Rural church services in some denominations were sometimes conducted in homes.

David Schwartz, who anointed himself as Bishop, began his reforms based on certain articles of faith that he passionately proclaimed as essential to salvation. Whereas, the Old Order Amish had already asserted their own exclusive possession of truth, David reasserted his version of exclusiveness for this group only. Strict conformance was as basic and fundamental to the Amish Christians as with the Old Order Amish--with special revelation from God to him alone and with him as the sole spiritual interpreter. Whereas scores of Amish congregations located in different states fraternized with each other, this Amish Christian group had the sole "key to the heavenly kingdom" and did not fraternize with anyone else. Perhaps seventy-five to one hundred Amish sided with David, including my mother's parents, Daniel and Catherine Mazelin. Daniel was early elected an assistant minister. A scattered few, such as my father's parents, David and Marian Nussbaum, came originally from splinter Mennonite groups to join this congregation.

With the zeal of recent converts, the Amish Christians had new light, the reformer's passion to create the righteous community, the assertiveness of those with newly found truth. They confirmed their inherited exclusiveness and separateness; and now in 1894 there was a fresh assertion emanating from the vigor and power of a reformer and the building of a renewed sense of community.

In appearance, and demeanor, during the first decade

there were few changes. The Amish Christians spoke the Swiss-German dialect, used Martin Luther's German translation of the *Bible, Martyr's Mirror* and *Ausbund.* Each of those practices was continued with worship services in German for the next forty years. No layman ever had any voice in church government; the Bishop ruled autocratically with his two assistants as confirming subordinates. There was no written or legal organization of the congregation.

In response to the wave of inventions and cultural changes in the early 20th century, what would the Bishop's revelations lead him to declare about their ownership and use? This list is long, although there were no sudden or drastic changes. Gradually his revelations permitted men to shave their beards, although he and his ministerial colleagues, and a few laymen, never did. Men cut and trimmed their hair but were admonished not to adopt worldly hairstyles. Women gradually discarded their black bonnets, white caps, and shawls. Dress styles were compromised; more colorful yet plain clothing was evident among them.

After two and a half decades, a church building was constructed. New home construction strayed from the simplicity of the Amish. Slowly running water, indoor toilets, bathtubs, automatic water heaters, upholstered furniture, electric lights and appliances won approval. Houses were painted white, barns and outbuildings were painted red, but untrimmed, justified for wood preservation. Telephones, then radios followed. Automobiles were grudgingly approved provided they were low cost brands and painted black. Farm tractors supplemented the horses. New kinds of farming equipment including powered grain threshing machines came on the market, among many other modern inventions. Would Bishop David Schwartz adhere to the pattern of the Old Amish who were noted for rejecting new inventions of convenience and efficiency, or would his reforms permit flexibility and modernization?

What held the community together between its deep roots in the Old Amish tradition and the temptations to compromise with alluring inventions of convenience? To the Old Amish efficiency was no reason for change; to society in general it was a key to progress. How could the Bishop overcome the traditions and practices of social and religious exclusiveness and stolid right conduct carried over from the Old Amish? Would he have fresh revelations? Initially, tradition joined with the total absence of any freedom of inquiry, exploring of ideas or expanding horizons through reading and discussion. Worldly ignorance reinforced by fear to do otherwise held minds and emotions captive. For many members, being snugly in the church with its rigid conformity was a comfortable security blanket--a safe place.

Perhaps community cohesion was generated less by spiritual love for the brethren than real or figurative tall fences, with peril to one's soul for trying to learn what lay beyond the enclosure. It was perilous to one's status to express doubt, discontent, curiosity, inquisitiveness or a challenge to the revelatory claims of the Bishop or to exceed the bounds of acceptable behavioral practices that he enunciated. Prompt excommunication was the predictable penalty for any courageous, obstinate or defiant members. That brought complete (shunning) social ostracism--being totally cut off from all sense of community within and condemnation to eternal perdition. Who dared to seek solace from the heathen world beyond while consequentially being condemned to perdition?

Church members and their children had the conditions of life and death defined for them. They were prohibited from exposure to other ideas through education, attending any other church or having contaminating discussions with anyone outside the fold. Complete isolation, avoidance of exposure to competing information served to stunt three generations of church members and their children, encircled by prescriptive social and cultural illiteracy.

The Amish principle of the dominance of community over the individual prevailed. The Amish Christian Church adopted additional forms of solidification. The Amish, at that time, sent their children to public schools through grade eight. The Amish Christian Parochial School was an extension of the home and the church with teachers and students all connected with the Church. As the Amish Christian Church progressed no member families of the church sent their children to public schools. No students at the parochial school came from outside the church. The school building was directly across the road from the church, a constant reminder how the two institutions were interwoven. When the school grounds were too wet, the children played games on the church parking grounds covered with a heavy layer of porous cinders.

Everyone was of Swiss or Swiss-related descent and all member families at home spoke conversational Swiss-German dialect. The Amish Christian Church used its own school as a powerful means of solidifying the exclusiveness of the church, as did some Missouri Synod Lutheran churches north of Decatur, Indiana. However, the Lutherans believed in higher education; the Amish Christian Church sided with the Old Amish practice of prohibiting any education beyond the eighth grade.

There was no school board to provide oversight or to formulate and set policy. All policy was determined between the Bishop and the principal of the school, which during my time, were father and son. Earlier, the Bishop's assistant, Jacob J. Schwartz, was teacher-principal, then absentee principal for several   years.

The sharpest single rule was to teach absolute obedience and conformity. Rigid unwritten rules reflected their strict policies. An example was the prohibition of going to outdoor toilets except during recess or the lunch hour, with the result of occasional "accidents." To interrupt class time by running to the toilet, no matter how urgent, seemed to offend the principal. Also illustrative of rigid rules was the procedure in dismissing classes for recess or the end of the school day. The principal pressed an electric bell button signaling the students to rise from their seats, stand in the aisle without whisper or conversation. The next bell served to order the lowest grades to march in two columns out to the anteroom, down into the basement, or outside. Each pair of columns was followed by the next pair until all had recessed. Rarely, the principal paddled one of the students. The sequel to any punishment in school was certain assurance of punishment at home. The culture of the home and the church was effectively re-enforced in school.

The Amish Christian Bishop gradually became more open to the use of new inventions than were the Amish. The Amish were not permitted to own an early steam engine, tractor or powered threshing machine; Amish farmers, as a group, contracted for service with an owner of such equipment.

In contrast, the Amish Christian farmers bought a steam engine, and later a tractor, to power the purchased threshing machine. They formed an exclusive threshing ring for their own church members. Typically, twelve to fifteen farmers constituted a threshing ring based on the number of workers required for efficient operation of the equipment. Every member raised wheat and oats; some raised rye, barley, soybeans or buckwheat. One farmer-operator provided the tractor for a fee while another serviced the thresher that was jointly owned. Six farmers, on a rotating basis, each provided a flatbed wagon and a team of horses, four or five men in the field pitched grain sheaves onto the wagons that hauled the sheave-loads to the threshing machine set near the barn. The grain flowed through the tube from the machine into burlap or special grain bags. Three or four men slung the fifty to sixty-pound sacks over their shoulders and carried them into the grain storage bin either in a separate granary or sometimes located upstairs in the barn. Usually, the owner or someone he had engaged trampled the fiercely blown straw onto a stack, the most miserable job of all.

When finished on one farm, the crew and equipment moved to the next member whose grain was ready for threshing. Members lived close or few miles apart. Farmers who were not church members, living among members, were puzzled as to why a threshing ring could not consist of adjoining farmers rather than some distant members of one congregation. Each different grain ripened at varying times during the summer requiring two or more threshing rounds among members.

The hostess who invited wives or daughters of participant members to assist her served a heavy noon dinner and sometimes an evening supper. To be invited signaled a social honor. Periodically, mornings and afternoons, the hostesses also served water and lemonade to workers wherever they were stationed without interrupting the work schedule. The threshers' workday in midsummer heat was often twelve hours long in a rush to store the grain before a rain shower.

A threshing ring was another chain in the exclusiveness. I cannot recall a non-church member ever joining the ring. As the farm population grew, the Amish Christian church had two threshing rings; in each ring one of the sons of the Bishop provided the tractor for belt power. The provider was regarded as head of the ring. At the end of the season, each member paid a few cents per bushel to finance the costs of operation and to pay for the threshing equipment and maintenance. My uncle, D. D. Mazelin, my mother's brother, was for many years the bookkeeper and treasurer for each threshing ring.

Another bond was the silo-filling routine in late summer and early fall season. Nearly all members of the ring had a small dairy herd and a round, vertical silo, twenty-five to thirty-five feet tall, to store green chopped corn silage for cattle feed. In September, before the corn was ripe, the silo-filling ring also consisted of church members. They shared the work of cutting corn (before hybrid seed) seven to nine feet tall, loading it on wagons, hauling it to the corn chopper set next to the silo, with an eight-inch metal tube as tall as the silo and extending on the inside, to blow the chopped corn in from the top. One man inside the silo walked circles tamping the ensilage to eliminate air pockets and avoid spoilage. Workers sometimes continued in chilly autumn drizzle. Although wet corn stalks were heavier and messier, they provided equally good ensilage. My own experience of working in those conditions gave me a lifelong aversion to being outdoors in chilly, rainy weather.

Most of the members also had a fruit tree orchard of one or two acres. The church members with orchards were comparably joined in two spray rings. Each ring employed a young man to operate the fifty-gallon spray tank. The pressure sprayer with long hose powered by a gasoline engine was mounted on a four-wheeled trailer with pneumatic tires. The sprayer was towed from orchard to orchard by an auto or small truck. The spraying cycles required a variety of chemicals from pre-blossom to near harvest, five to seven times per season. D. D. Mazelin, in addition to serving as the bookkeeper-treasurer for the silo filling and tree spraying rings, was also the chief chemical advisor. He knew the chemicals, proper mixtures and exact time of spraying all of which he gleaned from the County Agricultural Agent and bulletins published by Purdue University, the land grant institution for Indiana. My brothers, Elmer and Alvin, each sprayed regularly for more than one season. Occasionally, I filled in for the regular person. At this writing both suffer from advanced cases of Parkinson's. Elmer, a retired professor of physics, is convinced that the source or trigger of his malady is the chemicals used when combined with the genetic tendency. Medically, at this writing, the causes of Parkinson's disease are still being studied. (Elmer died in April, 2000, Alvin in December, 2000.)

In addition to these organized activities, there were many kinds of exchanges or trades of services, labor or products between neighbors. To a large extent neighbors, as members of this faith community, were not necessarily persons who lived next door. When a farm family moved, in preparation and on moving day, neighbors gathered with wagons and horses to transport household goods, farm equipment, livestock, grain and other animal feed. Neighbor's help was simply contributed; no commercial movers were involved. If a farmer was ill at planting or harvest time neighbors brought horse and tractor power and equipment and worked together in a "frolic," as they said in Swiss-German, until the task was completed. Quilting became a social event for the women. Butchering a cow or two hogs was a family and neighborhood undertaking. Unmarried women, typically called "old maids" were sometimes regarded as candidates for charitable or low paid domestic workers.

Each of these organized operations and informal neighbor to neighbor activities contributed to the bonding of the exclusive church community. In constructing a new house, barn or outbuilding much labor was donated. For many years these shared activities and responsibilities served also to fortify the Bishop's position. When he proclaimed that he was the revelatory spokesman for the Lord God, his assertions frightened and proscribed the minds and conduct of his followers. The doubters and challengers sometimes defied him, including three of his sons and other relatives. The power of excommunication, however, prescribing total isolation from family and friends was stultifying. A few rugged individuals who were excommunicated simply departed and did not look back. These included two of the Bishop's six sons. A third son, with his wife and daughter, endured multiple excommunications, and finally returned to the church after his father's excommunication. As with any person who has essentially absolute power, ultimate dissolution of the organization was predictable. The only question was, when?

One can conjecture that the Bishop lost an opportunity to implant and cultivate a durable Christian utopian community. Had he understood more of the basic principles of shared leadership and utilized the wisdom of some non-family lay persons that might have helped. He seems to have regarded the completely closed society with himself the theocratic head, restricting all persons to grade school education, and manipulating obedient family members to become successors as the prevailing model. This proved not to be durable.

When the Bishop and his cohorts separated from the Old Order Amish, they had experienced excommunication and life-long shunning by their own families who remained in that church. The Bishop of the Amish Christian Church used excommunication as his chief weapon much more frequently and more harshly than did the Amish. In my view, he frequently did so as a means of solidifying his power and authority.

Nearly all members of the Amish Christian Church were farmers. The bonding forces were not only the faith but also the exclusivity of the school, the threshing, silo filling and tree spraying rings, as well as nearly every kind of neighborly social intercourse. All of these forms of association confirmed and nurtured the closed society for nearly three generations.

Within this faith community there was a certain security that also made members feel they could not belong anywhere else. When in the 1930s the community was shattered many members felt that they could in no other place establish durable church membership. During the depression years of the 30s, some families, including our own, found a certain economic security in shared financial support. However, by the World War

II years, economic conditions had sufficiently improved so that this was no longer a bonding factor. The painful dissolution of the Church occurred by stages from about 1935 to the mid-1940s. What had been the cohesive, exclusive community for more than forty years was no more.

Until this writing, I had never connected all these factors and the extent to which the Bishop and his family dominated the shaping of matters of faith and worship as well as community. He was the author and sole instructor of the church catechism of all youth in the process of becoming members. Consistent with the Old Amish practice, there was no missionary activity. Persons from outside the Amish Christian Church joined as members only during its early years. To my knowledge during the last twenty years of the congregation only young people from church families joined as members. The church had become a totally inbred community.

The Bishop's eldest son, Noah, was elected as a minister to replace Jacob J. Schwartz when he was excommunicated. Paradoxically, this served not to solidify the Bishop's power; instead, growing numbers of members saw this as an excess of hierarchy. Among the three nominees proposed by Church members, election occurred by lot. (Three hymnbooks were placed on the pulpit; each nominee took one. One book had the election slip, "You are the one." Selection by lot, a tradition from the Amish church was interpreted as evidence of God's choice.)

The abandonment of the Amish Christian Parochial School for financial reasons, as described in another chapter, was an early step in the disintegration of the community. It was also symbolic of what was ahead.

As the Church disintegrated by stages, strong animosities developed between some of the members who departed and some who remained. The membership dissolution and changing farming conditions combined to accelerate the gradual dissolution of the various agricultural rings. What once had been a cohesive community of faith was shattered into splinters. Many persons were profoundly disillusioned. The formerly powerful, autocratic and proud Bishop David Schwartz during his later years became a disturbed, broken, and very contrite man.

Forsaken by his family, his only remaining support came from one widowed daughter, who stood with him to his death.

At his death, an undated statement of confession and remorse was found among his personal effects. Originally written in German, it was translated into English by an unknown person or persons. The typewritten English version that consists of two single-spaced pages begins with, *"I am a very sorrowful old father. My eyes overflow with tears when I think about of my past sins."* Intermittently, he is very specific and asks God for forgiveness. *"I openly confess that I inherited from Adam an honor-seeking nature, and did not recognize my sins, and because I thought too highly of myself, my pride would not allow me to humble myself. When I was rebuked about my sins I was not honest enough to admit it. I did not want a name that (indicated) I was such sinner. But, Alas! What shall I say, I am guilty and confess it. For denying it is a greater sin than the wrong I did. I am truly sorry, and I hope the dear Lord will keep me that I am not found in such things again. Jesus Christ said, 'Be ye therefore perfect, even as your father in Heaven is Perfect.' (Matthew 5:42.)"* After describing the kinds of sins in sixteen paragraphs, his concluding statement is *"Oh, how sorry I feel for all my sins."*

For forty years, having rejoiced in founding and leading this God-inspired utopian community, in David Schwartz's years following excommunication he agonized as he watched the turmoil in his church end in total disintegration. Perhaps no former member suffered greater disillusionment.

Chapter 8: School Amid Transitions

1924-31

When I was completing the eighth grade in the Amish Christian (A.C.) Parochial School in April 1931, several internal and external events and forces were converging. At the time I did not realize the meaning and significance of them. In retrospect, several of them were very important in providing opportunities that were timely and propitious for my further education. The severe economic depression of the 1930s, no school board, no organized financial plan, combined with deteriorating effectiveness of the Bishop's leadership, and the plight of the seriously underpaid teachers, led to the jarring conclusion that the A. C. Parochial School could no longer be adequately financed.

How was this school financed? Built in about 1910, the structure was a solid brick building with slate roof, English basement, steam furnace, electric lights. It was actually superior to the nearby one-room public schools. The building was constructed with gifts from church members and their contributed labor. Support for heating, lighting and maintenance of the church building across the gravel road from the school, the school building and teachers' salaries all were dependent on monthly offerings received at the church or special gifts from church members. There was no tuition charge and no fees; teachers had no contractual salaries.

Mom's parents, on whose land the school was built, had a large two-story house with full basement. The former schoolhouse located several hundred feet at the side of the orchard. Enrolment had become too large for the building. It was moved to become their summer kitchen. Her father then gave the two-acre tract to the church where the new brick school building was constructed. Whether he gave this at his initiative and generosity or under pressure from the Bishop, I have never known. Also, in Adams County records I find no evidence of transfer of title to the real estate. Apparently, there was no legal entity for the school tract.

From my first day, school was a wonderful place; there I was not cold in the winter. I could succeed and be recognized for what I did. I enjoyed the challenge and stimulation of reading, arithmetic, geography, history; easy learning of facts and information about the larger world were very exciting. Short plays, misnamed dialogues, only recently allowed by the Bishop, were fascinating and I was chosen to act in one. I learned by singing occasionally that I could carry a tune and was thrilled to sing in a small a cappella chorus of boys. The school had no piano, organ or other musical instrument. Even in the first or second year I secretly contemplated, "Lifelong school is what my life should be; early I turned my thoughts to becoming a teacher. Wouldn't that be a grand way of spending my life, teaching grades one through eight in a country school."

The small library, of perhaps two hundred books, praised by the county school superintendent, was reportedly better than the ones in the nearby public schools. In the late 20s, J.D.R. Schwartz, principal and teacher, borrowed a projector, black and white, without audio to show an occasional evening film, such as tapping rubber trees in some African countries, and the steps involved leading to the production of the completed auto tire of those days. As one might expect, the Firestone Tire & Rubber Co. made the film available. Tickets cost ten cents, a major movie event. A movie at school was especially exciting because the church prohibited any attendance at commercial theaters.

In 1929, to listen to President Herbert Hoover's inaugural address the principal strung a wire antenna, perhaps fifty feet long tied to a tree. He brought a primitive radio and suspended classes as we listened to the president's speech. Although we couldn't understand more than a few words, I remember that as a great historic event. The Adams County Superintendent of Schools also frequently commended A. C. Parochial School for its disproportionate share of high scores in the countywide annual examinations earned in each subject even when taught by uncertified teachers.

At the beginning of my schooling, my teachers had only an eighth grade education with no formal teacher training. The church ruled against any formal education beyond the eighth grade just as their Amish predecessors. However, during my elementary school years some of the teachers completed correspondence courses and evening classes at extension centers.

My mother finished the eighth grade, my father completed the seventh. My grandparents had irregular, very short school years, completed about the third grade. In the farming community, farm work frequently interrupted school attendance especially for planting of crops in the spring and harvesting in the fall. In the early decades of this century school attendance was voluntary.

So, for me to think of teaching was visionary beyond my being able to talk to my parents about it--in fact, I seemed unable to talk to anyone about my dreams. The Bishop appeared to choose the teachers for that school, and why would he ever consider choosing me? A hopeless dream! But the dream persisted as I listened to my teachers, one of whom was teaching grades one through four, the other, five to eight. In my first school year my uncle, D. D. Mazelin (my mother's brother) was my teacher. .From his early youth he was afflicted with progressive muscular dystrophy. A sturdy railing was installed on the inside stairway to enable him to enter the building onto the stairway landing that was at ground level. The railing enabled him to climb that half story. To write in standing position, he had to be put his tablet on the tall steam radiator at elbow level. He could not bend to write on children's desks. He greatly enjoyed teaching. However, at the end of my first year in school the Bishop ruled that his physical impairment compelled him to retire. Amos R. Steury, the Bishop's nephew, was named his successor.

When the new teacher arrived, several of my classmates and I were double promoted from grade one to grade three. I do not remember that we were told why but I remember my delight in moving ahead so rapidly. I recall two incidents in my third grade year, that illustrate the basis for administering discipline. In reading class each student stood up and read aloud by turns. One of the pupils mispronounced a word. I raised my hand "Did he read that right?" Mr. Steury, as a beginning teacher, didn't answer my question but replied, "Only the teacher corrects the reader. Now go stand in the corner." Another time in the heat of a game on the playground I lapsed a few words into Swiss-German for which I was punished, "In school you speak only English".

No one talked about choosing a career or goals in life; parents were almost all farmers. A few were carpenters, or painters, perhaps a half dozen of the younger people were employed in small home town factories. Women were homemakers or served as domestics. Education was considered only as basic to the simple rural careers. Education for the sake of knowledge or the joy of learning was considered an alien concept. High school and college were regarded as pathways to evil, endangering one's Christian faith. Careers for members of the church were limited to repetition of the work of parents and relatives, a condition brought from the Amish background.

When I was in about the fourth grade, the Indiana legislature passed the law requiring pupils to remain in school through age 16. Required quality of school buildings and equipment were also upgraded. A. C. Parochial school building and facilities conformed to or exceeded state school legal requirements. So, at the prompting of the principal, the Bishop decided that the school should add grade nine rather than have any of the students attend a public high school. No one in that church had attended high school. J. D. R. Schwartz, the Bishop's son, was then principal and teacher of the upper grades 7, 8 and 9. My teacher, Amos R. Steury, was assigned to teach grades 4, 5 and 6, while a new teacher, Agnes Schwartz, the principal's niece and the Bishop's granddaughter, taught grades 1, 2 and 3 in the basement of the school. Part of the basement area was renovated with a wooden floor, new small chairs and movable tables--real innovations. On our floor desks were screwed to the floor, desktops had inkwells with covers. We used wooden penholders with pens that required blotting. There were very few fountain pens in school. Under the desktop there was a shelf for books. My desk provided the seat for the student in front of me; I sat on the seat of the desk behind me.

While in school, it never occurred to me that all the teachers, excluding my Uncle Dave, were closely related to the

Bishop. But on reflection years later I could not help but wonder why. Were the Bishop's family members and relatives so much better qualified or was this part of the strategy to enhance his power and authority?

After teaching the ninth grade for two years, the superintendent of the Adams County Schools, Clifton E. Striker (twenty years later he was principal of Monmouth High School in the first year that I taught there), disapproved Mr. Schwartz teaching the 9th grade that constituted the first year of high school. Advancing state teacher certification requirements brought pressure for Mr. Schwartz to do additional study toward state certification even if he only taught in the first eight grades. So, having completed some high school courses by correspondence and passed the General Education Development (G.E.D.) test, often regarded as high school equivalent, he was admitted as a special student at Ball State Teachers College to register for summer term courses. I believe he did so for two or three summers, by which time the Great (financial) Depression had become serious.

Though I have never known any figures, the non-contract salaries of the three teachers were token and much below subsistence level. Mr. Steury lived with his parents on the farm; Miss Schwartz, an only child, lived with her parents; for subsistence neither of them had to rely on a salary. Mr. Schwartz was married with one child at the time. In summer and during holidays he did carpenter work. He also sold a popular brand of made-to-measure men's suits. The county superintendent of schools strongly urged all of the teachers to work toward state certification.

Mr. Schwartz was a strict, rigid yet excellent teacher. He prepared well for his classes. He enjoyed poetry, in both seventh and eighth grades the textbooks for literature and poetry were titled *Good Reading.* I greatly enjoyed both the poetry and prose; much of it was memorable, much more so than the literature that I later studied in high school. For this I credit the teaching of Mr. Schwartz who was an uncertified teacher with many years of experience. (My high school literature teacher, a graduate of Indiana University, was a beginner with required certification credentials.) In grade eight in one grading period I received my only "F"; when I inquired of Mr. Schwartz he said that he believed I was not doing as well as I could. "Whatever is worth doing, is worth doing as well as you can," he admonished. He was correct; for me it was a painful way to learn this lesson. He also enjoyed teaching geography, history, arithmetic and German. Despite his limitations, he generated the love of learning more effectively than most other teachers that I had through high school, college and graduate school. In fact for a long time he was my hero.

Years later I learned that he also had clay feet. Some people in the church assumed that he was engaged to a particular young woman and anticipated their marriage. Then suddenly the wedding of J. D. R. and Edna Habegger was announced in church. In less than seven months a daughter was born.

In the depth of the financial depression, the cost of operating the parochial school became a serious burden on the members of the church. Parents of children paid no tuition. Further the county school superintendent became adamant that on graduation from the eighth grade, students not yet sixteen, must attend public high schools typically through the sophomore year to age sixteen. Thus, during my seventh and eighth grade years, those ninth graders who had not reached age sixteen attended public high schools either in Berne or Monroe.

Let's look at a school day that began at eight o'clock and ended at three thirty. Recitations of the various subjects were interrupted in mid-morning and mid-afternoon with fifteen minute recesses. At lunch in early years we kept our metal buckets in the basement where we were seated at long picnic type tables. When the lower grades were moved to the basement we carried a folded newspaper to be placed on the highly polished desks to avoid scratches. The desks, in contrast to those with carved initials in the public high school, were impeccable. The lunch containers were stored on shelves in the basement; at lunch time we were formally dismissed to bring them upstairs each to his own desk. With our lunch buckets closed we waited breathlessly to hear the principal seated at a students desk to say, "Siet jetzt shtill", (Now be still) while we were expected to think a silent prayer. When he said "Amen," we charged into our meat or egg sandwiches, a piece of lettuce, turnip, radish or cabbage, a small half-pint jar of canned fruit and a piece of pie or cake. As soon as we finished lunch, we rushed to the outdoor playground unless it was raining. Snow and cold were no deterrents. (Paradoxically, though speaking Swiss-German was strictly forbidden the principal made an exception in calling us to silent prayer! I never heard any teacher pray.)

What games did we play? Nearly all boys played the sports in season. In spring and fall softball was popular. When we couldn't afford an official softball we used a sponge ball from the five and ten cent store. We used homemade bats. Occasionally a family provided a commercial bat. Seasonally, boys in the upper grades played basketball on a ground court. It was a very slow game, with very little bodily contact. There were no professional teams, and no three pointers. After each two point score the ball was returned to center jump. In winter months shinny (sort of a land hockey) was the game. The equipment consisted of a sponge ball, shinny sticks cut in the woods from small trees or a tree limb with an end crook. In my last year Mr. Schwartz introduced tennis that he had learned at Ball State Teachers College. Younger children had sturdy, concrete mounted, chain supported swings, a seesaw and a merry-go-round. The older girls rarely played any games; they either watched the boys play or palled around with close friends.

As a school of the church, there were certain paradoxes. There were no religious exercises; there was never a spoken prayer. We had no Bibles at school, German or English; we had no hymn- books and sang no hymns. The principal stored some secular songbooks; occasionally we sang "America" or "Santa Lucia" or other secular numbers for opening exercises. He had a strong tenor voice cultivated by private voice instruction.

We studied no religion. I don't remember seeing a Bible in the school rooms; we never had any Bible reading. We heard no slang, vulgar or profane language; that was strictly forbidden. And of perhaps equal significance was the fact that we learned our English from the grammar books. Character building obedience was abundantly practiced with stern rigidity. All

71

pupils remained in their assigned seats. We were not permitted to get a library book in a bookcase in the entrance hall. We had to get those during recess. Whispering to a neighbor or passing a note brought punishment. Unsolicited comments from students were not welcome; questions that showed too much curiosity were inadvisable. Pupils were occasionally punished for inappropriate behavior while walking several miles between home and school.

I was a very sensitive, rather shy boy. I was very observant but did not share my innermost thoughts with anyone and did not make friends easily, a characteristic that I later observed in each of my parents. I also was not very good in athletic activities and sports, often the last one chosen for a team in softball, shinny, or other games. I was not a natural leader, more of a loner, not gregarious, also evident in my parents. Not having any sisters, I felt different or odd. When I was teased, such as being called Sammy or Sambo, (as the son of Sam) I responded more in anger than with humor. Such a response encouraged the teasers. It seemed to me that teachers were not helpful in fostering personal development; I was too shy to ask them for help. However, I found compensation in mental activities and in every school subject.

In some respects, school and church were distinctly separate. School was in English; church services and catechism were in German. Lay, uncertified teachers taught school; only the Bishop was qualified to teach catechism most of which he wrote. That was entrusted to no one else. Only ministers taught Sunday school in church for young people not yet church members. No church announcements were made in school. No school announcements were ever made in church. The church building focussed on adults, with indoor toilets, lavatories and drinking water with no equipment or provisions for children. Parents did not visit school; there was no Parent-Teacher Association. The school had outdoor toilets without foundations for years. After they were upset each Halloween the principal had foundations poured with concrete pits. The wooden structures were securely bolted to the foundation. A hand pump on the outdoor well provided drinking water. For sanitation each student carried a collapsible tin cup. Yet, in church communion wine was served from a single cup.

The church was not only in difficulties because of the severe financial depression, but it began to show significant signs of internal disintegration. From 1931 on, tensions mounted, more members were excommunicated and the Bishop was more often challenged and defied. His first wife died on March 7, 1933, eight days short of their 50th wedding anniversary. He married his widowed first cousin on May 14, 1933. Marrying a first cousin was illegal in Indiana. His troubles were multiplying. I began to wonder whether the church might not endure; this church that was declared by the Bishop to be the only true church--standing alone against the whole world.

In September 1931 with very confused feelings, wondering what the future would hold, I rode the new school bus to enter Monroe High School. This was the second school bus in Monroe Township that took students from the farms to high school. The enrollment, grades nine through twelve, was somewhat more than the number of students in our grade school.

The full impact of the devastating effect of the depression was still ahead. All the while I was hoping that by some unimaginable miracle I would yet be able to become a teacher, perhaps in a public grade school. But how would I ever go to college, since one now had to go to college to become a teacher? How could I ever finish high school? Having skipped third grade, I gained a year and would be sixteen years old the summer after finishing the junior year. I greatly enjoyed high school and as a sophomore, I took five courses each semester rather than the usual four. No research papers were required; the library probably had no more than 500 books. No art or music course was offered although there was a mixed chorus. For the first time I heard stirring records of the "Anvil Chorus" and the "Pilgrims Chorus" my only exposure to classical music. I won first place in U. S. History in a county examination, and third place in Latin. Virgil Wagner, principal and teacher of history chose me to represent Monroe High School in the Adams county competition.

During my preparation, he invited me to his home for

dinner. I vividly recall Dad picking me up that evening at the Wagner home. Dad had to crank the old Model T; it would not start. I was terribly embarrassed when Mr. Wagner came to the rescue by sharing the cranking. Finally, after both of them were exhausted the obstinate car started. Why did we always have such old cars? I said to myself, "I will never have an embarrassing old car." (This was the only time that I can remember being invited to a teacher or professor's home until the chairman of my doctoral committee, Dr. Shirley Hamrin invited Jan and me as guests.) I greatly admired Virgil Wagner; I regarded him as a model for me.

If only the state law required one to finish high school, that might give me a glimmer of hope. My parents were already telling me that as soon as legally possible, I must stay home to do the farm work. Dad could earn some extra money doing carpenter work and hopefully save the family farm from being taken over by the mortgage holder. What a frightening prospect this was for my parents and in turn for me with my dreams of becoming a teacher.

Out of school association with girls outside our church was strictly forbidden. Yet I found some of the high school girls very attractive and with well-developed and appealing personalities. I felt that Neva Fricke, second daughter of a Quaker family living in Monroe, was the most attractive girl that I had ever seen. She was a brilliant student, had striking brown eyes, with shoulder length wavy, dark brown hair. She was a year ahead of me. Her older sister, Esther, was rather plain like our neighbor girls with uncut hair and her younger sister Mabel, in my class, did not measure up. Later I became quite infatuated with one of my classmates, Dorothy Schaff, another very bright girl with deep brown eyes and black, well trimmed hair. She was puzzled why I did not ask her for a date. All I could do was taking girls out on dates in my imagination!

I remember the death of only one student during high school, Mervin Hahnert, the son of our rural mail carrier. In my freshman year he was a handsome, popular sophomore who died very suddenly of what was termed "strangulation of the intestines." I found his death very difficult to bear. Later, another student in my graduating class, Marjory Holloway, died in childbirth during the summer following graduation. The father was not publicly identified; Marjory's parents reared the grandson.

Since neither of my parents had ever been inside a public school, their perceptions of what happened in high school were based on hearsay from neighbors or business people in town. They feared I would adopt foul language and slang that was very prevalent in such contrast with grade school. I might adopt values foreign to our church and family. I might become interested in playing or attending inter-school athletic contests (the high school had no gymnasium; boy's basketball, baseball and track were the only inter school sports). Commercial entertainment such as movie theaters was off limits. Gaudy clothes were strictly forbidden in our school and church. During my first two years of high school we were permitted to wear only black bow ties. (The Bishop who made this rule had never seen a tuxedo; I hadn't either.)

Compared with a regionally accredited, intellectual and cultured high school Monroe high school was dismally inadequate. No laboratory sciences were offered. I had two courses in biology and one in agriculture, but no chemistry or physics. Paradoxically, my brother Elmer earned a Ph. D. in physics.

Understandably, my father and mother envisioned no careers for their sons that would require high school education, much less college. My father especially was convinced that no matter what I wanted, finishing the junior year in high school as required by law was absolutely all the education I needed and would get. While mother was very subdued in her statements, her own love of school and her secret longing to be a teacher caused her to be quietly sympathetic to my predicament. Perhaps it reminded her of her unfulfilled yearnings many years ago. Did she secretly wish that what she did not accomplish her son might somehow attain? She kept the secret in her heart.

The psychic pain and agony of working on the farm while my friends in the senior class continued was almost more than I could bear. The fact that all other students from our church also quit at age 16 was no consolation to me. Many of them were pleased to have completed their formal education; conformance was what we had been taught. My dreams were rebellious; would church transition open new doors?

As I rebelliously and painfully labored at the harvesting of crops, had I only known the wise observation of Joseph Campbell, "I feel that if one follows what I call 'One's Bliss' the thing that really gets you deep in the gut and that you feel is your life, doors will open up! Through your own inner experience, the divine mystery is revealed."

Amid the pervasive confusion within the splintering Amish Christian Church I believed that God had a plan for my life. I placed great faith in the quotation of Jesus by Matthew 6:33, "But seek first his kingdom and his righteousness, and all these things shall be yours as well." Looking backward more than sixty-five years, my blessings have far exceeded my fondest dreams.

Chapter 9: Father

Dad was named Samuel at birth, a strong biblical name (spelled the same in German and English). He was addressed as Sam, except jokingly on occasion, he was called Sammy. He signed his name Sam D. Nussbaum, except for formal legal documents that he would sign as Samuel D. The "D" was an initial only; it was the custom in that community in his generation to use the first letter of the father's name, David, as the middle initial. This practice was carried over from the Amish where use of biblical names in large families produced many persons with the same first name and the same last name; the distinguishing part of the name was the middle initial or occasionally two initials. They also used nicknames; a black haired man was called "Black John" while a farmer with an apiary became "Honey Joe", a man with hilly land was "Hilly Jake."

Samuel, born on September 30, 1891, was the eldest of six: three brothers, Jacob, Philip and Menno, and two sisters, Sarah and Elizabeth. It was one of the smaller families of that generation. Sarah was nearly four when she died from a combination of diphtheria and whooping cough, from which several siblings also suffered. For Samuel this caused a long-term left ear infection that impaired his hearing. This also produced chronic drainage often attended by pain, especially when he suffered from a cold or upper respiratory infection. For most of his life, he wore cotton in that ear.

Sam was 5 feet, 7 inches tall an inch and a half taller than his father. In his youthful years this was about the average height for a man. He was small boned, of stable average weight for his height. He had well-developed muscles and was strong for his size. Sam combed his light black hair, only partly gray in later years, of medium thickness slightly parted toward the right side. He sometimes wore a belt; he much preferred suspenders for work or dress. For work he usually wore bib overalls with black or brown leather shoes. For Sunday dress he wore only black shoes with a medium or dark gray suit. He rarely, if ever, hung up his clothes. Most often he placed them on a chair in the bedroom. His general health was good with the occasional cold. He was never hospitalized. His life was carpenter work. Among many patent medicine remedies, non-tobacco Dr. Blosser and Cubeb cigarettes were recommended for the common cold. For some years Dad sold to acquaintances who occasionally bought a carton. He earned a few cents on a pack. When he had a cold, I remember that he rarely smoked in search of relief. Mom disapproved; after some years Dad gave it up. I do not remember ever seeing him smoking tobacco cigars or cigarettes. The church forbade their use.

His mother, Marianna, (some records read Marian) of the Habegger family, immigrated with her family to the United States from Switzerland when she was about two years of age. She had almost no formal education. She could not speak a well-structured, complete sentence in English and understood English only when spoken slowly and distinctly. I do not remember ever seeing her write in English. She could not carry on a conversation in English. All family conversations were in the Swiss-German dialect. Sam's father, also had no more than a second or third grade education, was the son of an immigrant from Switzerland. Samuel was born east of Berne; early the family moved to another farm northeast of Berne where he lived in a brick home next to a large log barn and other outbuildings. This log barn, one of the last of its kind in the community, was demolished and a new one built by Samuel in 1952.

When my parents were married on April 8, 1917, they lived with my father's family for nearly three years until they bought our family farm some 2-1/2 miles northwest. My mother's parental home was nearly the same distance southwest so that three residences formed approximately an isosceles triangle. One of the few songs I recall him singing, on the rarest of occasions for he could not reliably carry a tune, "Be it ever so humble, there's no place like home." That was his home for the rest of his life.

A brief history of his family provides a context to Sam's life. His mother suffered chronic depression all her adult life and was frequently very moody. She found very little joy and no fun in life. At the time of her death she had been essentially bedfast for seven years, probably as much by emotional as physical causes. When her husband, who had a good sense of humor and was given to frequent laughter, showed his vibrant personality, she would criticize him abruptly for being so light-hearted (Liechtsinnig).

Both of David's parents were born in Switzerland. David C. attended the Berne Mennonite church where his mother, Regina, and his father, John C., were very active members. When David C. was about eleven years old, his father was one of seventeen men in the congregation nominated to become the minister. Although her husband was a nominee, David's mother shared in the nomination of Sprunger. From among the nominees named by members of the congregation, the lot chose the elected one. Using this process, Mennonites believed that God made the final choice. Seventeen identical hymnbooks were placed on a table, each man picked up one. Samuel F. Sprunger, age 19 picked up the book that had the "elected" slip in it.

Two years later, on November 23, 1870, John C. died at age 34. David, the fourth child, had three older sisters and one younger brother. At age 13, he was fatherless. His mother married her husband's widowed cousin, John E. Nussbaumer, also a Swiss immigrant (the children shortened it to Nussbaum.) Even today in Switzerland nearly all families have retained the full name, Nussbaumer, which is translated as a grower of a particular kind of nut trees.

David's oldest sister, Catherine, married Peter M. Neuenschwander, a young immigrant minister from Switzerland. For a time, Peter served as an assistant minister in the Berne Mennonite Church. In 1879, he led a group away from that congregation mostly because he felt the new church building was much too ostentatious and started his "Schwander G'mein" named after him. That building was very modest compared with the present structure dedicated in 1912. The records do not show exactly what happened with David's family, whether they also left the Berne Mennonite Church at the time that Peter M. and his cohorts left. I believe that later, as a devout Mennonite minister, Peter M. would not have presided at the marriage of my grandparents without their first having been baptized.

Records are clear that Peter M. Neuenschwander presided at the wedding of David C. Nussbaum and Mariann Habegger (names are variously spelled on the marriage certificate). The Indiana State Board of Health marriage certificate, filed in Adams County Indiana Recorder's office, shows the date of marriage as October 15, 1889, but the signature of Peter M. Neuenschwander certifies that he solemnized the marriage on October 12, 1889. Probably the 12th is more authentic. They were married in Adams County, the exact location is not indicated. David was age 22; Mariann was 26.

The *History and Membership Record Book, Amish Christian Church 1894-1936* compiled by the Bishop David Schwartz shows that my grandparents joined that church on August 15, 1896, when Samuel was almost five years old. In joining, I believe they were baptized a second time, (he was age 29, she age 33), some seven years after their marriage. What brought them to the Amish Christian church is not clear. The Amish Christian church evidently recognized as valid the baptism of those who were baptized as Amish and were in the groups that left the Amish to become the Amish Christian church. Although the records are not explicit, I assume that David Schwartz, the Bishop, refused to recognize other baptisms as valid. (This is not documented.) In a letter written to me, dated August 3, 1994, Tillman Nussbaum son of Adam, who was a half-brother of David C. from their mother's second marriage, states: "If my memory serves me correctly, when my uncle (and) your grandpa, David C. Nussbaum, lived with us for a while many years ago, he had much to say about his brother-in-law, Rev. Neuenschwander, and of course many other matters of the early family and church life. I recall that David C. did not wish to talk much about his own baptism but felt satisfied of his last baptism by David Schwartz."

Grandma Marianna Nussbaum died January 3, 1934. After the disintegration of the Amish Christian church, Grandpa was restless and searching. In 1940, he joined the Apostolic Christian church that did not recognize baptism by any other denomination. He was again baptized on October 16, 1940. He died September 8, 1947.

Dad was baptized on May 5, 1912 at age 20. There was military conscription in 1917 but because of his ear infections he thought he was disqualified. The church would have required him to be a conscientious objector to war. deferred or classified as physically disqualified. He never talked much about his early years on the farm, his school days, or his life as a boy. Obviously, he occasionally was mischievous from his reports of John J. Hilty, his teacher, who threw chalk at boys in mischief. Dad was one of the victims; he once was hit on the forehead without noticeable damage. He liked arithmetic, but he expressed no joy about school days, distinctly in contrast to Mom's experience. He also did not get much encouragement from his parents. They had no books in their home except a German Bible, Martin Luther's translation, and only the local newspaper, and a farm magazine. Even when I was very young, I remember Dad often falling asleep with a book or newspaper; he could sleep soundly sitting in a chair or church pew. Reading was never a pleasure, nor did duty compel him very often. He never read a book. Were these times of real fatigue or was the tendency to sleep in church, in the evening sleeping while sitting in a chair rather than going to bed related to or derivative of his tendency to chronic depression? Dad was a person of few words; he almost never spoke ill of another person. Early, he admonished us that we should not to be sharply critical of someone else; perhaps we did not understand their words or actions.

As a youth he worked on the farm, except for childhood diseases apparently in good health. He early felt that his father was an inefficient "tinkerer", not given to diligent application of himself. In contrast, Dad seemed always to like competition related to efficiency and physical endurance. This was evident in games with his brothers, in cutting and shocking corn, shocking wheat or oats, pitching hay, milking cows, or raising a huge barn frame ahead of schedule. Later with his own sons, he really enjoyed racing in mathematical computations, playing checkers or give away, mill or similar contests, even spelling. He had a quick calculating mind especially liked the challenge of different uses of the carpenter's square in construction. As a late teenager, when his younger brothers could help on the farm, he developed an interest in carpentry, construction of houses and barns. At 19 or 20, he was employed as a carpenter with a construction group of neighbors. He learned quickly and readily earned respect as a bright, promising young carpenter. One of his fondest memories from his early twenties was a two-day sightseeing trip to Chicago—meaningful equivalent to today's extended visit to a foreign country. It was a momentous winter venture by several young men who had never been a hundred miles from home.

Transportation to and from work was mostly on foot or by horse and buggy; there were very few automobiles. He became interested in a motorcycle, bought one when he had saved enough money. Despite his mother's strenuous objections, he rode about on dirt and gravel roads like a young Spartan. Some of the courting he and Mom did was riding the motorcycle which had to be kick-started. By today's standards it was devoid of safety devices. Mom would occasionally agree to ride the rear carriage, which was without fenders or chain guards. Did he court anyone else? I don't know. He was admired for such boldness on the forefront among his age group.

But things changed when he got married. No respectable young married man failed to own and cultivate land. A farmer did not live apart from his work; he lived on the land and worked it. Farms then contained minimally forty acres but usually eighty. Horses were the only motive power for farm use. Farm equipment was minimal: a walking plow, disc harrow, spring tooth harrow, drag or roller, grain drill if you could afford it, a farm wagon, a sled, a corn planter, grain binder pulled by two, three or four horses. Most farmers had a few cows to milk, pigs to feed, chickens for eggs, and sometimes a few sheep. Life was simple; if you couldn't afford all the equipment, you borrowed gratis from established relatives or neighbors.

Dad and Mom began farming with two horses, three or four cows, a few chickens and pigs, almost no implements on the 75-acre farm purchase for $13,000 (about $173. per acre--a very high price). I never learned about the down payment or the size of the mortgage. The rudimentary house and barn were only a few years old; side buildings included a granary, buggy shed, two corncribs with wagon storage between, an attached hog house, and a temporary chicken house. There were only a few trees in fence rows. Immediately, they planted some fruit trees and established a garden. A silo needed to be built for ensilage storage used as cattle feed. State sanitation inspectors increasingly scrutinized milk-processing plants (though primitive by today's standards) who then required expensive cattle barn renovations and milk handling procedures.

For three or four years, Dad was excited with this new venture. There was endless work, building fences, drain tiling, fertilizing and spreading lime. Cash money was slow in coming, a few eggs and a little milk to sell, and after some months fattened hogs to be marketed. Dad soon realized that to get ready cash, he could earn it much faster doing carpenter work.

He employed Joe Schrock, a late adolescent living next door, as his hired farm hand who worked for perhaps $5 per week. Furthermore, Dad soon realized that, at heart, he was not really a farmer; being a landlord was more appealing. As the oldest, I was too young to be of much use on the farm and for a few years, Joe, a six-footer, worked hard. Joe was the eldest of six children of Katy Schrock, our next door neighbor, immigrant from other states, whose husband deserted the family and returned to Arizona. Joe was nine years older than I was; his family was desperately in need of income, so when he reached 17 and was out of school, he sought non-farm employment where he could earn more. Incidentally, their family owned no horse, so they borrowed one of our horses to pull their surrey that carried seven persons to church, until collectively the children had earned enough to buy an old Ford. Noah, the second child, was employed at the Bishop's farm as soon as his skills were marketable. From time to time Susan, child number three and more frequently Esther, child number four helped Mom for 50 cents per day.

When Joe left in about 1926, Dad had no hired hand. I was too young at age 8 to be very useful on the farm except for chores and Dad was again compelled to devote his time to farming with only an occasional day for carpentry. Finances again became very tight. In 1929 came the financial crash, the collapse of the stock market followed by the most severe depression in the twentieth century. My parents had borrowed to the hilt during the prosperous twenties. They hoped to reduce the huge mortgage and other debts by constructing a 125-foot chicken house for Leghorn chickens, and developing a fine herd of registered Holstein cattle.

At about this time, farmers were told that they could greatly increase egg production by awakening chickens long before winter daylight. Power line electric energy was not then available in many rural areas. An electric generator, a Delco plant, was purchased. A kerosene motor drove a generator with power storage in sixteen liquid-filled batteries. The artificial light awakened the chickens at 4:30 a. m. in the winter to begin feeding and thereby stimulate egg production. This previously owned Delco machine worked--sometimes, and became an unreliable source of illumination to stimulate the early morning feeding. Irregularity disturbed chickens that thrive on habitual routine, and the egg production was far below expectations.

Then in 1931, in the early part of the depression when testing of cattle for tuberculosis was becoming established, our whole herd, except one heifer, reacted positively to the test. Each animal had to be sold for slaughter not for human consumption; reduced market price was supplemented by state subsidy. What a catastrophe! In the midst of financial crisis, this was enough to dismay the sturdiest of farmers. Our best horse died of overeating growing corn plants when cattle and horses broke an unreliable fence between the pasture and the cornfield. This fine young black horse named Pet was the only fatality. Shortly before the TB crisis, one of the best cows died suddenly from undetected causes. Layer on layer of disaster for Dad, who was genetically given to worry, and his sporadic responses were not always logically calculated.

To compound the difficulties, though Elmer and I had reached ages 11 and 13 when we could be of some help, carpenter work was no longer available. Building construction and renovation were nearly at a stand still. As a carpenter, Dad was unemployed in the midst of the farm crisis. There was no unemployment insurance, no subsidized government programs, no government grants, or emergency loans, only farm mortgages.

The family never had any insurance policy whether health, medical-surgical, life, property, casualty or liability; the auto and farm buildings were not insured. The church prohibited commercial insurance; even lightning rods on buildings were forbidden.

During the 1932 and 1933 years, in the depth of the financial depression, Dad suffered mental and emotional depression; for six to nine months, he was an outpatient with a psychiatrist in Fort Wayne. One of the ministers of our church, Noah D. Schwartz, the Bishop's oldest son, provided transportation for Mom and Dad to go to the clinic, and paid most of the bills with church funds. We had no money for these medical expenses. There was no Medicare or Medicaid; there were no state or county agencies to offer assistance. Dad's ailment was compounded by more than the usual infection in his ear, continued from childhood diseases. In his frustration, instead of going to bed, he would sit in the dining room chair by the hour, moaning about the hopeless financial distress. Falling asleep intermittently, he refused to go to bed as if to inflict punishment and discomfort on himself for his financial failures. Mom would try in vain to have him get bed rest, often for half the night. During this distressing time, he would try to figure out whom to blame for the evil recession, condemning the stock market, the robber barons who brought about the crash or those wealthy investors who would collect the interest paid by the scrambling farmers and unemployed factory workers. When the Peoples State Bank in Berne closed the only stock that he owned became worthless. I lost my savings account of $7.21. He firmly admonished me never to buy anything on the stock market.

The farm did not produce well in those years; selling milk, eggs, and hogs every six months, were the key sources of income. But more often the grain harvest was not large enough to feed the livestock for the whole year, requiring grain purchases. Frequently, I had to drive the team of horses with the wagon to Monroe or Berne to the grain elevator either to grind our grain or the grain we bought mixed with a commercial supplement. Supplements to grain feed were manufactured in Decatur or Fort Wayne by Wayne Feeds or later McMillen Feed

Mills. The most painful part of the trip was for me again to tell the manager of the elevator "charge it." I sensed that the manager was not pleased with our credit record. Sometimes the manager told me firmly, "Tell your dad to come in and pay some of your account."

The very best land on the farm was the black loam on each side of the creek, encompassing some 25 acres often flooded by heavy rains in spring and early summer. Acres of corn, wheat or soybeans were seriously damaged or destroyed. Sometimes a second crop such as soybeans or buckwheat could still bring a fall harvest. Other parts of the farm were not flooded, but lacked adequate tile drainage as well as good fertilizer for maximum production. Unable to afford the best seed corn, we relied on planting seed from last year's crop. In some years the corn yield was only 35 to 50 bushes per acre. Hybrid seed was not yet available. Today such land properly tilled, tiled and fertilized using hybrid seed corn yields 175 to 200 bushels per acre. Similar contrasts could be made regarding oats, wheat and soybean yields. There were not enough financial resources to invest for such basic improvements. Lack of adequate horsepower often delayed preparation of the seedbeds and planting.

Then 1934 and 1936 were years of severe drought, almost killing the crops for lack of rain. To compound the drought, chinch bugs and grasshoppers attacked what remained of the growing corn and other crops. There were no effective insecticides, though a variety of home remedies were tried with hardly any noticeable effects.

Dad saw some of the neighbors with better land or more capital to invest in drain tiling, lime and fertilizer produce much better yields, which generated in him frustration, jealousy, and anger--even self-hatred. Periodically he would try with enthusiasm, sometimes on impulse, a small-scale venture such as growing capons. He planted a small patch of peppermint plants from a basket of roots purchased in northern Indiana. He observed the highly successful peppermint farmers in northern Indiana. Planting a bushel basketful of peppermint roots he envisioned similar results on our farm. He did not learn the steps and stages of the mint culture. Failing to achieve first year results his interest waned. At other times he planted sorghum cane, soy beans, then rather new to Indiana farming, sugar beets, several acres of pickles, an acre of sweet corn, or pop corn. To get successful results from any of these crops required specialized knowledge, specific practices and long term nurture. None of these crops was durably successful. Growing fruit trees, especially apples, was one of the most productive investments.

Dad undertook some side jobs. Also, he tried two apiaries of honeybees. Certainly the bees were useful in fertilizing fruit tree blossoms. Quite apart from production of honey, bees were essential for the carrying of pollen in season. Our family especially enjoyed honey as a spread for bread with butter and on fried mush for breakfast. In fact, we never had nearly enough for a season. As a profit venture, it was not successful. One of the obstacles to success was that Dad looked at the results being achieved by successful farmers, without understanding process.

He wanted to emulate or achieve positive results that he variously observed among other farmers, without adequately understanding all the components that a given project required. Yet, such endeavors often lent temporary relief from his depression, giving him fresh hope. When a project failed to produce the expected results within his tolerable time frame, the genetic tendency toward depression was compounded by situational stress. Since he really didn't like farming in the first instance, such odds became psychologically and emotionally overpowering.

During the winter of 1933-34, some of President Franklin D. Roosevelt's national projects began to take form. Dad was finally able to get a carpentry job at Homestead, a federal housing project in Decatur that paid 32-1/2 cents an hour. In financial desperation and also with understandable enthusiasm he was able once more to engage in the work that he really liked. Again, this required someone else to do the farming. In June 1934, I was 16 years of age--old enough to become a legal high school dropout. In those days at Monroe High School, there were far more students who dropped out than continued to graduation. So, Dad compelled me to stay at home that fall and winter to do the farm work. He needed to keep the farm from bankruptcy. From the perspective of his seventh grade education, he was convinced that three years of high school were more than enough for any one, and certainly for his son. I had already done nearly every aspect of farm work since aged 12, so he made me a full-time farmer, at least for the time being.

It is difficult for me to imagine anyone unhappier or more distressed at having to quit school than I was. Not only that, but Dad could not understand and was not in any way sympathetic to my point of view. He had never been inside a high school and probably knew no one even remotely connected to our family who was a high school graduate. His perception of the worldliness of high schools was compellingly reinforced by the church in which he had grown up, and the only church he knew. So, for that year, which should have been my senior year in high school, I shed tears, rebelled in vocal complaint and groveled in my misery, while taking care of the farm thinking of my privileged classmates whose understanding parents were very supportive.

Yet, I could also understand the financial distress that confronted my parents, and the calamitous prospect of losing our farm and our home. During that whole year, I wondered whether the God of heaven whom I trusted, had any way imaginable which would enable me to complete high school. Not to finish would forever kill my dream of becoming a teacher, the threatened destruction of a vision of hope.

Dad never developed close friends. He was socially very reticent and he seemed constitutionally unable when bills were past due to muster his courage to talk with creditors to cultivate their patience and forbearance. Though Mom prodded him repeatedly, he could not bring himself to follow through on so difficult an undertaking, when he saw no really satisfactory resolution. Lacking close friends, he could neither share with anyone the depth of his innermost pains of many kinds, nor was he able to talk through with anyone a systematic plan of attack regarding his financial dilemma. He also had no hobbies, in which to engage him; being constantly reminded of his inadequacies by Mom was obviously painful. Dad and Mom were not attuned to discuss rational alternatives to their financial incapacity.

Several years later, he formed his own firm for barn and house construction and renovation that he greatly enjoyed. This work gave his life purpose and meaning. On an occasional Sunday afternoon he would suggest to Mom that she join him in a visit to those sites where the owners had praised him for excellent work--nothing he did on the farm ever brought commendation. But Mom saw no point in sharing with him what he enjoyed very much, this one activity that brought him commendation.

Some years later, when I was in college I observed the long term effects. Dad had quite a different personality on site when engaged in his carpentry projects in contrast to his personality at home, even when his financial distresses were finally resolved.

Dad always found delight in seeing his sons respond courageously to his mentoring and nurturing in construction work. He was thrilled to watch me carry heavy green barn rafters walking on an eight-inch sill twenty feet above the ground. Later, when Mom objected that Carl was too young to work with him on a barn roof, Dad tied a cord of one-inch rope around Carl's middle as a safety device. Carl nailed shingles all day. Dad found delight in proving that his sons could do what Mom fearfully believed they could not and should not do. I can recall only one major injury from construction that he suffered. Building an addition to a large barn, while standing on some sheaves of wheat in the haymow of the old part, he slid down as his thumb was caught at the joint of an angling brace with a vertical beam. It was badly fractured.

He would have preferred each of his sons either joining him in that career or to have bought a farm nearby--provided one farmed the family home place. Though several of us learned much about carpentry that has been invaluable, none chose it as a career.

Had I continued uninterruptedly in high school, I would have graduated with the class of 1935. Since I was unable to undertake my senior year as stated earlier there seemed to be no hope. Yet, I was always thinking and praying for some miracle to enable me to finish high school. I considered some alternatives. I thought of trying to finish high school by correspondence courses. That had no appeal. The high school principal, Rolland Sprunger, who was given this office when Virgil Wagner left after my sophomore year, was a rigid administrator not given to flexible accommodation. So I wallowed in my misery.

This was compounded by another set of conditions. In the fall of 1934, most of my friends and age-mates in the church were baptized and admitted as church members. This was the typical age at which to be baptized. Mother was very upset with me that I had not presented my case to the Bishop in convincing terms to be included in that group. She was unsettled, probably embarrassed that her eldest son was so casual about making his profession of faith. Probably the more so because she was devout and her father had been a minister until his declining health prevented him from continuing. Also, there were the early signs of deterioration within the church, causing me to wonder what lay ahead for this singularly independent, self-proclaimed only "true church."

Jacob J. Schwartz, preacher since 1895 was excommunicated by his colleague Bishop David Schwartz. Turmoil ensued; some families left the church. With whom could I really talk about this in complete candor? Was I willing to surrender my future to the restrictions then in effect? No member had ever graduated from high school; was I to be another one? How painfully lonely were these thoughts as I harvested the crops, milked the cows, fed the livestock, planned the next season's crop rotation, plowed the fields, purchased seed, repaired fences and farm equipment during the cold winter months? Was this the best that life had to offer me?

In that winter a salesman came to the house who represented himself as selling a correspondence course that could lead to a civil service appointment. If successfully completed it would assure one of passing the civil service examination. I signed a contract. On subsequent reflection, I checked with the postmaster who insisted that no one could offer a course with such assurance. In frustration and anger, I canceled the contract and lost my $10 deposit. Now what?

I was further confused; what was I going to do? If only Virgil Wagner was still the high school principal I would seek his advice. He had died of a stomach ulcer during the summer of 1934; I found his death, though he had moved some distance to a much larger high school, almost unbearable. He had believed in me; in my sophomore year he had encouraged me, taken me to his home for dinner and coached me in U.S. history, my favorite subject, in preparation for the Adams County competitive examinations. He registered me and I won first place. This was the first signal in competing outside A. C. (Amish Christian) Parochial School which let me believe that I could really compete with excellent minds. How good was I? I wondered, for the grade school had no accreditation; Monroe High School lacked regional accreditation. In fact, none of the rural high schools in the county were regionally accredited. I earned almost all "A" grades, without much strain, but what did that mean? I also placed near the top in Latin, but Harvey Habegger, my close friend, won first place.

Sometime that spring I summoned my courage to talk to my former grade school teacher and principal, J.D.R. Schwartz. Would he give me any encouragement? Did he have any advice? Growing out of the conversations, I hit upon a plan. I realized that I had taken extra courses in my sophomore year; that prompted me to visit Rolland Sprunger, the high school principal. If I harvested the farm crops in the fall of 1935, attend school only in the spring semester could I graduate with the class of 1936? After careful analysis of graduation requirements which were very traditional, we agreed that if I took five courses instead of the usual four plus a correspondence course in civics from Indiana University, I would have enough credits to graduate.

Now, could I convince my father and mother? During that year I worked occasional days with Dad on construction, but all the money that I earned was used for farm and family needs. I was unable to save any for future use. Though the total financial strain was a little less, there were so many unmet needs. The list is long: new and repaired farm machinery, need for better horse power, improved dairy herd, higher quality hogs, deferred building maintenance among many other needs which had accumulated during the depths of the depression. And by now, the family had grown to nine to feed, clothe, to buy schoolbooks and pay medical bills.

Dad at first strongly resisted my plan to return to school. He said, "it wouldn't be so bad if you were the only one finishing high school; but if I let you, the brothers will get it into their heads that they also want to finish." That he was not prepared to face. Mother was more open, and considered the plan thoughtfully. After several months of imploring, they finally agreed. There was light at the end of the tunnel! For the first time, there was some distant hope.

Dad expected that when I finished he could persuade the younger brothers to quit school as soon as they reached age 16 at the end of the sophomore year.

I also made my delayed confession of faith--spring of 1935 on April 9--and was the only person baptized. According to church records, I was the last one baptized before the church began the fatal process of disintegration and dissolution; on May 3, 1936, the Bishop, David Schwartz was excommunicated. On this occasion there was a major departure mostly of David Schwartz's relatives and other sympathizers as well as those who were simply disgusted with the persistent turmoil.

Paradoxically, Jacob J. Schwartz, earlier put in the ban had been readmitted to the church and was once more elected as a preacher. It was he who excommunicated the Bishop. Now, Jacob J. Schwartz was in effect, the head of the church and several families who felt they had been unjustly excommunicated over the past decade returned and were reinstated as members. Two men among them were elected as deacons. It was then widely proclaimed that they had been falsely accused and excommunicated by the former Bishop. One of these two was the Bishop's son, Joseph and wife. The other was David J. Mazelin, Joseph's in-law and a cousin of my grandfather. He, his wife and daughters had repeatedly been chastised by the Bishop. The parents were twice excommunicated.

In the midst of this ecclesiastical turbulence, I completed

the fall farm work in 1935 and made plans to return to high school at the beginning of the spring semester near the end of January 1936. I followed through on my plans, was able to complete all the required course work and was graduated with the class of 1936. However, Principal Rolland Sprunger ruled that although I had the highest grade average in the graduating class, I was not eligible to be valedictorian because I was an "irregular" student. Similarly, the girl with the second highest average who had transferred to Monroe High School from Illinois at the end of her junior year was not eligible to be salutatorian. He named the student with the third highest average, James Habegger, valedictorian and the one with the fourth highest average, Francille Harvey, salutatorian. The principal remembered that in his graduating class in another rural county high school he expected to be valedictorian had not a girl with a higher average transferred in for her senior year. So, I was the victim of a promise he made himself out of his disappointment when he was "outdone by an invader." At Monroe High School, the graduating class did not wear robes. By selling a 150 pound hog for $5.30, I was able to buy a new mail order suit from Sears Roebuck & Co for my commencement. Why worry about being valedictorian when I can really graduate?

While in high school some church issues were raised. The Bishop did not allow any member to attend a service in another church. The high school principal occasionally invited a minister from the community to conduct a brief chapel service. Most often, the minister of the adjoining Methodist church was chosen; occasionally the pastor of the Berne Mennonite church was invited. That was a new experience. I had never heard a sermon in English; the ministers were not old, bearded men! We had to ask the Bishop whether we were allowed to remain in the assembly room during the twenty to thirty-minute chapel service, a new problem not previously faced. Most of the high school students from the Amish Christian church had not yet been baptized and were not members; the Bishop decided that we should remain. When I graduated baccalaureate and commencement services were held in the Methodist church. I did attend with my parents, although they were hesitant.

The winter of 1936 was the coldest on record to that date and may still stand in the records today. Schools remained closed several intermittent days because of temperatures at least twenty degrees below zero, Fahrenheit, often with fierce winds and heavy snow. But for my life there were new hopes for the future. Incidentally, Elmer and I had a debate concerning the positive and negative results of the automobile on society; Elmer, with his sense of humor, took the negative and won handily. I also was in a play, which previously would not have been allowed by the church; but the church fences now had holes in them and I thoroughly enjoyed my participation. Unbelievably, this goal was now achieved, I graduated from high school. None of my classmates from A.C. Parochial School completed high school; they had all dropped out at age 16. I was not aware that any of them at that time were very much concerned, though Harvey Habegger, some ten years later after military service did earn a degree in engineering at Indiana University, Fort Wayne. So far as I know, none of my other classmates ever did, although my cousin, Gerhart Schwartz, instead of graduating in 1934, returned to school to graduate in 1938. He and I became roommates all four years in college.

Now, how do I get to college? After my graduation, Elmer would be a high school junior in the fall; again I would have to do the farming. This time, Dad did not strongly object to Elmer's continuation though he was already 16; Alvin was a freshman. I took a state examination, a general knowledge type, competing for one of two tuition scholarships awarded in each county. The scholarships paid for tuition at any one of the four state colleges and universities; Purdue University, Indiana University, Ball State and Indiana State Teachers College. And, another major disappointment! I continued the farming and worked as time permitted with Dad's construction projects. During that year, we reached a grudging but tentative understanding that when Elmer graduated in 1938, I might that fall, consider college provided I would earn my own way. So, another two-year weary delay toward my goal of becoming a teacher. Mom was mildly sympathetic, yet confused with the dissolving church which had been her anchor. Dad had become a little less obdurate but far from agreeing that I could attend college some day--much less now.

During Elmer's last year in high school, I began quietly to make plans to attend that fall following his graduation in 1938. On inquiry, I learned that the State Scholarship Board was willing to grant me a state scholarship based on the examination completed two years earlier covering total tuition at Ball State Teachers College which was $66 per year. On application for student employment, I was promised a job in the college bookstore at $.30 an hour. My cousin, Gerhart Schwartz, grandson of the Bishop whose family had left the church some years earlier, returned to high school and graduated in Elmer's class in 1938. He too, decided to attend Ball State. We shared a room in a boardinghouse across the street from the campus in the home of a World War I widow, Lucile Duncan. So, by the fall of 1938 I had been able to save $30; and with my parent's half-hearted assent I was off to college, confident that left to my own abilities and financial management somehow I would earn what I needed to become a college graduate.

In Dad's thinking, having had no experience with high school or college, he had difficulty realizing that to me the four years in each constituted a unit leading to a diploma or a degree. Since his formal education ended with the seventh grade he never received any diploma; school was only a series of years during which one could quit at any point. Thinking that each year was rather independent of the others, he always hoped as he had while I was in high school, that I would regard a little college as enough.

I do not recall that he ever gave his assent for me to attend college; but his resistance lessened. After I had worked the farm essentially for four years and reached my 20th birthday, (Elmer had then graduated from high school) I was as determined as ever to go to college. Ball State teachers College was only fifty miles away. I would be home every few weeks for a weekend, and he seemed glad to offer me carpenter work on Saturdays. He often seemed puzzled as to just what it is one would study in college; it seemed to have nothing directly to do with any job which he knew. But, he raised few specific questions for he could not fit that in the realm of his own experience or knowledge. Except what I earned in carpenter work, he never gave me any money and never asked about my finances. However, we maintained a cordial relationship.

Overall, both the financial and family situations had greatly changed. Elmer did the farming; Alvin, during his high school years, lived and worked at Grandpa Mazelin's. Dad's contracting business was doing well; he employed several carpenters and other workers. He got contracts to build houses and barns; he had many renovation and remodeling jobs. He developed a reputation for good, reliable work. His ability to outbid many of his competitors gave him great satisfaction.

As the defense economy greatly reduced unemployment many people began to emerge from the ubiquitous depression. For the first time since they bought the farm, more than twenty years ago, he began to get a sense of financial well being. He was able to make major improvements on the farm; paint the buildings, put a new roof on the house, build a large shed for farm equipment and his construction tools (increasing value and variety). His registered Holstein herd had been redeveloped, milk production was good, REMC electric power lines finally provided power to illuminate all the buildings. Younger, sturdier horses provided more field power; he bought better implements, improved drainage and added lime and fertilizer; and increased grain and hay production. He installed indoor plumbing, improved the kitchen, piped both well water and soft water into the house and finally bought a new electric powered washing machine.

Personally, the depression from which he had suffered so much was now in the past. He and Mom, as well as some of my brothers and I joined the Evangelical Mennonite Church after the disintegration of the Amish Christian Church. Though Dad was not enthusiastic, this church did offer a spiritual focus for the family, and the family participated regularly.

Apparently, Dad had assumed that I would not return to college after the first year. In late summer of 1939, when he realized that I was determined to return for a second year, he chastised me severely. He did not want me to return to college, for reasons unexpressed. Perhaps he felt that I was becoming too worldly or wasting money that could more productively be used elsewhere.

However, two events stand out in my mind as most significant that brought about a complete change in his attitude and perspective. During the fall of my junior year, Ball State instituted Father's Day. Fathers of all students were invited to spend the day on campus, meet the faculty, attend classes, be guests at lunch and participate in special events. By then, my status on campus was well established, several faculty, my Ball State Book Store employer, Ruth Kitchin, and President L. A. Pittenger had favorable comments about me. Dad was obviously very pleased, greatly enjoyed Father's Day and returned home with a subdued pride and a very different view of what college was. From then on he was more able to relate to what I was doing, and reluctantly endorsed my college graduation--if the military did not draft me before then. As between these alternatives, he understood college much to be preferred. After that I do not recall that he ever again tried to dissuade me.

The second event was my discovery. In June 1942, Mom, Elmer, Dad and I were riding on the way to my Ball State commencement. I vividly recall Dad saying to me, "Leo, don't you think Reuben (my second youngest living brother) should finish high school?" Reuben had completed his sophomore year; unknown to me, he was determined to quit at the legal age of 16. I was not aware that during the year as Dad learned of Reuben's plans, Dad had not only tried to persuade him to finish high school, but had invited to our home the high school principal and on another occasion the county superintendent of schools to add their influence. "Leo, don't you think Reuben should finish high school?" I was stunned; I could not believe what I was hearing. I replied, "Dad, I cannot imagine why you would ask me this question; have you forgotten how hard you tried for years to keep me from finishing high school?" He thought a moment, then with a suppressed smile, acknowledged, "Perhaps even Dads can change their minds." That moment was indelibly etched in my mind, as were few other conversations in my whole life. Despite Dad's best efforts, Reuben quit high school at age 16, the only one among the six of us living.

Mom and Dad attended my Ball State commencement, proud to see me graduate with an excellent academic record and a certificate to become a teacher issued by the State of Indiana, hopefully to be used after World War II ended--if I survived. My dream of becoming a teacher, after years of delays, was again to be postponed four more years.

Immediately after graduation, I had a job waiting for me in the accounting department at Waco Aircraft Co., Troy, Ohio. This was June 1942, our nation was involved in World War II. I had been deferred from military service since Selective Service registration in October 1940 to complete my bachelor degree at Ball State. I now was eligible to be called to active duty. At Waco, in August I met Janet Gladfelter; we promptly fell in love and were married on November 25, 1942. Earlier that month I had already been inducted into the U.S. Army.

In other chapters I will deal with my four college years, six months at Waco, thirty-eight months in the Army, and our full, richly rewarding, abundant marriage and family life, as of this writing for nearly sixty years. In this chapter on Father, I will cover only those points at which we were in association with Father until his death on March 23, 1953.

The nations wartime economy was quite prosperous for those not in the military. The farm turned more profitable under Elmer's management with accelerated prices of farm products. Dad's contracting business, though more defense related in character, also turned prosperous. The farm became free of debt; he renovated the house and other buildings. For the first time in their marriage Dad and Mom had no financial worries. In turn, Elmer, Alvin, Milo and I were all drafted into military service. We served in various parts of the world; Reuben and Carl were left to do the farming. Reuben, for a time, with the shortage of certified teachers and his formal education limited to two years of high school, but with a brilliant mind, taught in an orphanage in Illinois.

When I returned from the Army service in February 1946, Dad stood ready to help us build a home in Decatur, Indiana where he had much of his contracting business. This was only three miles from Monmouth School where I taught in high school for the first two years. He greatly enjoyed Jan, his daughter-in-law, never having had a daughter, and his granddaughter, Felicity. As he ended his workday he often found it convenient to drop by just about time for dinner at our home. We all enjoyed our time together, even more because of the long separation during the war years. During the thirty-eight months I was in the Army we saw him very rarely, only on furloughs for a few days.

In 1948, we moved to Huntington, Indiana where I joined the faculty of Huntington College. He helped us move and was saddened that we were now thirty-five miles from them. Occasionally, we left Felicity and Luther, born in Decatur, with them when we took a trip. They also visited us.

In August 1951 we moved to Evanston, Illinois where I was going in residence to complete my doctor of philosophy degree at Northwestern University where I had been attending summers. Again, he gallantly loaded furniture on his pick-up truck and trailer to help us move nearly 200 miles from Huntington. Quite in contrast to the years when he resisted my completing high school, he raised no objection, though perhaps no less puzzled, what all this endless education was about.

During times when we saw him he was congenial, but at times I did sense some form of depression. Having reached his 60th birthday, he talked about retirement and took on somewhat fewer contracts. He and Mom, with Noah and Martha Mazelin, took an automobile trip to California; probably the only extended vacation Mom and Dad ever took. Mom reported that Dad did not find this very rewarding, that he showed more signs of depression. His having less work was not enjoyable; he seemed abstractly worried. Carpenter work had been his life, demanding work kept him occupied; without hobbies, without close friends, without interests in reading or travel, life may have seemed vacuous. I was not aware that his condition was so serious.

When I completed my Ph.D. degree at Northwestern in June 1952, I accepted the position as dean of the College of Liberal Arts at the University of Dubuque in Dubuque, Iowa. On March 23, 1953, Milo, with his wife, Violet, lived in Wilmore,

Kentucky where Milo was attending Asbury Seminary. During spring vacation, Milo who was home to earn some money working with Dad, called with a tragic report. That morning Dad had taken his life by his own hand. We were shocked and distraught wondering how Dad might have been helped out of his distress. The genetic tendency toward chronic depression and lacking avenues of relief seemed to have overpowered him. The whole family joined Mom in grief and sorrow. He was sixty-two years of age.

Chapter 10: Mother

Mom, whose given name was Margaret, (her name at birth was Margaretha in German) was the oldest of eleven children with three sisters and seven brothers. In birth order Margaret, Jacob, David, Peter, John, Barbara, Noah, Benjamin, Martha, Leona and Amos. (Peter and Amos, died in infancy). Her family called her Maggie as did nearly everyone else. To my Dad, she was Mama, not addressed by name. In turn, she did not address Dad as Sam, but only as Papa. In Swiss dialect, parents were Mama and Papa, the same as in English. As we boys grew older, she became Mom, more formally, Mother. She was often "Mom" to a number of her twenty-two grandchildren, and great-children.

Reared on a farm where physical labor in all seasons was endless, her father's records show that at seventeen years of age, she was paid the handsome sum of $50.00 per year, while her younger brothers earned $100.00 annually. She seldom commented on the inequity; girls in her mind and experience did not have and probably were not entitled to equal status. She regarded her father's decisions as correct and not to be challenged. If she harbored doubts they were not expressed. In many ways she, as the eldest, was her father's pride. She was very respectful and deferential to him; he was a kind yet stern and commanding father. He chose his words carefully, within my hearing rarely expressed tender affection. When she turned 21, he gave her a gold watch with a hinged cover. She wore it rarely dangling from a black shoelace instead of a gold chain. In the Amish tradition, that her parents left when she was two years old, a decorative necklace would have been regarded as a prideful adornment. At her death I was given the watch still in running order with a gold necklace, a gift which she seldom wore. In later life, she regarded it as a cherished possession. To my painful regret, the watch was stolen when our home was burglarized.

My brother, Elmer, recalls conversations with Mom concerning her lack of good health during her early 20s. Her physician prescribed more walking. Her parent's farm had a wooded tract at the back end of the eighty acres where they had placed a small chicken coop. She was assigned the care of the chickens which required a twice-daily walk of three quarters of a mile. (It is difficult for me to imagine a prescription that required more walking for the oldest of nine children that lived on a farm with no modern conveniences and required endless physical labor.)

Physically, Mother was of small stature, about five feet three inches tall, small-boned. She probably never weighed 120 pounds. Her posture was quite erect until later life when she developed a slight hump back. She wore her straight, long, light-brown hair parted in the middle pinned in a bun on the back of her head. As long as I can remember her hairstyle did not change. She never visited a beauty parlor. Her eyes were light blue. For reading, sewing or other fine work she wore simple, white steel rimmed spectacles, usually with small oblong lenses. She was of light complexion, very sensitive to sunburn; for outdoor work she always wore a wide-brimmed hat. Unless dressed for company, she always wore an apron. Until mid-life she wore the same style dresses of mid-calf length and high black, low heel shoes. She had small hands, average length fingers and small feet. For most of her life she had a hurried pace, energetic and frequently was seen running upstairs, one step at a time. When asked who was the most influential person in her early life she promptly named her father's sister, Aunt Anna Steury, whom "I always admired as a kind, Christian woman, always willing to help others, yes, us too. She would visit the sick, and help in anyway that she could."

Mom was convinced she had a good mind. Though restricted to eight years of schooling, she very much enjoyed school, was very proud of her top grades. She had a keen and accurate memory. She memorized many biblical quotations, some poetry, mathematical tables, and such practical information for daily use as cooking or baking recipes. While in the eighth grade, during the teacher's illness she felt excited and flattered when she was asked to teach a class. Mom may have done some additional study with her former teacher, John Hilty, because of her love of learning and her secret dream of becoming a teacher.

From school days on there seemed to be a low-key competitive spirit between Mom and Emma Habegger Steury, classmates in school. Emma was keen-minded, an engaging personality, a niece of the Bishop, and especially loyal and deferential to him.

Emma was chosen as one of two teachers by the Bishop and the principal, Jacob J. Schwartz. Although not directly verbalized, I felt that this resulted in understandable sense of jealousy against Emma. In any case, Mom had a deep and frustrated desire to be a teacher which she occasionally expressed and must have passed on to me and some of my brothers, as the saying goes, "in mother's milk."

She seemed to find subtle, unexpressed vicarious satisfaction in my continuing education beyond eighth grade. She did not express envy, jealousy or feelings of injustice in my educational opportunities that had been denied to her. She offered mostly unspoken assent, a certain "sinful pride" in admiring her sons one by one, progressing through high school, college and beyond.

As a grandparent, I think back about my grandparents ending their formal education in the third grade. I cannot recall that any one of them ever questioned or commented to me about my aspiring education. Now, as the oldest grandchild on my mother's side of the family I wonder what they thought of my graduation from the eighth grade, high school and college. None lived to see me earn the Masters or the Ph.D. degree.

I vividly recall Aunt Leona asking my mother, "Is there something wrong with Leo that he isn't able to finish his school? It's taking him so long." From Leona's perspective, she knew of no relative who had ever gone to high school.

Mom was diligent in letter writing, especially when her sons were away from home, at work, in college, in military service or later living at a distance. Her spelling, punctuation and grammar were flawless, her manuscript meticulous. She greatly enjoyed receiving letters.

From childhood Mom enjoyed reading. She never had a library card. In her youth she would not have been allowed to use a public library; the closest one was in Decatur, ten miles distant. Her reading consisted of an extremely narrow range of subjects and authors. Until about age 40, most of her reading was in German (church and Sunday school were also in German), including her *Bible* during her later years in English. Although a slow reader, she dutifully read the *Bible* from Genesis through Revelation many times. *The Martyr's Mirror,* catechism books of the Amish Christians and Mennonites she read in German. *Prince of Peace, Black Beauty,* and *Bunyan's Travels* were books she read in English. After joining the Mennonite church, she read church periodicals, some missionary reports and books by evangelical Christian writers. For most of her life, time for reading was limited to Saturday evenings or Sunday afternoons.

In later years the variety of her reading was slightly broadened in books given by sons and daughters-in-law. Books by Billy Graham, E. Stanley Jones, D. Elton Trueblood or Douglas Steere were all interpretations of Christian faith and living. She would urge Dad to do more Bible reading, for which he showed very little interest. In mid-life, as she acquired more household conveniences, she often said that duty required her to use more time for reading that provided spiritual nurture.

In her youth, courtship in the Amish Christian church was firmly regulated by the parents, often carried on by letter, even in a small close-knit congregation. Dating outside the church was not permitted. She never shared with us much about her courtship and engagement, but she evidently was deeply in love with the Bishop's son, John. She had saved a box of letters (found by one of my brothers snooping where he wasn't supposed to) between them, probably when they broke up he returned hers, which she had written to him. Their courtship was serious; whether they were engaged I do not know.

As John matured, he wearied of his father's church, turned into a rebellious and defiant young man that finally caused his father to excommunicate him for being "a proud and carnal son, absolutely disobedient" as shown in church records. He was effectively disowned and permanently shunned. He promptly moved to the city of Fort Wayne, thirty miles distant, lived there, married and reared a family.

Had she married the Bishop's son that would have been a coup in social standing and church status--to marry the prince.

Did she consider joining him in his rebellion, then to marry him? Possibly, but she did not reveal her innermost thoughts to us. In her father's household there was never the kind of defiance or open contentiousness as there was in the Bishop's family. The Bishop's family was repeatedly, if not continually, fractious.

By contrast, the Nussbaum families of which there were three (my grandfather's and two others) did not rank very high on the church social scale. Rather than marrying up from her role as daughter of minister number three, she married someone on the descending social scale. One can conjecture that her parents took painful if unexpressed note. (Ironically, Dad's sister, Elizabeth, did marry one of the Bishop's less rebellious sons, Peter, parents of Gerhart, my college roommate.)

Could Mom compensate in some ways, or was she destined to find marrying down on the social scale a handicap in her own personal and social development? That question never occurred to me in childhood, but as an adult, I often wondered. However, to such a question she would probably not have given a candid reply. Did she revise her thinking as the Amish Christian Church disintegrated and the Bishop sank into disrepute? We will never know.

Mom seemed to me to have a complex of feelings toward the Bishop, finding a conversation of any substance with him difficult if not impossible. Whether she felt he was the obstacle to her marrying John, she never really said, but I early observed that she never seemed comfortable in the presence of the Bishop.

Mom and her siblings felt that the Bishop did not accord their father the respect which was his due, perhaps in part, because Daniel Mazelin (number three among the ministers) had at times spoken his determined mind when he differed with the Bishop's domineering views.

These feelings were intensified when around 1928, Grandpa Mazelin suffered serious loss of voice volume and clarity of speech, which fundamentally handicapped his preaching. At that time, the Bishop was reported to have said that God was stilling the voice of the man who often challenged him. The Bishop didn't have to dislodge his periodic adversary, God did it for him. Later Grandpa Mazelin's ailment was diagnosed as

Parkinson's disease from which he suffered for some 35 years.

During the decade of the 1930s and until the death of Mom's parents (her mother on August 10, 1944 and her father on January 6, 1946) lived in their original home, at times with as many as ten persons, an over-crowded home indeed. At maximum, Daniel, with advanced Parkinson's disease, Grandma with open sores from varicose veins, Dave and Leona with disabling muscular dystrophy, Martha, employed outside the home, Noah and wife, Martha, Ben and Naomi with two sons, Harry and Roy Stanley lived in that home. Ben was the farmer, Noah the carpenter. During high school, my brother Alvin lived there to assist with chores, especially to aid Dave and Grandpa. To care for the incapacitated required significant nursing talents. The human relations, the stresses and strains and the physical labor together greatly challenged human endurance and required the patience of Job. As the patriarch, Daniel, declined in mind and body, the tensions became almost unbearable to some family members. Who was in charge? Sometimes the unhappiness spilled over to Mom as she listened to complaints and to some of the seemingly unsolvable complications. Life was even more complex because of many visitors to the home, especially to visit Dave, whose friends were scattered in many parts of this and other countries.

As several of her younger siblings were married during the years of severe financial depression in the 1930s, they recalled their Father's gifts to Mom at her marriage 14 to 18 years earlier. His generosity included a cow, a horse and $500 in contrast to a Westminster chimes mantle clock or a small amount of cash for her brothers and sisters.

There were few retirement facilities or nursing centers; community mores expected family members to care for invalids and members of the older generation. Mom's parents and her brother, Dave, died at home. Only Leona, when bedfast with muscular dystrophy and complications, resided in a nursing home for the last few years of her life. Noah, Ben and spouses were given the farm in exchange for their commitment to care for the parents, Dave and Leona for their respective lives.

Mom, as the eldest child was ever loyal to her Father and

to her church. Rarely, she hesitantly revealed her inner doubts, conflicts of mind and unanswered questions on some subjects, especially related to Christian faith. But usually she repressed them lest she engage in sinful misadventure. For her, Doubting Thomas was never a comfortable role model.

My mother was a disciplined, strong-willed, determined person in matters related to her faith and other subjects about which she was confident that she knew enough, ever awed by many of the mysteries of existence. She was uncompromising concerning honesty and personal integrity. She had an unfailing trust and faith in God as relayed and revealed in Jesus Christ. She believed devoutly in prayer, practiced it fervently in her "closet with the door shut." I do not remember, except while teaching us childhood prayers, ever hearing her pray aloud. Grace before and after each meal and family prayers were always spoken by Dad in German. When Dad was absent Mom led us in silent prayer with bowed heads and hands folded beneath the table. She did teach us childhood prayers in German as she put us to bed. The most frequent one was..."Müde bin Ich, Geh zur Ruh." (I am tired, I go to rest) She believed in God's eternal system of justice, of reward and punishment, and steadfastly agreed with Paul's statement that, "All things work together for good of them that love the Lord."

In my younger years my perspective was too limited to appreciate the long-term significance within which she applied this assertion. But I did adopt as one of my fundamental principles an admonition of Jesus quoted from the Sermon on the Mount in Matthew 6:33, "But strive first for the kingdom of God and his righteousness and all these things will be given to you as well." With my much longer perspective I find this to be a proper ordering of life's priorities.

Mom was a literalist, soft but plain spoken, no idle words, plain living without frills. For most of her life, she could not afford all the essentials; had she desired them, there was no money for frills or luxuries. Though she could share and enjoy a laugh at humor or a joke, her mood usually was serious and sometimes somber. Jesus' prescriptions concerning use of language – "Swear not at all" (Matthew 5:34) -- she meticulously observed. Jokes about religious persons were never acceptable. Reading novels was frivolous; reading had to have a serious purpose, such as spiritual growth, building of character, or information useful in one's work. Reading for fun was using time unwisely. Education for intellectual contemplation, knowledge for knowledge's sake or theoretical conjecture had no appeal. Such mental exercises might lead one onto wrong paths and could readily lead to false beliefs and endanger the true faith. She never wearied of well doing and in her own ways was a "Second Mile" person.

She probably never went shopping except with a specific purpose or for a definite need, window-shopping had no appeal. Casual or non-essential purchases were unknown to her. She faithfully remembered each birthday of her sons and daughters-in-law with an inexpensive affordable gift, sometimes a small check.

I do not remember hearing or seeing her express verbal endearment, affection or love to my Father, or seeing them kiss in spite of the agape "kiss of love" prescribed by the church. Similarly, I did not observe affectionate verbal or behavioral expressions between grandparents or married uncles or aunts. Bodily contact for affection, hugging, touching, stroking, kissing--except very young children--was not practiced. Distinctions between agape and erotic kisses were not discussed or explained.

Calling parents by first name? Forbidden. I was once scolded for saying to a visiting neighbor who met me in the yard, "Sam is in the house." And grandparents, Grandma Nussbaum, not Grandma Marian; Grandpa Mazelin, not Grandpa Daniel. Yet, inconsistently with regard to first names, ministers were referred to but not usually directly addressed in Swiss-German as Diener Dan, Diener Dev (David) (Diener meaning Servant). These terms and conversations were all in Swiss-German; the subtleties cannot really be translated into English. Social direct address by name, in any form was not the general practice.

Mom was a very private person who did much unexpressed thinking and reflecting on her own. Her thinking was probably within the boundaries that she had either learned from her parents or in her church, for she had very little exposure to ideas. She did not read popular magazines.

She listened to radio in later life only for Christian religious broadcasts. She did not own a television, did not see a commercial movie, a theater or attend an instrumental musical concert. She avoided a public athletic contest, a county or state fair, a circus, a dance, a fashion show, a stage play, a public lecture. She did not engage in politics and, so far as I know, voted in an election only in mid-life after joining the Evangelical Mennonite church. She avidly listened to religious choral music, English or German, on rare occasions in her church. She enjoyed singing hymns or gospel songs. To venture outside her very parochial upbringing, she would have regarded endangering to her own spiritual well being, perhaps interpreted as doing some things which Jesus would not have done. As was forbidden by her church, she did not attend another church service until the Amish Christian Church disintegrated when she was middle-aged. Once she made the painful transition, she was equally loyal to the Evangelical Mennonite Church that she and Dad hesitantly joined. Apparently they believed it to be the best alternative among the denominations that they knew.

My brother, Milo, as pastor, served two of the Evangelical Mennonite congregations in the Morton, Illinois area for his whole career. He served thirty years in one congregation that grew from a handful in a storefront to several hundred members, in a complex of buildings with a wide-ranging mission program. In his very effective pastorate, I believe she saw him as the model son. Being proud of one of her sons was not a matter for discussion outside the family. In any group of five or ten people, she rarely spoke but was a very intent listener. Taking the initiative was not in character. Occasionally, she would write her own thoughts on paper if only for self-clarification, which she might show to no one else.

She did not own a bathing suit; did not wear a dress in length less than half way between her knees and ankles. She never wore slacks or pants, not even when she hoed weeds in the cornfields or husked corn in cold weather. She could not have publicly addressed any group of people; she was all her life constitutionally shy. When on exhibit for any reason, she was frighteningly embarrassed, became very nervous. She never lost her ability to blush. Innately, she was persuaded of the correctness of St. Paul's prohibition of women speaking in church, and she was quite comfortable for herself to observe this admonition as the proper role of women concerning leadership in nearly all respects. I remember how offended she was when in her middle age, the town of Berne had a woman postmaster; she regarded this as very unseemly. However, she did teach a Sunday school class in later years for her widowed colleagues that I believe gave her great satisfaction and fulfillment. In an otherwise English language church, elderly widowed class members used German language Bibles. It was a comforting return to the language of their earlier years. .

She loved flowers, planted and tended them assiduously; every spring, she planted and cultivated her large vegetable garden. For nearly fifty years she spaded the soil by hand and meticulously filled each furrow with fresh cow manure. What fertile garden soil that produced! With loving care she prepared the soil, planted the seeds, nurtured and cultivated the growing plants and enjoyed the harvest with the fulfillment of a symphonic composer or a published poet. She shared in the creation of freshly edible vegetables: lettuce, peas, green beans, tomatoes, shelled beans, turnips, carrots, cabbage, rhubarb, ground cherries among others. Only after her seventy-fifth birthday did she give up the vegetable gardening, with joint-aching regret. Sweet corn, potatoes, more cabbage and turnips were grown on a larger tract in one of the fields. She would cut flowers for a vase but did not use them as a formal dining table centerpiece. She greatly enjoyed the fine-grained leaves of the asparagus plant, but I do not remember her ever serving or eating fresh asparagus though she harvested and enjoyed nearly every other kind of home grown vegetable and fruit from the garden and orchard.

Some fourteen months after my parent's marriage, while they lived with my Dad's parents, I was born. The other six brothers were all born on the family farm home with the family physician attending and usually assisted by Mom's mother. Grandma Mazelin would stay for a day or two after which for ten days or two weeks either Martha or Leona, Mom's younger unmarried sisters, or one of Mom's many cousins would come to the house and fill mother's work role. When the helper left, Mom with another addition to the family who required regular breast-feeding, carried on the exhausting work as usual. So far as I know, she never had any serious complications and struggled as best she could to carry on normal household and family duties.

For most of her life, she suffered periodically from corns that grew on top of some of her toes. The family physician found no cure. I don't know whether she ever went to a podiatrist. As a mother of seven boys, she stood alone as woman, as female--increasingly frustrated as each successive birth yielded another boy rather than a girl companion, who could become a colleague and co-worker. I believe after five sons, my parents changed physicians, from Dr. Ernst (German spelling) Franz to Dr. Amos Reusser, both of whom practiced in Berne. Their medical education consisted of interning with an older practicing physician. Some friends interpreted changing physicians as an extra effort to have a daughter. Ironically, living only two miles away Dan and Katy Steury, double first cousins to my parents, had six living daughters, no sons.

When there were only two children, Mom helped in the fall harvest season. She took the horse and buggy to the cornfield to shelter the sons from the chilly weather as she assisted Dad with the husking of corn. Dad would tear apart the corn shocks, lay the corn stalk bundles on the ground for husking. Mom and Dad husked the ears, and piled them on the ground to be dumped into the wagon bed at the end of the day. Dad tied the husked stalks in bundles, then placed them upright in larger shocks later to be hauled to the barn for cattle feed. She often fretted that our cornfield, after the husking, was not as neatly swept as the fields of some other skillful farmers. Dad was less concerned and wanted to see the basic work done without a detailed manicure. With the birth of the third son, Alvin, she found the housework fulltime demand on her time and physical energy. (Incidentally, at this writing I still have the first boots I owned as a two-year old accompanying Mom in the cornfield.)

In my early years Mom envisioned ideally, that each of

her sons would become a farmer within a few miles of the home farm as our home farm was to her parents and in-laws. Among my brothers, Reuben bought the home farm from her; Carl bought a farm about five miles away. Her four older sons did not buy farms and among her siblings Noah and Ben bought the family farm.

She was always worried about not having enough money to meet minimum needs, especially in the weeks approaching the semi-annual farm mortgage payment in February and August. (Because of this, I had imprinted on me early in life that these two months represented six-month intervals!) Other debts were also burdensome, but this one was so crucial, during the long depression years. Much of the farm year was designed to have enough income at those times so as not to fall in arrears and risk foreclosure and lose the farm. On occasion, they borrowed part of the money to make the mortgage payments. Weekly milk checks helped, but some major income item was also required, such as the sale of broilers, fattened hogs, large quantities of eggs, an excess cow or heifer, or that extra income Dad could earn in carpentry.

When a car killed a wandering chicken, she ran to the road to salvage it for dinner. I was perhaps six years old, when I saw it happen. As she stewed it for the evening meal, I told her that I could not eat any of it, "I was not going to eat dead chicken." My stomach rebelled, and for perhaps twenty years or so, I never ate chicken. Even today, when I see stewed chicken as that one had been served, I pass it. She was very frugal, nothing should go to waste.

As her Father, she never learned to drive a car. When we had the gear-shift Star, I recall Dad persuaded her to try, in our driveway, backing toward the road; the front right fender that already had a break, hooked the fence. Dad slammed on the brake, the car stopped. She asserted that she would never try again, and she didn't! Her husband and her sons were her chauffeurs.

Seasonal debt at the local bank, with the note co-signed by one of my grandfathers, to buy seed or fertilizer was an annual occurrence. Or it happened because of a poor harvest, to buy grain feed for the cattle, hogs or chickens. There was always interest to be paid, some amount on the principal and the note renewed. Mom and Dad had no market-negotiable collateral. More often Grandpa Mazelin, who had an excellent credit record, would co-sign the note or, Grandpa Nussbaum with lesser credit rating did so. To take the renewal note to one of them was always embarrassing, even agonizing, and sometimes prompted shame. Mom felt apologetic for not making a larger payment or paying the note in full.

Grandpa Mazelin had a reputation for paying his obligations when due; though his words were few his very look and example were in their own ways accusatory. Grandpa Mazelin's farm operation was something of a model of orderliness, systematic planning, good productivity, everything done on schedule. He was known to assist other relatives with short-term loans to help them get started in new farm ventures.

Dad's worries were general without well-considered plans for solutions; Mom's were the conscience-demanding kind that required punctual attention to creditors, with apologies and explanations if there were even danger of being late. She never succeeded in transforming Dad to be more like her father, but the years of effort were frustrating and often anxiety producing. Yet, she never forgot her subordinate role as a woman. Until Dad's death, I believe that she neither sought nor had the authority to sign checks, although they co-owned the farm and co-signed all legal contracts.

Paradoxically, she helped observe growing family conflict among her siblings as her father's undiagnosed Parkinson's became an increasing handicap. After he lost his ministerial post, he was less and less in command of the family. On the family farm, Mom's brothers and sisters became engulfed in confusion as to who was in charge and who would take care of whom; her mother's varicose veins became a major handicap. Uncle Dave and Aunt Leona suffered disablement with muscular dystrophy. The patriarch suffered; none could take his place. As the oldest child and a woman, Mom felt helpless yet with nagging guilty conscience compelled to help find solutions.

To my mother, time was God's gift, never to be wasted or

used for frivolous or trivial purposes. I'm not sure she ever took a real vacation before age 60; she refused ever to ride a boat, she had a deep fear of water. She didn't mind her sons and Dad playing checkers, give-away or mill. Though she knew the games well, she had no interest in playing them, but she enjoyed watching a close contest. I sensed that though she would relish winning, for a woman to be openly competitive was unseemly.

She was always busy, perpetually and dutifully at work that she could not escape caring and feeding seven growing boys. Rarely did she have temporary household help, during my years at home never took the family to a restaurant. She was always engaged in cooking, baking bread, canning fruits and vegetables, dressing chickens, in winter season with other family members slaughtering a cow or butchering a pig. She never served less than twenty-one full meals per week unless, on an occasional Sunday noon we went to Grandma Mazelin or extremely rarely, to Grandma Nussbaum. There were no holiday celebrations, no holiday travel and rarely changes in the daily routine. Summer family picnics--never. Grandpa Nussbaum had his unique description of picnicking. He said, "Why do we want to eat in the woods? When I was a boy we ate in the kitchen and went to toilet in the woods. Now all this is reversed; we eat in the woods and go to toilet in the bathroom." (For variety and kinds of foods served, see Chapter 3.)

Beds to make, dishes to wash, clothes to launder for nine people. (in good weather dried in the sun, hung on the clothes line) Ironing and mending every week, she frequently faced a malfunctioning washing machine engine, or clothes wringer. Seven boys with few spare clothes generated the need for lots of mending--much of it because in depression years she had no money to buy new clothes, or enough time to sew them, which she also managed to do on her treadle machine. During the depression years of the early '30s she sewed her own dresses and many of our shirts--often for everyday wear, made of Wayne or McMillen Animal Feed bags bleached white to remove the color and printing. For her, dresses were made from a single pattern, the same style and length though with different colors and fabrics.

114

Could the boys be domesticated? To some extent for selective duties, frequently, at best, responding reluctantly and at worst rebelliously. One or two enjoyed baking cakes or cookies, one or two did occasional cooking of limited dishes but not for the whole family. Some liked to iron handkerchiefs, some would hang out the clothes on the line after washing, or take them off the line when dry. All took turns to carry in water from the nearby cistern or drinking water from the distant well next to the barn. All were routinely drafted to wash and dry dishes. The older ones had to help with the animal feeding, stall cleaning, milking and gathering eggs. Frequent litanies heard in the dining room and kitchen, "It isn't my turn, Mom; I did it last night; I did it twice since Leo dried dishes". But all of us showed up promptly to eat all meals; we ate meals as a family--the exceptions were very rare. And, Mom had prepared them, boys set the table, brought in wood for heating the kitchen stove and for all family members old enough to walk, there were always tasks to be done in the house, lawn, garden and orchard as well as on the seventy-five acre farm.

With seven boys on the farm, twelve years difference in age between the oldest and the youngest, five were in school at one time. Childhood and seasonal diseases not only reduced the work force mornings and evenings and added to Mom's work, but at times illnesses were serious and two or three times life-threatening.

Victor, the second youngest was killed at age nine in a bicycle-pickup truck accident, hit by his uncle by marriage. He was pedaling home a mile and a half during noon lunch hour to pick up his new baseball glove ordered from Sears Roebuck mail order house. The shock of his sudden death brought a very solemn time in our home for weeks. And, no one in the family ever heard a word of regret or apology from the uncle. His auto insurance paid funeral expenses and the cost of a new bicycle. Mom and Dad wanted no more from the insurance company. Mom was firm in her refusal to make any money from Victor's death.

Childhood diseases invaded our home regularly, colds, mumps, tonsillitis, two varieties of measles, scarlet fever from which Reuben suffered permanent, severe handicaps. Milo suffered from pinkeye complications that required long treatment and left his vision in one eye permanently impaired. Victor developed mastoiditis that he suffered for several months. Seasonal flu occurred many times, respiratory infections were frequent. Alvin fractured a leg when he fell out of the haymow. The fracture was above the knee. Instead of using a cast, Dr. Franz placed his leg in a traction frame mounted on his bed with a tightening hand screw. His foot was wrapped in felt. After two weeks, although Alvin complained day and night about the growing pain in his heel, Dr. Franz refused to remove the device and examine the foot. Alvin was bedfast for eight weeks. When the felt was removed, a doubled corner of the felt lining had worn a hole in his heel the size of a nickel, a quarter-inch deep. He had a life-long mutilated heel. That ended Dr. Ernst Franz's medical services to us, although some friends attributed a different reason for the change in family physicians.

As an infant Carl had pneumonia. Dr. Amos Reusser had given up the case as hopeless and Carl's death appeared imminent. Dr. Edwin Nyffeler, the family chiropractor, was more tenacious. At the most critical time, he applied battery heated copper plates to Carl's chest and back for several hours, and within twenty-four hours the crisis had passed.

Elmer, in a race down an old straw stack, broke an arm; when he got up, he said, as he looked at his wrist, "It doesn't hurt much, but it is crooked." When do you go to the physician? When do you call him by phone to ask whether you should take prescription No. 1, 35, 91, or some other? And, when do you just hope whatever the ailment, it will wear off, especially when the family cannot afford another doctor bill? All these afflictions and complications were, in the end, hardest on the mother who had to tend them all. On Saturday nights in sequence, family members had baths in the wooden wash tub, set in front of the open oven door to get token heat on cold winter nights. And, tomorrow morning at nine o'clock is church or Sunday school for the whole family.

Ironically, when I was named Leo, I was given no middle name. I am confident Mom did not know that there had been thirteen Roman Catholic Popes named Leo. Each of my brothers in succession was given a middle name. I was disturbed and demanded that I also have a middle name. My parents added my middle name legally--the name of my choice, Lester. I continued use of the name or initial during my whole life. How ironic that each of my brothers has mostly ignored the middle name or initial.

She was a faithful devoted, caring, loving mother who lived according to the standards of her own upbringing. She served all of us with unusual energy and devotion. She was uncannily frugal in depression times and painfully determined that the imperiled farm must not be lost. For years during the depression, she agonized seeing little hope for a financial resolution. Her distress was very painful and deep.

In the years of World War II, she was deeply pained as she saw four of her sons in military service. I was in the U.S.; Elmer in Europe; Al as an officer in Okinawa in the west Pacific zone; Milo in India and China. She did find financial relief. The farm became debt-free, our home was renovated with central heating, electrical light and power, modern plumbing, refrigeration and freezing equipment along with a variety of conveniences and appliances. For the first time during her 50s she finally had her bills paid on time, owed no one and enjoyed some discretionary income. But, the persevering strain and pain of getting to such comparative financial well-being left many permanent scars on her mind and spirit. Perhaps the more so because some of the financial relief was attributable to a world war in which four of her sons were compelled to serve, a double insult to her deep faith-commitment to pacifism---opposed to all war. Some of us elected non-combatant military service, some regular service. Reuben was spared military service because of physical limitations; Carl, after the war, was drafted and elected optional Civilian Public Service.

During the war years, Grandpa Nussbaum had been a widower since January 3, 1934 when Grandma Nussbaum died. For some time, he lived with his youngest son, Menno, his wife Genevieve and daughter Doveanna on the home farm that Menno bought. When the farm was sold and Menno's family moved to a

117

smaller home in Berne, Grandpa lived with Mom and Dad for several years. Mom always regarded Grandpa Nussbaum as a religious, mental and financial lightweight. However, during those days his Christian faith was stirred afresh with the demise of the Amish Christian Church. He took, very seriously, further explorations as he joined the Apostolic Christian Church, where he seemed to find genuine satisfaction. Mom regarded Grandpa's stay as a burden which she would have liked to avoid but felt it her duty to provide her father-in-law a home in his final years. He had almost no income and very few assets. Though in fairly good health, he found few household tasks which he enjoyed doing. He did help with snapping green beans, pitting cherries for canning, taking nutmeats out of cracked hickory nuts, peeling and coring apples, and similar tasks. Reading was of no interest to him. Although he was a very pleasant person, he and Mom could find few subjects on which to converse. In his earlier years, a sense of humor was an evident part of his personality. In his later years, his demeanor turned increasingly inward and his range of interests and activities became very limited. He died on September 8, 1947.

Mom's general health was remarkable. Except for seasonal colds and coughs and decaying teeth that necessitated an upper plate, she was astonishingly durable, especially considering her life--long exhausting schedule and physical exertion. She was never a hospital patient until, at age eighty-five, the last ten days of her life after she fractured a hip in a fall in the church basement. She died on September 14, 1978. With a funeral in the Evangelical Mennonite Church, she was buried in the adjoining cemetery next to Dad.

Ironically, she was spared moving to a nursing home that she had prospectively regarded as an almost intolerable confinement and unbearable invasion of her privacy. After selling the home farm at age eighty, she lived alone in a mobile home located some forty feet from Carl and Justine's residence. After raising sons, she had lived with Reuben and Estella for twenty-four years as an active grandma amid their six children on the family farm. Perhaps the prospect of institutional living even made death a preferred option.

Chapter 11: Youthful Activity: Plain and Fancy Mischief

In my generation, relationships with rural neighbors, and associations within and among families were remote from the law. If a party was aggrieved, even if it posed a potential legal case, I cannot recall a single instance among our neighbors that a person turned to the law for justice or recompense. One did not think of legal action as the basis for settling differences. Rather, there were efforts at reconciliation or mediation between the injured parties or grievances would simply be buried, sometimes carrying grudges. Social relationships might be affected. There were various ways of alerting repeated offenders from ready acceptance whether at a farm sale, ignoring them when passing on the road or in town by not waving, or not greeting with a "Hi" or "Good morning", or the more frequent Swiss-German equivalent.

Some offenses were dealt with by the church. If in the church, the Bishop might chastise the offending person. If committed by a school child, even on the road to or from school, the grade school principal might serve as adjudicator, perhaps followed with punishment by the parents.

In this rural setting, many forms of mischief, spontaneous or planned, humorous, or serious did occur but were either dealt with by the parties affected or frequently just ignored. Once, accidentally, I ran over killing a neighbor's dog. We still spoke, relationships were not fractured and there was no lawsuit. But then a farm dog was not a member of the family, sleep on the owners bed or eat Purina Chow. He slept in the doghouse.

On the two-mile walk to school, we passed many metal signs fastened to farm fences as advertising such as Babe Ruth candy bar, Butter Finger, Burma Shave, Pennzoil, and Coca Cola. Walking on the gravel road we often played marksmanship, throwing some of the large pieces of gravel at these road signs, with varying amounts of damage. Walking with the two Schrock children, our next door neighbors, this marksmanship became competitive. Who could make the biggest dent closest to the middle of the sign or within one of the letters? Over time, some of these advertising signs made of painted metal

119

started rusting, were unattractive, if not badly mutilated. Were we late for school? Never.

Telephone wire insulators made of heavy green or white glass, now a valuable collector's item, appeared every few hundred feet. They required keen marksmanship and were not easily damaged. But once in a great while a lucky marksman tossing a large piece of gravel would shatter one. That was a rare achievement worthy of adulation among kids but not reported to the principal!

Metal advertising signs during the depression years covered several square feet. When we needed waterproof roofing for our rabbit pens, these sufficed very nicely. Occasionally, my brothers and I and the neighbor boys removed them, carried them home and converted them to rabbit-hutch roofing. Were we stealing? We didn't think of it that way. We weren't arrested. Did our parents object? Yes, indeed. We did not return them, but we didn't get any more!

Birds were abundant: sparrows, pigeons, crows, meadow larks, killdeers, martins, swallows, red-winged blackbirds, bluebirds, bluejays, owls, occasional cardinals, wrens, red-headed woodpeckers among many others. Conservation of birds was not in our vocabulary, they were all fair game though a few were already protected by law. Sometimes birds were targets for rock-throwing. I remember one singing meadowlark, sitting on a fence post. I took aim, hit him squarely and killed him. While this was very unusual, I do recall that I was much pained by my success at marksmanship--probably the only success I can remember. This remained in my memory whereas hundreds of misses I have forgotten. Though illegal, we often took aim with a rifle and on the rarest of occasions would hit the bird--our youthful form of violence. The despicable black crows were too crafty ; we never hit them.

There were transient persons of various kinds, the Schmutz Jud (translated innocently, Dirty Jew) a squatty, itinerant peddler who carried two hand cases containing needles, buttons, thread, straight and safety pins, and other items that farm housewives required. Wearing his crumpled gray suit, oversize shoes, a wide-brimmed hat, he walked the dusty gravel roads of the community with his commodity bags of many compartments. He knocked on doors, was usually invited in where he proceeded to show his merchandise to the housewife. She might just need some black thread, four white buttons and two sewing needles for patching overalls. He saved her a trip to town. His profit--a few pennies. If it was lunchtime within an hour he might rest in his chair until the invitation to share the family meal. If he arrived in late afternoon, he would await an invitation to dinner and lodging. His offer to pay was usually declined. He was pleasant, always courteous, a wandering fixture in the community who returned every month or six weeks. He was also the butt of jokes, not in his presence. In this rural area he and the junk dealer in Berne were the only known Jews. I never heard his name; in the language of the community, he was "Schmutz Jud." We had never heard of anti-Semitism. His origin, I don't know; we never learned whether he had a home base. He was still coming when I went to college. (My brother told me that when he died in Ft. Wayne, he left an estate of $100,000 to a charity.)

Two other transient persons in the community were Grosz Charlie (Big Charlie) and Dutch Louie. They were itinerant workers, usually employed by the day. Big Charlie would dig ditches for drain tile, cut corn and put in shocks, husk corn, or replace a man on the threshing crew for a day. He was fed and housed and paid perhaps a dollar for a day's work. Where did he come from? I have no knowledge. What happened to him? Perhaps he ended up on the County Farm (the retirement home for persons without family or funds). He loved raw tomatoes picked in the patch. Mischievous boys would sometimes throw them to land near him and run to hide behind a building before he could see the attacker.

Dutch Louie did similar work, but was much less reliable and very temperamental. For his lack of dependability in quality and quantity of work the farmers gradually did not employ him; he disappeared I know not where. He was often the victim of cruel jokes by boys in the community.

Another apparently homeless itinerant was Peg-Leg. He wore a wooden leg shaped like the lower part of a crutch. He walked the roads during the depression, was pitied by some, the butt of jokes and comments by others. So far as I know he did not work, but roamed the community and lived off the good will of the residents, some who would feed him, or give him overnight lodging. We never knew his origin or his demise. He claimed that he lost a leg during World War I, occasionally regaled youngsters with stories, real or fictional, hoping to win favors in food and lodging. Many people in that pacifist community wondered whether he lost a limb in battle.

A different kind of regular visitor at the farm was the retail delivery person, or door-to-door salesman. The Watkins man, the Raleigh man each regularly scheduled with a wide array of home remedies, cough syrups, liniments, aspirin, pain tablets and shampoo, among others known as patent medicines. The national firms for whom they were agents were reputable even though many of the potions may have done less than advertised. The Fuller Brush man brought quality commodities for human and household use from hairbrushes to floor scrubbers. A regular caller the same day each week was the huckster. His Model T Ford chassis with a wooden custom-built body was large enough for a man to walk in the middle aisle. He carried a small array of groceries: white sugar, brown sugar, bread, baking flour, cookies, spices and candy. In a small chicken coop in the rear under the body, he kept a few chickens that he bought or traded for groceries. In buying them, he tied their legs and weighed them with a hanging scale. For years the weekly bread man brought fresh bakery bread, cinnamon rolls and cookies. We boys, tired of Mom's home-baked bread, regarded the light and airy, wrapped bakery bread as a luxury.

The jokes, nonsense and mischief among seven boys were many, sometimes harmless but at other times threatening if not perilous. Elmer was always spunky and daring. When he was no more than age seven, he would climb the ladder on the windmill despite Dad having wired a board over the first four steps to prevent kids from climbing. Elmer took off his shoes, deftly hooked his toes on the protruding cross bars of the ladder and up he went. There were birdhouses at the 30-foot level; he peered into them and scared the martins that nested there. He screwed up his courage, crawled over one of the crossbars of the frame, and hung by his bent knees. When Mom learned of this as one of the younger brothers ran to the house to tell her, she almost had heart failure. She early learned what it means to forgive seventy times seven. Elmer was frighteningly scolded; but his adventurous spirit was unsubdued.

One summer Clarence Schrock, his youngest sister, Marcella, Al, Elmer and I went swimming in the Blue Creek on a neighbor's farm. The water was warm, the sun hot and we all just dropped our clothes on the bank and went swimming. Really, none of us could swim; the water was too shallow, no more than two feet deep, but time slipped by. When we got home our parents wanted to know where we had been. "Fishing and swimming", said one of the brothers. Mom turned all colors, wondering what else we had been doing. That evening Dad had a visit with the mother of Clarence and Marcella and we were told that never again would we go swimming, boys and girls together. Their excitement far exceeded our understanding! At other times we boys did go fishing; no rods and reels, just a small branch from a tree, wrapping cord for a line with a small fish-hook and earth worms dug from the creek bank. Our only catch may have been a sunfish, small catfish or a crab.

A silly impulse can cause great damage. One day I was perhaps seven my mother was filling a bucket at the well with the windmill pumping the water. There was an extra hole about the size of my ring finger in the vertical shaft of the pump that moved up and down through a collar around the shaft. I said to my mother, "Look, my finger is taking a ride, as I inserted my finger into the hole." Instantly, she saw the danger to the end of my finger being crushed and pushed out the pin to disengage the pump shaft. My finger was badly injured, the nail came off, but the bone was not broken--thanks to a quick-acting mother. How often we boys were in peril through stupid kid's play.

Some years later when I was perhaps twelve, I was sent to Berne with the team of horses and wagon to grind some feed. I felt grown up and a little daring. The church had not really allowed anyone to go to the public swimming pool in Decatur, the only legitimate pool in the area, yet a few young people would sneak in, including some of my friends. I was envious. To be admitted required a health certificate from a physician, so I stopped at Dr. Reusser, our family physician; he checked my pulse, listened to my heart with the stethoscope and for ten cents signed a certificate. This shocked Mom They almost denied me using it; but when I got a ride with friends one evening, I went for my first dip in a real swimming pool.

Several years later, Grandpa Nussbaum at age 69 with pitchfork helped us make hay. That involved spreading loose hay on the wagon as the hayloader pushed it up from the ground. It was a fiercely hot July day. That evening he gamely joined two of my brothers and me dips in the old gravel pit west of Berne--no modern pool. At least we washed off the hay dust as we jumped off diving boards feet first not having learned to dive. Grandpa showed the kind of intergenerational sportsmanship that we almost never had with Dad.

On another hot August day, Elmer and I had been cutting weeds and vines on the banks of the Blue Creek where the county surveyor annually assigned each property owner whose land drained into the Creek a few hundred feet to be mowed and dredged. When the weeds were thoroughly sun dried we were required to burn them, to guard the fire while assuring a clean burn. The plot next to ours was that of an Amish neighbor, Pete Hilty, who was best known for his chronic constitutional stuttering. The plot was only a quarter mile from his barn. Out of sheer mischief we decided to set fire to his that was not dry enough for a clean burn. We were eager to have him come out and, in his excitement, so we could hear him stutter--which is exactly what happened. He was furious with us and stuttered in non-discernible, guttural noises. We said we were sorry, and helped him put out the fire. A case of transgression for potential legal action? Indeed. We knew the Amish man would take no such action against us; however, it was terrible cruelty to a neighbor.

One of the ventures that Dad undertook to increase income during the depression was to house a flock of chickens in an old chicken house with ground floor on an unoccupied farm a quarter mile east of our place. Perhaps at age eight, I was sent to carry a small bucket of shelled corn for their evening feed.

Having walked to and from school, four miles, this was a weary walk. So, on one evening a little over halfway there, I dumped the corn at the side of the road and went home. The next day when Dad went to feed the chickens, he could tell they were nearly starved; he demanded an accounting. I confessed, was spanked; next time walking was comparatively less painful!

Firecrackers, during our boyhood, were legal in Indiana. We looked to the Fourth of July, the only time that our parents allowed fireworks. It is a marvel that no one of whom I know was injured. Firecrackers ranged from the tiny two-inch, thinner than a pencil, to larger four-inch perhaps three-eighths of an inch in diameter. We tried many forms of explosion: drilling a hole in an apple, inserting the firecracker, lighting it and throwing it as high as possible. The apple was shredded. We set them off in tin cans which were bent into every imaginable shape. Squeezed into a crack in the top of a wooden fence post, the cracker made a frustrated noise. Roman candles came in small tube form, one end was lit and colorful balls of fire went skyward. Sparklers were made of solid chemicals wrapped around a wire; when lit they sparkled fiercely but were not hot enough to injure the bare skin. And mischievously, some of us even would throw one out on the road to scare a horse with buggy; punishment followed. Dad enjoyed the fireworks, though usually let the boys do the lighting. Mom would anxiously watch, always fearful that some accident would result in injury. Once a year, it was low-cost celebratory fun.

In early years there were no commercial celebrations with fireworks; but by the time I was in high school, Fort Wayne, thirty miles away, had a significant public fireworks display at least one or two of which I attended.

Our Schrock neighbors next door, had only one cow and most of their five acres consisted of ponds which had been created by digging clay for the former tile mill on their property. Pasture was very scarce on their small acreage. When Elmer was ten or eleven, Marcella Schrock the same age was often assigned the task of watching the cow for pasture on the roadside. Marcella's mother asked for Elmer to be with her to help watch the cow a quarter to half a mile from their home. With Elmer's insatiable curiosity, with no sister at home, he and Marcella agreed to remove their clothes in the tall grass and examine each other's bodies. Elmer then brought a report to his brothers about what he learned. His inspection reports fascinated us. As far as I know the cow was never injured by traffic!

Elmer was always the experimenter, the budding scientist who became a physics professor. During his junior year in high school while I was running the farm, we engaged a former high school teacher, Sam Lahr, to help with corn cutting. He drove a 1929 model Pontiac coupe; each morning he parked it near the granary and walked a third of a mile to the cornfield. Elmer had his required morning chores before time for the school bus. But instead of doing his work he decided to unlock Sam Lahr's car-- not to remove anything or do damage but to prove that he could. The window on the driver's side had sagged with age and remained open just a crack; the doors were locked or unlocked by a small inside handle about an inch long, with up and down motion. Pressed down, it was locked. Elmer tied a loop at the end of a binder twine, dropped the loop around the lock handle. This took some time, but finally he hooked it, the loop tightened around the lock handle. Apparently, the lock was broken; the door wouldn't open. So, he tugged and struggled; the string broke, one part fell inside the car. Elmer was petrified; Sam Lahr was not a generous or forgiving person. I was busily at work in the field husking corn; Elmer came running at top speed to beg me to bail him out. It was time for the school bus. He yelled that he had a very important test that day. He was really scared, "Please get me out of trouble!" What to do?

Would I fix it for him? Bail him out of what could be a real legal charge, or should he learn a harsh lesson--always compellingly inquisitive, the scientific mind asking questions and wanting to find out. I angrily told him to get on the bus and that I would take my harvest work time to deal with his contemptible mischief the best I could. In a nearby field unsuspecting Sam Lahr was busy cutting corn and putting it into shocks.

I returned to the car and surveyed the situation; if I didn't find a remedy, Sam Lahr would surely be vengeful, perhaps legally. If I try to bail out Elmer and fail to get rid of the evidence, am I a party to the crime?

In Elmer's desperation to get the car door open, he had also broken the door handle on the side of the driver. I remembered that Sam Lahr always used the door on the passenger side. Perhaps it had some defect. I formed a loop at the end of a metal rod, reached in to turn the crank to raise the windshield. Then I was able to reach in from the front with the same rod to unlock the door on the passenger side; I removed the string, the most damnable piece of the evidence, closed the windshield and locked the passenger door. I glued the driver's side door handle; everything appeared normal, no evidence of burglary.

Elmer returned from school frightfully anxious. He wondered each minute what he would do if he had to face Sam Lahr. He knew that he had been engaged in a criminal act, attempted burglary, potential auto theft. A few days later we noticed that the driver's side door handle had fallen off. Evidently Sam Lahr never suspected the attempted burglary, at least not enough to confront us. Did Elmer remember the lesson? Only for a time; it hadn't killed his curious experimental nature, the research scientist, the professor of physics. It was just one of his experiments that misfired!

One of the few trips Elmer, Alvin and I took was to Cleveland with some neighbor friends. We drove 200 miles to the city to visit the zoo and to attend a fair. During the day, Alvin was separated from the rest of us, I do not recall why, but we had agreed to meet at a specified place and time. We waited a long time for him. Finally, he showed up having been robbed of the money he had (two or three dollars), scared to death but unharmed. At that time, such an experience was rather unusual; today, unfortunately, quite commonplace.

For boldness, even reckless action, Alvin often was a leader. One evening, chores finished and supper over several of us boys were riding horses bareback, galloping up and down the lane which led to the fields. Dick, a brown horse of lighter weight and faster than the draft horses was a good runner and provided the best riding. We, in turn, were racing against the clock. Alvin was sure he could run him faster than the rest of us.

At full gallop he came toward the gate, just as he entered the barnyard, Dick stumbled, flopped hard heels over head, landing on his back. Alvin could have been crushed, but fortunately, he was flung to the side as he landed on the ground, shaken but not seriously hurt; the horse showed no evident injury. We never raced Dick again.

I never saw Dad use a gun, so far as I know, he never owned one. But his Dad was a lover of guns and an avid marksman. Grandpa owned a .32 calibre rifle, a .22 calibre rifle, and at least one shotgun. While he hunted occasionally, he kept the guns to shoot undesirable birds such as crows, sparrows and sometimes pigeons. When we butchered pigs or a cow, he always shot the animal and wielded the sharpened knife to cut the jugular, to draw as much blood as possible to improve the condition of the meat.

Grandpa Mazelin, on the other hand, wanted nothing to do with guns. He left that to the boys. As to guns, we boys saw Grandpa Nussbaum as a model. Sparrows were abundant, crows were in nearby wooded lots, and pigeons were messy on the barn roof and in the haymow. Finally, we convinced our parents to let us buy a gun from Sears, provided we took lessons from Grandpa Nussbaum on gun use. He was an enthusiastic teacher, very insistent on using all safety features.

We had fun at marksmanship, shooting apples off fence posts, tin cans and other forms of targets. It was a challenge to hit a sparrow at a few hundred feet; pigeons were sensitive to being followed and crows were downright crafty. We never shot a crow, but we killed many sparrows and pigeons. In aiming to shoot sparrows, we often missed the sparrow and hit the metal ridge roll on the top of the barn. Over the years it developed many holes each of which brought verbal spankings from Dad. But a bullet through the tail of the windmill brought punishment; that was strictly forbidden. Each hole brought with it a fringe of rust. At times, we took aim at a telephone wire insulator, but a neighbor having fractured a telephone wire brought a telephone official's warning which ended that sport. However, letters on metal advertising signs fastened to farm fences were delightful targets, though had the law been applied each bullet hole was a criminal offense.

We never had a gun accident that injured anyone. In the cow barn I was watching in the back for sparrows when I thought I had the gun on safety but triggered it accidentally a few inches from my foot onto the concrete floor. The bullet left its mark on the concrete as it ricocheted from floor to ceiling. That scared and sobered me in handling the gun for a long time. Each brother, in turn, having turned twelve or thirteen learned to use the rifle. The fact that we never had an injury was perhaps more miracle than sound judgment. Occasionally, we hunted rabbits and squirrels and were able to supplement our meat dishes, though several of us never developed much of a taste for non-domesticated meat dishes.

I never had a bone fracture while I was growing up, more fortunate than Elmer and Al. I did have an internal injury that at the time and for many years later I conjectured may have caused my chronic gall bladder problems. Milo and I were driving home from my grandparents with a team of horses and the box wagon which had a wagon seat which was fitted on top with slides, sliding forward and backward. It was located a distance from the front so that we could rest our feet on the edge of the front board. My feet slipped off and I fell forward and landed just below my ribs on the right side in the gall bladder area. Instantly, the pain was so bad that I had Milo drive the team, and lying on the wagon floor, I agonized terribly as we drove the two miles home instead of going to town for some feed. For several days the pain was unrelenting, I do not recall having any medical attention. Slowly, it diminished; in a few days I was back at work.

Years after that, I suffered severe stomach area pains after eating certain kinds of food, especially if I had a very large meal. Occasionally, I had medical attention with no clear diagnosis. Perhaps nearly thirty years later our family physician in Sherman, Texas did all gall bladder tests then available and found that my gall bladder had no evidence of stones yet had quit functioning. He suspected cancer and scheduled surgery. The gall bladder was effectively dead, filled with extremely fine sand. The surgeon said he had never seen a gall bladder like this one yet did not believe that all this could have started from the injury that I described. He didn't convince me. After the removal I never had any of the symptoms.

Skating was a wonderful winter sport on the Hilty pond across the road formed years earlier when clay was removed to make drainage tile. In depression years, there was no money for skates. We never saw shoe skates; skates were clamped to ordinary work shoes. One Sunday afternoon, rummaging around the upstairs storage area of Grandpa Nussbaum's rendering and laundry shop, I found a pair of old, rusty skates. They had been Uncle Menno's; he hadn't used them for years. I could adjust them to fit my shoes. Yes, he would let me have them; what a find! Learning to skate with skates clamped to one's shoes was a great challenge. Skate blades were dull and had to be sharpened with a hand file. Even when firmly fastened skates, after a few shoves, came loose. Balancing oneself on the ice was one of the lesser complications; if only one had sharp, securely fastened skates. Over the years, we found better skates. After the chores were finished, supper over, dishes done, with kerosene lanterns, we traipsed over to the Hilty pond to be joined by next door neighbor kids. In spite of all the initial handicaps, skating became an important winter sport.

.An innovation in the depression years was the electric fence, proclaimed as a boon to farmers in simplifying fencing chores and dramatically reducing initial costs. From a central source, low voltage, low wattage, single uninsulated electrified wire was mounted on insulated posts around a pasture area. Animals avoid electric shock; one or two shocks for a well-grounded cow with a damp nose touching the wire would teach her a memorable lesson. We bought one of the contraptions and fenced a pasture area, and cattle responded as expected. Electrical wattage was adjustable and weeds had to be kept mowed to avoid grounding. Quickly, we boys found it appealing to shock each other and try our endurance at shockability. Elmer was very durable, took full hold when well grounded, even to the extent that the rhythmic shock brought muscular spasms. Milo and I tolerated less intensified power, by taking off our shoes or standing on damp ground. Elmer won, hands down! While electrified fences became widely used, initial claims had been overstated, not otherwise unknown in the world of advertising.

As the oldest of seven, I often felt that I needed to prevent the younger brothers from carrying out boyish pranks. But on occasion, I got into mischief. In winter cattle were fed corn fodder; they ate the leaves, tassels, and husks. The bare cornstalks were piled some forty feet from the barn and burned. European corn borers winterized in the stalks and propagated a new generation in next season. One Sunday evening during chore time at dusk, without thinking how the fire appeared, I set fire to a pile of cornstalks. It was just dark enough that the fire reflected on the end of the barn. While there was no wind or serious visible hazard, some elderly church members were driving about a half a mile away going to supper with friends. They saw the side of the barn lightened by fire and drove over asking for kettles to help put the fire out. The stalks burned quickly and there was no harm. But at the next catechism class, the Bishop chastised me as a bad example for my younger brothers in my ill-considered action. All I could think was, "Thank God, the barn didn't burn."

Why do the names of Alvin, Reuben, and Carl show up so rarely in mischief? Alvin worked and lived at Grandpa Mazelin's home all four years while in high school, peak years for mischief making. Reuben and Carl were yet too young; their mischief making will have to be documented by one of them. By that time I was off to college. Whether they were purer than their elder brothers I can only conjecture.

Imagine the hazards of the law, the perils to neighbors, the danger to lives if parents were to rear seven boys on a farm or an urban setting in this litigious, gun-toting, murderous era. Perhaps those were the good old days.

Chapter 12:

A Valiant Life Undaunted by Calamitous Handicap

1898-1965

David D. Mazelin: A Source of Inspiration

In many ways my Uncle Dave, David D. Mazelin (he always signed his name D. D. Mazelin), my mother's brother, had sterling qualities of person and character which deserve admiration and emulation. He meant so much to me for his determination, courage, persistence, keen-mindedness, humility, diversity of talents and continuing adaptation. A most unusual man of dauntless courage with an indomitable spirit he displayed phenomenal capacity for survival and a remarkable resiliency of character to surmount the most formidable adversities with inner strengths and a peerless ability for adaptation. Although at the time, I was only dimly aware of his profound impact on my life. In retrospect he, simply by being himself at all times, influenced me more than any other person. My inability to persuade him to write for posterity reflections of his kaleidoscopic mind, his agonies of body and spirit in the midst of overwhelming adversities and his humility amid conspicuous achievement shall always remain one of my deepest regrets. The intellectual life, in terms of scholarly enterprises and academic attainments, was not a part of his legacy or that of any member of his family.

Uncle Dave, even more than my Mother, was quietly supportive of my going to college although I do not recall that he ever explicitly said so. Somehow we were on similar wavelengths, especially when my plans to attend college became very specific and even more so once I was an active student. He was the only relative with whom I could meaningfully talk "college language" or discuss my college experiences. We could connect, for he too had been a teacher in the classroom. He greatly enjoyed teaching and suffered terrible emotional pain when he had to leave it.

He was born on March 10, 1898, the second son and third child of Daniel and Katherine Mazelin. Apparently normal at birth, by age six he had difficulty with stair-steps and climbing ladders or trees. In his pre-adolescent years his muscular dexterity seemed different from that of other children; he was not as agile or as strong as most children of his age. This was most evident when he played athletic games. He was often embarrassed as other children made fun of his awkwardness. The family physician could not make a diagnosis and did not know any medication or treatment that he could recommend. In the rural area where his family lived there were no orthopedic specialists available. Moreover, it was not customary to seek consultation from medical specialists beyond the family physician who had not attended medical school but had served as an intern with an older physician who in turn had learned in the same way from his predecessors.

As he grew into adolescence, the muscles in his back were not of normal strength. By late adolescence his walk became a distinctive labored gait, with toes pointed somewhat outward and back slightly arched to compensate for muscular weakness. He could not walk fast, his balance was delicate, he could not run, and when standing up from a sitting position he would increasingly need to use his arms braced on a desk or table to become upright. His muscles were rather flabby, and he faced many limitations in physical movements. At age 20, his condition was finally diagnosed as muscular dystrophy; several years later he was finally told that there was no known cure for his affliction.

No one in the community had heard of muscular dystrophy. In contrast to his physical deficiencies, his mind was sharp and acute, probably well above the norm. I am not aware that he ever took an intelligence test. In adolescence he was not able to help with the farm work or with the daily chores of milking, feeding, or cleaning stables. He was very limited in his use of garden tools. He faced the puzzling decision about choosing a career. The church restricted his formal education to the eighth grade; rural career options always included hard physical labor. Furthermore, his condition seemed to be progressive. What he could do at a given age in adolescence might no longer be possible two or three years hence. How could he be useful in the family? Who would support him financially? Who would take care of him if he became totally dependent on someone else? These and related questions are answered in the succeeding contents of this chapter.

As automobiles became available, Uncle Dave enjoyed the empowerment of driving but by age nineteen he was no longer able to start the hand-cranked Model T Ford. His brother, John, bought a Star, one of the few low-priced models with a self-starter. Because there was no driver's license requirement or legal driving restriction, Dave could drive again.

A new brick building for the A. C. Parochial School had been constructed next to the road on the corner of the Mazelin family farm. The growing enrollment had required two teachers, and Dave was selected to teach the first four grades for a token salary. Indiana teacher certification laws were leniently regarded. Although he was not legally qualified to teach, he confidently taught the first four grades. For nine years, beginning at about age eighteen, he greatly enjoyed teaching. As his lower back muscles continued to weaken he could no longer bend over to help pupils with their deskwork. Going up and down the inside English half-basement stairs, even with a sturdy railing, became a great strain. He could not use two sets of outdoor steps to the first floor that had no railing. With great reluctance he accepted the decision of the principal and the Bishop that he must end this satisfying career. What career could he next consider?

Those who are normally agile give little thought to the muscle requirements needed to change bodily positions, walking, running, sitting down, or rising from a sitting to a standing position. Again, he had to evaluate his very limited options. What kind of work could he do by himself without requiring help whenever he needed to change positions? All stairs, even those with sturdy railings, were extremely difficult for him. One of his brothers carried him upstairs to his bedroom. He had to take inventory of his assets, his interests within the context of his physical limitations, recognizing that what he could do then might not be possible two or three years later. He could still walk on level, indoor, non-slippery surfaces. Smooth concrete surfaces with no steps were negotiable, but walking on grass more than a few steps was difficult and increased the danger of falling. When he fell, he had no muscular control or restraint whatever. Thus he was always at risk of falling hard with danger of severe fractures. His bones lacked the usual muscle cushion. At the time their home had no indoor plumbing except a hand pump beside the kitchen sink that provided soft cistern water. They installed a toilet stool and lavatory in a downstairs closet. Several years later his brother built an all purpose first floor room that contained his bed. In his whole adult life he suffered the embarrassment of needing help for his daily toilet.

When Dave discovered that, sitting or standing, he could use a small portable typewriter. This opened new career opportunities. Despite the muscular weaknesses and limitations, resting his fingers and hands against a solid surface made them exceptionally steady and have delicate control of his finger movements. His handwriting was a model of expert calligraphy. He ordered books and catalogs and learned varieties of lettering styles and sizes. After purchasing a text on double-entry bookkeeping he mastered the basics. He learned to read music and played a simple foot-pedal organ; using a musical instrument was on the leading edge of what the church permitted. With a clear tenor voice he enjoyed singing. The church had forbidden photographs, but as soon as the Bishop permitted cameras Uncle Dave purchased a good model and mastered its use.

All those life developments must have come at an enormous psychological cost. One wonders how he could help from becoming bitter and resentful as he faced his increasing limitations. Could any outlets for his developing talents help him make a living? He was very anxious to know how rapidly his condition would decline, however he could not get a medical prognosis.

Even with his handicap, at any given time Uncle Dave never was a single career man. While teaching school he also was a barber to his brothers, nephews, and occasionally, nieces and neighbors. He used a hand clipper in combination with barber shears before they had electrical power. Until I was ten years old, when our hair was shabbily long, some evening Dad would call Uncle Dave and ask: "Is it convenient for us to come over for hair cuts?" Rarely did he say "No." We boys, depending on our size, sat on various household chairs and props in the large dining room, temporarily converted into a barbershop. In depression days Dad paid him a quarter for each haircut. When Dad didn't have quarters Uncle Dave still provided his service without obvious resentment. In later years with an electric clipper, braced his right elbow clutched in his left hand. The procedure required a wrist movement rather than an elbow movement. As his muscular control declined, barbering became impossible.

Uncle Dave not only was secretary and treasurer of the combined spray rings, but also became the local authority on chemicals to be used, their mixtures and spraying cycles. Concurrently, (described more fully in Chapter 7) he served the two threshing rings operated by church member farmers for many years.

In 1942, at age 44, Uncle Dave injured his hip in a fall after which he was never able to walk. For the remaining twenty three years of his life, he spent most of his working days sitting in bed. His only mobility was to be carried, bent at the hips, slung over a man's shoulder or sitting in a hand-operated wheel chair. Later the Muscular Dystrophy Association of America gave him an electric wheel chair that he used with great delight and enjoyed a new measure of independence. During his last years, he was too weak to manipulate the controls of the electric wheel chair. Even when he was literally confined to his bed, Dave was always working.

All day long he sat erectly in bed with his legs flatly stretched in front of him, at a right angle to his upper body. A small tray served as his desktop where he did all his work. He continued in this manner of accommodation until near the end of his life. Although with his weakened muscular condition, sitting in bed this way did not cause him to feel the strain that other people would suffer. Writing and receiving letters were always very important to Uncle Dave. At various times in his life he corresponded with scores of people around the world. Because he was a dependable correspondent, he also exchanged letters with relatives and friends in Switzerland and at times with other handicapped persons. During World War II when he was bedridden, he wrote often to persons in military service, especially his nephews, other relatives and former pupils. In earlier years he used the typewriter but gradually, due to his limited arm movements, he wrote only in longhand.

Uncle Dave's first cousin, Noah Steury, head of a novelty manufacturing company in Berne, Indiana, made frequent trips to Switzerland to buy music box movements. Noah often brought him Swiss photo calendars, some small and others as large as twelve by fourteen inches. With Uncle Dave's love of elegant photography, he greatly admired the artistic quality of these calendars. This was the only visual art form they displayed in their home. The church prohibited displaying artistic paintings and sculptures. With his aesthetic sensitivity and talent, though uncultivated by formal education, he found fulfillment in producing high quality photography that offered yet another career for many years.

As soon as the Bishop permitted cameras Uncle Dave purchased a good model that produced black and white pictures. Soon he upgraded his camera to one of the better accordion types with tripod. He enjoyed taking family and group photographs; over time family photography became a source of income. He studied film developing and printing, using the enclosed common family wash room where he practiced the process. He enjoyed considerable success as a modest entrepreneur. Not only was he limited by physical handicaps; he had to improvise within the limited workspace that was also used by most of the other members of the family of nine or more. Over the years these experiences mysteriously generated in him adaptability, a mellowness of personality, and a remarkable level of tolerance. With his active and inquiring mind Dave always was thinking of new ventures within the range of his abilities.

Contemplating a major venture in 1937, he imagined an undertaking so vast that most persons without physical limitations would find forbidding. The circumstances that spawned the contemplation required a bit of historical information. The Mazelin immigration from Menilot, France took place in 1840. Shouldn't there be a celebration or recognition of this event on the 100th anniversary in 1940? Among families the Mazelin clan was not particularly large; most of the descendants lived within a hundred-mile radius. Shouldn't there be a family history for posterity? As far as he could determine no such record was extant. He had read few family histories. But he knew no authors with whom to confer as to the scope of the work and time or cost such a project entailed. How does one begin?

Propitiously, Uncle Dave's earlier experience with publishing gave him some encouragement. Since its founding in 1894, the Amish Christian Church had used the historic German hymnal *Ausbund*, a copy of the hymnal found in our home. It had no musical score. In 1931 the Bishop, prompted by close members of his family who occupied designated positions in the church, decided that a new hymnal was to be produced by the Economy Printing Company of Berne, Indiana. The family members included J.D.R. Schwartz, the Bishop's youngest son who served as song leader; his oldest son, Noah, who had been elected deacon; and Joseph P. Habegger, the Bishop's nephew who was an elected minister. Uncle Dave was asked to help with typesetting of the musical scores and text in the German language. None of the authors had any experience with a publishing project of this magnitude, and for Uncle Dave typesetting was a completely new undertaking. He learned to set type with a pair of hand tweezers. For the hundreds of hours that he devoted to this task, I don't believe that he received any compensation. It was as if he were paying a debt which he owed the congregation. The prevailing attitude among many community leaders was, "How fortunate this handicapped person is that we found useful work that he could do." I do not know whether the authors who devoted endless hours to selecting and assembling hymns and tunes, a massive undertaking, were compensated. Uncle Dave's attitude was one of painful longsuffering, while he learned and performed the task faultlessly. In retrospect, it was a splendid experience of preparing him, ten years later, to become author and publisher of *The Mazelins in America, 100 Years, 1840 to 1940.*

Ten years earlier the church Bishop would have frowned on such a venture as too much self-exaltation. By this time, however, the Bishop had been excommunicated; his dominance no longer prevailed. Having graduated from high school I was planning to be the first member of the family to attend college in 1938. Trusting my opinion, Uncle Dave and I had several conferences to discuss his plans to publish a family record.

Uncle Dave had accumulated some cash from his various enterprises, mostly from his photo finishing. He decided to wax bold once more and begin the authorship and publication venture, though privately acknowledging that he might not succeed. His household family reluctantly promised full support without understanding what such a project would entail. He began to outline the basic family tree, to prepare questionnaires to gather data about the different generations, to plan how to organize the data and determine the cost of postage (at that time first class cost three cents). He talked with a printing establishment in nearby Berne about the cost of typesetting, printing and publishing. He had no subsidy and no assurance of financial assistance if the costs exceeded his resources. Obviously, the publisher offered no advances! Gathering, organizing and verifying data required many months; to save money he did the typesetting with a pair of metal tweezers while sitting in bed. What an incredible achievement!

Hardcover in a variegated dark maroon and black, *The Mazelins in America, 100 Years, 1840-1940*, Peter Mazelin Branch, (the only known immigrant Mazelin family), was finally published in March 1941, after many months of tedious and exhausting labor. Uncle Dave included a number of black and white photos of historical importance, among them one of his parents and the former Bishop and his wife cradling and binding wheat. There is no photo of the author. The only fact Dave gives about himself in the family record is "David D., March 10, 1898, Berne, Indiana, Photo-finisher and compiler of this book." Dave makes no reference to his handicap or the agonizing conditions under which this extensive collecting of data, organizing, writing, typesetting and publishing project was accomplished. One heart-rending incident that I recall being told: His brother, while taking a lock-up set type that included several pages, dropped and spilled it. It had to be totally reset. An intimate observer said that was the only time he ever saw Uncle Dave explosively angry. From the scanty resources available to him he assembled an introduction of forty pages briefly describing the immigrants' experiences, their travels within this country and deciding where to establish their new home. Beyond the introduction he decided to keep the biographical information brief in a volume of 262 pages. Because church membership in that community was a key index to the person's identity and a majority of Mazelin descendants belonged to this church, he consistently included it in the biographies. Of the 731 Mazelin descendants listed, 595 were living at the time of publication, 136 having died since the first arrivals in 1840.

Uncle Dave's modesty and self-effacement are evident throughout the book. He gives far too much credit to persons in his short preface. It reads as follows: "The author wishes to make acknowledgment and express his deepest gratitude to all those who so willingly and generously contributed of their time, information and help in any form in the gatherings and compiling of this work. Especially does he wish to express his gratitude to Sam Nussbaum of Berne, Indiana (not related) and Leo Nussbaum of Monroe, Indiana, for their great help in assembling and compiling the contents for this publishing." His acknowledgment touched me deeply. There is no mention of his own family.

I know that Uncle Dave regarded the completed project a painful and tedious success. The book sold rapidly, and soon those who sought additional copies were disappointed to learn that there were no more available. Certainly among family members his authoring and publishing was regarded as a highly notable accomplishment, without really understanding the distinctiveness and significance of the completed book. One piece of evidence: when his brother, Ben, later wrote a brief biographical summary of Dave at the request of the tri-weekly

Berne Witness, he did not mention Dave's authoring and publishing this family history. Uncle Dave never disclosed to me whether his income exceeded his expenses. I suspect that if there were any gains from the publication they were slim, even with all his contributed services. As was so characteristic of him, he under-priced his product.

For several years, Uncle Dave wrote articles for publication in local newspapers and farm periodicals, some of which brought him modest compensation. On completion of the book project he needed some rest, but a typical traveling vacation was impossible. On one later occasion, my brother, Alvin, who had been his "valet" during high school days (and nick-named him Barney), an agreement which applied only to the two of them, took Uncle Dave to Chicago for two days by commercial plane. Wherever he went, he was either carried on Alvin's shoulder or transported in a hand-pushed wheel chair. This may have been the only time that he slept in a bed other than his own. (Uncle Dave was never a hospital patient.) Between 1938 and his death in 1965, whenever Uncle Dave left the house, he was picked up from a sitting position and carried over the right shoulder either to the automobile, or after 1957, to his motorized wheel chair given by the National Muscular Dystrophy Association. During my college days and later, I greatly enjoyed taking him in my car for a drive through the countryside. Dave possessed an extraordinary eye for detail. Through his keen observation of nature, the flowers, the fall colors of leaves, the visible birds, changing landscape, the condition of farm crops, the attractiveness of well-manicured farmsteads, he enriched my life by articulating his observations.

Even before Uncle Dave published the family record, I was greatly interested in learning about his feelings and thoughts when as a teenager and later he realized that his muscular condition would probably limit him for life. My conviction that he should write this for us, for other handicapped persons with less self-discipline and fortitude and for posterity, was intensified after he successfully published *The Mazelins in America, 100 Years, 1840-1940*. What was even more remarkable was that he did this without completely giving up several of his other endeavors, including some photography, seasonal record keeping for organizations.

Although he greatly enjoyed people, visiting in person or at a distance on the telephone or by correspondence, he was a very private person. For hundreds of friends he was an attentive listener. He always patiently heard my pleadings that he should write about his coping with life as a severely handicapped person. I stressed that this was another way for him to help other people, with which he did not disagree. In fact, the consistent comment by visitors was that they hoped to bring this bedfast person some cheer. On departure, however, they most frequently remarked that they gleaned far more from him than they brought. But after some reflection he always said that he did not wish to put himself forward as one who had done something unusual or out of the ordinary. He could not bring himself to want to do this kind of writing. Whatever arguments I could muster, none changed his resistance.

While I can in no way propose to express his thoughts and feelings, I believe that his accomplishments should be factually recorded. That has prompted me to include a chapter in my lifetime reflections lifting up his life as worthy of admiration, respect and empathy-- especially for our children, who were old enough to remember him in his latter days. After 1951, because our family lived in Illinois, Iowa and Texas--and a year in India-- we rarely saw him and then only on very brief visits. Perhaps the grandchildren, each in his or her own way, can derive some inspiration from the facts of their great uncle, an extraordinary person.

Dave assembled a large collection of photo albums, most of them from his own photography and a large share from his own development and printing. He aspired to meet some professional portrait photographers; he was most curious about the varied lighting devices that they used. Although he experimented widely with portrait photography, he was never fully satisfied with the results he achieved. So far as I know, he never had the opportunity to visit a professional portrait studio, but he often studied professional photographs of his nephews and nieces trying to gain some new perspectives.

In his last twenty years, less innovative persons would have joined the lines of the unemployed; but not this persistent and tenacious victim of muscular dystrophy. He revived his stamp collecting which he had earlier put aside for want of time. His interest was enhanced because the U.S. Postal Department produced far more new stamp issues. Moreover, both the artistic and the historical qualities of the new issues appealed to him.

Always eager for new experiences his reputation as a versatile, talented and innovative person spread widely in the community. Because all the religious studies and worship of the Old Order Amish were in German, mastery of the language was very important to the Amish people. An Amish neighbor, Ernie Schwartz, who was eager for his sons to become more fluent in the German language asked Uncle Dave to tutor them. For many months while sitting in his bed he tutored them weekly. Learning rapidly, both the boys and their father found him a very effective and engaging teacher. The parents of Palmer Steury, a mentally handicapped adolescent, (a first cousin once removed) asked Uncle Dave to apply his talents to help Palmer accept his limitations. Uncle Dave accepted the challenge. This was a new experience---a physically handicapped person teaching self-acceptance and adaptation to a mentally limited person with whom he could meaningfully empathize. Palmer became a dependable factory custodian who was so employed until retirement age. He and his parents were generous in praise of his teacher's help.

Uncle Dave's impeccable handwriting was always something of an exemplary calligraphic model. Paradoxically, his declining muscle strength did not lessen the steadiness and control of his hands and fingers. Sometimes he used a back brace for support. His bed was his desk, his workshop, his dining table, his bath room where he was helped with toilet needs, where he read and wrote. He was not a wide reader of books.

Now he returned to an earlier interest in calligraphy. He developed a variety of lettering styles, each with a highly professional appearance. His work was of such quality and his prices so modest that his reputation spread by satisfied customers. Once more, this entrepreneur was in business. He had always tended to under price his services, so perhaps for the first time he could rely on his talents to produce a moderate income. He lettered posters, small signs and diplomas, a wide variety of certificates. Orders came from high schools, colleges and universities, churches, clubs, and studios. I remember that he filled one order from a university for 169 honor roll certificates.

Uncle Dave kept daily diaries for most of his adult life. The typical contents included the mundane details of everyday life: the minimum and maximum temperature; unusual weather conditions which he frequently compared with weather conditions in other years on the same date; and rare notations when he was ill or not feeling well. His diaries also reported on any notable condition in the family or in the community such as a major illness or an accident, visitors from a distant place and how he used his time for a major part of the day. Here are a few examples from 1965, several months before his death on July 22:

January 5
"30 degrees, calm, fair and clear. I worked on citations again for Chuck Gage of St. Louis. 58 high for the day. Our new county agricultural agent came in here tonite for the first time."

January 13
"High winds all nite, blowing snow into huge piles, still snowing. 12 degrees. Snow storm continued all night and is still going strong this morning. Roads are a mess. All schools are closed far and wide. 2000 motorists stranded southwest of here and hundreds of them everywhere from Mississippi River to New York. This storm is a monster. Bens went to see Roy at the hospital again this p.m. He is feeling fairly well. A bit lonesome as few people could go anywhere. No mail today. "

January 25

"I mailed 31 citations to Chuck at St. Louis.
Have lots of work on hand again.
Harry's children here p.m."

January 29
"Today they launched from Cape Kennedy in
Florida the largest or rather the heaviest rocket
ever put into orbit. It was about 19 tons. It
will appear as bright as Venus at night. My,
what all things useful the billions are wasted in
space. One wonders just how long the
taxpayers of the nation can provide enough for
everything--$100 billion a year."

February 3
"6 degrees below zero. Another cold and rather
windy morning. I am doing some of Leona's
cards again. [His youngest sister, who also had
muscular dystrophy, who paints water color
greeting and seasonal cards] Funeral of James
Yoder this p.m."

This is Uncle Dave's last entry in his diary. Was he
aware that he would not write in his diary again? We were living
in Texas at that time, and I have no available information on that
question.. However, what is evident even in the few samples,
from his diaries, although he sensitively reported any ailments of
family members, he rarely commented on his own. His hundreds
of friends and acquaintances held him in high esteem as is
suggested by the registration of three hundred fifty-five persons
at the funeral home where his body lay in state for two days.

I have read most of the diaries that were given to me by
his sister, Martha, who was the last survivor among his siblings.
Because my brother, Alvin, had lived in their home for four years
and helped daily in caring for him, I felt it only fair that I give the
diary collection to him. As was so typical of Dave, he never
revealed his deepest feelings, and he told no stories about
himself. All of his records of himself were very impersonal. He

often used diaries to compare seasons with those of previous years, including the dates when fruit blossoms were first visible; dates of completing corn planting, the first frost; and the end of the corn harvest. He recorded observable events and conditions without revealing much about himself. As I mentioned earlier, he was consistent with his steadfast refusal to write about himself, or so far as I know to express his most intimate thoughts or feelings to anyone. In reflecting on Uncle Dave's long years of adaptation I must wonder how he managed such controlled emotional conditioning and restraint.

There must have been periods of *fear* as he faced the unknown future, *dread* as he increasingly had to rely on others, *anger* at the accumulating frustrations, *despair* as he was forced repeatedly to leave one career that he enjoyed in search of another, *hopelessness* in the face of new limitations accompanied by unanticipated obstacles, *hurt* as he dealt with bluntness or cruel comments, *shame* and *aversion* as he increasingly had to call caretaker brothers, sisters and sisters-in-law, as well as caretaker nephews, to meet his every bodily need. Someone else's arms and legs had to bring him whatever he could not reach from his bed. The miracle of his life is that amid all complexities of existence he was dauntlessly persistent and rarely morose. As he aged, he grew so much in attitudes of good will, graciousness and mellowness of personality and in a spirit of forgiveness and generosity.

From some of his occasional comments, I inferred that prayer was an integral essence of his life, yet I never heard him pray. Prayer is not mentioned in his diaries. He was always grateful for what he had and exhibited an attitude of thankfulness for those who helped him. All these qualities pervaded his life. However, we shall never know the real sources and magnitude of his formidable courage. We can learn much from his dauntless determination and tenacity, and, I give thanks for what his life has meant to so many persons.

For me Uncle Dave with the qualities of character, attitudes and actions served as a model. Jan and I were attending an educational conference in a remote location in Colorado when we were notified of his death. Unable to attend the funeral, I took a long, solitary walk that night and wept bitterly as I celebrated the memories of the person I so greatly admired.

Chapter 13: Reflections on My Way to College

1938

When Elmer graduated from high school in May 1938 he agreed to become the interim farmer. Now, I wondered, am I really on my way to college? Two years earlier on the basis of a state examination I had won a tuition scholarship to my choice of four state institutions of higher education: Indiana University, Purdue University, Ball State Teachers College or Indiana State Teachers College. Annually, two such scholarships were allotted to each county in Indiana. The Board of Control granted me a scholarship that I had earned in 1936. On 4-H Club trips, I had visited Purdue in West Lafayette. I liked that campus with its large elm trees and attractively landscaped buildings. As the state's land-grant institution its principal programs were agriculture, engineering and home economics. I wanted a history major, which Purdue did not offer. Two of my favorite high school teachers, Virgil Wagner and Jacob Smuts, were Ball State graduates and Ball State was closest to my home. Because a major means of travel for holidays, vacations and home visits would be hitchhiking, proximity between college and home was important.

During my sophomore year in high school Virgil Wagner, then the principal of the school and also my history teacher, for $1.50 sponsored a school bus trip to the Ball State campus. Although I do not remember that he ever encouraged us to go to college, I later wondered if he might have used this trip to prompt us to think about college. That is what I ended up doing. We were told that Ball State had some eight buildings and one thousand students, an impressively large number in contrast to Monroe High School with seventy students. In my freshman and sophomore years of high school we had four teachers, including the principal; in my last two years there were five teachers. The high school was on the second floor. The first through the eight grades were on the first. The basement was shared; the largest room with its smooth concrete floor in winter weather was occasionally used for very limited physical education exercise.

The school lacked a gymnasium and had no showers or dressing rooms in the building. The Ball State campus with its several large attractive brick buildings, large classrooms, and a huge gymnasium with a swimming pool stood in striking contrast to our tiny high school.

The summer of 1938, with all the usual late summer farm tasks, seemed to drag more slowly than other summers. I do not recall that my parents ever gave their approval for me to go to college; they had given up saying, "No." Moreover, it seems, they clearly understood that I was determined to go. Now that Elmer was doing the farming and I had turned twenty, I strongly felt that it was time for me to move in a career direction which was neither farming nor carpentry. On an occasional day, I joined my Dad in carpenter work; my pay was forty cents an hour. At the end of the summer of that year I gave Dad all but $30 of my earnings for general family use.

Now that I cast on my own, I was so challenged, frightened, threatened that I knew I did not dare fail. The loneliness of the risk did not permit failure for I could never face myself or those whom I defied by casting my lot in my own direction. In perspective, this resulted in too little joy, too few times for the occasionally frivolous, too few hobbies, and explorations not directly contributing toward my vocational goal. Also, too much caution in spending money lest I might have to float a loan. I let nothing divert me from my central goal of succeeding in college to become a teacher even for penurious pay.

I staked my future, God willing, on thirty dollars cash, a state tuition scholarship that was annually renewable with a grade point average of at least 3.25 (index of 4.0), a promised job in the college book store at thirty cents an hour and my assertion of financial independence. Ruth Kitchin, the female book store manager, selected me as an employee on the basis of my employment application, my photo and my high school record. From birth, my human relations had been predominantly male. In grade school my three teachers were all men; in high school I had two women teachers in Latin, biology and economics. But a woman boss in the work environment I never had. I did not feel any prejudice, but it would certainly be a new experience for me. I often wondered why did she choose me? I also wondered if I could make that transition from farming to clerking in a bookstore. That was another challenge.

Gerhart Schwartz, my first cousin and also the oldest of seven, was a year older than I was. He also planned teaching as a career, but had quit high school at age sixteen at the end of his sophomore year according to legal attendance requirements. His father, a farmer, earned extra income from a milk route picking up ten-gallon milk cans from farmers and delivering them to the local milk condensery. This became Gerhart's job, along with helping on the farm. Any doubts about his becoming a teacher rapidly disappeared while loading those hundred-pound cans. To compound his obstacles, his mother, Elizabeth, my father's sister, had died while he was in high school. By completing correspondence courses, he was able to return to high school in the fall of 1937 and graduate with the Monroe high school class of 1938.

Gerhart and I decided to be roommates in college, because our frugality was a shared necessity. There was no men's dormitory at Ball State. Elliott Hall, a traditional, Indiana limestone, modified gothic residence was under construction but not ready for the fall opening. Women lived in Lucina Hall. Many students lived in rooms in private homes. On a trip to Muncie, we looked at various rooming houses. We rented a second-floor room at 424 North McKinley in the home of Lucile Duncan, a World War I widow, who had a high school age son and daughter. Her husband had died following World War I of complications from mustard gas contamination on the battlefield in France. The room, diagonally across the street from the campus, was very conveniently located. For two dollars per week bedding was provided, and we shared an adjacent half-bath without shower or tub with three other residents. Each week Mrs. Duncan cleaned the room and changed the bedding. The family bath with tub on the first floor was also available to the roomers. Though inconvenient, for me this was luxury having grown up in a home without indoor plumbing. We shared that room for three years; in our senior year we decided that we wanted one year of residence hall living in Elliott Hall. The cost rose to two dollar forty cents per week.

Gerhart, grandson of the former Bishop, and his family had changed membership from the Amish Christian Church to the First Mennonite Church in Berne. That had engendered some alienation between our parents, but Gerhart and I did not let that affect our good relationship. The Amish Christian Church was in the process of dissolution; my family had not joined another congregation, although we were exploring alternatives. Having declared our financial independence from our families, Gerhart and I had to rely on our own resources.

Recognizing what the burden of debt had done to my parents over the years, I developed a strong aversion to borrowing money and paying interest. I was determined to graduate from college debt free. Was this realistic? In retrospect, I recognize that I worked too many hours each week; this prevented me from much additional reading, more disciplined writing and bull sessions with my friends and colleagues. Was it detrimental to gaining the best education? Much later, I learned that I was seriously deficient. Friends cautioned me that teachers' salaries were very low especially in rural areas where one thousand dollars per school year was generous. Did I want to live such a penurious existence all my life? How could I support a family on that income? I did know that when I married, I would not be able to afford seven children--then, a rather typical family.

Trusting God for guidance, I knew that many things could go wrong, many missteps could lead to unplanned debt. What could I do to show myself to be totally responsible for myself? After talking with several life insurance agents, I bought an ordinary life policy for $1,000 from O. F. Gilliom, with Lincoln National Life Insurance Co. By reputation he was the most successful life insurance agent in the community. The annual premium was $17.13. In case of my death, this hopefully would pay for my funeral expenses and any debts. Considering my assets, the annual premium was a significant but, I believed, essential expenditure. My parents never had any insurance--life, medical, liability or property. From today's perspective that is incredible!

Having grown up in the Amish Christian Church, I already had deep inferiority feelings and no other social, religious or political connections. I was indelibly impressed and puzzled by the Bishop's claim that this was the only true church and that to associate very much with anyone outside that congregation would leave me spiritually corrupt. Even the Mennonites regarded our church as odd. We had been emotionally and spiritually secure in the insulated A. C. Parochial grade school, but in the public high school we were then exposed to the larger society. Also, the Nussbaum families ranked low on the social scale. As the oldest in the family I was often pressed to carry responsibilities beyond my physical ability, such as being sent at age twelve by Dad to do a man's work on a threshing crew. The men often reminded me that I was a kid trying to do a man's job. I had no escape.

Unschooled in the social graces, I felt this also inhibited my personality development. Would this be a handicap in college? Yet, college would also offer me a fresh start; no one at college would know my parochial background. This could be a new beginning. At no previous time in my life was I ever as seriously engaged in pondering burning questions about my future. At no previous time was I as perplexed in trying to arrive at the best decisions.

This was time for serious reflection, a time to ask whether going to college was the correct decision. I pondered the poem by Robert Frost, "The Road Not Taken"

"Two roads diverged in a yellow wood,...
I took the one less traveled by,
And that has made all the difference."

Had I adequately considered some of the many other options? Who would bail me out if I failed? After the delay in high school graduation from 1935 to 1936 and two more years of farming, was I now ready to undertake the collegiate venture? Why were all my age mates from the church content with one or two years of high school? Why were Gerhart and I the only

152

freaks who insisted on a college education? Would I be psychologically maimed, perhaps for life, by the continuing deep financial depression? Would we perpetually live in a financial depression?

I had been admitted to Ball State. I was dubious, even frightened, as I anticipated the new level of competition I would face from graduates of prestigious high schools. I wondered how would I deal with my deficiencies contrasted with those from homes with many books, those who were regular borrowers of books from libraries with time to read? Or with those who had been exposed to quality cultural arts, who played musical instruments and had a repertoire of musical knowledge? I really believed that my inferiority would be conspicuous to those whose parents were college graduates, where ideas and enriching experiences were discussed and the intellectual life was as integral to the home life as meals and sleep. How could I compensate for my deficiencies in family travel? We didn't even have a globe or a map in our home. Having to work for subsistence from the day I arrived at Ball State, could I ever make up for the layers of deficiencies? Would my accent seem foreign since I had spoken only Swiss-German (Schwiezer-Dütch) in my family and High German in church until age 15? These were sobering, anxiety-producing thoughts.

Lurking in the background was a gnawing concern about the war clouds that were evolving in Europe. Would our country become involved in another war? Would Hitler continue to snatch one country after another? How would the momentous turmoil in Europe affect my college? Could that once more interrupt my college plans? Having grown up in a peace church, which prohibited all military participation, how could I face a proposed universal military draft? This prospect would certainly pose ominous consequences for me.

I scarcely recognized what in later years became crystal clear. College to me then was not an intellectual venture; it was a requirement for certification to teach. Reflecting now on my understanding at that time, I did not comprehend that a college education should be a mind-opening, intellectually challenging, life-transforming set of experiences. College was only the gateway to a career that had certain requirements for entry. That very narrow and restricted understanding not only greatly affected my whole attitude about a college education but also my selection of courses during my first year. I did not have good advice and I did not even know what or whom to ask.

As I pondered my fears, hesitations, and apprehensions, I asked myself, "Why would I want to engage in a career that was so alien to my family background?" I believed that my mother always had wanted to be a teacher, though she rarely talked about it. Perhaps I was fulfilling her dream a generation later. It seemed that I had a vocational calling, a divine summons that had its own schedule of delays, pauses and forward motion. If this were a divine summons, despite all my limitations, what strengths would I bring to this venture?

I had endured many frustrating situations: crops destroyed by drought and floods, insufficient horse power for soil preparation and planting, obsolete equipment for soil preparation, inadequate commercial fertilizer for maximum results, and low quality of seed grain. I learned to temporize and to find alternative solutions, usually having to compromise and settle for less than the best. Painful frugality had become constitutional, and chronic lack of money grossly distorted what farm life could be. Yet, surviving these multifaceted limitations and challenges imprinted some character-building lessons from which I benefited in the years to follow. Perseverance and prevailing amid sequential adversities conditioned me to take advantage of new opportunities. How I looked forward to a more favorable juncture of circumstances.

I was thoroughly disciplined by hard work, committed to fulfillment of promises made, honest in all circumstances, persistent in adversity, and efficient in the use of time, even when engaged in multiple tasks. Critically viewing a frustrating situation and finding possible alternative solutions, I had often practiced. Based on my high school record, I was convinced that I had a good mind. My concern was to apply all my resources to the fullest. I was questioning whether I could make the shift from mostly physical labor on the farm to academic and intellectual pursuits.

The Ball State Bookstore job assured me of regular earnings for food, books and other minimum essentials. Further, it placed me in one center of campus activity where I would meet and could come to know faculty, students and administrators. I had a ready ability to remember names; I quickly learned that we all enjoy knowing someone interested enough to call us by name. I was proud of my reputation for trustworthiness and dependability. My moral training, though at times extremely rigid, served me well in whatever predicaments I found myself. That training was grounded in a strong religious faith, though I was striving to be more flexible and open than the teachings of my church. For example, I no longer felt it necessary to believe that those not of our strict faith were all condemned to perdition.

I was fortunate in having a sensitive and caring housemother in Mrs. Duncan and a compatible roommate whom I had known all my life. He and I shared many of the same anxieties. One of our differences was that Gerhart often had great difficulty in making decisions, whereas I believed in gathering the best information available, and then I acted on it. He was habitually late whereas punctuality with me was almost constitutional. As our children will readily testify, they were often reminded that we shall depart at nine and a half minutes past ten o'clock. And we did!

Blessed with good health I found regularity of meals and sleep essential to my wellbeing. On reflection, I began to realize that perhaps my greatest asset was having concerned parents and brothers, and knowing that in any emergency I could readily return home. Moreover, in the event of failure, I still would be welcomed by my family. My brothers were open-minded about my going to college, even though at the time they were not enthusiastic. But my parents exhibited different attitudes. My mother anxiously watched me depart for college and my father was somewhat bewildered in his opposition. However, we never became estranged and never had a break in our relationship. The door to college was finally opened, and it was time to enter courageously.

Chapter 14: The Dream Becomes Reality

In 1938, packing for college was simple. It included one mid-size piece of luggage, several card-board boxes that contained folded clothing, a simple toilet item kit with tooth brush, a small container of salt in place of expensive tooth paste, a razor with extra double edge blades, and shaving lotion from the five and ten cent store. My wardrobe consisted of one good dress suit, some extra pants, sports coat, several ties, three or four dress shirts, two pairs of shoes, sox, underwear, cotton handkerchiefs, one casual jacket, one topcoat, no hats. Bare heads in all seasons were fashionable and more economical, but not very warm. Another very important item--several pint and quart jars of canned fruit which served as our dessert between the evening meal and bedtime. With no refrigerator we stored canned fruit on the floor in the closet. We ate the open fruit jar dessert over a limited number of days to keep it from spoiling.

Elmer and Milo drove Gerhart and me to Muncie—fifty miles from Berne--in the family car. We were not crowded including minimally adequate clothing. Neither of us had a pre-college personal library, typewriter, lamps, room decorations, radio, stereo, record player, TV, computer, or other equipment. The conversation was bland, not revealing our inner anxiety.

Our room was scantily furnished: two single beds, thin mattresses, two study tables each with flexible elbow lamp, two straight chairs, one four-drawer dresser without a mirror, one ceiling lamp, and a well-worn carpet in the center of the room. The wallpaper was drab and well aged. There was no artwork on the walls. Because we had none at home this absence did not disturb us. The only mirror was in the bathroom. We had no telephone. We shared a small corner closet with a clothing rod, wall hooks and one hat shelf. Mrs. Duncan, soon affectionately addressed as "Mom Duncan," cleaned our room once a week. Each week I sent laundry home via parcel post in a special cardboard container covered with light canvas, conveniently posted in the bookstore postal substation. In a few days Mother returned my laundry, washed, neatly folded--sometimes with a letter, and home baked cookies that Gerhart and I shared.

Although she sent no cash, she dependably and faithfully provided laundry services and cookies. On reflection, I realize that I did not adequately thank her.

Gerhart less often sent his laundry home. His mother deceased, his younger sister, Frances, was the housekeeper for the family. I was often pained to see how few communications Gerhart received from his motherless family. He was also disturbed about his widowed father's conduct. With vivid memories of their mother, Gerhart and his siblings had strong objections to the woman his father was courting. However, his father persisted and later married her, much to the distress of the children.

Three other college boys lived in what we labeled the "House of Duncan:" They were Daryl Murphy from nearby Ohio, an average but serious student; he shared a room with rotund, happy go lucky Kenneth Wilson from a nearby community. Ben Early, a more polished and handsome youth, lived in a single room.

Mom Duncan served no meals; deciding where and what to eat was a challenging new experience for me. At home I had always taken for granted Mother's planning and preparing three meals each day; there was always enough food on the table to eat one's fill. Although some dishes were not always what I would have preferred, the food was nourishing, tasty and plentiful. At home, I gave no thought to the cost or having to pay for the meal. As a family we always gave thanks to God for the blessings that ours. Suddenly, I had to decide not only where and what to eat; but always what could I afford? My reserves were minimal; now I had to plan and budget, something of a shocking realization. At home, each meal was served in the same place--the family dining room table. Now there were several locations for my meals, as well as different times, places and menus. I wondered about my ability to establish a routine that would economize on time and money? Nearby were two campus hangouts the Tally-ho and the Pine Shelf. One block in the other direction was a rooming house owned and operated by a Mr. Peterson that served breakfast, lunch, and dinner family style. Pete served the noon meal to all comers--mashed potatoes, pork or beef, two or three vegetables and dessert for thirty cents. Many of his customers were boys reared on the farm who thrived on heavy noon meals.

I soon discovered that not being engaged in physical labor I could economize by skipping breakfast. I gorged myself with Pete's family style noon meal followed by a moderate a la carte dinner in the Lucina Hall college cafeteria. Wieners and pork chops were two of the lowest cost meats. Chicken was also low cost, but still suffering from my deep aversion to it, no matter how it was prepared, I would not touch the dish. Cole slaw, rather than some other salad, was a steady menu item. Occasionally I ate jello. I often ate another canned vegetable, typically corn, green beans or peas. There were no frozen foods. Water was my only beverage. Ice cream was an expensive luxury that I could rarely afford. I still have my detailed financial records; the cost of my food ranged from $2.75 to $4.00 per week. Depression food prices still prevailed.

A few words about the founding of the college. Ball State had an unusual history. During the early part of the twentieth century It had been a private two-year normal school to train teachers housed in one large three and a half story building. When the State of Indiana raised teacher training requirements, the five enterprising, wealthy Ball Brothers presented the state with an offer. Their Mason Fruit Jar Manufacturing Company was located on the other side of Muncie. They offered to acquire and give the normal school building and land to the State of Indiana provided the institution is named Ball State Teachers College. The state accepted the gift. That transaction occurred in the year of my birth, 1918. Later a sculpture was erected. It consisted of five Greek pillars symbolizing the Ball Brothers in an arced formation facing University Avenue. It was named "Beneficence;" the students soon nicknamed it "Benny."

Twenty years later, when I entered Ball State, John H. Heller, editor and publisher of the *Decatur Daily Democrat* was President of the five member State Teachers College Board. Frank C. Ball, Vice-President of the Board, was the only surviving member of Ball brothers. The Ball family was also instrumental in establishing the Ball Memorial Hospital built across University Avenue from Ball State Teachers College.

The bookstore was in the Administration Building about 500 feet from the "House of Duncan." Even before registration, I presented myself to Ruth Kitchin, the manager. She impressed me as very energetic. Her penetrating gray eyes suggested an alert, discerning mind that commanded immediate respect. In her early thirties, she was well established in her manager's position; she had completed two years of college and then decided to be a manager rather than a teacher.

The bookstore had been attractively renovated in an arced arrangement with light, varnished wood paneling, attractive glass counters and exhibit cases. Students bought new and used textbooks, supplies, modest jewelry. The store stocked a few non-text books. The postal substation sold postage stamps, money orders, a depository for letters and packages including many weekly laundry containers. Self-service laundries are a convenience unknown at that time.

The bookstore opened at 7:30 a.m. As soon as I had registered I brought my class schedule to fit my hours of work with the other student workers. The rate of pay was thirty cents an hour. The required attire all year was a dress shirt with tie, even on Saturday mornings. In winter season, a dress jacket was also required. Immediately I was assigned to be a clerk; as soon as I learned the postal rules I also handled postal sales. Textbook boxes by the score were being unpacked in preparation for the opening of classes. Twelve hundred students all bought either new or used texts; this store had a virtual monopoly. To become efficient I had to learn shelf locations, book titles,and prices.

.Ball State operated on a twelve-week quarter academic calendar, the academic year beginning in early September and ending in June. Freshmen had several days of required orientation, tests in spelling, penmanship and English to determine each student's course placement. I probably had a perfect score in the spelling test; spelling was always easy for me. I was placed in a second level of English composition and literature course. Embarrassingly, however, I was assigned to a Zaner-Blosser remedial penmanship class. (No one had heard of computers invading the college curriculum or offices.) After five

159

weeks of corrective practice I was dismissed. Each freshman was assigned to a non-credit library science course for six weeks.

One of the traditions strongly emphasized from the first day was no smoking anywhere on campus for students, faculty, administration and staff. The very few addicted professors literally stepped off the curb onto the street so as not to violate the tradition. To my knowledge, the source of the tradition was never documented. I never heard anyone relating smoking to a concern for health. Also by tradition, all freshmen had to wear "green beanies" (a green skullcap with a short visor) for the entire first quarter. Concurrently, freshmen had to step off the sidewalk in deference to upperclassmen that requested it. At age twenty, I found this insulting but I did conform.

Classes began on the hour for fifty minutes, starting at 8:00 am and met four days each week. Punctuality and regularity of attendance were emphatically required. The fall quarter courses included Written and Oral Expression, Primary Sight Singing, Personality and Business Efficiency, Intermediate Typing, World Civilization, Men's Glee Club, Library Science, and Fall Sports and Games. Six quarters of physical education were required. I wanted a history major along with business education, which would provide the so-called practical side of my education. Teacher certification required a sequence of courses in general business, accounting, business law, typing and shorthand. History, sociology, political science and economics constituted the entire social science department. State certification to teach the social sciences included courses in each of these four disciplines that totaled sixty-eight quarter hours of the 192 required for graduation. I decided to take this route while adding a minor in English.

I aspired to develop some competence in music for which I had no background except singing one year in my high school choir plus a few months of private voice lessons during my farming years. I soon learned that I had no talent for sight singing, but I nevertheless doggedly persisted through the course. I had failed to distinguish correctly between enjoying music and performing it. I registered in a studio piano course in the winter quarter 1938-39 with a native Viennese professor of organ and piano. His patience exceeded my persistence; despite a grade of "C" for the winter quarter I registered for a second course in the spring. With my heavy course schedule combined with work, I practiced far too little. I learned to play the piano very modestly, but Professor Owen taught me some music theory that I really cherished, and he generously gave me a "grace mark A." Having failed to earn a place in the College Choir, I joined the Men's Glee Club that offered open membership. I persisted and enjoyed singing in the Glee Club; in my junior year I earned a place in the College Choir and the special Choral Society that with community voices performed *The Messiah* in December.

At 10:00 am on Wednesdays no classes were scheduled; that time was reserved for an optional convocation. A faculty convocation committee, with no student participation, planned these programs. Programs varied from talks by Ball State President, Lemuel A. Pittenger, History Professor Robert LaFollette, Poet Robert Frost, to national newspaper columnists, prominent radio commentators and vocal and instrumental soloists. Other programs focussed on political and cultural events of the day. I was literally starved for this augmentation of my education, for it helped to fill a huge vacuum in my life. Despite a very tight schedule of classes, study and work I rarely missed the free convocations. The chairman of theconvocations committee lectured his classes reminding them of the significance and value of this part of their education. Hundreds of students attended although some found this a convenient time to "chew the fat" at the Tally-ho or the Pine Shelf. Evening programs for which students were charged admission included a traveling orchestra, a Don Cossack male chorus from the Ukraine, Nelson Eddy, the Indianapolis Symphony and others of similar prominence. What a thrill, for the first time, to hear an orchestra play the "Blue Danube" and "Tales from the Vienna Woods." These programs were very memorable. I never dreamed that I would visit Vienna several times. Tragically, when we visited and cruised on the Danube it was no longer blue but a muddy gray and brown!

The College also addressed student health. All freshmen were required to submit a complete health record including a tuberculin skin test and small pox vaccination followed by a personal interview with the female college physician, Dr. Amelia T. Wood, a rarity in those days. Not having known that there were women physicians, this was another new experience. My skin test was positive; this required a follow-up chest x-ray that showed a healed lesion on one lung. Drinking milk from our tubercular cows, described in an earlier chapter, may have infected me. I knew of no other family member who had a positive skin test or any known tuberculin infection at that time. I have never had any further known effects.

One evening Daryl Murphy at the House of Duncan came in with an embarrassed look, eager to give us a report. He had completed his interview with Dr. Wood, the college physician; as usual, she scrutinized his health record to clarify any information. "Mr. Murphy," she said with a puzzled look, "I don't understand your answers to two of the questions. Are your menstrual periods regular? Do you have any special problems?" Daryl squirmed in discomfort as he revealed to her, "I didn't understand the questions and I didn't notice the section was for 'girls only'; I was sitting between two healthy looking girls and put down the same answers as one of them did. I thought what was good for her was also good for me." Daryl had no sisters, no sex education and totally ignorant about the physiology of women. Dr. Wood advised him to have some dates that should bring some gradual enlightenment. We all roared with laughter that he felt compelled to share his ignorance. In his naivete, that was evident in other areas of life and living, Daryl was planning to major in biology.

There were four fraternities on campus, two local and two national. Fraternity members were in a minority but exercised disproportionate political power. Soon I was asked to consider joining; in my ignorance I asked many questions. I was hesitant; when I learned of the additional costs involved and the time encroachments, I decided that fraternity membership was not essential to my well being. This was not the end of the pursuit by fraternities although I never did join. Gradually, I declared myself an active non-fraternity or Independent leader.

After two weeks of classes I developed a cold, felt lousy and for three days stayed in my room. "Mom Duncan" brought me some chicken and rice soup; a day or two later she made her own diagnosis. "You don't have a fever and your cold is not bad. Your trouble is homesickness, more than anything else," she pronounced. She was an experienced housemother and often, it turned out, a clever diagnostician. As I reflected on her comments I slowly came to realize that she was correct. I had never been away from my family for this many days. The cold hung on the usual fourteen days, but I became immersed in my classes and returned to work in the bookstore. The drastic transition from the daily rural farm routine surrounded by the family brought with it emotional and physical debilitation. My pride and determination did not permit me to call home, but I did wonder whether the family really missed me. They hadn't joyously wished me success, but reluctantly watched me go. Even in dreams I was back milking cows for many weeks, conversing in Swiss dialect, clear evidence that the subconscious was active. I had always been instinctively shy; it took me longer than many others to establish strong friendship bonds with other students, male and female.

Over the weeks, in classes and in the bookstore new relationships were slowly developing, new connections and friendships were formed. With my very limited experience in dating, I wondered whether some of the attractive classmates would consider going on low cost dates. How much would my restricted upbringing haunt me with interference in good relationships and friendships? I had an occasional date and found that many girls understood the need for frugality from their own experiences.

Some of my academic initiation was exceptionally challenging. Dr. Charles Van Cleve in English class assigned a research paper on a subject of our choice with certain rigid requirements. All data must be noted on thin 4x6 paper specially ordered by the bookstore; and the data had to be meticulously recorded according to his strict system. I chose Woodrow Wilson, President of the United States at the time of my birth. Never in grade or high school had I been assigned a significant research paper. I discovered with his unique system that I was probably no worse off than students who had other methods of recording research data. I also learned that I was not the only student who had never written a research paper. So I set out to learn fast enough to catch up with students who had training and experience in research.

From my first day in Sight Singing class I learned how musically ignorant I was. Professor Palmer introduced us to vocal music beginning with Palestrina through the European classical era, discussed musical composition, assumed we knew basic, major and minor keys and could individually read and solo assignments when called on in class. I learned how absurd it was for me to be in this class. Many students who were majoring in music had extensive vocal and instrumental training and choral experience. Happily, in history and business courses I thrived; by the end of the first quarter my plan to major in each was confirmed. By the end of the freshman year I squeaked by with a scanty 3.25 average. I had learned much about college in general and had only begun to sort out where best to concentrate in pursuing my educational goals and importantly, cultivating my newly established intellectual interests.

Chapter 15: Immersed in College Life

1938-42

Gradually, I perceived dimly that college was more than a set of courses; it was a comprehensive and life-changing experience. What a change in life's routine this involved. Consider some of the specifics in transition from farm to city. I changed from wearing patched bib overalls, unwashed socks and heavy work shoes, to a dress shirt, tie, dry-cleaned pants, and polished slippers. My principal endeavor was a shift from physical labor to intellectual pursuits; from prescriptive family living shaped by farm animal needs and nature's daylight and dark, to flexible, individually adaptive schedules often at odds with nature's routine. These were contrasts in the changed agenda. From prescriptive practices of the church family, I gradually moved toward open-ended curiosity and explorations. I moved from a very restrictive security to an anxiety generating freedom of uncertainties; and from a life that offered many answers to questions that dared not be asked to an arena which posed a growing list of questions with virtue acclaimed in tentative answers and suspended judgments. Mind opening questions became more important than closed minded answers.

On the lighter side, I was amazed at the extent many students became engrossed in trying beer, wine and liquor. Frequently those who came from homes that had no alcoholic beverages with parents who had shielded their children from ever tasting wine or beer began to consume alcoholic beverages more and more indiscriminately. Fraternity and sorority affairs sometimes became drunken parties. I learned that students whose systems had not been conditioned by alcohol were more vulnerable to intoxication. To me, having grown up with wine and beer in the home, I found no appeal to overindulging. In fact, I believe in my whole college career that I did not consume an alcoholic beverage a half dozen times. On the one hand I had no such inclination; on the other hand I could not afford it.

For me with my prescriptive pre-college life, these contrasts became profoundly troubling. Attending the Amish

Christian church services was as prescriptive as breakfast, dinner and supper; thinking and speaking had their rigid boundaries. The rapid erosion of the church that had been so potent a force in my life was now past; the surviving members were asking, "Is anything salvageable or shall we abandon the disaster?" My family had not yet been able to agree where to go, having realized that rebuilding was not an option. We were determined that the church destruction must not shatter family solidarity. As the oldest, and because of age, the only one of the brothers who had yet become a church member, I felt some family responsibility in the decisions to be made. The church that had been so central in my life now was a vacuum. With whom could I meaningfully discuss my dilemma concerning this specific problem? Could I somehow set aside this current confusion to deal with the other transformations that I faced? My troubled condition prevailed for many months. It affected my level of efficiency and total concentration on my college work.

I wondered whether I should attend church, and if so which one. That was a haunting question. The Wesley Foundation in the nearby Methodist church was very active. Gerhart and I, sometimes together, at other times separately attended churches of various denominations. One year I joined Wesley Foundation students at a regional conference at Northwestern University (founded by Methodists). We stayed in residence halls on Lake Michigan. I was greatly impressed with this campus and with the leaders at the meeting. I never dreamed that some day I would earn my Ph. D. degree at this prestigious institution.

These were exploratory learning experiences, in contrast to our pre-college indoctrination. At times we attended the United Brethren Church with an avid member and friend, Ben Ervin. One visit to the Nazarene church concluded our interest in that denomination. We explored; we visited the old stone downtown Presbyterian Church that in our junior year came to new life with a young pastor, Lewis Weber Gishler. The congregation began to make plans to move across the river to the campus area. Once or twice we worshipped with a high church Episcopal Congregation, with contrasting ritual and ceremony. We visited the Disciples of Christ with weekly communion service. (Coincidentally, years later, Gerhart and I geographically far apart in our careers both were elected elders in the Presbyterian Church.)

Every few weekends when I didn't have to work in the bookstore on Saturday morning, I hitch hiked the fifty miles home. This too was because of my frugality when hitchhiking was not regarded as hazardous. It also offered some different learning opportunities; many drivers shared their own stories. Some drivers talked about themselves, others asked many questions. I got many kinds of advice. "Why would you want to be a teacher, salaries are terribly low. You can't raise a family on that income."

In addition, I discovered that hitchhiking involved certain skills. I soon learned before getting into a vehicle to ask the driver who offered a ride where he was going. To be dropped entering a town is much less productive than on the departing side. If offered a short ride, should I take it or wait for a longer one? Truck drivers were sometimes especially interesting. I often asked questions; some drivers talked politics, others about the war in Europe. Hiking after dark was not advisable. Drivers on four lane roads offered far fewer rides than those on less traveled two lane roads. Rural drivers were more accommodating, but rarely traveled very far. By graduation time I had become a confident, veteran hitchhiker who felt that the trip was sometimes more meaningful than arrival at the destination. That became valuable experience even in my army days

On Saturdays when I went home I was a carpenter with Dad to supplement my income. I discovered how important were free meals at the family table, both abundant and good. On Sunday afternoon a brother, uncle or friend happily returned me to campus. Some relatives enjoyed a certain pride in associating with the first college student they had known, perhaps seeing a campus for the first time. On occasion someone drove me to Bluffton to connect with the Muncie interurban—a single electrified passenger car on railroad type tracks.

Each trip home meant reliving the cultural transition from college to farm conditions and return, English to Swiss-German, conversations about the realms of learning and ideas turned to persons, events and routine of the day. Gradually, I learned that these weekend interruptions, however important in other respects to my family and to me, were academically distracting. It was time that could have been productively used in supplementary reading, enriching study, or rewriting papers.

Other weekend activities came to the fore. Virgil Smith, director of financial aid located across the hall from the bookstore in the controller's office, whom I saw every day, invited me to sell tickets at home football games—a few more dollars. Sometime during the second quarter, sales were over and I attended the game. On occasion the large downtown Masonic temple that provided banquet meals called on college students as waiters and servers. The pay was better than at the bookstore; I was on their favored list of students. In two Christmas seasons, between classes and during part of the vacation, I worked in the Muncie Post Office hand sorting and bundling mail. There were no zip codes or automatic sorting machines.

On occasional weekends a fraternity or sorority sponsored an open dance. The theater department produced plays, the music department offered vocal and instrumental ensembles. Each year the convocation committee sponsored a major program series for paid admission. Included were programs such as a leading orchestra, the Vienna Boys choir, a Don Cossack chorus, a Metropolitan vocal musician, or other features to which the Muncie community was invited. By college and university standards today, this was a lean series; for those of us from rural high schools this was a cultural feast.

Illustrative of its cultural limitations, the bookstore stocked mostly textbooks and related course readings; the bookstore did not stock or promote broad non-textbook reading. Supplementary reading was to be found in the college library or by special order. Few students had a significant number of books in their own libraries. Most students were not conditioned at home or high school to regard broad reading as essential to gaining an education, though I was probably an extreme example. My personal library at graduation was negligible. College library book purchases were meager compared with current practice; the library ordered most of its books through the bookstore. There were no facilities for inter-library services. Some faculty gave individual orders to the bookstore manager.

I held two summer jobs, sequentially, after my freshman year. At times I worked at carpentry with Dad. Uncle Ben Mazelin became involved with the Agricultural Adjustment Act (AAA), a complex of farm programs that provided various kinds of federal government assistance to farmers, initially on a voluntary basis. Programs included crop insurance against loss due to floods, drought, crop damage by pests and fungus and payments to farmers for idling acreage to help raise farm prices. For the first time, aerial photos were used to determine the acreage of particular crops. I measured with a surveyor's wheel were to validate the acreage of each crop. I was employed for a few weeks to do spot measurements, both on participating and non-participating farms. During the Roosevelt era, many heavily mortgaged, financially desperate farmers were anxiously awaiting cash from these new programs. Other farmers of independent mind without farm mortgages were firmly opposed to any government participation and refused any cooperation. On one such farm where I was assigned to do measurements, with gun in hand the farmer chased me off his premises. He wanted no part of this "new Roosevelt Socialism." Summer learning had many dimensions!

Following my sophomore year I painted my parent's barn and adjacent buildings, excluding the house, with a brilliant, glossy Montgomery Ward red generously trimmed in white. (Incidentally, I believe the paint applied in 1940 was the last time the barn was painted.) When the paint job was finished, Frances Judy and her parents invited me to join them on a ten-day trip to Michigan. Her father and I shared a room; Frances and her mother shared one. That trip was my only vacation.

Another summer for a few weeks I worked on the night shift in construction of concrete grain storage bins more than one hundred feet tall. I used a wheelbarrow to haul eighty-pound cement bags from the railroad car a few hundred feet to the concrete mixer. When construction reached the top, I went up the open elevator to help remove the wooden forms and drop them to the ground. I was not attuned to work at such heights. If I needed any confirmation of the importance of college this summer provided abundant testimony. The labor union charged temporary employees an hourly fee; I never understood why but I had no deduction. I celebrated my financial cash bonus.

Working at night and sleeping during the heat of the day with no air conditioning was enervating and physically exhausting. And working at ground level then suddenly at a height of one hundred feet was somewhat nerve wracking for me; going up in open elevators then dismantling scaffolding and dropping it piecemeal to the ground did not appeal to me. Carpentry closer to the ground was much more satisfying.

This recitation concerning subsistence testifies to the trappings of mind with which I was burdened in my transition toward immersion in college. Far too slowly I became engaged in the intellectual encounter and mind-challenging venture.

Back to college. As a naive young man from the farm, I assumed that all professors would be well-balanced human beings, if not models, and that they reared socially adaptable, well-adjusted progeny. I was surprised to learn how wrong my assumptions were. Some of the faculty seemed to me, and to some of my fellow students, to be quite eccentric. Several faculty couples were childless or had exceptional children, perhaps socially maladaptive or peculiar.

From early in my college career I was searching for a role model, personal or professional, among the faculty. In this quest, I did find some negative professional models, men and women. Several professors devoted all class time to lectures, many of them were dull and uninspiring. In some classes I felt that challenging questions were neither invited nor well received. Some faculty answered student questions with a show of impatience, eager to return to the security of the lecture. The Socratic style of teaching was rarely practiced. I knew that when I began teaching I did not want to emulate them; I found no one whose teaching style I believed deserved to be completely adopted. I did glean worthwhile segments that have served me well in my career. Dr. Harry Fitch as a man, counselor, diligent teacher with scholarly inclinations, husband, father, churchman, given to humane service probably came closest. He used the Socratic method of teaching, with well-formulated questions. A keen observer of individual students, that often led to increased self-understanding, he was one of the first people to suggest that I should pursue a doctorate. Some twenty years later on a leisurely world tour, he and his wife visited us for several days at the University of Mysore in India where I taught for a year as a Fulbright lecturer.

An important aspect of my college years was a desire to understand human personalities; that was further stimulated through the courses in psychology. I was increasingly struck by the distinctive individualities of college professors and the inter relationship of their personalities and their effectiveness as teachers. Were they more interested in their subject specialties than in being effective teachers? Were they genuinely interested in making sure that the students learned? With some faculty I felt that reading their lecture notes appeared to be the principal objective; if the students learned well that was a happy coincidence.

I was curious about their individual faiths, personal qualities, families, and life styles. Before college, I had never met a college professor. Dr. Robert LaFollette, my favorite history professor, was not known to participate in any denomination, never made reference to his personal faith. However, he was emphatic in his admiration of Ralph Waldo Emerson and Harry Emerson Fosdick, who was a popular radio preacher and pastor of the Riverside Church in New York City. Having no radio, only occasionally did I hear him on Sunday afternoon. His delivery was non dramatic but intellectually powerful. That prompted me to read some of his books, for example, *The Modern Use of the Bible.* What a discovery--he didn't interpret the Bible literally! I had never heard of that; I not only read his book, I absorbed it. Dr. Fosdick was both mind opening and faith renewing. *The Man from Nazareth* portrayed the human side of Jesus. I learned that Dr. Fosdick had been Presbyterian but was alienated as too liberal. The Rockefeller family, American Baptists to which Fosdick shifted, built the large Riverside church near Columbia University. My curiosity turned to books such as *How Odd of God to Choose the Jews,* by Lewis Browne, challenging the claim that the Jews were the chosen people. These readings set my mental pot boiling; having grown up being spoon-fed with biblical literalism, I was a stranger to the realms of sharply conflicting and contradictory ideas. Yet that is the basic nature of college. I became skeptical; I was puzzled. Slowly I came to the awareness that one need not render a judgment of true or false of what one reads. Most issues have multiple interpretations, none of which may be either fully true or false; one must learn to be tentative and suspend one's judgment even for extended periods of time. This discovery was of profound significance and essential to a liberal education. Dr. LaFollette had his own methods of promoting tentativeness; I am greatly indebted to him for these evolving insights. In all his courses he required a critical reading report written on one of the books on the supplementary reading list beyond the required texts. He graded these himself, often with penetrating comments. As chairman of the social science department he made this a departmental requirement of each professor.

At least one departmental faculty member treated this very superficially. Mr. Lawrence Hurst, associate professor of economics, was a very weak link in the department. After a few weeks in his course, I doubted that he read the reports but probably placed a grade on the paper based on the quality of the student as formed in his mind from earlier reports. On the front of the page I wrote a critical report. On page 2, the backside, I wrote a letter to my mother. My hunch was confirmed; the grade was"A."

Dr. Paul Royalty, the new Chairman of the English Department, taught a course, "The Bible as Literature." When I learned in my freshman year that he was indifferent to organized religion, I wondered how the Bible could be literature or history? I thought the Bible was the word of God, the foundation of Christian religion. In my senior year when I had become far more open-minded, I realized that I should have taken the course but then could not work it into my schedule. I had come to realize that the Bible had many dimensions pertaining to poetry, literature, history, metaphors, Jewish and Christian interpretations of religion none of which was written during a scientific era.

This was a state institution; I understood that discussing one's personal faith with faculty was not standard practice. There was no college chaplain. My hesitation led me not to make direct inquiries, but I hoped to understand by inference and indirection. Before college, I had learned not to ask probing questions about Christian faith but to accept fixed answers. Were questions now safe? With my natural shyness I had been conditioned to think privately but not to ask. Certainly, the nature of my questions was greatly changed, having gone through various stages of doubt and skepticism.

Claude Palmer, Professor of Music, directed the choir at First Presbyterian Church. Ruth Kitchin, bookstore manager, a Presbyterian, told me that Dr. Van Cleve shared her denominational choice. Much later I discovered that President Pittinger was another Presbyterian; Mr. Winifred Waggoner, Controller, was Methodist. His son, Junior, in my class became a friend.

Professor Harry Fitch, Chairman of the Department of Education, a respected gentleman, had a son, Ray in my class, who seemed to be an intelligent, well-balanced person. I envisioned them as compatible father and son. Dr. Floy Hurlbut, Associate Professor of Science, taught geography in the science department. Not realizing the fundamental significance of laboratory science, I chose courses in geography to fulfill the science requirement. I was in three of her courses: "Environment and Man", "Geography of Europe" and "Geography of Asia." Dr. Hurlbut was an authentic conservationist ahead of her time and believed that one should experience geography by visiting the region to supplement book knowledge and map study. During the spring recess she took the class in "Environment and Man" to the Smoky Mountains. (She also was a disciplinarian. Having instructed us about appropriate conduct, she shipped one young man back to campus after he created a mid-night disturbance in the hotel.) The region then was ideal to study the flora and fauna in relation to the environment; now commercialization has altered much of the natural landscape.

Because Dr. Hurlbut was born in China, the daughter of missionaries, she taught geography of China with a passion, greatly concerned with Japanese invasion but was confident that over the centuries the Chinese people and culture would prevail. She avoided any report of her view of Christian missionary endeavors.

Reflecting on the changes in the political map of Europe since World War II, brought about by Hitler and Stalin combined with the dissolution of the Union of Soviet Socialist Republics, created fresh awareness of the millions of helpless victims and refugees. When I consider the European turmoil during my lifetime since World War I, one cannot help but wonder whether the energies and power struggles between nations can ever be sufficiently harnessed to solve the Europe's problems peacefully.

Based on his publishing record Dr. Eldon Burke was probably one of the best scholars on campus. Dr. Burke, professor of history, and a devout Quaker who taught courses in English history. He was a rather private individual. In my senior year I wrote a major research paper on the British regard for and attitude toward Mahatma Gandhi and his Independence movement which was in the news almost daily. Knowing of Gandhi's steadfast opposition to war prompted me to undertake this study. What I learned added to my motivation to apply for a year's study and teaching in India that led to a Fulbright faculty appointment in 1958-59. Facing the imminent certainty of military conscription after graduation, I had several soul-searching conversations with Dr. Burke as my senior year was drawing to a close. His own irresolution about his future in response to the war may have made our conversations less helpful to me than I had hoped. At the time he was considering whether to engage in the work of the American Friends Service Committee, although he was well past military draft age. I believe he finally did so.

Among teachers colleges I believe Ball State overall was in the upper ranks. The Ball State library was regarded as somewhat unusual for having open stacks; some libraries were still considered more as repositories where safeguarding of books took precedence over providing readily accessible resources for reading and research. To roam the stacks of the library was for me a stunningly eye-opening and mind-challenging experience. As I much later realized, to my knowledge, Ball State, during my student days, did not have a truly distinguished teacher or a nationally ranked scholar. Nonetheless, many of the faculty members were caring, diligent persons totally committed to their profession, with many Masters degrees and Doctor of Philosophy degrees earned at major universities. However, as a student I was never invited to a faculty home.

Beginning my sophomore year, my academic direction was clear, I had a new self-confidence. I earned straight A's. With my bookstore work, I knew many students by name. With election of class officers, I ran as Independent for the class presidency, against Doyle Collier, a member of the Navajo local fraternity. (The name Navajo did not relate to members any more than a Greek name would signify that members are of Greek ancestry). The four fraternities and some sororities generally lined up in his support. I did not conduct much of a campaign, even had inner doubts whether I wanted to win, and lost by two votes. Though I lost, this did much for my self-esteem. I had established myself as a student, a campus leader, and as a reliable employee in the bookstore where I was very visible to the campus community.

Overall, the sophomore year was very good; with all A's my cumulative academic record was more than adequate to retain my state scholarship. That was never again in doubt. Budgeting my money was well ordered; my social life took form. I could afford occasional dates to movies, to college events, and an occasional dance. Two fraternities again pursued me, but I declined; by now I felt that I did not need them. In retrospect, with my tendency to be a loner, I might well have benefited.

In the annual junior class drama, I had one of the lead roles. My only clear recollection is that Gerhart was the student director; I competed for the part and won. I was a crippled man with cane, and I cultivated a pronounced German accent.

My only other venture into drama was during the sophomore year when I was paired with an attractive junior brunette, Louise Kistner. She had a steady boyfriend, Mac, a prominent gymnastic athlete, but the play led to a feeling in both of us that we were in love. Mac was conspicuously jealous; instead of being seen together on campus, we exchanged feverishly written notes through campus mail several times a day. This wore down after two or three months and evaporated. I had dates with several college women, and occasionally in the tight schedule of first year student nurses at Ball Memorial Hospital with Frances Judy whom I had known from pre-college days. This turned more serious; after the sophomore year. After that we dated frequently, but never exclusively. Nursing students then had many hours of floor duty; their schedules were often rigid. That undulating relationship endured until graduation, when it ended. We had many good times together, never had a fight. To me her personality lacked vitality and drive. Neither of us was really certain that we wanted to get married. We were never engaged, but her parents were very kind and supportive of me. I enjoyed being with them.

During my junior year I was introduced to a traveling salesman named Oliver Graham; he lived with his aging mother in eastern Muncie. I believe he introduced himself when I visited the church of which he was a member. He was a traveling salesman and a very pleasant, engaging person. He called me when he was in the city; I liked him and he seemed determined to establish a close personal friendship. As one of the few people that I came to know beyond the college, I valued our relationship. He loved music, played a large variety of classical records in his home. Then Ollie invited me to be his guest at the Indianapolis Symphony; occasionally invited me to dinner with him and his mother. He invited me to spend the night at their home; I declined. One evening after dinner he suggested that we take tub baths. Finally, in my naivete I realized that he was a homosexual and that his solicitous attentions to me took on new meaning.

He was frustrated with my failure to respond to his overtures; I was relieved when he understood that he and I had different goals in our friendship. This was my first experience in dealing with a homosexual individual. After my graduation when I moved from Muncie, our friendship ended. In the army and in later life and in further psychological study I learned much more about the many dimensions of homosexuality. What I had read in books had become a personal experience.

My experiences in the bookstore were important in my college career. The bookstore manager employed only students; she was always addressed as Miss Kitchin, never Ruth. She was very cordial, yet maintained her distance in relationships, as was the practice by the faculty. She was always fair, even-handed and showed no favoritism. I remember that when several students were going to a conference, Miss Kitchin entrusted me with her late model Chevrolet. On the return trip in a small town, perhaps 30 miles from Muncie, cheerily conversing, I got my first speeding ticket, driving ten or fifteen miles per hour above the speed limit. At 8:30 p.m. they conveniently had a justice of the peace on duty; I could pay my $5 ticket without having to return later.

Miss Kitchin was an effective and efficient manager and commanded nearly universal respect among students, faculty, and administration. She addressed students by first name, but faculty never. The term Ms. had not been coined; in class the faculty also addressed students as Mr. Adams or Miss Whitacre. Faculty were addressed as Dr. Hydle if they had a doctorate; if not, Mr. or Miss, rarely as Professor. Looking over a catalog roster of women members of the faculty, I believe that none of them was married. On the administration and clerical staff rosters show only two who were married. I can only recall three or four male faculty members who were not married--at least one was regarded by students as homosexual. Formality in personal address was consistent with attire; casual dress in the office or classroom was not acceptable. In the four years at Ball State I was not aware of, nor was there any news in the college paper, which suggested inappropriate sexual conduct by faculty or administrative staff. Human relationships probably were more akin to the Victorian era than to relationships toward the turn of the 21st century.

In college residence halls the sexes were rigidly segregated; no person of the opposite sex was permitted anywhere in the residence hall other than the public lounge or adjoining lounges. Women residents had to sign out and in, adhering to set hours enforced by the adult head resident and the dean of women who was Miss Grace DeHority. Non college property owners who housed students were expected to enforce similar rules and were frequently regarded as "in loco parentis." Forbidden sexual relationships between students took place in secluded or remote places or in automobiles, not often in hotels where registration was generally supervised with the intent of assuring appropriate marital status. Motels and automotive vans appeared during and immediately after World War II.

Paradoxically, the men's Blue Key organization (originated at University of Florida), of which I was a member, persuaded Miss DeHority to approve a pajama dance on campus at 4:00 a.m. on Saturday morning. Blue Key membership was limited to about sixteen men who were leaders on campus, and I greatly cherished my membership. Incidentally, when Ball State and Indiana State Teachers College Blue Key chapters agreed to mount a Victory Bell, the winner of the annual football game would claim the bell for a year. Our chapter had it mounted in a sturdy wood frame. We needed transportation to Terra Haute. The controller's office scheduled the Ball State auto, a large Studebaker; Mr. Waggoner, the Controller, designated me as driver. We proudly exhibited the Victory Bell at the initiation ceremonies when the game began. Humbly, when the game ended, we had to leave it there.

I was also elected to two other national honorary societies, Pi Gamma Mu in social science and Pi Omega Pi in business education. Ball State did not have a chapter of Phi Beta Kappa. I had matured intellectually, emotionally, socially, religiously, and greatly improved my self-esteem. I felt that I was respected and well regarded by many faculty and fellow students, although I formed close friendships with only a small number of persons. I was ready and eager to begin my teaching career. At age 24, I had been fully focussed on my college career and up to that time had not considered marriage.

The "bookstore gang," as we affectionately called ourselves, developed a close camaraderie. Occasionally, we held a picnic or dessert at the home of Ruth Kitchin or at the home of friends; two or three times my mother invited the gang for a Sunday noon meal at our home. Some of the gang were uninitiated in farm life and found this an exciting new venture. Though a lot of added work for my mother, she especially seemed to enjoy these guests. On the first occasion being totally unaccustomed to entertaining persons outside her formerly closed society, she noted with great surprise how eagerly each person, male and female, helped with food preparation and dishwashing, quite different from her tradition. On subsequent occasions she eagerly looked forward to entertaining this group.

The work in the bookstore was a good learning experience about a small non-profit business operation. During my junior and senior years I was also assigned the bookkeeping for the bookstore; the records were kept across the hall in the controller's office. Daily summary transaction totals from the register tapes were recorded in a journal, posted in a ledger all by hand. At the end of each month I prepared a trial balance. Costs of heating, lighting, custodial services, maintenance, renovation were not charged to the bookstore records. The only inventory of assets was merchandise for sale; inventory was taken annually at the end of the fiscal year, June 30.

I had developed a high enough measure of trust not only with Ruth Kitchin but also with the controller and his staff that I was entrusted with combinations of two safes and access to the business office archives. Bookstore employees were given strict instructions about confidentiality of all business matters; I remember hearing the controller in anger chastising an employee who had failed in this respect. On occasion I had to visit the archives for pertinent information. I took the occasion to look at non-related information such as Ball State President's princely salary of fifty–five hundred dollars annually. I was discreet in knowing; I never told anyone that I knew. I never dreamed that I would become a college president and could not imagine that as president I would earn that much per month plus housing, maid service, country club membership and generous expense funds. At that salary President Lemuel T. Pittenger drove a handsome Packard often parked in the bookstore lot. I developed a friendly relationship with him; on one occasion he offered me a ride to Portland, Indiana part way home for the weekend. I accepted with pleasure.

I learned much from the work experience and the human working relationships in the bookstore and the controller's office. In many ways Ruth Kitchin was a model in her relationships with administrators, faculty and students. At the same time she did not bend the rules to provide special favors; however, she was very accommodating whenever that was possible. She expected loyalty, respect, punctuality, and complete dependability; she accepted no shoddy work, gossip, half-heartedness, or discord among the staff. She had a sharp memory including detail; a promise was meant to be kept. In the four years of work in the bookstore she rarely chose a student whom she had to dismiss. The staff in the controller's office was well disciplined, courteous, efficient. All those are traits that I came to regard as essential and tried to emulate.

During my college studies I discovered that I was not the authentic scholarly type able to concentrate on a narrow specialty. I learned that I was not content without seeing the big picture and how the parts and pieces fit together. I was able to relate to all kinds of people. Observing her, I absorbed some of the essentials in developing team work. At the same time, I was not what is termed a natural leader. Although I enjoyed administrative responsibilities I had to cultivate and develop leadership ability. I greatly enjoyed the classroom as a student and as a teacher; however, I did not win student loyalty by depth of scholarly ability. I earned respect from students by knowing my subject, explaining it clearly, and treating them fairly and evenhandedly. Dr. Ralph Noyer, Dean of the College, had a reputation among faculty as the brain. I am not aware that he ever taught a course. Although, he had a kind of remoteness, once you came to know him, he was clearly the intellectual among his colleagues. With scant tolerance for shoddy thinking, he was both respected and feared by members of the faculty. He was a leader through his brilliance and assertiveness; faculty rarely challenged him in matters academic or intellectual. Though I had very little personal association with him, when I later applied for a Ph. D. program at Northwestern University, Dean Noyer wrote a very persuasive letter of support. It never occurred to me that I would become an academic dean for a total of eighteen years.

As my college days were ending, I clung to my plan to become a teacher. My deferment from military service ended at graduation; once more I was delayed in pursuing my career. I had ruled out business as a career and had given no thought to becoming an administrator. In the choice of my college curriculum, it was clear I was committed to high school teaching. I had shifted from elementary level to high school level, but had not considered a career in college. I completed two terms of student teaching, one in history, the other in business education. In sharp contrast to some individuals who early in life have well formulated career plans, my struggles had convinced me to keep my goals modest—hopefully attainable. Long term plans evolved very gradually.

At graduation Ball State did not award summa, magna or cum laude. A cumulative grade point average (g.p.a.) of 3.6 was required for graduation honors; my g.p.a. was 3.552. I had not known what the honors level requirement was; more time devoted to extensive reading and study and less to pursuits for financial remuneration could have served me well to raise the academic average. Advanced degrees were not yet in my plans. At graduation I had a reached a status among faculty and students of which I was proud, and had developed a new level of self-confidence. Financially, I was debt free and had even invested in part ownership of a horse and a colt, hogs and some grain valued at $105.37. My records show that my rate of pay at the bookstore had risen to forty cents an hour, an increase of 33 1/3% in four years. My cash expenditures for all purposes during my college years totaled approximately $1,400, with a state scholarship to cover tuition costs of $264.00. I had conferred on me a Bachelor of Science in Education degree. The State of Indiana granted me a certificate to teach high school students; I was eager to begin my career. For some two years I had been deferred from military service until graduation. Now I would be reclassified as available to be drafted.

Chapter 16: The World Beyond

June 1942-December 1942

When we were graduated in June 1942, Gerhart, my roommate, and I had an opportunity to enlist in the navy to earn commissions as officers. He and I discussed this at length. He accepted. I declined. Neither of us knew when we would be called to active duty. Although in some respects I found the naval commission appealing, I could not make the commitment to become a military officer. At the initial Selective Service Act registration in October 1940, I registered as a conscientious objector to military service, indicating that I would perform Civilian Public Service. The United States was not yet at the war. On December 7, 1941, Japan attacked Pearl Harbor and the next day Congress declared war. During the preceding two years of war in Europe, President Franklin D. Roosevelt had repeatedly promised to keep the United States out of the war. All this changed when Germany and Italy sided with Japan that destroyed a large part of the U. S. Navy at Pearl Harbor. With his "Blitzkrieg" Hitler had already ravaged much of Europe with astonishing success and was devastating Great Britain with air warfare. Feeling the savagery of Hitler pursuing his goal of *Deutschland Uber Alles* and the threat to all of Europe, would I still refuse military service?

In hand to hand combat, or any form of combat, could I kill the enemy soldier who may be in battle only because he had no other option? Yet, did I want to refuse to help overcome the savagery of Hitler? Now the struggle of conscience was immediate and critical; among the options available, there was none that was going to satisfy me. I wrote to the Selective Service Board in Decatur, asking that they reclassify me from 1-O to 1-AO, for non-combatant service that was available only in the U. S. Army. The Board informed me that I was reclassified.

I had established my membership in the Evangelical Mennonite church during my sophomore year, before my registration, where my parents and some of my brothers also joined. I would have been supported in whatever category of service that I chose. The church adhered to its historic position as a peace church; nonetheless, it supported the decisions of individual members in dealing with the military draft. I was not prepared to become a combatant. When I started college I feared our nation becoming engaged in the war, and I was deeply troubled about this matter throughout my college career. I had attended some meetings of the Fellowship of Reconciliation, suspiciously regarded by the Federal Bureau of Investigation (FBI) as a Communist-related organization. I was interviewed at least once by an FBI agent. I read extensively concerning the positions held by Mahatma Gandhi, Toyohiko Kagawa, Rufus Jones, Georgia Harkness and other pacifist writers. (I could then not have dreamed that I would meet Mr. Kagawa in person after the war or that I would devote a year to teaching and study in independent India, Gandhi country.)

At graduation time, with the probability of my being drafted into military service within weeks, no school board would consider offering me a teaching contract; so, I decided to choose another direction. George Prickett, who had been a student colleague in the bookstore, had graduated at Ball State. He sent word that he had a job at Waco Aircraft Co. in Troy, Ohio. The company had government contracts to build military gliders and was employing people by the scores. George advised me to come to Troy confident that I would have a job as soon as I arrived. (I had a minor investment in the 1941 Ford principally owned by my brother Elmer. Having two other vehicles, the family permitted me to use this one for the time being.) I went to Troy and was immediately employed in the accounting division without regard for my draft status. I found lodging in the same private home where George lived. With its rapid growth, this small company acquired space in vacant residences and other buildings wherever available. I was located in a residence with two other men in the cost accounting section. The company had what were then widely popular government "cost plus fixed fee" contracts. I was employed at $50 for a 40 -hour week with a declining scale of payment for overtime. If I worked overtime, each succeeding hour was at a reduced hourly rate. My two colleagues were career bookkeepers or accountants with no college degrees.

I quickly won the confidence of the supervisor; in a few weeks they appointed me head of the cost accounting section. With some bookkeeping experience and courses in corporate accounting, I rapidly learned Waco's system of cost accounting.

The industrial world of work was different from college. Many employees had little or no college education and few persons with college degrees. This was not a realm of ideas, and there was little time for reading. Where would I find friends and dates? We were in the midst of war conditions facing records and figures. Almost daily we missed another worker who was called to military service. We wondered whether there would be a future.

Food was more costly. However, in contrast to college, I ate breakfast; I felt flush with funds. I went home perhaps one weekend each month where Mom's cooking was still "free."

One morning a telephone caller informed me that George Prickett, who rented a room in the same house, was in jail. The plant superintendent wanted me to be a reference for George who had been picked up by police during the night as a "peeping Tom." He was released and went back to work. Although George firmly denied to me that he had been window peeping, I could not decide whether I believed him innocent or guilty. In a few weeks George left Waco Aircraft Co.

When I left the farm for college, I assumed that as soon as I was employed fulltime I would help pay off some of the long overdue debts to relatives and acquaintances from whom my parents had borrowed money during the depression years. Some of the debts were small. From my first paycheck I paid $5 to one of the patient creditors. After a few weeks, I had him paid in full. Then I made a personal visit to a great uncle to learn the amount still owed him. Each week until I was called into military service I made a payment; he was very pleased. However, when I returned home after more than three years of military service I was delighted to learn that the thriving war economy had enabled my parents to become debt free.

Although I enjoyed my work in accounting and was delighted with the confidence and respect that I readily won from my superiors, I also confirmed my unwavering intentions that after years of sequential delays my career will be teaching. People, rather than figures, must be the central focus of my career. The prospect of gaining wealth in the corporate world did not appeal to me.

I had dates with several young women in the Company and at the Congregational church that I attended, some stimulating and some dull. One evening while working overtime in the main office, I observed a very attractive, energetic young woman who, I learned, worked in the traffic department. I was introduced to Janet Gladfelter, and we had a very brief conversation. I called her the next day, and we arranged a date on August 25. She lived in Vandalia, a few miles from Troy. Following the movie, "Mrs. Miniver," over a snack at a restaurant we had a long, scintillating conversation. She was very intelligent. We talked about ideas. She had greatly enjoyed her first year of college at Bowling Green State University, and was enamored with her sorority. I took her home and driving back to Troy, I thought and felt this was different. Our intellectual, religious and social interests meshed at many points, although differed at others. For me, the evening together was a very fulfilling personal experience. I became aware that my regard for Janet might be truly serious. We talked by phone at work; we had dates to movies, and sometimes only for conversations.

After several weeks I met her parents. On Sundays I attended her Lutheran Church in Vandalia where her father was pastor. Her mother regularly invited me to Sunday dinner in the parsonage next door. Conversations with her father were intellectually stimulating, about college, his seminary, biblical subjects, politics, the war. I remember one Sunday her parents joined us at an evening church service in Dayton. The erudite preacher's subject was "The Valley of Dry Bones" based on the text from Ezekiel. How I wished I had heard such sermons in my youth.

One weekend Janet went with me to meet my family. By then we knew we were in love. Occasionally, we watched air traffic at the Dayton airport in Vandalia a few blocks from her home, wondering what the future would hold for us. Would air travel be part of our lives if we outlived the war? On October 10, we attended the Ball State Homecoming football game against Bowling Green State University that Janet had attended. In a close game Ball State won. Being two young people who did not believe in wasting time, at the end of that day we became secretly engaged. We agreed that no announcement would be made. Her father had intended that after an employment interlude of a year, she should complete college, then law school and become a high salaried practicing attorney.

Events moved swiftly. My draft board notified me that I must report for induction into the army in November. I resigned from Waco Aircraft Co. in mid-November. Jan and I considered marriage either before I left for military service or after I was located in the Army. Her parents were adamantly opposed to our marriage at that time. My parents with whom I had a harmonious relationship raised no objection and deferred to our judgment. In the atmosphere of total war with no end in view, we had very long, painful conversations deciding what to do. In effect, on November 25, 1942 we eloped to Berne, Indiana where my pastor conducted the wedding ceremony in the parsonage. We then notified her parents. As anticipated, their reaction was so strongly negative that reconciliation required many, sometimes painful, years.

However, years later, the professional successes that Jan and I achieved in teaching and educational administration brought frequent praiseworthy comments from them, especially from her mother. Frequently, she expressed envy of the academic life style we had. They acknowledged that ours was the kind of life they would have wanted for themselves. (By 1955 her parents still lived in Ohio. Her father sought a rural pastorate near Dubuque, Iowa where I was dean of the college at the University of Dubuque. He also sought some affiliation with the University seminary, possibly teaching Greek. My best efforts to facilitate his appointment were not successful.)

But I am getting ahead of my story. I was on a two-week furlough from the Army for the wedding and brief honeymoon. My parents arranged for Jan to live with them until we could know whether it was feasible for her to join me at the army base. She was promptly employed at Central Soya Co. in Decatur, Indiana and I was off to an unknown destination in the U. S. Army.

In times of peace it is very difficult to remember all the effects and disruptions which attended the conversion from a peace time economy to a war economy. Whatever was needed for the support of the military effort had the highest priority from food, clothing and shoes, rubber, gasoline, lumber and hundreds of consumer goods. Rationing of essential materials for civilians prevailed for years. Factories whose products were not essential to the war effort were either converted to manufacturing of war material or closed. Employees moved readily to factories producing goods in support of the military. Anxiety levels were high and decision-making in this climate of uncertainty involved high risks. Families experienced unprecedented disruptions; the social fabric suffered new and larger stresses. Millions of young men and thousands of young women entered the military services thereby opening employment opportunities without precedent for women of all ages. In such a time, decisions to marry or not to marry were both painfully difficult and precarious. Because of the long separations with diverging interests and the urgent need for companionship, many marriages during and after the war did not endure. Jan and I did not suffer long separation. Our risky marriage venture hastily undertaken, turned out to be a very good one for which we have been continually grateful.

Why has ours lasted, as of this writing, for 60 years? Some reasons are fairly obvious while others are subtler. Both of us strongly agreed that we married for keeps. We both came from strong, durable families. We each had a deep commitment to our Christian faith, although not denominationally irrevocable. Our basic values were similar, though with very different cultural roots, we agreed that our mutual trust must never be violated. Our intellectual pursuits were substantially rooted, though in different directions. And, perhaps most significantly, we were able to be together during most of the time during my military service in such striking contrast to millions of others who were separated for years. These considerations made a world of difference. We had indeed been more fortunate than we could have imagined.

Chapter 17: The Quartermaster Corps

November, 1942- February, 1946

Military troop travel was mostly by rail. At the end of my two-week furlough in December 1942, Jan and my brother, Milo, took me to the Fort Wayne railway station. We bid sad farewells after which they returned home while I boarded the train for Toledo, Ohio to the collection center of Army recruits already inducted. There we were provided GI (Government Issued) haircuts, dress and fatigue uniforms, necessary documents, minimal equipment such as dog tags with serial number and blood type, barracks bag, mess kit and shaving kit. Then we were routed toward our unknown destinations and training camps. As I learned later, most military travel was to destinations unknown to troops. Retired railway coaches were revived for military travel. Accommodations were minimal and food was plain. We traveled day and night; at intersections our coaches were switched to other trains. After eighteen hours we arrived in Petersburg, Virginia, from where were bussed to Camp Lee, four miles from the city.

We were issued a manual of U. S. Army regulations. Military abbreviations and acronyms pervaded the printed regulations, and soldiers were known as G. I.' s.

We were marched to our basic training company located in a recently constructed, simple two-story wooden barracks. Each of us was assigned our metal bed, mattress, pillow and footlocker. The supply sergeant issued each of us sheets, pillowcases and one blanket. (An Army blanket issued more than forty-five years ago, at the time of my discharge, still occupies an important place in the trunk of our car). The corporal explained army regulations. He showed us how to wear our hats, ties, belts, make our beds; place our heavy, high, brown, shined shoes in a fixed place under the bed; fold our socks, hang our uniforms on a rod at the head of the bed and place our hats on the shelf. He also showed us how to open the windows to ventilate our non-air-conditioned barracks. Each day we were told what to wear--fatigues or dress uniform.

Each item, without deviation, must be exactly in its place and be ready for weekly inspection. At night our billfold must be inside our pillow cover--the only safe place. We met our company commander and drill sergeant, who taught us Army regulations on saluting officers and formations for reveille and retreat. One non-commissioned officer sounded the trumpet summoning all basic training companies to platoon formations at morning reveille and evening retreat. There was a single mail call each day.

We learned how to march: left foot first, toes turned slightly outward, thirty-inch rhythmic steps, how to stand at attention, at parade rest, eyes forward, eyes right, to swing our arms, with shoulders back and head erect.

Army offered no room for individuality; strict conformity was the order of each day. The military program was designed to develop automatic obedience to orders from above. The army set the time to go to bed, the time to rise, time and conditions of formation for reveille, formation for retreat, how to wear our single color clothing, what, when where to eat. We were ordered how to relate to fellow soldiers, to non-commissioned officers, to commissioned officers and when we may leave camp. We were instructed how to make our bed, when to change sheets, and arrange our clothing in the footlocker. Each day was organized according to specific army regulations. We were told how to prepare our weekly laundry lists of GI clothing for the camp laundry. At one end on the first floor of each barracks was a latrine that included lavatories, urinals, toilet seats and showers, without partitions. In basic training, we had nightly bed check by the charge of quarters. Rotating duty was shared by all privates, such as KP (kitchen police) which mysteriously I was never assigned. Nighttime guard duty I did draw. Radios and record players were prohibited. (TV and computers were still in the future.) Books were not to be conspicuous. Newspapers could be purchased at the PX (Post Exchange.)

I completed the eight weeks of basic training required of every soldier at Camp Lee. In basic training each soldier was issued a rifle and taught by a lieutenant how to dismantle, reassemble, clean, care, use and store it. No ammunition was issued. Marching with and without rifles, we went on extended marching drills by platoons and companies. Physical conditioning included long marches, running, jogging, pushups, rope climbing, crawling on our bellies. We were taught many army regulations related to military training and activity. We were out in the field sleeping in tents, eating out of mess kits, cleaning our mess kits by scrubbing them with sand. Along with rifle practice on the rifle range, we learned to crawl with our equipment under barbwire on the ground for long distances. Ammunition was issued only when we were positioned on the rifle range.

I was no stranger to a rifle. Grandpa Nussbaum had taught me good marksmanship and the care of a gun. A precision marksman, he claimed that he once split the bullet of a .32 caliber on the sharp edge of his knife mounted in a vice. I had hunted game but in contrast to hunting animals and birds, on the rifle range I was shocked to see the target was in the shape of a human head and upper body. Nevertheless, I did earn a good marksman medal.

We ran obstacle courses and at mealtime we were always very hungry. Food was plentiful without being elaborate and I gained weight. Always conscious of its principal purpose as preparation for death dealing action, I did not relish my basic training. As a conscientious objector to combatant service I questioned the need to carry a rifle and practice on the rifle range. The officer told me firmly that there was no escape from this training but that my status will be considered in assignment to duty. Fundamental questions still plagued me. Did I belong in the army? Did I have a right to refuse combatant service in fairness to others who were without grounds to claim conscientious objection?

There were no telephones in the barracks. Telephone service was available only at central telephone booths; calls were restricted to off-duty hours in the evening. Standing in line waiting for a telephone followed by continuing busy signals made telephone calling very tedious and difficult. Telephone technology was not as advanced as today; it took much longer to make a long distance call. I wrote to Jan several times each week; letters were the most reliable form of communication. In emergencies, we used Western Union telegrams; obviously, there was no FAX or e-mail. U. S. postage was free to service people by including in the return address name, rank and serial number.

For the first time in my life, I experienced racial segregation. Complete racial segregation was required in the military and legally imposed in civilian life throughout the South. Except for one student in my class at Ball State, I had never known any black person. Military troops were separated as white or colored. Any person who had one-eighth black ancestry was classified as colored even if in civilian life he had "crossed" and had been accepted as white. Companies were divided by race. Colored officers were very rare, most colored companies had white officers and some white non-commissioned officers. Military exercises were conducted in segregated companies.

When races shared public transportation on buses and trains, laws throughout the South required colored to sit in the rear with whites in front. When some passengers were standing in the aisles and a seat became available whites had preferred seating. Commercial airlines, operating under federal regulations, did not segregate passengers. In the South, there was no mixing of races in hotels, restaurants, hospitals, theaters, athletic events, churches, schools and colleges, libraries, auditoriums, stadiums, mortuaries and cemeteries, use of drinking fountains, toilets or other so-called public facilities. Actually, blacks were denied equal access to all public services. In some southern communities, when whites met blacks on the sidewalk, blacks were required to make way for the whites. In lines waiting for services or to make a purchase, blacks were expected to step aside and defer to whites. I interpreted racial segregation to be a legacy of slavery, in glaring contrast to the preamble of the Declaration of Independence and the democratic ideal. In addition, to me it was in opposition to the admonitions and teachings of Jesus; I found racial segregation abhorrent.

In 1896, the U. S. Supreme Court, in Plessy v. Ferguson case, approved racial segregation to be in accord with the U. S. Constitution under the "separate but equal" doctrine. The ruling embraced all public accommodations, including public schools. Despite the ruling, however, the already existing separate public schools in the South remained patently unequal. They were grossly under funded. They had inferior equipment, books, supplies and other necessities for teaching and learning. Inferiority was the dominant characteristic of education for colored children. I witnessed the results of this inferiority in the colored soldiers I encountered at Camp Lee. Many could not read or write, even though they had had some schooling. Illiteracy was widespread. This was a serious obstacle to efficient basic training but much more so in technical training, the next step in the military. Although in college I had one course on the history of the South, I was astonished and deeply distressed by what I saw and learned here. The course did not include explanations of the racism in the U. S. and the divided sub-cultures that it created and sustained.

After completion of basic training, troops were assigned to a technical school. Some of the best were given the option of applying for officer candidate school located at Camp Lee. I had declined that option. The technical schools functioned to prepare troops for services rendered by the Quartermaster Corps. There was a shortage of clerk typists. The typing school had 160 typewriters in one room with every typewriter occupied for two-hour intervals throughout the day. Instead of assigning me to a school, I was appointed to teach typing. For daily eight-hour shifts, three of us were teachers helping students to improve typing techniques, check their typing errors and proofreading.

At this time it seemed that I might be at Camp Lee for a while. So Jan left her job at Central Soya Co. in Decatur, Indiana and moved to Petersburg where we found a one-room lodging. With her experience in selling shoes, she was immediately employed. I was permitted to spend nights in town but had to return to my company in time for reveille.

Camp Lee bus service to Petersburg was frequent and we were delighted that I was able to commute unless I had night duty.

For a few weeks I was assigned as clerk typist to Captain Hyll, a career officer, who was named camp director of a new program, Army Specialized Training Program, (ASTP). It was designed to select prospective engineers and send them to college for accelerated study while remaining in the military. Captain Hyll was responsible for selecting privates who either had some training in mathematics or the sciences or who showed a high aptitude for engineering and other technical programs not available at Camp Lee. I handled all the correspondence and conducted preliminary interviews. When the military quota was filled this short-term recruitment ended. Captain Hyll, a cigar smoking, rotund, lethargic career officer, seemed more interested in idling away time than in seriously addressing the tasks at hand.

In the one mile walk to my workplace, my inflexible Army shoes so seriously rubbed and traumatized the tendon in my left heel that bursitis developed. For three weeks, I was confined to Camp Lee hospital with a cast on my left leg from toe to knee. Complete immobilization was prescribed as the best cure for bursitis. Fortunately, after work in Petersburg Jan was able to visit me for which I was very grateful. I have never had a recurrence of the bursitis.

The hospital had no private or semi-private rooms for enlisted men; all beds were in a large open ward. In an adjoining bed was young Henry from More Coal, Kentucky. He was a genuine hillbilly, friendly, and gregarious with a great sense of humor. He had very little formal education, but he could talk for hours about life in the remote coal mining areas of his community. On one of her visits Jan asked him, "Where is More Coal?" His sparkling reply was, "There are only two ways to get there; one is to ride a mule; the other is by 'shank's mare.'" We understood going by mule, but "What is shank's mare?" He gleefully taught us the meaning of the expression that is also defined in the unabridged dictionary— "to go on foot, to use one's own legs."

After my return to duty, I was called to the headquarters

office. The non-com stated, "So you've been in the hospital for three weeks. Do you know what you missed?" "No one has told me," I replied. "You were on orders for shipment to Europe, and we had to scratch your name." I was shocked and fearful of his next statement. By then I was expecting the worst, when he said to me, "We have an opening in classification here in the Headquarters Company. How would you like to be assigned here?" I was breathless, stunned. "I would find that very appealing." He sent me to another building for an interview with Staff Sgt. Henry Labovitz, who was head of the limited assignment section in classification. After the interview, Sgt Labovitz asked me to join him in his section. He noted my college degree with courses in psychology and testing. There began a new phase of my Army career that turned out both interesting and often challenging.

I had often pondered what seemed to be the mysteries of military assignment. Is all a matter of chance? Or is there human carelessness or some divine predestination? As I gained experience in sorting quantities of the Form 20, I discovered that what had seemed so mysterious became rather transparently evident. (The IBM generated Form 20 was a single card that contained summary information on each soldier, including name, serial number, education, work experience, test scores, gender, race, special talents, physical limitations, if any, military training and classification. The data were punched into the card on the edges. Cards stacked upright in containers were sorted with a long needle). We received military orders for a specified number of troops with certain qualifications to be shipped to a designated location on a given day. We lifted the selecting needle to pick those who appeared qualified according to the punched Form 20. If we needed more we sent others until the quota was filled. An officer signed the transmittal shipping order, and the "victims" never knew what anonymous clerk made this happen. Those of us doing the sorting to fill orders, rarely knew what awaited the troops after they left Camp Lee. I often wondered as a participant in this process what may have happened as a result of my anonymous participation in a series of events.

My job also included individual counseling such as helping soldiers out of difficult personal dilemmas. I much preferred this more human part of my job.

After a time Jan accepted a civil service position at Camp Lee, as secretary to the medical supply officer at the Camp hospital. For living quarters, I was transferred to Headquarters Company outside the bounds of basic and technical training. I was soon promoted to Private First Class. Restrictions on my movement were considerably lessened. Unless assigned to night duty, I could spend the night with Jan in our temporary home. For all travel we had to rely on public transportation or "shank's mare". Most of our weekends were free of assigned work. My duties did not require homework. We visited some of the many historic sections of Petersburg and environs, including Richmond with an occasional trip to Washington, D. C. We planted a garden on one of the plots made available to area residents on the edge of the city.

Our Limited Assignment section processed individual soldiers with physical, emotional or intellectual limitations. We worked in close consultation with medical officers at the hospital, mostly by telephone. Medical officers in specialties including psychiatry determined the diagnosis and restrictions that applied to a soldier's condition. We then had to determine what kind of training or duty was most appropriate in reclassifying the soldier, "Limited Assignment." Occasionally, we had to determine the authenticity of a soldier's complaint or was he "goldbricking." (the military term for shirking duty or goofing off.)

We dealt with scores of individual conditions. Examples are the trigger finger with a missing joint or a non remediable stiff joint; vision of less acuity than required for general service; physical injury suffered during basic training; severe allergic reactions of the skin or upper respiratory tract to certain stimuli. Other conditions were serious emotional problems, bedwetting, homosexuality, and physical ailments aggravated by military exercises. With appropriate medical consultation, we also had to determine whether a current condition was remediable and whether "Limited Assignment" was temporary or permanent. Although we were non-commissioned officers in the Quartermaster Corps, we often acted under the authority of officers in the Medical Corps.

When troops completed eight weeks of basic training, they were assigned to a technical training school. Sgt. Labovitz and I joined other non-commissioned officers in individually interviewing soldiers to assign them to an appropriate school. These schools included cooking, baking, laundry, fumigation and bath, tent repair, truck driving, auto mechanic, typing, supply clerk and others that involved the services rendered to the Army by the Quartermaster Corps. To make an assignment we took into account the soldier's education, work experience, test scores, and to the extent possible individual preferences within the range of competence. White and colored companies were interviewed separately on different days, segregated in conformity with military regulations of the time.

Although we had troops from all parts of the country, vast numbers of colored soldiers from the deep South had very little schooling. Many could read little or not all. Their vocabularies in so called standard English were extremely limited, so much so that I was ignorant of many words that they used. Some who were illiterate had no test scores. Scores dependent on their reading level were of little value in determining how and where they should be assigned. Yet, many of them had levels of intelligence that enabled them to function well in some of the army schools requiring only manual tasks. Some had non-literary talents that could be very valuable; some had had work experience that was applicable to certain military assignments. Many colored soldiers, reared in the black-white vertical society, had poorly developed personalities. In Southern practice they were often ignored as if invisible. "Speak only when spoken to" was a rule of segregation always with, "Yes, sir or no, sir."

Occasionally, our communication with colored soldiers brought unexpected humor. We posted on a large blackboard the list of Quartermaster technical schools. I asked an innocent looking soldier which of the schools he would like to attend.

He replied, "Suh, A cain't read." He listened intently to the list that I read to him, "Cooking, baking, auto mechanic, truck driving, tent repair, fumigation and bath." He perked up, "Suh, A takes fo'nication an' bath." My clarification led to a downcast look that prompted me to start over in order to help him understand his misuse of words. Day by day my ignorance of Southern culture was slowly being diminished.

The vast majority of the colored soldiers came from the deep South. However, there were some remarkable contrasts among high school and college graduates from northern states. We discovered a few persons with professional degrees in law, engineering or on the way toward a medical degree. Some of them had "crossed" racial lines. They made glaringly evident the injustice and gross impropriety of using skin color as a classification or category. Most of them were profoundly unhappy and some were deeply depressed but could find no escape or resolution to their dilemma.

Jan and I became members of Second Presbyterian Church in Petersburg. Jan had been a Presbyterian since her father was a Presbyterian minister until she was 16. I decided while in college that I would become a Presbyterian. I liked that form of church government and I viewed with favor the educational requirements for the ministers among other reasons.

The pastor of Second Presbyterian was the Reverend W. B. McIlwaine Jr., a widower, perhaps age sixty. He lived on a small rural family estate, Sysonby, with his maiden daughter, Babs, and his mother who was in her eighties. His mother remembered the War Between the States and the long siege of Petersburg. Her father had been one of the surgeon generals of the Confederate Armies. Although I had a college course on the History of the South, I found her long oral dissertations mostly foreign to what I had previously learned. My education was greatly enriched by a Southerner's version. Visible remnants of the war were a cannon ball lodged in the wall of the church, along with war monuments and replica about the city. She took me to a memorial chapel with a brilliant, stained glass window for each of the Confederate states where she exposited at length. Now that I am nearly the age that she then was I have forgotten much of what she taught me, but I will never forget the intentness and reverence of her critical elucidations.

Dr. McIlwaine became a staunch friend during the thirty-eight months that I was stationed at Camp Lee. His family often invited Jan and me to Sunday dinner. Their Negro "mammy" lived in the "nigger" house a few hundred feet from the mansion. (These were the terms they used.) She was their faithful servant, cook, and maid and had reared the daughter, Babs. She remained nameless to us! She served their multi-course meals in grand style. To summon her from the kitchen, where she ate alone, Dr. McIlwaine rang a miniature bell. On some Sundays she attended church service, seated alone racially segregated in the balcony. Jan and I shared the back seat with her in Dr. McIlwaine's Buick while driving from church to Sysonby. However, each person clearly knew and accepted his or her place and station in life.

At one Sunday dinner we met Frank and Helen Jane Montgomery; Frank was an officer in the military reserves stationed temporarily at Camp Lee. We developed an enduring friendship; after the war we visited annually for many years even though we lived in distant states. We also visited with two couples who became friends from Berne, Indiana. Max and Virginia Sprunger and Simon and Elma Schwartz were stationed at Camp Lee for a short time.

In November 1943 Jan called me after a medical appointment. "I am pregnant," she excitedly told me. In the ensuing months we both eagerly looked forward to parenthood knowing that this would bring a major change in our lives. On August 12, 1944 Felicity Ann was born in the osteopathic hospital in Dayton, Ohio. Jan had stayed with her parents in Vandalia for several weeks planning for the birth. By a coincidence, both happy and sad, I was given a three-day pass joining other grandsons to serve as a pallbearer at my Grandmother Mazelin's funeral at Berne, Indiana. After the funeral I *drove hurriedly* to Dayton and arrived just in time for the birth of Felicity. Jan's mother quickly christened her

"Lisha", proclaiming "that four syllable name was just too long for everyday use." (That name stuck until graduate school.) I was ecstatic and proud, having a daughter, in contrast to my having grown up with six brothers and no sister. Jan and I were genuinely delighted. Even though, having had only sisters, Jan was eager for a son. I had planned to hitch a plane ride from Wright-Patterson Airfield at Dayton, Ohio to Richmond, Virginia but the weather grounded planes. Trains from Cincinnati toward Virginia had already departed. With painful regret I *hurriedly hitchhiked hundreds of miles* back to Camp Lee.

Jan and Lisha stayed with her parents for a few weeks until I had a furlough to bring them to Petersburg. My dad, enthusiastically, had built a solid oak baby bed with up and down slides on each side, for Lisha, his second granddaughter. We shipped it to Petersburg and the three of us traveled by train via Cincinnati. We were able to move from a one-room to a small two-room apartment. A family! Eagerly and proudly we watched Lisha grow. We did not dream that we were rearing a Professor of English and Women's Studies at the prestigious University of California at Los Angeles (UCLA).

The war restrictions imposed many added housekeeping chores such as Jan's washing and wringing by hand bed sheets, pillowcases, diapers, underwear, socks, dish and bath towels. Washing machines could not be purchased; there were no public laundries. Even today, her hands show the results! Happily, my clothes went to the Camp Lee laundry. Refrigerators, new or used, could not be found. The iceman delivered our daily allotment of ice for the antique ice box. New electric kitchen equipment had disappeared.

The war seemed never ending! We began to process rotated troops from Europe, many for retraining in anticipation of major offensives in Europe to be followed by an invasion of Japan.

My work had become highly routine and repetitive, there were no intellectual, organizational or administrative challenges. The days and weeks passed much too slowly. "Frozen" in my position, I was promoted to sergeant. I had an unsought offer to transfer to the finance division within Camp Lee with another promotion in rank. I could not gain release for any other assignment. I wrote to my Selective Service Board requesting a reclassification to 1-A. It did not loosen my "frozen" assignment. I thought I was making myself available for new challenges feeling that I was very much "underemployed." I was again astir with career aspirations. Impatiently, I found it difficult fully to appreciate how fortunate I was in my assignment when contrasted with millions of others, including my three younger brothers scattered around the world. Elmer was in Europe in the medical corps; Al was an officer in Okinawa; Milo was in the medical corps in India and China.

In April 1945 I was given a three-day pass; a friend took care of Lisha. Jan and I had been eager to see plays and shows in New York; servicemen and women were given substantial ticket discounts. We attended stage plays, musicals and visited museums; we had a delightful, fully crowded time. On the train to New York City, we learned that President Franklin D. Roosevelt had died at Hot Springs, Georgia. Vice-President Harry S. Truman was inaugurated president. Early in the next month, the war in Europe ended. On May 5, 1945 Germany surrendered. After the devastation of two atomic bombs on Hiroshima and Nagasaki, Japan surrendered on August 14, 1945. What worldwide excitement that generated!

"Now, surely I would soon be out of the army!" However, being frozen in position I had to help process troops moving back from Europe and other fronts. Newly inducted troops replaced those being discharged. From the army's point of view, my separation from military service had a low priority. Finally, in February 1946 my turn had come; I was transferred to Indiantown Gap Military Reservation in Pennsylvania where on February 13 I was discharged. With my discharge papers snugly tucked in my handbag, I took a bus to Pittsburgh where I boarded the Pennsylvania railroad train to Fort Wayne. There I was met by Jan, Lisha who was already six months old, and my brother, Carl. What a joyous time!

Jan had preceded me home by a few weeks; we had

known the end of army service was getting close but no specific date could be established.

The school year in mid-February were too far into the semester to get a teaching position at that time. However, teaching positions for the fall became available. While I was still at Camp Lee, Connersville, Indiana east of Indianapolis sent me a contract based on my record and recommendations without an interview. I signed with delight. Jan traveled to Connersville to find an apartment or home for the fall; everywhere housing was very scarce. During nearly four years of war almost no new housing had been constructed. She could find nothing suitable, returned to my parents' home in despair. She prevailed on me to resign my first teaching position, which made me very unhappy. Finally, after these many years I had a teaching job with no place to live! How ironic! I did resign.

Jan's father had plans for my employment. If Jan wasn't to become a high salaried lawyer, his son-in-law should become a high-level business executive. Her father recalled my rapid advancement at Waco Aircraft Co. before my military service. He had enthusiastically scheduled an interview for me with a major electrical manufacturing firm in the Dayton area. I thanked him for his thoughtful effort; I was pained to have to disappoint him again. However, I was determined that I would not again be diverted from my career goal. I learned of two teaching positions that were open within a few miles of my parents' home. I signed a contract with George Schieferstein, township trustee, to teach at Monmouth high school located three miles north of Decatur. The school year of eight and one half months at a salary of $1,925, was typical in a small rural high school.

I had a teaching position for the academic year 1946-47, but no home and no car. However, now I was a civilian. Again, I had to pay for my own postage! Once more I could decide where to live in a non-segregated society. I could choose when, where and what to eat, which color and materials of clothes I would wear. It was my decision when I would go to bed and when I arose, what color sheets and bedcovers I use, where I work and leave my job at a time of my choosing for a better one. It will be my decision to move from one location to another. Once more I have degrees of freedom that I have not enjoyed for thirty-eight and one-half months.

Chapter 18: Beginning My Teaching Career

1947-1951

Dad with his construction company was engaged in renovating and building new homes in Decatur, Indiana. Dad and Mom invited our family of three to live with them while Dad offered to build us a home in Decatur. Carl, too young for military service, was the only brother living with them at the time. Elmer, Alvin and Milo were still in military service. Reuben, physically ineligible, was an uncertified teacher in a church school for orphans in Illinois.

Jan and I purchased a corner lot on West Monroe Street for $325. On one side was a long established home, on the opposite side across the street a new two-story home was under construction. Across Monroe Street from our lot was a cultivated farm field. We visited with the president of a local bank that eagerly granted us a mortgage at 3½% interest. The city of about 6,000 residents had a negligible residential building code; there was no drainage, foundation, structural, heating, electrical or plumbing inspection. Getting a construction permit did not require a blueprint. There was no sewage disposal plant; sewage and drainage were joined in one system that drained into the St. Marys River.

Although many building materials were still scarce after the war, Dad, as a building contractor, had friends in the lumber and building supply businesses. He was able to purchase the basic building materials in Decatur. We used asbestos shingle siding because many kinds of lumber were still scarce. (Then asbestos shingles were not regarded as hazardous.) Jan and I went to Fort Wayne, about 20 miles away, to buy plumbing and some electrical fixtures, as well as a gas floor furnace. Natural gas, electrical power, telephone lines and drainage connections were already available on Monroe Street.

Dad did the drawings in preparation for construction of our one-story, four-room home. The outside dimensions were 24x30 feet with an eight by four foot front vestibule including a guest closet. Dad found enough hardwood flooring for the living room; the two bedrooms had pine floors, the kitchen and dinette floor was covered with linoleum. With our respective talents Jan and I helped in construction. She painted inside walls and woodwork, and kept the place in good appearance during construction. I did much of the wiring, some carpentry and plumbing. We began construction in March 1946 and were proudly ensconced in our own home in May.

How was our home furnished? Furniture was still scarce; many furniture factories had been unable to buy lumber and materials for furniture manufacturing during the war. Fortunately, Jan's Aunt Sade was a partner in a Dayton, Ohio furniture store. She was generously helpful in our purchasing a living room carpet, a couch and chair set, floor and table lamps, a dinette table and chairs, bedroom furniture and drape materials that Jan sewed.

A childless friendly neighbor, who was a plumber and welder, furnished used steel pipe and aided me in sturdily mounting a pair of home made swings in concrete footings. Later between the swings on the support pipes, I suspended a wooden cross bar to swing by the arms or for chinning. To Lisha the swings quickly became indispensable. These swings, disassembled, accompanied the family to Huntington, Indiana, Evanston, Illinois, and two locations in Dubuque, Iowa. Reassembled and remounted the swings became, to each of our children in turn, and often for their neighborhood friends, an essential piece of backyard equipment that brought them endless enjoyment. When we moved from Dubuque to Sherman, Texas the children, ages 16, 13 and 11, decided they had outgrown the swings.

My dad greatly adored Lisha and Jan, because he never had a daughter and he rarely saw his only other granddaughter. He gave Lisha a little brass hammer so that she too could learn to be a carpenter. After work he often stopped in and never declined an invitation to the dinner table that accommodated four persons. During the summer, while working with Dad in Decatur, I usually walked to work, or some other worker picked me up and took me home.

Automobiles, both new and used, were extremely scarce, for auto factories had been converted to manufacturing of military vehicles. One day Dad spied a 1929 Chevrolet coupe that was priced at $200. Its wood frame was badly rotted, but the weak engine would run and with effort the sagging doors closed. The disintegrated fiber top leaked badly. The windshield wiper was hand operated. This was the best buy we could find; Jan and I named this clunker "Clotilda." When it rained, while riding in Clotilda, I always wore a raincoat.

On a Thursday and Friday in October, schools closed for the annual teacher's institute, sponsored by the Indiana State Teachers Association. In 1946, Jan and I attended the institute held in Fort Wayne. On our way home, we met a drenching rainstorm. Jan held an umbrella over our heads so that I could see the road. With my left hand, I energetically operated the windshield wiper. It was hazardous! Shortly thereafter, our friendly neighbor, the welder, came to the rescue. He ripped out the canvas part of the top and soldered a three square foot piece of galvanized metal to join the metal fringes. Now it was rainproof! After a few months the motor of "Clotilda" gave up.

I tried desperately to buy a new streamlined Studebaker from the dealer in Geneva. Having ordered a new car months earlier, I could never find out where I stood on the waiting list. In this sellers market new car dealers had long lists of very impatient potential customers. New cars still had government-controlled prices. Rumors prevailed of dealers accepting sums of money "under the table."Used cars, however low or high the mileage, sold at whatever the market dictated. Finally, during the winter I found a two-tone green very low-mileage 1946 four-door Chevrolet at a used car dealership priced at $1,850. Was the mileage accurate? I had no way of knowing, for in those days a skilled mechanic could easily turn back the odometer. Compared with pre-war prices, the $1,850 asking price was outrageous. Jan and I talked it over aware that we were at the mercy of the market. We bought the car. I said to her "We have no choice; but I'm confident we will never again pay this much for a car!" What foresight! Every 5,000 miles the motor required a new water pump.

We enjoyed watching Lisha grow. She enjoyed her swing everyday and romped in the yard. She looked at and learned letters on the "refrigeberator" door. I sowed lawn grass seed and planted a small vegetable garden. Jan did much to decorate and make the house a real home. I did carpenter work with Dad building new homes until school opened in September. Jan, the experienced saleslady, worked two days per week in a local shoe store. To add to our income, Jan and I served as bookkeepers for a nearby automobile service station. We became active in the First Presbyterian Church. I taught a Sunday school class. We chose a physician, Dr. James Burke, an insurance agent, Kenneth Runyon who was a fellow church member, and a lawyer whose name I cannot recall to handle our legal contracts. We already had a banker. With no money to invest we had no need for a broker.

School opened after Labor Day. I drove to Monmouth school, a township consolidated grade and high school. At age 28, I finally launched my career. To my astonishment, there I recognized my principal, Clifton E. Striker, the former county superintendent of schools when, twenty years earlier, I was in grade school. (At that time, he occasionally came to observe the teaching and near the end of the school year he brought uniform county-wide printed final examination questions in each subject.)

I was assigned business subjects, including two sections of typing, shorthand, general business, bookkeeping and rotating study room supervision. I was appointed school treasurer. There were four teachers in the high school plus the principal who also taught several classes. Cash receipts from the cafeteria, basketball games and sales of special order books were entrusted to me. There was no school safe. I locked them in my desk where they remained until Saturday mornings when I made the weekly bank deposit. The principal wrote all the checks. Choral music was important but there was no band or orchestra.

From the first day, I enjoyed my teaching. I had

excellent rapport with my students. Most of them came from Missouri Synod Lutheran farm families, and were well disciplined. Students represented the full range of abilities and levels of motivation. Grading on the curve was then current practice. There were "A" grades and an occasional "F." I do not remember any rebuttal on grades either from students or parents. I had good relationships with the principal and the other teachers. Basketball was popular and the only seriously competitive inter-scholastic sport for which the families were avid supporters. In the spring season, with its fickle weather, baseball games were often cancelled. At events that brought them to school, I felt that I was well accepted by parents. However, only once were we invited to a parental home, the home of August Selking who next was elected the township trustee. Student attendance was excellent, except for illness.

Our son, Luther James, was born in Adams County Memorial Hospital in Decatur on January 13, 1947. I informed Dr. Burke that I would like to be present in the delivery room. Having seen natural birth among farm animals as long as I could remember, why not be present to give Jan all the encouragement that I could. In contrast to the practices at birth today, he found my request rather insulting, as he firmly refused. No doubt, I was ahead of my time. Any disappointment I felt about the delivery room request was dispelled in now having a girl and boy in our family. Lisha did not demonstrate symptoms of feeling competitive with her invading brother. Luther was a contented baby, good-natured, but always hungry. They peaceably shared the second bedroom.

At school in winter and early spring, students suffered the usual contagious diseases. After weeks of exposure to mumps among students, I contracted the childhood disease. In childhood when each of my brothers had mumps I was spared, now, I had a severe case. Although absent some ten school days; I made a full recovery. Because breast-fed infants seem to have a natural immunity to the disease, Luther, two months old, shared my bed but escaped infection.

During my first year of teaching I began graduate study

at Ball State. With Decatur teacher colleagues on Saturdays and evenings we commuted to the college campus. The school year ended uneventfully; I signed a contract for the next school year. The state legislature adopted a new salary schedule for public school teachers; my contract salary was increased from $1,925 to $2,700. With credit for my years of military service, this represented a gain of 40%. Looking back over my professional career this was my largest percentage salary increase ever.

During the summer I learned that my principal, Clifton E. Striker, was fired by the township trustee. The new principal was a middle-aged man, whose wife was a teacher. Doyle Collier, a classmate at Ball State, became the industrial arts teacher. Part time, he sold life insurance with his stepfather's firm. He had no interest in an advanced academic degree. Commuting with two other teachers, I continued my graduate studies at Ball State during the summer of 1947, evenings in the academic year following, and the summer of 1948. I was getting close to a Masters degree that was required for a permanent high school teaching or a principal's license. Jan's father volunteered an investment loan so Jan and I ambitiously purchased two adjoining lots on the other side of Decatur on Mercer Avenue. Engaging my father's construction firm, we built two more homes. These homes were larger than our abode, a story and a half with full basements. Occasionally, I was able to squeeze in a few hours of carpentry. Jan and I hoped to make a profit by selling the homes.

However, a family of four, we needed more space. In the fall of 1947, we sold our first home and moved to one of the new homes on Mercer Avenue. We took out a mortgage and repaid Jan's father the money that he had invested. Lisha, who found a good friend in the Kocher home across the street, seemed to her proud parents to be very bright. Luther was growing too rapidly to be as eager to walk as Lisha had been. But he was already venturesome, and I overlooked some of the obvious hazards for active toddlers in a home with three stairways. When Lisha started to crawl we were living in Petersburg, Virginia in a second floor apartment with a stairway that had no guard. I taught her how to crawl downstairs going backwards and she never fell. When Luther learned to crawl we had three stairways, two inside the house and one outdoors, each one with a door. Once the door to the basement was left open and he rolled down the stairs. His head suffered a bantam egg sized bump. My lesson: instead of building fences teach the children safety precautions!

I was delighted to return to the classroom for my second year. Now students knew me, I had established good relationships with them. Teaching the same courses, the second time was easier. It seemed strange to see the principal and half the teachers new. The principal appeared to be inefficient, poorly organized and at times a bungler. I had hoped to learn good administrative practices from him. Instead, I found myself more often a critic of what I regarded as inept performance. I had to remind myself that I was not there as an administrative critic; I must be the best possible teacher.

At church I was appointed superintendent of the Sunday school but taught a class only occasionally. Jan and I had formed some valued friendships in Decatur; we played bridge with Anita and Bob Macklin, a partner in an automobile dealership. That developed into an enduring friendship. Jan was busy taking care of Lisha and Luther and organizing the new home. She learned that a plumber who had a high school education, living across the street earned 40% more per year than I did; that aggravated both of us. Yet, she was fully supportive in my pursuing a Ph. D. degree that would lead to college teaching or administration. My life had been so crowded with activity that I had not seriously considered study beyond the Masters degree until Dr. Harry N. Fitch at Ball State stimulated my thinking by strongly suggesting that I enter college teaching; that required a doctorate. If I were to pursue a doctorate I was intent on earning it at a first rate university. Obviously, I was not an academic specialist; I was clearly a generalist. I was consciously in danger of expending my energies in too many directions. Had I lost clearly defined, well-focused goals? My career had been long delayed; could I make up for lost time? I had written an original research paper for the Masters degree; in the fall 1948 I was only one course short of the degree.

In addition to my other commitments, Doyle Collier persuaded me to earn a license to sell Columbus Mutual Life Insurance on a spare time basis. He stressed the commissions I could "easily" earn. I sold a few policies. I even learned that I could earn a good living selling life insurance, but I had no abiding interest in becoming an insurance agent.

I registered with a placement agency that notified me of vacancies in teaching positions across the nation. I was eager to upgrade my position to help compensate for the delays in starting my profession. I was offered a third contract at Monmouth at about the time that I learned of a position at Huntington College in Huntington, Indiana, about 35 miles away.

Jan and I visited the tiny campus dominated by old College Hall that "contained administrative offices, recitation rooms, an auditorium, the library, the print shop, literary society rooms and a lounge."(quote from the College catalogue) The College, with an enrolment of about 300 students, had recently changed from two-year to a four-year institution but it was not regionally accredited. It was owned and operated by the United Brethren in Christ Church, a small, very conservative denomination. On our second visit there the president and the dean were very solicitous. They offered me a contract at a reduction of $100 from my salary at Monmouth. They also offered small faculty housing on a large lot with detached garage for $35 rent per month.

The Academic Dean and Professor of Foreign Languages of the College, Wilford P. Musgrave, and one post-retirement faculty member, Luther Warren, had earned doctorates. The degrees of other faculty members were bachelors, some had masters degrees, two persons who also taught in the seminary had Bachelor of Divinity degrees. The president and dean gave me three titles: assistant professor of business, director of student life for men, and director of evening classes. Salary deficiency was off-set with titles!

I was excited to have two offers--one to continue at

Monmouth, and the other from Huntington College. Jan and I considered many angles. Was teaching in college important enough to reduce our annual income by $100? Having taught only two years at Monmouth might cause the prospective employer to infer that I was dismissed. Were we really willing to sell our new home and move into a much smaller one? Did we want to leave our newly acquired friends and begin over in a new community? Without my Masters degree what were my chances of getting an offer from a stronger college at a higher salary? All of her life Jan had been accustomed to moving with her family every two or three years. She was readily adventurous. Accustomed to living in one farm home for 20 years before college, I had been disturbed by the unsettledness that attended military service. If college teaching was my career direction, I had to realize that beginning college teachers were sometimes paid less than high school teachers. As a struggling private college, Huntington had no legally required pay scale. If I were to undertake summer doctoral study at a university in the Chicago area, at Chicago or Northwestern, there was excellent railway service between Huntington and Chicago.

Boldly, I accepted the Huntington offer after Jan and I had considerably agonized over the $100 salary cut. We hastily sold our home at public auction and moved. We had already survived some high-risk decisions and actions; this might turn out to be a propitious move. Some of our friends had their doubts. My dad accommodatingly turned his truck and trailer into a low cost "U Haul" for us. Although he had become accepting of his sons' high school education, even college, but this move was especially puzzling to him.

Our small new home in Huntington was located on Fruit Street in a row of faculty housing. We had a detached garage that housed the car and a heavily used sandbox for the kids. The ubiquitous swings were remounted, and there was ample room for a garden. Lisha and Luther shared a bedroom with bunk beds. Adventurous Luther played in the fresh tar in the street. His mother cleaned him with firm prohibitions. But he did it at least once more. He also experimented by inserting a hairpin into a wall plug. He blew the fuse, but fortunately was not injured. Already a venturesome child, he exhibited strong individuality. The children quickly found playmates across the street. College students, including the president's daughter, were readily available for babysitting.

Jan quickly had the house in order. Within a few months she was selling *Childcraft,* a childrens' encyclopedia on which our children were reared. She won a free set. I moved into my office in the new men's dormitory to begin my double duty as teacher and administrator.

Elmer Becker, President, with B.A and D.D. degrees from Huntington College, was very personable, of middle age, an experienced father but much more minister than educator. He had no military service, but he ideally envisioned young men's rooms ready for inspection at any hour. Having grown up with six younger brothers and endured my share of military inspections, I was unprepared to be the disciplinary inspector! I was more of a realist. In those years, each college residence hall had a surrogate "father" or "mother." I engaged Mrs. Lucile Duncan, my former housemother at Ball State in whose home I had lived ten years earlier. She sold her home in Muncie where she had served as a docent in the art gallery at Ball State. She and I had similar expectations in dealing with college men.

My class enrollments ranged from five to eighteen. Being very energetic and eager for extra income, in the second semester I added an evening course in Principles of Accounting. Jan was one of the students. Yes, she earned an "A." On Saturdays we drove to Ball State where I completed my last course for the Masters degree. Jan also registered for a history course. On one Saturday, we had a novel experience—the only time that I ever ran out of gas. Luckily, we were close to a service station.

The majority of Huntington College students were members of the very conservative United Brethren Church, mostly first generation and generally unsophisticated. Very bright students were few. Admission policy was essentially open. The College had very strict rules—no smoking, no dancing, no drinking for students and faculty. That was a completely dry three-year period in our lives. Weekly chapel was a requirement for students and faculty; as a graduate of a state college I found this a new experience. Many of the assemblies and chapel services were dull and not meaningful or interesting to students.

We became involved in the community; we joined First Presbyterian Church. We wanted an educational Sunday school for our children. The minister, David Robert Hutchinson, argued that couples with young children would not attend both church and Sunday school. Furthermore, he pointed out that there was no room for a young couple's class; there were only small rooms for young children. I challenged him asserting that we could meet around the long table in the kitchen. Couples could rotate to have coffee ready for the class to begin on schedule with discussion of assigned reading for a full hour. I promised to lead the class and argued that attendance at church service would also increase. Very skeptically he agreed on a trial run. We named it the Coffee Class. I chose books that were on religious and spiritual issues meaningful to that age group. During the first year, summer included, we averaged twenty-six in attendance. Reading the books generated vigorous discussion; durable friendships were formed or intensified. Young families attended the thriving Sunday school and church attendance increased notably. After two years, Mr. Hutchinson was delighted. At his recommendation I was nominated and elected a member of the session, ruling body of the congregation. More rooms were needed for Sunday school and plans were begun for an addition to the church.

I became an active member in the Junior Chamber of Commerce. From my youth I was a conservationist; while in grade school my parents gave me a simple Montgomery Ward fountain pen, for me a real treasure. It survived grade school, high school, college, the military years until then. One snowy Sunday morning, I discovered that my pen was missing. Where could I have lost it? I remembered that on Saturday my car was parked on the other side of the campus. I returned to that spot, and mysteriously, there I spied the pen stuck in the snow---happily recovered once more!

Early in our stay, President Becker called me to his office one day; he showed me a letter from William H. Danforth, chairman of The Danforth Foundation. Mr. Danforth was establishing a national program in colleges and universities to stimulate faculty-student relationships. He invited Dr. Becker to appoint a member of the faculty who, with the spouse, would be designated Danforth Associates. In that era, college and university tradition, especially in public institutions, faculty-student association was limited to the classroom.

The Foundation wanted couples to help build closer faculty-student relationships, by inviting students into their homes, and engaging them in educational and social activities beyond the classroom. The Danforth Associate couple was invited to the Danforth Conference at Camp Miniwanca for a week preceding Labor Day on the east shore of Lake Michigan near Muskegon. The Foundation would pay travel expenses, meals and lodging in wooden floored tents, offer a week of educational programs led by prominent speakers, and $50 to entertain students in their home during the ensuing academic year. I recalled that in my college years I was never invited to a faculty member's home. Would Jan and I accept such an appointment? We accepted with eager anticipation. The program led to many rich experiences beyond our fondest dreams and an evolving relationship with the Danforth Foundation that endured for 25 years. In our future activity, the program did indeed promote closer faculty-student relationships.

In subsequent years, Jan and I attended the week long Danforth Conferences at Camp Miniwanca six times. Mornings were committed to lectures followed by discussion groups, afternoons to recreation and evenings to songfests or religious services seated on the sand dunes, while observing the setting sun across Lake Michigan. Most of the lecturers were nationally and internationally known. Among the prominent ones were: the world renowned Toyohiko Kagawa from Japan,

James Muilenberg, Allen Wehrli, Douglas Steere, Roland Bainton, Ruth Isabel Seabury, all distinguished seminary professors, and Benjamin Mays, president of Morehouse College, who later became chairman of the Atlanta, Georgia school board. Jan and I also established friendships with college and university faculty couples from many parts of the country. Amazingly, fifty years later we still have "Sarabelle," an exotic sand, wind and water worn piece of drift wood from the dunes. It occupies a prominent spot in our retirement home. Our participation in Danforth Foundation events, national and regional produced some of our fondest memories.

During the first year at Huntington came an invitation to return to Monmouth high school as principal. August Selking had been elected township trustee succeeding George Schieferstein. Mr. Selking had several children in Monmouth school, and expressed his respect for me while I was teaching there. He learned that I had completed my Masters degree and had received a license to become a school principal. He, with his student daughter, Margaret, came to Huntington to try to persuade me to return to Monmouth as principal. Mr. Selking wanted to upgrade the school; he urged me to be the key instrument in that process. Jan and I extensively discussed this offer; it was very flattering. Importantly, it provided some assurance that I was in the right profession. However, by then my aspirations had irrevocably turned toward a doctorate and college teaching. I declined Mr. Selking's offer to his deep disappointment. I have never regretted that decision.

In this crowded year another very important event occurred. On March 30, 1949 our third child and second daughter, Margaret Sue, was born. She was named after her two grandmothers. From the beginning she was a very contented child, eating, sleeping and sucking her thumb. She was well accepted by her older brother and sister. Our small home was full, three children in one bedroom. This was an unfortunate scaling down of home space, convenience, heating and ventilation. The crowded conditions were not only burdensome for Jan. Our physician, Dr. Thomas James also convinced us, that it affected the health of the family. I tried valiantly to persuade President Becker that we needed more space but he claimed complications because the home was financed by the Federal Home Administration. In our third and last year at Huntington College he finally accepted a plan to enlarge and improve the house. However, the project had not been started when we moved to Evanston many months later.

In our second year at Huntington, Luther contracted rheumatic fever. We attributed it in part to the poor ventilation in the house combined with his frequent tonsil infection. The prescriptions for rheumatic fever at the time were to prevent the afflicted one from becoming excited, kept quiet and sedate without walking, with plenty of rest. The only medication was aspirin. Luther had been walking very well, and keeping an energetic boy off his feet was a major struggle for his mother. Several members of the Coffee Class offered to be helpful; one mother with noble intentions brought a small puppy that Luther instantly loved. However, Dr. James ruled out the pet as generating too much excitement. Painfully, we returned the winsome little puppy to the donor. Lisha had started school and had reached the age at which she was helpful in caring for Luther and Margaret. After a few months when Luther recovered, he had to learn to walk again. In due time his tonsils were removed; happily he suffered no physical damage.

During the first year at Huntington, I requested application forms for a doctoral program from three universities, Chicago, Illinois and Northwestern; I applied at the University of Illinois at Urbana-Champaign and Northwestern in Evanston, Illinois, fronting on Lake Michigan. In due course I was admitted to both. I chose Northwestern because of the restricted number of doctoral students and the convenience of rail travel between Huntington and Evanston. In the summer of 1949, I began my studies toward the Ph. D. program that required one year in residence and competence in French and German. Northwestern did not require the Graduate Record Examination. Instead, I completed the eight-hour Ohio State Examination that tested both knowledge and endurance. I do not recall the score but I was notified that my performance was satisfactory.

I continued to enjoy my teaching at Huntington College; students were responsive at different intellectual levels. Many students used the library only very sparingly. The College catalog of 1950-51 contains this statement, "For a number of years the library has been located on the second floor of College Hall and occupies four large rooms. The book collection consists of over 16,000 volumes covering various fields of learning." The very modest collection included many gifts from ministers' personal libraries on their retirement, and substantial "weeding" was needed. The library had a token budget for acquisitions.

Many of the students showed minimal writing skills, although there were a few notable exceptions. Most of the faculty were members of the supporting denomination, United Brethren in Christ. Their work was generally routine. Intellectual vitality, creativity and innovation were rarely evident. Conduct of faculty meetings was low key and uninspiring. Debates of significant intellectual or curricular issues seldom occurred. Wilford Musgrave, the Academic Dean, was weak and unimaginative. Reputedly among students his teaching was very pedantic. In the president and dean, I did not observe either one to be a strong leader or model in his position.

In many respects, I was unfortunate to begin my college teaching at Huntington College. Not regionally accredited, its institutional priorities were misguided. Instead of being surrounded by model educators, many of my administrative and faculty colleagues were only marginally qualified for their positions. The buildings were inadequate, and much of the equipment in the science laboratories, the gymnasium and other facilities was obsolete. Despite all the financial academic needs, the College began a football program. In addition to being underpaid, the faculty was much too small. Faculty commitments of Christian faith, which I did not sign, were essentially those required for membership in the supporting denomination. To circumvent the faith requirement, President Becker employed more degreed and competent faculty part-time. However, they were omitted from the faculty roster in the catalog, perhaps so as not to be visible to the Board of Trustees that contained several Bishops of the United Brethren in Christ Church. I saw much that needed improvement; but in this place I could not experience quality in teaching and learning. How could one advance from this level of college education to the challenges faced in a college or university of top quality? How could I rise from the midst of faculty and administrators many who were not employable in a stronger college? For me who entered the profession with many limitations, this was indeed a formidable question underpinning my aspirations. As I ardently desired to overcome my deficiencies, to earn the Ph. D. at a first rank university and advance soundly in the profession were the challenges that I faced.

Chapter 19:

In Pursuit of the Doctorate at Northwestern University

1949-1952

In the summer terms of 1949, 1950 and 1951, I was registered in courses and seminars in education and psychology at Northwestern University leading toward the Doctor of Philosophy degree. Early every Monday morning I kissed Jan and the children good-bye and boarded the Erie Railroad passenger train for Chicago. The two and half--hour ride provided good time for study. At the Chicago station I boarded the elevated train--the "L"--for a forty-five minute ride to the University campus in Evanston. Much of the week was spent in Deering Library. I ate meals in one of the nearby cafeterias and roomed in one of the fraternity houses fronting on Lake Michigan. On Fridays after my last class I made the return trip to Huntington to be with the family.

My pace was wearying. At home, Jan took care of the children, canned vegetables from the garden, washed, sun-dried and ironed clothes, and kept the house and lawn in good condition. Her tasks were doubly difficult during the time of Luther's illness with rheumatic fever and when Margaret suffered a broken nose from a direct hit by one of the swing seats. Valiantly, Jan managed remarkably well during the weekdays. When I returned home each Friday evening I provided her some relief from the manifold home maintenance tasks. On weekends the family shared each meal around the kitchen table. Unless illness interrupted all family members were in Sunday school and church.

In the masters degree program at Ball State, I had focussed chiefly on counseling combined with courses in educational administration. At Northwestern the doctoral program courses built on those sequences. At Ball State, psychology and education courses were in the education department. At Northwestern some counseling courses were in the education department, while psychology courses were in

221

this department. One of my most memorable and career-shaping courses was taught by Dr. Rudolph Dreikurs, an Adlerian psychiatrist, Professor of Psychiatry at Chicago Medical School. Since I completed that course, several of his books have had a prominent place in my personal library. Among them are *The Challenge of Marriage, The Challenge of Parenthood* and *Psychology in the Classroom*. Several of my earlier courses were based on the psychology of Sigmund Freud or Carl Rogers. Although at the time Adlerian psychology had fallen into lesser repute, Dreikurs made it come alive with ready application in parenting and teaching. Other courses and seminars were also very demanding. Later, while in residence I completed one quarter of internship in the Vocational Counseling Center on Northwestern's Chicago campus.

Many doctoral candidates feared the French and German language requirement as a formidable obstacle. Some students settled for the Doctor of Education degree that required more courses but no foreign language. I was determined that I would not compromise my pursuit of the Doctor of Philosophy degree. Northwestern required that both language requirements be completed before the student was permitted to address the subject and undertake research for the dissertation. I had completed two years of Latin in high school. Cognates in Latin, German and English helped me learn French more rapidly. I completed the five-week course offered especially for doctoral students and I passed the examination. Because I had studied German vocabulary, reading, grammar and writing for six years of my grade school, followed by a year of German in high school and participated in German language Sunday school until I was fifteen, I took the examination to determine how much I needed to study.

The timed examination required translation of classical German into written English. I anxiously awaited the results. Papers were graded with a numerical score; 70 was passing, my grade was 69 1/2! I was dumbfounded. On inquiry, I learned that the examination was prepared and graded by Professor Hoffman, a native of Germany and head of the department of German. Reportedly, he was determined that no doctoral students would pass the German examination without real mastery of the language. In my appointment with him he was formal but courteous. I said, "Sir, I do not understand why you graded me within one-half point of passing, yet made no comment on my paper to tell me where my errors are." He smiled and replied, "Mr. Nussbaum, I see that you know much German; but I believe that a little review would be good for you."

I borrowed books from the library written by Johann Wolfgang von Goethe, Heinrich Heine and Johann Christoph Friedrich von Schiller, among other classical German authors. On weekends with the help of a neighbor native to the German sector of Switzerland I translated readings into English. I also reviewed vocabulary. Again I, with about forty other students, tackled the German examination. I was notified that one other student and I were successful. Professor Hoffman did not return the paper or give me the score. Hallelujah!

The chair of the doctoral committee is the key person in interpreting the expectations of the department of study and interpreting the standards of the university. The chair can be a significant facilitator or a dedicated obstructor in determining the length of time required by a doctoral candidate to complete the requirements for the degree. My chair was Dr. Shirley A. Hamrin, Professor of Education. Other committee members were faculty of the Psychology and Education departments. At every turn Dr. Hamrin was as eager as Jan and I were for me to receive the degree; he pushed and pulled in my favor. He arranged the date for my qualifying examination. After Dr. Hamrin read my answers to the examination questions he did not issue a grade but spoke very positively of my writing. "You are now ready to proceed with the research for your dissertation;" he said encouragingly, " I expect to see you in that doctoral graduation line next June."

In those post-war years, housing on and around the campus was still very, very scarce. Northwestern had retained some metal Quonset huts that were rented to married graduate students. These huts were even smaller than our home in

Huntington. However, I placed my name on the waiting list in the summer of 1950, hoping for Jan and the children to accompany me while I was in residence beginning in late summer 1951. The housing office gave me little hope that a vacancy would occur, even when I registered, and in subsequent months prospects continued to be dim. I made many other rental housing inquiries among residents in the campus area. In summer 1950 I learned of an available apartment in the home owned by the widow of a Free Methodist bishop that was just a few blocks from the campus. In applying I assured her that we would be fully responsible renters. We signed an agreement for the academic year 1951-52. There was hope!

However, a few months later the owner wrote to me that the status of a very loyal member of her church overrode our agreement therefore she was renting it to her rather than to us. What could we do? Take her to court? Publicize her lack of integrity among her neighbors? Even if ordered by the court to reinstate our agreement would we want to share a home with a humiliated, angry landlord? We decided that we better start our search once more. As I undertook my studies again, Jan and I were very distressed.

Because I had resigned from my teaching position, we had to vacate the home in Huntington in August; what were our options? Jan's mother and father who lived in Greenville, Ohio, said they were preparing the upstairs rooms in the parsonage. If we found no housing, Jan and the children could reside with them for the year while I continued my commuting to and from Evanston. Jan and I considered this as the last resort. We had dealt with other problems that at the time appeared insoluble; faith combined with unrelenting action sometimes turns up answers that we could not have imagined. As I commuted home on Friday before the last week of summer term I struggled with the dilemma. I had faith; now, what should be the action?

On that Friday evening and Saturday Jan and I tried to explore all our options. We decided that on Sunday afternoon we would drive to Evanston; I would complete my classes and examinations. She would devote all her time for one week to searching for housing. We called my mother who lived 35 miles away who said she would be delighted to care for the children for that week. The children enjoyed visiting grandma, grandpa and romping on the farm. As we drove to Evanston, with bestirred minds we made a list of ways Jan could tackle the seemingly impossible housing search. Commuting by the "L" Jan stayed with relatives who lived in Cicero, another west Chicago suburb. I returned to the fraternity house. Our list of possible quests was forbiddingly long, yet Jan attacked it courageously. We read the real estate sections of newspapers; including the canvassing of adds of large estates in Evanston, Skokie, and New Trier. Perhaps they might want a live-in gardener and offer a garage apartment. Jan would visit real estate offices to study their listings and read the few newspaper listings of rental property.

Monday morning Jan visited Quinlan & Tyson real estate office near the campus. She learned that minutes before her arrival a large three-story home with a full basement was listed for rent, located on Orrington avenue about a thousand feet from Northwestern's main library. The husband of the couple, with three young children, was recalled into military service related to the Korean War. Realizing the scarcity of housing for families with young children, they considerately offered to rent their home for a year to a responsible family. A back wing contained rooms with separate entrances. The owners permitted renting rooms to graduate students. On the third floor there was an apartment suitable for a young couple. The location was ideal; renting rooms should be easy. For a renter prospect to view the property, Quinlan and Tyson required a deposit of $100 with positive reference reports as to character, reliability and financial accountability.

After Jan looked at the home she called me with breathless astonishment. The rental agent called Dr. Hamrin and our bank as references. Dr. Hamrin assured the agent that whatever agreement we signed would be carried out faultlessly and that we were financially accountable. We signed a contract to lease the home for one year; the monthly rental was $250 (annually $3,000. We had no medical, health or liability insurance.) plus telephone, electrical power and gas bills. In effect, we committed ourselves to become sub-landlords; we had approximately one month to move from Huntington, Indiana to Evanston, to rent and furnish the student rooms, and get myself organized for research on my doctoral dissertation. We had to acquire furniture to supplement our own combined with what the owners left.

Back in Huntington in a few days, we packed the family into the car and headed off to another adventure. Once more Dad brought his truck and trailer, gamely loaded our few pieces of furniture, and headed for Evanston, a distance of nearly two hundred miles. When we arrived we placed each piece of furniture. Then Jan took inventory of what more was needed to accommodate two double rooms for students on the second floor and the apartment on the third floor. I shopped at the Salvation Army, Goodwill, and other stores that sold previously owned furniture. I even built some small worktables. Because of the convenient location, in a few days we had rented our rooms to four single men and the third floor apartment to a young Garrett Seminary couple, who readily served as our resident baby sitters. One of the young men, a graduate student in music, became the piano teacher for Lisha. For our family's needs the home was ideally commodious. The children had a play ground in the backyard. We had a large dining room; the owners left their dining room furniture and the piano. The study off the dining room was spacious and conveniently arranged. Bedrooms and baths were well arranged for room renters. The children slept in one room.

The large, heavy wooden storm windows were stored in the basement. With extension ladders, I installed them before winter set in. After being confined in the small residence in Huntington, our family greatly enjoyed the spacious home with playrooms in the basement during inclement weather. Lisha attended school, Luther had an early January birthday. After testing, the school declared Luther at age four and a half ready for Kindergarten. In the evenings, Margaret, at age one and a half, was already Lisha's pupil. The nearby streets and the city of Evanston at that time were regarded as safe, quite in contrast to the safety concerns of today.

How was this entrepreneurial enterprise financed? When we moved in we had less than $500 cash. Our income consisted of approximately $330 per month from the Veterans Educational Program, popularly known as the G. I. Bill, plus income from rented rooms. The G. I. Bill also paid tuition at Northwestern. Fortunately, we had no debts and no credit cards. When Jan had the household organized, she ambitiously took an evening waitress job at the Huddle, a student restaurant-snack bar on the ground floor of the Orrington Hotel about four blocks from our residence. In the spring quarter while writing the dissertation I taught two 45-minute bookkeeping classes in mid-afternoon at New Trier High School, approximately five miles from our home. Fortunately, we had a positive cash flow, lived moderately and at the end of the year had more cash than at the beginning. We even bought very attractive, like new, Duncan Phyfe dining room furniture from a family in a large Evanston home that periodically shed its furniture and decor. In early fall, late spring and summer Jan and the children, with great enjoyment, used the Lake Michigan beaches adjoining the campus. The family attended First Presbyterian Church, several times enjoyed the Brookfield Zoo, Chicago museums, and Evanston parks. The children remember that their mother took them to movies on Saturday. Regrettably, Jan and I were so busily occupied that we could attend only a few of the many cultural, educational and athletic events at the University.

Relocation consumed a lot of time and energy. In the weeks between the end of the summer quarter and the beginning of the fall quarter, I made very little progress toward the research related to the dissertation. School counseling as a field of study had considerably evolved during the World War II era leading to state counselor certification. Counseling involved testing and personality inventory to refine vocational selection and predict vocational success. Compared with today's instruments, processes, and diagnostic tools those instruments of data collection and analyses were indeed crude.

I completed a counseling practicum on the Chicago campus at The Vocational Counseling Center. As part of the Evening College, beyond the typical age of undergraduate students most clients were seeking vocational guidance or career redirection. We used such instruments of that day as the ACE Psychological Test, Strong Vocational Interest Inventory, Kuder Preference Record, The Minnesota Multiphasic Personality Inventory, Wechsler-Bellevue Adult Scale to provide data about the client.

The client registered, stated his/her reason for being there. Then the head counselor assigned the client to one of the graduate students. Typically, client problems were related to unhappiness with a job, seeking guidance in changing careers, or trying to understand why he or she had been fired from a previous position. Not infrequently the client may have found it easier to establish rapport with the counselor by expressing surface issues, hoping that if the climate felt safe, he could gradually move toward the underlying or deeper problems. Some clients seemed to express concerns or anxieties by layers as if peeling an onion; perhaps it would take many layers of peeling to uncover the heart of the problem, the central issue or concern.

One client whose case was assigned to me I well remember as a prime example of this process. The man was employed in the Chicago mayor's public relations office; his initial statement was considering changing his job. When I suggested administering some of the tests and inventories, he pleaded that we postpone the tests. He said he needed to tell me more about himself. He served in the military during the war as an enlisted man. His wife worked as a civilian and over time they purchased a number of War Bonds that they tucked away in a bank safety deposit box.

After he returned from military service a daughter was born. He advanced in his work and later accepted a position in the mayor's office. His wife was very eager to buy a home. He hesitated but finally acceded. As they approached the settlement date he became extremely anxious, as was obvious by the anxiety that he exhibited. Why was he anxious?

Sometime earlier he had a homosexual encounter in a restroom with a man who turned out to be a plainclothes policeman. He was arrested at the scene. This put him in grave legal jeopardy and shattered his self-image. In negotiation, the officer proposed to release him for a specified sum in payment. The client was beside himself, totally unnerved. What would this do to him and to his family? The substantial sum that the officer demanded represented most of what he and his wife had saved in War Bonds. He gathered the War Bonds, signed his name, forged his wife's signature and paid his blackmail.

With the home purchase settlement date just ahead how would he explain the absence of the War Bonds to his wife? His anxiety knew no bounds! Further, he had recently developed a highly conspicuous, several inch radius bald spot on the back of his head. He interpreted this as divine labeling of him as a culprit; perhaps he committed the "unforgivable sin against the Holy Spirit.". What shall he do? This session was followed by several more. When the quarter ended; he was assigned to another counselor.

The Practicum and testing, interviewing and classifying of military service men had given me considerable experience in counseling. However, I did not feel that should be my career, although many of the cases were very interesting and challenging. My mind and heart were set on teaching. Dr. Hamrin had offered me dissertation material based on a proposed study to interview and analyze top executives of major corporations to compare effectiveness of different styles of leadership. An association of corporations offered to finance the cost of the study but I declined that offer. Because the association was financing it I would have to meet their requirements that might take longer to conduct the research and write the dissertation than I had planned. Also, I did not want to engage in a project that might divert me from higher education. I felt that I had endured enough diversions and delays.

I settled on a dissertation project that dealt with the problems of college students from the students' perspectives. Counselors, administrators and faculty at a college or university observe student behavior, hear student complaints and criticisms, conduct interviews either at student or staff initiative learning student problems at whatever level students choose to reveal them. They keep records, render decisions and make judgments based on what they learn. As studies have shown, it is difficult for some students to reveal their innermost thoughts or problems to a person employed by the institution, despite assurances that all information is completely confidential. If a professional counselor in no way connected with the college or university were to interview a random sample of students about their concerns and problems would those results be significantly different from what the employed staff knows or perceives.

I presented my thesis topic and plan to Dr. Hamrin; he raised a number of questions and made suggestions that resulted in several modifications. After he approved the plan, I submitted it to President John R. Emens, of Ball State University with the request that I conduct the project on that campus. After discussing my plan with the Dean of Students, Dr. O. T. Richardson, Dr. Emens gave his assent.

The student sample was selected and I conducted the interviews and collected the data. The IBM Center in Evanston punched the data into cards that were then standard procedure. In principle, the cards were similar to the Form 20 used in the U. S. Army. That was the most widely used system for recording, manipulating and analyzing research data. Incidentally, I found some errors in the punching of the data cards. Admitting the mistakes, the Center gave me a discount that was meaningful in the budget of a doctoral student.

To celebrate the New Year, 1952, I began the tedious task of manipulating and analyzing the data. Sorting cards with the needle reminded me of the Army experiences, except that these data were all mine! The tasks were greatly facilitated by having my large, private study with suitable desks and tables. Having known other students who suffered disastrous loss of dissertation material, Dr. Hamrin insisted that as soon as I had a draft of a chapter, I place a carbon copy in the safe in his office. (Copy machines were not in vogue.) I composed on my manual typewriter. Corrections on the original and carbon copies, however, were tediously made with an eraser. The penalty for typing errors was inordinate time consumption and messiness!

Jan was a fast typist, so when I completed a draft and proofed it, she prepared the revised copy, greatly speeding up the process. Late afternoon each day, I deposited a copy of the newly typed pages in the safe of the College of Education. With our multiple tasks, the stresses on each of us were very exhausting.

By springtime, I had made good progress in writing the dissertation. Dr. Hamrin, always accommodating and prodding, critically read each chapter. I made suggested changes and produced the final copies. By late April, I submitted the completed dissertation and the attendant summary. Professor Hamrin of the Education department and Professor Irwin Berg of the Psychology department were the principal members of my doctoral committee. Together they set the date for the final oral examination by all the members of the committee. Although I was confident, as I approached the examination date I was nevertheless highly anxious. Just suppose I did not pass! When I considered all the sacrifices that Jan and the children had made, all the time and energy we had expended, what would I do now if I failed?

When I entered the room, the committee was assembled. They probed me with questions about my choice of subject, my research plan, the collection of data, the analysis procedures, the principal findings of the study. Was I planning to prepare this for publication? I hesitantly admitted that I would prefer not to have to look at these data any longer

Dr. Hamrin turned to the future. "What kind of position do you plan to seek for next year?" "What do you expect to do ten years from now?" To each question, I replied with vague answers because I had been too intensely occupied with the dissertation that I had not thought much about the future. At the conclusion, he said to me, "Ten years from years from now you should be a college president." I was greatly surprised; I had not entertained such a goal. Then I remembered that he had once told me that he had been elected to the presidency of Hamline University in St. Paul, Minnesota. However, before he took office he had a severe heart attack. As he recovered his physicians advised him not to take such a strenuous position. Later, I often wondered if he were projecting his aspirations onto me.

In dismissing me, Chairman Hamrin asked me to wait in an adjoining room. In a few minutes I was invited back. Dr. Hamrin told me the committee voted unanimously that I passed with commendation. He added, "Prepare yourself to receive the Doctor of Philosophy degree at commencement on Deering Meadow." I sincerely thanked the committee, and especially Dr. Hamrin for all his help and sustained encouragement. As I walked home to inform Jan, I said a prayer of thanksgiving. We had reached another milestone.

On June 16, 1952, dressed in my doctoral cap, gown and Northwestern University hood, I marched to the commencement site on the spacious Deering Meadow; somehow I was less confident of how much I knew than I was at my eighth grade Adams County commencement in 1931. I was so much more aware of the vast gulf of "unknowing" that by contrast, my knowledge seemed miniaturized. Our family rejoiced together at the cultivation of the life of the mind. Now, what adventures lay ahead?

Chapter 20: Professional Career Advances

1952-1958

The Superintendent of Schools at New Trier, Dr. Mathew Gaffney, where I had taught bookkeeping, at his initiative invited me for an interview. Here was the prospect of a position, not yet fully described, in one of the best high schools in the central part of the country. What a possibility! Could I be lured back into a high school teaching or an administrative position? Jan and I discussed this at length. New Trier was an upper-scale income community, the school system was excellent, housing was very expensive. Did we want this urban setting in which to raise our children? Could teachers afford to live in the area, or did they have to commute from areas where living costs are lower? I was flattered by the invitation but declined the interview; I decided to pursue a college position.

When I inquired at the University placement office, I learned that many small colleges had teaching and administrative positions open. I prepared my resume' and sent it to the presidents of a number of mid-western colleges, most of them related to the Presbyterian Church. I decided to apply only to private colleges where teaching was the central purpose. With smaller enrolments I would have opportunity to know students as individuals. In a private college, without cumbersome state regulations, changes in curriculum, policies and practices could be more easily achieved. In a smaller institution I would have a more direct impact on policies and closer working relationships with faculty—I could make a difference.

Some presidents replied that they had no appropriate position open, while others did not respond. Two presidents wrote at length about their openings at Alma College in Michigan and at the University of Dubuque in Iowa. The president of Alma College wrote several pages in longhand about the head of the business administration department position trying to persuade me to come for an interview. The

President of Dubuque, the Rev. Dr. Rollo LaPorte, replied promptly to report two vacancies, one as dean of the college and the other as dean of students. I learned that Dr. Milo Rediger, interim dean of the college for the past two years, was returning to that position at Taylor University, Upland, Indiana. -Among the various openings these two appeared worth exploring. When Dr. LaPorte came to Chicago to talk with me, we had a congenial meeting me at the Planters Hotel after which he invited Jan and me to the University for an extended interview.

The State of Iowa had a historic reputation for quality education. Though Jan's family had lived in more than one city in Iowa, I had never been west of the Mississippi River. We drove to Dubuque, fascinated by the city of rolling hills overlooking the mighty Mississippi. Founded in 1852, The University consisted of a College of Liberal Arts and a Theological Seminary, with total enrolment around 500 students, about 400 in the College. There were two Roman Catholic colleges in the city, Clarke College for women and Loras College for men. After two days of interviews I told Dr. LaPorte that I was interested in becoming the dean of the college. With my limited experience in an inferior college, I had not learned how scant my qualifications were for the position. Some faculty were at the College before I was in the first grade; at age 34 I did not consider how they would interpret my audacity were I to accept the position as academic dean. Colleges and universities did not have faculty search committees at that time; faculty and administrators were appointed at the discretion of the president with board approval.

I discussed the position with Dr. Hamrin; he thought it would be a good challenge for me. He told me the position should pay a minimum of $5,000; I accepted the position effective July 1, 1952 at a salary of $4,500 with subvention for an eight-room residence across the street from the campus and a promise of free tuition for Jan to complete her degree. Two years earlier, Dr. LaPorte had appointed Dr. Elwyn A. Smith, about my age, as Dean of the Theological Seminary. From my present perspective, a wiser president would not have appointed either one of us because we had inadequate experience. Administrative changes were waiting in the wings. Within the year of my arrival, the Board dismissed Dr. LaPorte who returned to the ministry, and appointed in his stead the Rev. Gaylord Couchman, a local Presbyterian minister, to the presidency.

My appointment was effective July 1,1952 just after my thirty-fourth birthday. Our home lease in Evanston ended in mid-August and the home in Dubuque was not vacant. I began my work as scheduled while the family remained in Evanston. The children still fondly recall summer days at the beach on Lake Michigan. I lived with the Mihelic family; Dr. Joseph Mihelic was Professor of Old Testament in the Seminary. On weekends I returned to Evanston.

I moved into the office of the dean of the college in Steffens Hall adjoining the president's office; his office had a window air-conditioner, mine did not. The office was located directly above the basement chemistry laboratory, at times very odiferous. I was introduced to the staff and to faculty who were on campus. The seminary dean, faculty and staff were located in another building.

Dr. Milo Rediger, my predecessor, whom I had once met, years earlier, had already returned to his previous position at Taylor University where my brothers Elmer and Milo graduated. Dr. Rediger left the office in good order, with some part-time faculty yet to be appointed. I was immediately introduced to a controversial issue on many liberal arts campuses. Faculty opinion was divided on whether home economics, accounting, typing and shorthand courses should continue to be offered. Liberal arts purists were eager to delete all those vocational course offerings; others with a more practical turn of mind were strongly persuaded to continue and expand on those offerings. With the president's support, I made temporary or part-time adjunct faculty appointments to teach these courses allowing time for further consideration. I made no friends among the liberal arts faculty; gradually I learned that this was a minority view. The next year by faculty vote typing and shorthand were dropped. A few influential Dubuque alumnae brought their influence to bear so that home economics was retained although enrolment was very small. Accounting, for which there was great student demand, was retained; I agreed to teach accounting for the time being until a faculty member could be found.

In mid-August a moving van from Dubuque transported our furniture to the two-story home on University Avenue, with a full basement; the house was much smaller than our rented home in Evanston. Once more we had to scale down. The move was rather uneventful with a messy exception--in loading the van the driver placed a can half-full of lard on top of furniture and blankets. In transit in the summer heat the lard melted, the upset can poured lard over the contents below! Never before had I seen such a morass of molten lard, greased blankets, comforters and furniture!

Our family was warmly welcomed; the children quickly found playmates and friends. Schools were within walking distance for Lisha and Luther; Margaret had a playmate her age next door, Alex Hansen. A faculty family lived in each home on the long block, with one exception, the home of a shoe repairman. The academically indoctrinated children called him Dr. Sieg. He enjoyed the "honorary degree." The childless couple, generous with cookies and candy, became good friends of the youngsters.

Our family quickly discovered Eagle Point Park on a bluff several hundred feet above a lock and dam in the Mississippi River. Summer picnics, beautiful oak, hickory, elm and maple trees, play equipment combined with watching freight traffic move through the locks attracted persons of all ages. We joined Westminster Presbyterian Church downtown; I became active in the Kiwanis Club. Jan registered for courses at the University to complete her degree as rapidly as possible. She found friends among faculty wives, especially a close neighbor Pat, spouse of Dr. Edward Thorne, newly appointed theater professor also from Northwestern. Jan and I developed friendships with young couples from the church, Kiwanis Club and especially with our pediatrician, Dr. John Graves and his wife Jane. I quickly learned that the academic dean must not establish close friendships with selective faculty members. He must be an even-handed dean to all members of the faculty, never to give the appearance of possible favoritism.

The University, founded as the German Theological School in the Northwest, had a history of educating ministers and missionaries, while having accepted financially needy immigrants from central Europe and Mexico. The institution gradually developed into a college of liberal arts and a graduate theological seminary; it had regained its regional accreditation that had been lost during the financial depression of the thirties. The physical plant was old and the financial condition was weak. Faculty members in the College included a combination of very devoted men and women with Masters degrees and many years of service joined by post World War II appointees with doctorates. In contrast, most Seminary faculty had doctorates. Salaries were marginal with no well-defined salary scale. New appointees were paid what the market required; after some teaching experience most of them would move to a stronger academic institution. Faculty members in the first category included William B. Zuker, Professor of Chemistry, who also had the title of vice-president and secretary to the board; Anna Aitchison, Professor of English (Phi Beta Kappa); Dorothy Taylor, Professor of Physics; Hazel Rothlisberger, Associate Professor of Mathematics; and William G. Rozeboom, Registrar and Professor of History. They and some of their colleagues, among 35 full-time faculty, including C. T. Peterson, Professor of Physical Education, were largely responsible for the survival of the institution. Their teaching experience was mostly at Dubuque. They had not been engaged in professional organizations for so long that they had lost interest in doing so. When I offered Miss Aitchison and Miss Rothlisberger an all-expense paid trip to attend a regional professional conference they refused the invitation, claiming that they would not know any other faculty members in their disciplines. Several departments had only one full-time faculty member--a very serious deficiency.

The dean of the college and the dean of the seminary

operated quite separately with distinctive student bodies between the college and the seminary. Each presided at the respective faculty meeting. There were no University-wide faculty meetings and very little association or sharing between the two faculties. In recent years there had been no dean of men or women in the college; Frank Bretz was appointed dean of students. He was a rather prissy person, lacked the large vision, the effective organizing ability, and the inner psychological security required in such a position. After two years he moved on.

Admissions policy in the college was inadequately defined; in fact, admission was granted to nearly all applicants. The catalog claim of the University "to serve the whole Church and the World" was slightly reflected in its student body with about 4% international students. There were also some exceptional students. In my third year two seniors in national competition won Danforth Foundation Fellowships for graduate study planning to make college teaching a career. Both of them were highly successful as professors and administrators in distinguished universities. But the disparity between them and the wide range of students of lesser abilities required faculty to teach across a wide academic spectrum.

In athletics, the coaches in football, basketball and track programs, and particularly the Athletic Director, Kenneth E. Mercer, who had been a professional football player, recruited some talented athletes who were very marginal students. Academic ineligibility in sports often thinned the athletic squads. The coaches and the Academic Standards Committee of the faculty, that included William B. Rozeboom, Registrar, who with mathematical rigidity, wanted the college standards enforced. Understandably, Mercer and Rozeboom were often at odds. As dean, I was in between the combatants having to enforce the Committee's decisions with athletes and their parents. The Reverend Gaylord Couchman D. D., had become president on April 1, 1953 during my first year. Because of the change in presidents, the board decided to delay issuing of faculty contracts from the usual date of March 1 until April 15. That won no accolades for me.

Couchman had been an athlete in a college that had not survived. He faced the specter of raising additional funds to replace the lost tuition income from failed athletes. From my perspective I saw no future for the institution by retaining athletes who were failing students. The University had almost no endowment and suffered a serious deficiency in cash flow. Without a good development staff, fund-raising devolved mostly on the president. A large percentage of the alumni were teachers, ministers, missionaries, and in other social service careers. Very few had accumulated significant wealth. Support from Presbyterian congregations was diminishing; when church budgets had to be cut the colleges were often the first to be deleted. The percentage of regular alumni donors was much below national averages. Fundraising by President LaPorte had been far below expectations.

In addition to a lack of capital funds, building maintenance was badly in arrears. The library, located in rooms in Steffens Hall, was woefully inadequate. The bookstore, across the street, shelved mostly textbooks. Residence halls were obsolete. There had been no new construction on campus in more than twenty years. The current business manager was a young mathematician with no appropriate experience. When President Couchman took office, he named a friend, former minister and admissions officer, The Reverend Harry Turner, as business manager. When I asked President Couchman what were the qualifications of Mr. Turner, he pointed out that he very frugally managed the finances of his family of four children. It seemed to me an unlikely preparation to manage business affairs of an academic institution. The University, already in financial disarray, had a president and a business manager neither of whom with any academic experience or training.

It became obvious to me that I had not asked nearly enough questions before I accepted this position. Admittedly, my initial performance was inadequate, but I was a diligent and rapid learner. My office was open to all. I was a good listener. I learned of the history of the University, and faculty and student frustrations. I strove to resolve legitimate grievances, always

239

honored confidential information and practiced genuine integrity. Gradually, I won the respect of most of the faculty and students.

Even with prevailing low salaries I learned to recruit faculty and to upgrade with new appointees. Faculty candidates in mathematics, foreign languages, and the sciences were in great demand; qualified faculty members were scarce and very difficult to attract at the salaries Dubuque could pay. Elwyn Smith abruptly left the University in 1956; he held prestigious degrees but was not strong in cultivating human relationships.

Having survived the change in president, business manager, and dean of the seminary, I served on some national committees of the General Assembly of the Presbyterian Church. Educational leaders in the national church came to know me, and I participated in some consulting college visits. For example, I developed abilities for seeing collegiate institutions as a whole; in part by participating regularly in the Iowa Independent College Association, the Annual Stillwater Conference of Academic Deans, and annual meetings of the North Central Association of Colleges and Schools. I read widely in professional journals.

At the same time I greatly enjoyed teaching two courses each semester, either in psychology or teacher education. Students responded well; I challenged them not only with book learning but also in library research and regular writing. I developed a different and more personal relationship with students as a professor than as dean.

We continued to be active in Westminster Presbyterian Church. Periodically, I taught an adult Sunday school class; however, I was unable to develop the esprit de corps that I had enjoyed with the Huntington church Coffee Class. I was again elected to the Session of our church. During summer vacation months the seminary office of the University had more requests for pulpit supply than available ministers. At their request, I as an elected elder, sometimes filled pulpits fifty miles and more from Dubuque. I was active in the local and district programs of Kiwanis International. Jan and I became known and involved in the Dubuque community.

One of my auxiliary interests was The World Calendar then under discussion in several western countries and the United Nations. It was a stable calendar; each quarter had an equal number of business days. January, April, July and October began on Sunday, each with five Sundays and 31 days. The other eight months all had 30 days, except June and December each added a day labeled "W" as World Holidays. I spoke to various clubs and organizations; business people showed avid interest in equal business days each month. As a college dean I envisioned no further long debates to settle next year's academic calendar. Suddenly Secretary of State, John Foster Dulles, declared that discussions should be ended. I concluded that Dulles' assertion had made my meager efforts futile. I turned to more urgent matters.

Our family had a shocking experience in August 1954 when Jan was stricken with polio. We suspected that she became infected while we were vacationing at Strawberry Point State Park. Our family physician, Dr. Paul Laube, immediately put her into an isolation ward in the hospital. We were even more distraught because we knew about Salk vaccine but it was not yet available We feared that the children may also have been exposed. Life became very complicated; the family was scheduled to move from University Avenue to 2084 Grace Street, a larger home about two blocks away. As planned, Lisha, age ten, went to a week's camp; Luther, age seven, went with the Couchman family with his friend Johnny, on their summer vacation in Minnesota. An older student, Mary, became our housekeeper, helped with the move and took care of Margaret who was then five years old. I was in anxious distress, frightfully worried about Jan and not a very competent mover. Mary, a very mature person, and an experienced housekeeper, stepped in valiantly. With her help, the move was completed on schedule, even though many items were temporarily dislocated.

Jan suffered temporary paralysis in back and leg muscles; she returned to our new home from the hospital in about two and a half weeks. Immediately, she began physiotherapy at the University of Iowa hospitals in Iowa City.

That continued for several months; her back and leg muscles were permanently damaged. With extended therapy she made a good recovery. We were very grateful that the children avoided infection.

Jan valiantly completed her studies for the degree and graduated magna cum laude in May 1955. She was promptly appointed to a junior high school teaching position in the Dubuque Public Schools. Later, she greatly enjoyed teaching junior high level, especially seventh and eighth grades. Top leadership in the public schools was tradition bound and stale. As was the practice in employing married women, Jan was not given a contract but a letter of appointment with a salary $200 below that for male teachers with comparable qualifications. Dubuque had a large population of Roman Catholics with an Archbishop resident in the city; that school system was nearly as large as the public one. Problem students were frequently bounced back and forth between the two systems.

Lisha, and Mary Couchman three or four years older, who lived across the street, early exhibited their enthusiasm for teaching by enrolling faculty children, including Margaret Sue, in "Facultots." On some Saturdays and during summer vacations they taught games, athletic contests, songs, home made "movies" interspersed with Kool-ade and cookies happily furnished by the liberated mothers. They were cheerleaders, then, in turn, appointed themselves "Homecoming Queen," gathered lilacs for the "Homecoming Court;" this event took place on the open lot across the street. Margaret who was then age three fondly remembers the group and she acknowledges that the learning was durable. She recalls "Oh, That Jim," a silly little ditty that she was instantly able to sing at age 50. Luther formed a "brotherly" relationship with Johnny Couchman with heavy emphasis on athletics and other university and church events. They formed a football team "Skippers." Having started school earlier in Evanston, Luther was one grade ahead of Johnny. They also became good friends with the college athletic coaches. Both Lisha and Luther were assigned parts in college plays. Lisha, Luther and Margaret liked school and made excellent progress. Some teachers were excellent; a few were marginally competent.

Supplementing the home, the school and the close knit University community was in many ways an ideal place for our children in their developing years. There were picnics, plays, concerts, and church events, ice-skating, athletic contests, birthday celebrations and Christmas parties. We learned the benefits of a whole community helping to raise the child.

Summer vacations had become very important to the family because Jan and I along with the children all looked forward to our family time away from Dubuque. We learned of a large cottage available at Lake Ripley, Wisconsin at a price that we could afford. One summer the Frank and Helen Jane Montgomery family from eastern Ohio joined us; their children and ours were of similar ages. We continued occasional visits that had begun at Camp Lee, Virginia in 1942. Frank served as pastor of a Presbyterian Church in eastern Ohio; Helen Jane was a teacher. We had much to share about our professional positions. In swimming, boating, croquet and other activities the children were compatible.

One summer we traveled to Yellow Stone National Park via the Dakotas and Montana, areas that I had never visited. We stretched our money by staying in low-priced motels, carrying a portable canvas bed for Luther as the family slept in one room. Canned fruit juice and day old sweet rolls in the motel room served as our breakfast with a picnic lunch of bologna sandwiches with lettuce on white bread. We picnicked in parks. Dinner was full meal in a restaurant.

Another summer from Milwaukee we cruised across Lake Michigan; the sun was partially obscured by a haze while we basked on deck in the pleasurable temperature. By evening we were all unsuspectingly roasted, spent a miserable night and for days peeled by the layers. We visited extensive fruit orchards and an automobile assembly plant in Flint, took in some museums and enjoyed the state capitol.

Another summer we visited Rochester, New York, where my brother Elmer, with his family, was completing his Ph. D. in physics at the University. From there we headed east on the New York freeway via Albany toward Lake George.

The children shivered in a morning swim with water temperature around 40 degrees. We stopped at the marble quarries in Vermont and gathered some chip souvenirs. These trips were also designed to be educational as well as recreational. Jan gave each child an appropriate outline map of the United States on which they traced our journey, filled in the names of state capitals, state flowers, nicknames, state flags and major products. All cars had front license plates; they tried to identify as many different states as possible. Margaret wanted to know how much is a million; I told her to start counting. She tired after a few thousand. This helped to occupy the minds of impatient young travelers and somewhat reduced the friction among three energetic kids who were captive on a backseat. In parks along the way we took breaks for energy-releasing physical activity. Occasionally when they became too rambunctious I stopped the car and required them to run half a mile; the relief was effective but temporary.

When the backseat trio became uncontrollable, I placed the most offending one in the trunk among the luggage. (At this writing, such treatment would probably be regarded as parental child abuse.) As the two on the seat talked with the trunk occupant, this became a game rather than punishment; the trunk instead of "prison" became a preferred confinement. Each year the children looked forward to the summer trip. They discovered that they could often relate summer learning to what they were studying in school. We also involved them in planning the trips.

Personally, I learned that I needed regular vigorous exercise for my physical, mental and emotional well being. A university volleyball team was organized but frequently the game had to be cancelled because of too many absentees. One evening only C. T. Peterson, director of physical education and I showed. He suggested that we play badminton. I countered, "Do you mean that silly little game? He challenged me, "I can show you a rugged contest." I quickly observed that he was highly skilled, having taught the game for many years. As the good teacher, he started teasingly but in each game assured himself an easy victory. The next morning my muscles ached, but I was a convert. We played three times weekly; from October to mid-spring I never won a game, before I tasted victory. From then on we shared wins and losses. I was hooked; for nearly forty years this was my favorite sport— along with summer water skiing. In smashing the bird I probably spared many a student or faculty member from the effects of an overly aggressive encounter.

Paul J. Laube M.D., alumnus, secretary of the board and chair of the Faculty Relations Committee was very patient with a young dean and often very helpful to me. He was also our family physician and a friend. His experience included medical mission work in China before settling into surgical practice in Dubuque; he had much broader world perspective than many board members and President Couchman whose only non-Iowa experience was three years of seminary education in Chicago at McCormick Theological Seminary and summer fishing trips in Minnesota. His tenacious, deep roots in Iowa greatly limited his larger perspectives.

Our years in Dubuque provided many friendships with couples in our age range. Among them were Wayne and Edie Norman, George and Pat Cassat, John and Peg Law. George and Helen Maruyama were regular bridge companions. We were all members of Westminster Presbyterian Church that had moved from downtown to a new building on University Avenue across the street from the campus.

In the early years, I taught some courses in economic studies including accounting and typing when other qualified faculty members were not available. I continued to enjoy teaching; the classroom hours were among the best of the week. Students responded well even though my expectations were quite demanding. On my way to my office, I often asked myself why I ever left full time teaching. And yet, as I attended to the wide range of decisions to be made in the dean's office, I found genuine satisfaction. I disliked having to deal with the repetitive conflict between the athletic director, "Moco" Mercer, and the Academic Standards Committee with whom I found myself in agreement. Mr. Mercer tended to think that the value of a good athlete should take precedence over the published academic grade point average requirements. As the academic administrative officer for the Committee, I found myself in a continuing prickly relationship with Mercer as he reminded me that some of my predecessors had been more academically acccommodating, much to the displeasure of the academic faculty.

By 1956-57 because the College financial condition continued to be stressful and I loved the classroom, I taught two large classes in each semester in subjects rooted in my graduate study. In the fall semester I taught Introduction to Psychology with 50 students and Introduction to Teacher Education with 36 students. In each class I gave three final grades of "A." There were a few highly capable students; I required several quality papers in each course that involved library research and some critical evaluation. In the spring semester I taught the same courses with 52 and 25 students respectively. In Psychology I gave three "A" final grades; in Education one. The grade of "C" predominated in all classes, good spreads of "B" and "D" with only one final grade of "F." In these two courses more than one section was often available, but despite my high standards, students continued to flock to my classes.

When I came to Dubuque, I had not taught at a public college or university. I felt that it would be valuable to add that to my experiences. Professor Harry Fitch at Ball State University invited me in the first summer term 1955 to teach a class in Introduction to Psychology with 27 students and one in Teacher Education with 11 students. President Couchman, who failed to understand any benefits to be derived for me, reluctantly granted me leave for that five-week term; I agreed to count two weeks as vacation. I enjoyed the teaching and the renewal of relationships with faculty who had known me as a student. I was lodged with my brother Al and his family who lived in Muncie in the same home he and his wife, Maxine, have continued to live. I returned home most weekends.

That experience served to fortify my conviction that I did not want to shift to the large public university. The more personal relationships with students and faculty in the small private college were to me more satisfying and meaningful. It also served to remind me that as I approached mid-life I had no international travel or living. My life had begun as very parochial, had become interstate and regional. I had had very few international college students, really no international faculty. I felt that I needed international academic experiences to expand my horizons and enlarge my perspectives.

Furthermore, it inspired me to evaluate my status and experiences during the six years at Dubuque and to assess the future of that institution. In this process I began to assess the status, problems and pervading issues at the University. One conviction had become emphasized, in the words of my friend Carl V. Harris, "Just to dream with dreaming youth
Makes me a better man,
While we together find life's truth
And come to know God's plan."

The objectives of the University and the College of Liberal Arts were admirably stated; unfortunately, there was a significant gap between the stated objectives and their realization. The institution had lacked strong, academically competent leadership in persons prepared to make long term commitments. Funding of the University was not only seriously deficient but there was neither a clear program nor personnel to engage in current and long term planning and fundraising at the level that was so critically important. Too many highly competent faculty and administrative staff were rotational. After a few years of experience at Dubuque, they tended to move to stronger, higher quality colleges. One example representing several faculty members was a fine young classics teacher, Carl V. Harris, Yale Ph. D., who after two years was invited to return to his alma mater, Wake Forest University. He and his wife Lucille, piano teacher have remained steadfast friends.

The University had a long history of admitting small numbers of immigrant students who were helped in their preparation as stated in the motto "to serve the Church and the World." A few of them remained as faculty. A small number of graduates engaged in Christian missionary work in the Middle East and the Orient. I was concerned that this traffic was too much one-way; foreign students coming, but no students or faculty going. Quoting from one of the articles for the student campus newspaper I wrote, "Would not the campus life be eminently richer if each year some American students studied abroad for one year and returned to Dubuque to complete their undergraduate study?" In the same vein I challenged some of the faculty. But I found no positive response to my pleas from students or faculty. Furthermore, mid-twentieth century members of the board, faculty and administration lacked comprehensive international vision. I decided to follow my own advice to apply for an appointment as a Fulbright lecturer for a year at a university in India.

Furthermore, I was also greatly concerned that student personnel policies and practices were not organized and only erratically carried out. With its mediocre reputation the institution attracted and admitted too many academically and personally marginal students. Poor study habits, low academic performance, and insufficient motivation were significant factors in the low retention and graduation rates. As an example, I recall one sophomore student about to be dismissed for academic failure who came to my office to plead his case, "I can read good. But I can't understand what I read." Such results had cumulative negative effects despite the smaller numbers of high achievers who distinguished themselves in graduate schools, professions and careers. Hundreds of graduates have been eminently successful in teaching, medicine, social services, business and the Christian ministry. Unfortunately, their successes have not adequately served to raise the academic reputation even by the time of this writing.

An excellent case in point comes to mind. In the mid-nineties, post retirement in 1995-97 while at Eckerd College we received a grant from Fund for the Improvement of Post Secondary Education (FIPSE) to assist six colleges to establish an intergenerational educational program involving students, faculty, and retired persons. At Dubuque the project did not succeed. During the grant period, the chair of the board of directors at the University of Dubuque was a very successful former president of a national bank purchased by a banking chain. Having fired the short-term president of the University, the board elected the chair as acting president. I had not seen him since his graduation during my earlier years as dean. When I visited the campus, his first comment was, "You may not remember me, I am Bruce Meriwether. I was a very ordinary student in high school, on the basketball team. At the end of my first semester in college my grades were very low. You called me to your office and told me that I was placed on academic probation for one semester; if I did not notably improve I would be sent home. That was my turn around; my conference with you saved me." Under a new president last academic year, the University had an accumulated deficit of nearly two million dollars. This led to a drastic reduction of majors, a loss of students, a cut in faculty and a desperate effort to raise funds to cover the deficits—the hardest money to raise. Today, the University still suffers from inconsistent quality.

In the fall of 1956, I applied for a new venture as Fulbright lecturer at a university in India for 1958-59. In 1946 at the initiative of Senator William J. Fulbright of Arkansas, the Fulbright Program was enacted by Congress. He was a distinguished educator who had been president of the University of Arkansas before entering the Senate. He envisioned the educational and cultural benefits toward world peace and understanding to be derived from exchanging graduate students and professors. Professors from many countries were selected annually in national competition to teach or conduct research in another country. Graduate students similarly selected took courses or conducted research usually toward an advanced degree. From my student days I had a special interest in India, especially Mahatma Gandhi. I also felt that in my professional development I needed some international experience in a culture very different from our own.

At the time of my appointment at Dubuque, I was promised that after six years I would be granted sabbatical leave for one academic year. When I asked President

Couchman for his recommendation with my Fulbright application he hesitantly assented. I regarded my prospects of winning as very slim. Jan and I had talked over whether we could take such a venture if I should be selected. We did not tell the children or any of the faculty members. In the spring of 1957, I was informed that I was a finalist with winners to be announced by early fall for the year following. Jan and I were both eager and anxious but we did not spread the word.

In June, we were vacationing at my mother's home in Indiana. In a telephone call, The Board for Christian Higher Education in Asia, with whom I had earlier communicated, offered me a position for two years as the academic vice-president of Chung Chi College. The Board wanted an immediate answer. Two years was too long for the children to interrupt their education at home and to be away from their friends. I would not be granted a two-year leave, but would have to resign. Yet, this was a challenging opportunity if the Fulbright appointment did not come. I was in inner turmoil. Jan and I talked it over thoughtfully. We decided that I would decline the offer and risk the prospect of my winning a Fulbright appointment. With one bird in the hand and the other very desirable one still in the bush, it was a difficult decision!

In fall 1957, I was notified that I won a Fulbright appointment to India; sometime later I learned that I was assigned to teach at the University of Mysore, Mysore, state of Mysore (now Karnataka) in South India. In due course I informed President Couchman and it was announced to the faculty. My leave for the academic year 1958-59 at half-salary was approved by the board. The response of the faculty was very mixed; some were enthusiastic in their congratulations. I recall that Professor Anna Aitchison who had firmly declined my request that she attend a regional conference of professors of English came to my office with Associate Professor Hazel Rothlisberger. She addressed me. "Dean, now that you are going to leave us for a year to teach in India, I don't quite know what to say; should I congratulate you or give you sympathy? Why would you want to go to India? I don't understand." I was stunned, although I should not have been.

She had lived in Iowa her whole life, except while at the University of Wisconsin in Madison earning her master's degree. She had scarcely traveled outside the Midwest. She could not fathom any educator wanting to teach in a country as foreign and different as India. Her profound lack of understanding is an example of the entrenched parochialism at the University of Dubuque in 1957.

When we told the children Lisha and Margaret broke into loud, unhappy and prolonged crying. "We don't want to leave our friends for a whole year; you are really mean and cruel parents. Why didn't you ask us before you decided?" Luther was more restrained in his response. In days ahead as we talked about the adventure, the excitement of traveling halfway around the world and visiting countries in Europe, their resistance and unhappiness diminished.

In planning for my absence during the next academic year, President Couchman was unsuccessful in appointing a one-year replacement for me. He did the unusual, not on my recommendation. He named a trio, each on a fractional time basis, to carry the responsibilities of the dean of the college. None had any experience as an academic dean. The trio consisted of William G. Rozeboom, Professor of History and Registrar, R. W. Sandven, Associate Professor of Psychology and Dean of Students and John Knox Coit, Associate Professor of Philosophy. Although I wrote regularly to President Couchman and others on campus each month during our stay in India, I did not receive a single communication from him. I interpreted this as another example of basic lack of international interest, perhaps encrusted isolationism.

After commencement exercises in June, 1958 I rapidly completed the work of the dean's office. The eyes of our family turned toward India.

Chapter 21: Our Discovery of India
1958-59

Jan and I were mindful that this was another high-risk venture. We were concerned for the health of the family. We made thirteen weekly trips to Iowa City for a series of required inoculations against yellow fever, small pox, typhoid, tetanus and cholera. Financially, my travel expenses to India were paid; we had to pay for the other family members. We expected the costs to deplete our modest savings. Could we find a quality school for the children? Could we adapt to the strange and different culture? We couldn't help but wonder whether at year's end we will have found it all worthwhile. In preparation we read all the materials provided by the State Department and read and discussed several books on India. We were fascinated and significantly informed by a book authored by the daughter of Chester Bowles, highly popular in India as the recent Ambassador.

Why would a young family want to live in India? For me, there were several reasons. During my student days Mahatma Gandhi, the non-violent leader of the freedom movement in India, was in the news every week. The public press in this country favored the British view and was generally not supportive of Gandhi; some viewed him with disdain. This Hindu pacifist with his fervent disciples and millions of followers trying to secure freedom for India from the British Empire was to many Americans more of a puzzling curiosity. There were a few notable exceptions such as Norman Cousins, editor of the *Saturday Review*, William L. Shirer, then a reporter for the *Chicago Tribune* who walked with him from 1931 more than a year and developed a worshipful attitude toward him. E. Stanley Jones, a prominent Methodist missionary, was an ardent admirer of Gandhi; Jones admired Gandhi's pacifist practices. Jones acknowledged that some of his attributes and characteristics were better testimony to the Sermon on the Mount than that of most Christians. From his magnanimous and inclusive perspective Gandhi at times

252

declared himself a Hindu, a Moslem, a Christian and a Jew. Gandhi repeatedly refused to limit himself to the exclusively Christian requirements of E. Stanley Jones, the Christian missionary, who wanted Gandhi to profess his loyalty totally to Jesus Christ. Other individuals and news media had viewed Gandhi and India with varying degrees of support and sympathetic attitude.

Moreover, the Colonies in America freed themselves from the British by four years of violence; Gandhi succeeded in freeing India through non-violence, patiently exercised over a span of thirty years. How paradoxical! In a culture more than 5,500 years old I wondered what legacy Gandhi left for the nation after eight years? Were Gandhi's methods uniquely applicable because of his personality and leadership? Were the influences of the martyred Gandhi still evident in 1958? Would they wither away in nationhood? How had pacifism, generally considered as passive, developed into active power? Britain had massive military power; what were Gandhi's real weapons? Furthermore, I was increasingly troubled that Western education had excluded and was ignorant of Eastern history and culture, languages and thought, generally arrogating to itself an inherent superiority.

I was searching for answers, perhaps in part because of my youthful upbringing in a traditionally pacifist Mennonite church. Having written a major research paper in college analyzing the strongly negative British attitude toward Gandhi, what could I learn on site?

My assignment as a Fulbright lecturer in educational psychology was principally to Teachers College at the University of Mysore but with vague information as to the specific courses that I would teach.

Our travel information was sent to us by Dr. Olive I. Reddick, Director, U. S. Educational Foundation in India. Travel arrangements were made by American Express. We purchased individual round trip tickets with intermediate visits in each direction in Europe and the Middle East at no extra cost. Having been instructed to present myself at the University of Mysore in August, I packed several boxes of personal library books and test instruments shipped by freight. In preparation for departure we sublet the University owned residence at 2084 Grace St. furnished and locked our personal belongings in one room. We purchased five light weight soft red plaid plastic fiber pieces of luggage in addition to a small piece of hand luggage for each person. Pan American airlines insisted that we conform to strict rules for baggage weight for international travel. At the time of departure the children were thirteen, eleven and nine years of age, respectively. Lisha turned fourteen in transit on August 12.

We drove our 1956 Ford to Berne, Indiana, and paused briefly for a family visit, where we turned the car in to the Ford dealer for credit toward a new one when we returned from India. My brother drove our family to Vandalia, Ohio for a brief visit with Jan's family. On July 16, we bid them farewell at the Dayton airport. (Jan's mother gave us shoelaces to replace two broken plastic handles on the luggage! We found no handle replacements in New York.) We headed for New York on TWA Constellation aircraft. We scheduled a three-day stay to visit the United Nations, museums, the TV show Tic Tac Dough, Times Square, Rockefeller Center, Macys, and the Statue of Liberty among other sights. We saw the movie, A Night to Remember, that showed the sinking of the Titanic.

Already, the children expressed their individual grievances. Lisha complained that our economical lodging at the Congregational-Christian Service Center was too unsophisticated. Luther asserted his independent spirit when he, without our knowledge, left the United Nations debate and walked back to our lodging. Margaret wept because we did not buy the special Betsy-Wetsy doll. Our good friend Carl Harris from Wake Forest College in North Carolina joined us in the city and then escorted us to New York International Airport (now JFK) to bid us farewell as we boarded the Pan Am DC-6B four-engine prop aircraft headed for London. We made a refueling stop in Gander, Newfoundland. At 18,000 feet in economy class our meals consisted of two servings of sandwiches and beverages for the twelve-hour flight.

In London we were lodged for three nights at the

Regent Palace Hotel off Piccadilly Square, with the bathroom at the end of the hall. We were confused by the old non-decimal British coins and bewildered by traffic on the left. Tours took us to the Tower of London, museums, Buckingham and Kensington Palaces, St. Paul's Cathedral, Westminster Abbey, the London Tube, boating on the Thames. Jan and the girls saw some plays. We boarded a British Viscount for Amsterdam.

Amsterdam and The Netherlands were distinctly different. At that time the city and the landscape were meticulously clean in striking contrast to the condition on later visits. The Dutch used land and water interchangeably for transportation and commerce. They appeared to be healthy people, vigorous, energetic and diligent. Bicycles for all ages were a principal mode of transportation amid automobile traffic both in the cities and in the countryside. Luther and I rented two bicycles and greatly enjoyed an extended tour of the city. Shipbuilding was still a great industry. Milk, cheese, butter and chocolate production were very important for domestic and export consumption. We found the Dutch people friendly and cooperative with tourists; we enjoyed our three days among them.

We visited a farm with a small dairy where they produced cheese. We took a short boat trip to the isle of Marken with a cheese factory where we were introduced to a variety of cheese wheels. The people were mostly attired in traditional Dutch style wearing wooden shoes. In the museum we were fascinated with the historic Dutch paintings. Luther was so attracted to the dark Rembrandt paintings that we bought him a small, framed print of The Night Watch. Lisha purchased a Belgian painting, Four Negro Heads. The children were unhappy with the breakfasts that consisted mostly of bread and cheese; for lunch hamburgers and French fries were hard to find.

Heading for Istanbul we boarded KLM, DC 6B aircraft to Istanbul. Turkey in Europe and in Asia serves as the historic intersection of East and West. This was also our introduction to the extraordinary differences of the third world.

We arrived in Istanbul sometime after midnight. In going through customs we were given a variety of materials that I did not feel like reading that hour of the night. We checked in at the Park Hotel for which we had prepaid coupons issued by American Express. Shortly after we were in our rooms, the desk clerk knocked on the door. "Sir, we have one of the best exchange rates to convert U. S. dollars into Turkish lira. Will you need some Turkish money?" At the airport I had not any changed money. Innocently, I gave him two American Express checks, pleased to share a good exchange rate.

The next morning I read the materials given at customs. We were warned of a black market in lira and the only legitimate exchange was at a bank at the official rate. All exchange receipts must be kept subject to customs inspection at time of departure. I had declared the amount I brought into Turkey, but if I were checked how would I explain not having any receipts? I suddenly remembered a news report in a recent issue of *Time* magazine. U. S. soldiers who engaged in Turkish black market were hung by their toes! For three days I felt like a wretched fool, a potential criminal. Only on the last day did I realize that the AMEX checks exchanged were equal to the prepaid coupons that I had forgotten to declare. Saved! A lesson learned. (The official rate was 5.25 lira per U. S. dollar, black market 11. At this writing the official rate is 1,535,180 and fluctuating daily.)

The Bosporus Straits are a beautiful sight; the mosques are among the most elegant architectural and artistic creations anywhere in the world. We were introduced to the Moslem prayers from the minaret towers. We visited the Turkish Bazaar with its 3,000 open shops. We observed the striking contrasts of extreme wealth and utter poverty side by side. To my great relief, on departure we breezed through customs with no difficulty.

On the evening of July 28, we departed on Pan Am for Karachi, Pakistan, where we were introduced to hideous flies and intense heat. After a transfer delay of several hours we boarded Air India for Bombay, on an almost new British Viscount with a smooth flight at 17,000 feet. At the Bombay airport an agent of American Express Co. greeted us. He gave me some rupees, a reservation at the West End hotel, and a schedule of our flight to Bangalore the next morning at 6:45 a.m. on Indian Airlines. Our whole trip had been on aircraft with propellers; jet planes were not yet in civilian service.

On the long bus ride to the city air terminal my journal remarks on the culture shock we all experienced: "We saw a sample of the heavy Indian summer monsoon and a cross section view of Bombay--from utter squalor to the princely residences of West End. People were soaking wet sleeping on the sidewalks, doorsteps, doorways amid mosquitoes, rats, filth, and among wandering cows. Here it was in all its stark grimness." Many years later Luther remembered that "Bombay was the most God forsaken city in the universe. A year later coming from inland India, Bombay was the most cosmopolitan city. The perspective of the observer made all the difference."

The next morning we were sharply awakened at 4:30 a.m. We dressed in a great hurry and almost missed the bus to the city terminal and on to the airport. With the drastic time change we were all quite disoriented. The aircraft to Bangalore by way of Mangalore was an obsolete DC3 with no controlled air pressure. In the midst of the monsoon season we were abruptly introduced to its turbulence as we bounced around. Silverware in containers in the back of the plane raced clear to the front of the plane; we were petrified! We were told that several weeks earlier several passengers and stewardesses had been severely injured when the plane dropped several thousand feet. What an introduction to air travel in India as we were being served breakfast by two calm stewardesses! Finally, we landed safely at the Bangalore airport.

In Bangalore, we were comfortably lodged in another West End Hotel. We spent the rest of the day getting acquainted with our surroundings. At bedtime servants carefully enclosed our beds with mosquito nettings as they asked, "What time does master want bed tea?" Promptly at 7:00 a.m. a servant removed the mosquito mesh and served each of us with a pot of hot tea and a banana. After morning showers, we were introduced to an Indian breakfast in the dining room. Uniformed waiters served the meal in elegant style. We had fine British silverware and china for each place setting, a total of thirty-two pieces.

Then we called Bishop Cotton Schools to arrange for the attendance of our children as boarding students. We had decided to place our children in an Anglo-Indian school, not to a school connected with American missionaries or businessmen. The children needed to experience Indian society. We met with Warden Thomas of the boys' school and Head Mistress Constance Millington of the girls' school. They were very British and we discovered many of the schools' characteristics were representative of the colonial era. We discussed their curriculum, books and supplies and required tuition payment. We saw the required uniforms and were told the location of a reliable tailor who could measure, cut and sew the uniforms in one day. The girls also had to purchase two white frocks that they chose from pattern books for required Sunday Anglican church service. They had to be ordered from the tailor for later delivery to the school. We purchased the necessary items and returned to the hotel.

On the next day, July 31, 1958 Jan took Lisha and Margaret to the girls' school, and I took Luther to the boys' school and said our farewells. Regrettably, our departure was very abrupt but I was due in Mysore at my assignment the next day. In the girls' school, except for two Australians, our daughters were the only non-Asian students; at the boys' school Luther joined two sons of the British headmaster with the student body divided about one-half Indian and half Anglo-Indian ancestry. Could our children adapt to the different living conditions, food, beverages, dress, teaching methods, disciplinary requirements, and classmates of differing religions in a shockingly different culture after being in India only three days? We were deeply concerned; however, we saw no feasible alternative. Jan and I returned to the hotel as we anxiously pondered whether we were taking unmanageable risks. Were we being unfair to our children? Their answers then were an emphatic, "Yes." Today, their answers are as different as Luther's perspectives on Bombay!

The next morning we took a taxi to the bus station to await a bus to Mysore 90 miles away. Our tickets provided a reserved seat on this rudimentary, non-air-conditioned bus; after a time the agent announced that only standing seats were available. Luggage, placed on top, included fresh vegetables, live chickens, a rare goat with its feet tied, bundled clothes, and occasionally some human passengers. In the summer heat of 90-degree temperatures, safe drinking water was not available. The only safe beverages were hot tea or coffee. The air was filled with road dust. The bus halted occasionally at a roadside Hindu shrine for devout worshippers. Every stop in a village brought beggars to the open windows of the bus and travelers who dismounted were besieged.

Upon our arrival in Mysore, a lecturer on the faculty of Teachers College of the University of Mysore arrived in the official Jeep. He chauffeured us to the Hotel Metropole where we were lodged until we found an acceptable residence. We gained ready rapport with Principal A. C. Deva Gowda of the Teachers College who greeted us officially that evening. He was a sophisticated, scholarly educator who had studied and traveled in England and the United States. I soon observed that he was an effective administrator, knowledgeable, punctual, and systematic in the context of a culture known for procrastination.

Official opening of the University was June 25; by August 1 only occasional lectures had been given. Candidates for the degree Masters in Education were admissible through August 25. Texts were not generally available and library work was not expected. The entire educational process involved only notes taken by students at lectures given by the faculty followed by periodic external examinations. Examination papers were graded by outside evaluators. Mr. Deva Gowda was determined to change the system as he faced an all-pervasive cultural lethargy that was thousands of years old. He wanted me to understand their educational system so that I could become a colleague in bringing about constructive change.

Toward that end he had made some bold plans for me.

As I look back, I understand much more clearly how much confidence and trust that he had in me. Very early he explained that he had arranged with the Mysore State Department of Public Instruction to select and release forty senior high school teachers and vice-principals for a unique six-week course that I was to prepare and teach. He titled the educational venture as the "Career Masters Course." These educators were to be in residence at Teachers College beginning in early February. He wanted me to have ample time to prepare the syllabus while I was teaching other courses in the fall semester.

Within the first two weeks we observed the political importance of the former Maharaja of Mysore, now the Governor of Mysore State by appointment of the President of India, Rajendra Prasad. President Prasad visited Mysore City for a gala occasion at one of the palaces (Lalitha Mahal) for the laying of the Foundation Stone of a new Children's Center.

Moreover, I also learned of the elevated status of Mr. A. C. Deva Gowda as an educational leader. I was greatly disappointed that within a few weeks of my arrival at the University, Mr. Gowda was appointed Director of Public Instruction of Mysore State. In accepting the appointment he moved to Bangalore, capital of the State. Although he had a Masters degree from Leeds, Mr. C. Rangachar, a man of lesser stature and much more tradition bound, was named principal of Teachers College.

Mr. Deva Gowda assured me that his assumption of higher office should in no way interfere with my assignment; I should proceed courageously to design a course to accomplish the goals that he had in mind. He named a brilliant young Brahmin instructor, Mr. M. S. Satya Murthy, as my assistant. However, he insisted that I was fully responsible for preparation of the syllabus, planning and teaching the course to introduce these high school educators to Western methods used to guide students in choosing careers. Satya Murthy was to accept whatever I assigned him. With his understanding of the Indian culture and traditions, he could serve to warn me when he thought that I proposed to venture onto dangerous ground.

Mr. Deva Gowda and I immediately established easy

rapport. In contrast, other faculty members inclined to tell me what they assumed I wanted to hear. In India, accurate factual and statistical data and records were scarce, making it difficult to receive reliable information on many subjects. I discovered that the Indian modes of thinking were very different from ours. For example, if I asked one person what percentage of the Indian people spoke any English one might tell me perhaps ten percent, while another would state probably five percent. The same applied to historical information; prior to the British era dates and time periods were almost non-existent. I had to learn that my zeal for factual accuracy concerning many subjects had to be modified in order to establish rapport and mutual understanding. I could not assume that Indians would adopt my modes of thought and behavior.

In daily events, an invitation specifying six o'clock was a vague generality; guests might begin arriving an hour later. Stated time was a vague generality, not a specific. A date announced for the opening of school might be days or weeks ahead of the actual beginning of lectures.

In the market, the seller's stated price of a commodity was an invitation to bargain rather than a sum that the buyer be expected to pay. Servants given a shopping list and a sum of money did not return from a purchase of vegetables and fruit with a predictable amount of change. Buyer and seller bargained for each item; no third party would ever know exactly what the payment was. Servants had their own schedules of pocketing unannounced "commissions" for services rendered. We understood that a shopkeeper to servant transaction inevitably yielded lower prices than a "rich Westerner" bargaining with a shopkeeper or his servant.

The same principles applied to transactions involving contracts. The contract price was not the end of the transaction; the seller would expect some hidden sum as an unrecorded benefit. For example, we had an electric table oven. The agent of the government owned electric utility stated it would require an additional ground wire installation at utility expense. I went to the office time after time, "Yes sir, we will get it connected for you," was the typical response. But it never happened. After many weeks I inquired of faculty friends; at first they pled innocent. After we had established mutual rapport and trust, one of them asked, "Did you offer anything to grease his palm?" Naively, I admitted that I had not. Once I understood the system Jan and I decided that we would purchase our baked goods. I decided that on this item I would not adopt the Indian transaction mode. And neither would the Indian utility agent compromise his transaction mode. The oven was never connected.

We leased the unfurnished Palace Model Home built of soft brick then coated with a heavy layer of plaster that is given an annual coating of whitewash. As was the custom and at the behest of Indian friends we mounted a shingle naming it "The Iowan" and another shingle stated "Leo L. Nussbaum Ph. D." Some asked why I did not show each of my degrees. Indian practice was to list degrees such as, "Ramakrishna Vaitheswaran B.Sc. Honors" or even "Gupta Das B.A. Near Pass." The home was surrounded by a solid wall enclosure some three and a half feet tall with enough space for a small garden. My transportation was a Raleigh bicycle, the Cadillac among bicycles, parked in the locked garage next to the house. Jan traveled more elegantly in a three-wheeled motor scooter chauffeured by a young Moslem entrepreneur; a fold-down top protected her from the Indian sun. That reminds me of a shocking discovery that I made one morning while shaving. Conditioned to all faces, except for Jan, that were much darker than mine, I was astonished as a minority in skin color how bleached I really looked!

Indian merchants used various interpretations of the free-enterprise system. Jan did her cooking on a double spirit lamp (kerosene burner) and boiled all our drinking and bath water with an electric teakettle. We rented an obsolete, decrepit Leonard refrigerator shipped ninety miles from Bangalore, described as "one fridge in perfect condition." We found none among the dealers in Mysore. The monthly rent for the fridge cost more than our full-time house servant. Several dealers in Mysore offered rental furnishings such as bed frames, springs, chairs and tables. I asked three dealers to give me a firm bid for a list of furniture items. Two bids were very competitive but the third one was much higher. I told that dealer that he was way above the other two. "How does this happen?" I inquired. "Sir, I have not had much business recently so I have to charge more."

We learned about styles of dress. Mr. Deva Gowda was always attired in a dark Western style suit and tie; his appointments were meticulously on time. I always wore a shirt and tie with jacket except in very hot weather. Most other faculty dressed variously in Indian attire. Indian women and adolescent girls always wore colorful saris with a bare midriff between the choli and the sari. Girls were often barefoot; women wore sandals or flat-heeled shoes. Early in our stay we invited a few faculty and graduate students as guests in our home. With surprising bluntness, one of the faculty looked at Jan in her Western style dress without hose, "Madam, your legs offend me." Thereafter Jan wore the sari, except in our home when no guests were present. She discovered the pleasure of its comfort and versatility as well as the astonishing variety of colors and materials.

Eating Indian food required some adaptation. South Indian Hindus were mostly vegetarians and their palates were conditioned to heavily spiced foods. Spices consisted of red pepper, varieties of curry, hot peppers and a generous use of onions and garlic. Some Indian vegetarians ate fish that they called "the vegetable of the sea." Others enjoyed shrimp and prawns. Hindus abhorred beef that in only two states could be legally slaughtered. A few Moslems slaughtered cattle in the dark of night; our servant was able to buy meat on the black market. However, the beef was from underfed cattle, tough and edible only if finely ground. We early concluded that if we remained in India for some time we would also become vegetarians. Hindus, Moslems and Jews avoided pork; hogs were rarely seen. Some poor quality mutton and goat was available; chickens were always scrawny and not very palatable.

However vegetables and fruits were abundantly available in great variety. Fresh carrots, peas, green and shelled beans, corn, cabbage, onions, celery, turnips, radishes, red beets, potatoes and cucumbers could be purchased in the market nearly every day. Rice was a staple. Rice was bought in bulk that often contained some added sand or tiny white gravel to increase weight, a hazard to teeth fillings. Our servant sorted rice grain by grain. Fruit varied by season, included bananas, plantains, oranges, lemons, sweet limes, limes, papaya, mangoes, coconut fruit and juice. Occasionally apples were shipped from the North. We boiled all vegetables and peeled all fruit. A choice delicacy was the cashew nut, which sold whole for the equivalent of forty cents per pound. Freshly roasted cashews with fresh Nilgiri tea often served as our afternoon low tea. We slowly adapted to the Indian food. .At the end of our stay, although very hungry for good fresh meat, the whole family was addicted to very spicy food. Lisha especially enjoyed scrambled eggs blackened with pepper.

The stunningly different culture and traditions required many other forms of adaptation. The toilet in a separate little structure a few feet outside the kitchen had no Western style equipment. There was no toilet seat, only a "squatty," a hole in the concrete floor that required flushing with water poured from a storage bucket. Water had to be used very sparingly; city water was shut off from 9:00 a.m. to 4:00 p.m.; electrical power for residences was unavailable for the same hours. The water department claimed that the water was purified for drinking but after observing live larvae we concluded that only boiled water was safe. This Palace Model Home, as defined in Indian terms, one of a section of homes financed by the former Maharajah.

We lived next door to an Anglo-Indian family, an intermarriage of English and Indian that had no status among Hindus or Moslems, and who lacked any clearly definable identity in traditional Indian social categories. They were very pleasant neighbors. They had a large, well-fed dog in contrast to most dogs. One day they reported that the dog died from a Cobra bite. After that we did not go outside the house at night without a flashlight to illumine the path! Across the street was a closely grazed field of perhaps sixty acres on which individually owned cattle from the city roamed every day. Low caste women with pre-school children followed the cows, and picked up the fresh cow dung with their hands, and made patties. When dried in the sun they were cooking fuel. Fresh cow dung spread on the dirt floor and dried served as durable floor covering.

Trying to absorb the total environmental, cultural, human relationships, language subtleties, food, transportation, poorly functioning telephone system, was sometimes overwhelming. We had no telephone in our home. When we entertained the first guests of faculty and graduate students they seemed to stay interminably. How surprised we were to learn that guests do not depart until the host at his initiative says, "You may now take leave."

Learning rupee money transactions was very complicated. First we had to convert dollars to rupees. To compound the confusion, rupees were in two transitional money systems: the old paisa modeled after the non-decimal British system and the new decimal paisa. (paisa in Hindi, pice in English) Our servant, having mastered the money systems, was proud to teach us the value of two sets of coins.

I quote from my journal record of first impressions during our early days in Mysore. "Going to the shops, one first finds them abhorrent. Cow dung, horse manure, human excreta, urination beside the street, cows, oxen, scrawny ponies with carts, people sitting on the sidewalk, most walking barefooted. People wear every imaginable kind of attire. Much of the food is exposed to flies, sanitation in accord with Western conditions is almost unknown except for a sign that pointed to a slightly used, PUBLIC URINAL."

"Women must not show their legs, even though barefooted. No low necklines are permitted yet nursing a baby in public is often seen. Young children run around naked, many are carried on the hip wearing only a loose top--no pants or diaper. Urination by children and adults at the side of the street, usually in a squatting position is often seen. Defecation by children is frequently observed. In open areas they may share the morning toilet squatting in a circle, with bottoms out. Toilets never have paper, only a bucket of water to wash oneself with the left hand. The left hand is used for cleaning, never to take food or to give an item to someone else."

"Yet no mixed gender adolescent youth are seen in groups or as couples. Husbands and wives are not often seen together in the city. Most Indian women are hesitant to talk with

265

a man in public."

"Indians do not shake hands, but exchange greetings by joining the palms of the hands in front of the face. The Indian eats with his right hand, uses no napkins, no silverware except a small coffee spoon to stir the thick coffee with milk and sugar. He mixes his food on the plate, bowl or banana leaf with his right hand. At the end of the meal, some Indian men regard a loud burp as a sign to the host that they have been fully satisfied."

"Discrimination on the basis of 'caste, sex, race, religion or place of birth' is prohibited in the constitution. Legislation has been passed providing for universal education; begging is outlawed. The visitor is quickly told that there is a time lag between enactment of the law and its application and enforcement. The visitor observes that begging is everywhere with no evident effort toward enforcement. Caste is thousands of years old in Hindu tradition and its prevailing practices of discrimination are deeply rooted in Indian society."

"One is impressed with Indian dependence on government. Perhaps it is symbolic that, as in Britain, government always uses a plural verb 'are.' Industries that are nationalized include buses, roads, railroads, domestic airline, post office, telegraph, telephone, electric power generation and transmission, waterways, research institutes, police, insurance, many hotels, mines, schools, most colleges and universities, radio, television and many manufacturing industries. Government is the largest employer and regarded as the most desirable. To many young men, government employment seems to be the only avenue to respectable livelihood and appropriate status for a college graduate."

"Occasionally, there is a freakish twist in government services. The post office does not sell stamps to the retail customer. The post office has a private individual, seated at a post office window, who purchases stamps in quantity from the post office then sells them to them to customers. The reason given is the inability to hold individual clerks fully accountable without an expensive verification system. In banks two or three tellers count the money in full view before giving it to the customer. We are also advised to have stamps higher than 50 paisa cancelled in our presence to prevent postal employees from removing them and reselling them to the private stamp agent."

These quotations from my journal offer some of our early glimpses and interpretations of Indian society. However, in general the striking differences between the two cultures have not been greatly allayed; first impressions are mostly confirmed.

The preamble of the Constitution of India reads: "We, The People of India, having solemnly resolved to constitute India into a SOVEREIGN SOCIALIST SECULAR DEMOCRATIC REPUBLIC (Forty-second Amendment substitutes SOVEREIGN DEMOCRATIC REPUBLIC) and to secure to all its citizens: JUSTICE, social, economic and political; LIBERTY of thought, expression, belief, faith and worship; EQUALITY of status and of opportunity; and to promote among them all FRATERNITY assuring the dignity of the individual and the unity and integrity of the Nation; IN OUR CONSTITUENT ASSEMBLY this twenty-sixth day of November, 1949, do HEREBY ADOPT, ENACT, AND GIVE TO OURSELVES THIS CONSTITUTION."

In many respects this constitution is one of the most noble and idealistic of any nation in the world; its full attainment will require several more generations. After centuries of British rule, Mahatma Gandhi during his thirty-year leadership, and supplemented by government negotiation, was able to generate sufficient common cause among these diverse, ethnic, cultural and linguistic entities to win Indian independence. An ancient civilization was and is striving to become a new and modern nation. And we were fortunate enough to be there to observe the beginnings of the himalayan transition that will require many decades if not centuries! At this writing, India as a modern nation is fifty-two years old.

In so many ways our family was also in transition. Among Hindus with its hundreds of castes and sub-castes, we were not Presbyterians, we were Christians. We learned that the large umbrella, Hindu, encompassed sub-divisions of basic castes. "Brahman, is to study and teach, to sacrifice; Ksatriya, must protect the people, sacrifice and study; Vaisya, also sacrifices and studies, but his chief function is to breed cattle, to till the earth, to pursue trade and to lend money; Sudra, duty is only to serve the three higher classes--and it is better to do one's own duty badly than another's well." (A. L. Basham, *The Wonder That Was India*, p. 138) Along with the hundreds of sub-castes and those of no caste (outcaste) the system offered vertical status and social order.

Indians were committed to establishing a democracy. Can this be done? They reminded us of our racial and economic "caste systems." We were proud of our greater longevity, sanitation, medical services, hospitals and our valuing of life. They needed to reduce infant mortality, increase longevity, and improve the health of the general population, especially the outcastes. Indians reminded us that in our advanced technological culture we have accepted as a given, annually 50,000 deaths and millions maimed by automobiles, evidence of very cheapened human lives. Hindu vegetarians, to whom the cow was sacred, believed that we, violently killing animals for food, were denying the sanctity of all life. Sharing the Hindu home with a milk and dung-producing cow was abhorrent to us; they were confused seeing the dog as a lowly animal and could not understand having a housebound dog as an unproductive, expensive family pet.

Further distinctions extended to customs of courtship and marriage. How do you choose a life mate? Indians laud their parents as much better qualified and more experienced in choosing the life mate for their offspring. Parents choose a marriage partner from the same caste and sub-caste so that they are not too different in their expectations. To them evidence that Indians have the superior system is they have far fewer divorces; however, in rural society divorces are not socially acceptable. Indians challenged the merits of our falling in love and then marrying. How could that fictional falling in love possibly be durable? "Indian young people marry and grow into love."

Indians prize the joint family living together, especially in rural areas. This assures companionship for the children growing up with their cousins. In a large family all the members honor the older generations, daughters-in-law are subservient to their mothers-in-law, sons are all related and get along well, obedient to the father or grandfather. Baffled by the claims of smooth joint family relationships we ask, "Do all mothers get along so well with their son's wives?" "Of course, you must understand that the mother-in-law shared in the choice of the son's bride." The oldest generation is always assured of family care for life. Gradually, we begin to realize that in our culture the primary focus is on the individual, whereas in India the principal focus is on the family unit. We understand that it is difficult to evaluate one system as better, but the two systems are very different. The less one knows about the history and foundations of why and how things came to be the way they are, the easier it is to pass judgment in a narrow, prejudiced, superficial way. To be different does not mean that they are necessarily inferior. We became aware that in our ignorance of other cultures we often behaved arrogantly; we began to see why there was much truth to the recently published book, *The Ugly American.*

In discussions with Mysore Teachers College faculty, we learned of India's shortage of basic grains to meet the minimum food needs of the nation. We talked of over population as one of the world's greatest problems. We learned that India from the beginning of nationhood was one of the first nations to establish a cabinet-level Department of Demography in the federal government. Its basic purpose was to recommend policies to the government to lessen the rate of population increase. Although there had been some reduction in the rate of increase, results after eight years were disappointing. Some Indians were optimistic about the future. However, they strongly emphasized the himalayan task of changing the way mothers and fathers in Hindu culture think about their progeny. Each family believes that it must have sons to carry on the family tradition. Hence, the finest traditional greeting to an Indian woman, "May you be the mother of a hundred sons."

Historically, natural conditions kept the Indian population in check. High infant mortality, even more than 50%, floods, droughts, starvation, rampant disease such as small pox, typhoid, yellow fever, Bubonic plague, measles, polio, mumps, diphtheria and female infanticide among others caused a very heavy death toll. After centuries of devastating conditions, propagating successful family planning may require several generations.

Moreover, when the British established themselves, joined by Western missionaries and educators, they brought with them Western inoculations, hospitals, medical practice, improved sanitation, and purification of drinking water. All of these practices not only saved many children and adults from the ravages of nature. But the results also increased longevity in the twentieth century from an average of twenty-six years to more than fifty. Inadvertently, Western intrusion greatly contributed to the exploding Indian population. Jan and I were compelled to lay aside many of our presumptions. This was a year of not only teaching but also of vast learning.

University faculty challenged my belief that the overpopulation was a major world problem. "Dr. Nussbaum, overpopulation is not one of the biggest problems; rather the world's greatest problem is Western over-consumption." At first, my mind could not comprehend any basis to render such a judgment. I thought, "Surely there are no economic grounds for such a conclusion." The United States had millions of bushels of excess corn, wheat and other grains in storage. Moreover, in our conservation programs we had millions of acres lying fallow to limit productivity. Yet American people ate more than we needed for good health and physical condition. Did Indians have a valid point? Worldwide, economists contend that there is enough food production to feed all the people--and millions more--the problem is lack of an adequate system distribution. I could not help but acknowledge that they had a part of the economic truth in their comments.

On October 1 all the Fulbright grantees, lecturers, research scholars and graduate students, with spouses, were assembled in New Delhi for a two-week orientation and information seminar on India. We listened to lectures by embassy staff and upper-level Indian government officials. Topics included the geography, economics, religions, history, handicrafts, foreign policy, influence of Gandhi, the literature and languages. There were trips to many parts of the city. On October 2, Gandhi's birthday, a national holiday, we visited the Gandhi Memorial and placed jasmine blossoms on the simple

270

stone slab that marks the burial of some of his ashes. (October 2 is also our grandson, Marc's birthday.) Quoting from my notes, "A professor at the University of Calcutta who was secretary to Mahatma Gandhi in 1946-47 gave a personal account of experiences during those trying months before Gandhi's assassination. This alone was worth the trip to India." Jan and I celebrated Worldwide Communion Sunday in Delhi Free Church, an international congregation affiliated with the Church of North India. This was a high moment!

We met Ambassador Ellsworth Bunker, a stolid New Englander, who was much less popular and admired than his predecessor, Chester Bowles. Mr. and Mrs. Bunker held a reception for the Fulbright group where we had the rare privilege to meet Senator William J. Fulbright, the initiator of the Fulbright program who was in New Delhi to attend The World Bank Conference.

Our group had an hour's conference with Prime Minister Jawaharlal Nehru in his pressroom. Mr. Nehru was also his own foreign minister. Slightly more than five feet tall, his stature rose rapidly as he spoke about his vision for India and answered our many, varied questions. He was an avid Fabian Socialist and perceived the private sector to be auxiliary. His insistence on a non-alignment policy of refusing to join either of the power blocks won him disdain from the American government, especially from John Foster Dulles, Secretary of State. Nehru's great admiration of Mahatma Gandhi pervaded his comments and, later in his radio broadcasts to strengthen nationhood, he would fervently appeal to the people in the name of the Mahatma (great soul). Fulbrighters rose to standing ovation, then bowed low with palms joined, Nahmaste. One of the Fulbright professors from Central State College, Wilberforce, Ohio had posed two sculptures of Mr. Nehru, offering him the choice between the "conceptual likeness" and the "visual likeness." He chose the "conceptual likeness" as he humorously quipped, "Naturally, no one would not choose "visual likeness" when one can have "conceptual likeness." Later that week, Senator Fulbright graciously accepted the "visual likeness."

For months there had been domestic and international

conjecture as to who would succeed the aging Nehru, India's first and only Prime Minister. *Time* magazine had floated the name of Morarji Desai, Finance Minister, who leaned politically more toward the private sector. Known as a teetotaler who drank cow's urine did not deter the Republican administrations from advocating him as a successor to Nehru. Not viewed with equal favor among most Indians, *Shankar's Weekly* often combined astuteness and humor. They reported the introduction of a new cocktail, "Morarjin," compounded from tap water, goat's milk and unadulterated bootleg liquor imported from prohibitionist Bombay's well known secret distilleries.

At the end of the first week of our orientation was the beginning of the Indian harvest festival of Desara. Schools, including Bishop Cotton, had a holiday; Jan left New Delhi by plane to meet the children in Bangalore and escort them by taxi to their first stay in our Palace Model Home. In Mysore, Desara festivities were among the most important of the year.

Orientation activities were in recess on Sunday; I decided to travel to Agra to see the world famous Taj Mahal. Early Sunday morning, on the railway depot platform I met a Swiss pharmaceutical salesman; we agreed to share an air-conditioned train compartment and formed a friendship both interesting and beneficial. Our family had arranged for a week's visit in Switzerland on our return trip home. He proposed that he ask his favorite travel agent to plan a Swiss round trip for sightseeing by rail and water. Later, that became the high point of our homeward journey. Hans Schönmann and I greatly enjoyed our Taj Mahal visit and our friendship endured for years until his untimely death in Basel.

The Fulbrighters had become a cohesive group as we completed the second week of the conference and said farewell to resume our respective assignments scattered all over India. I returned to Bangalore by British Viscount aircraft from where I took an obsolete bus to Mysore to rejoin the family. The family was fully acclimated to mosquito nets carefully tucked under the mattress of the poster beds; later I installed mosquito screens on the barred windows, much to the consternation of our Indian friends. They contended that screens would deter the breezes

272

from flowing through the house.

Our family reunion was delightful; the children quickly adapted to our new home. They played four-square ball on the flat roof in the hot sun, went for walks, read, and rode rented bicycles. Luther and I played badminton at the sports club. We attended horse races at the nearby track and visited the lions, tigers, and many other animals along with exotic birds in the zoo only a few hundred feet from our home. Opposite the flatland of Mysore, scenic one-thousand-foot high Chamundi hill posed an exhausting hiking challenge.

One evening while cycling, darkness overtook Luther and me; a policeman charged us with improper lighting and marched us to the police station. After identifying myself as a visiting Fulbright professor at the University of Mysore and bowing to the chief with deferential apology we were released to walk--not ride--our bikes home.

The family attended various Desara festival events amid all the holiday glamour. The former Maharaja of Mysore royally attired in glittering gold uniform and golden crown ensconced in a lavishly decorated howdah atop a large elephant led a parade several hours long. Elegantly uniformed policemen astride their prancing steeds served as guards. Rows of highly painted and decorated elephants sauntered amiably. Uniformed musical bands, college students and school children, military units and civilian organizations including Rotary International club members marched to celebrate a long Mysore tradition. After dark, the main palace grounds surrounded by high walls and huge gates was glamorously illuminated with thousands of light bulbs posed on every architectural edge; this offered a stunning sight as if in fairyland. We were escorted to Krishna Rajasagar Gardens a few miles from the city where holiday illumination created another fantasyland as we walked amid the flowers, shrubs and water fountains. There we were served our evening meal amid glamour beyond our most ecstatic imagination. That too was Mysore, India, memorable beyond possible description. In my opinion, I have never witnessed a holiday celebration anywhere else in the world that exceeded this one.

That wonderful family time and the school holiday were

over too quickly; the children rode a taxi back to Bishop Cotton Schools in Bangalore. They had made some friends, were more comfortable with the heads of the schools, and were adapting to the Indian food and lodging. At least they accepted their return to school with less reluctance.

My teaching schedule had become heavier; I was assigned lectures to the undergraduate psychology class at intervals focussed on particular topics. A new graduate course on educational administration for which I was responsible had mysteriously appeared in mid-semester. I gave the students library assignments with extended reading; I noticed the looks of consternation but they did not question the assignment. However, a few days later at the opening of class the students had delegated one member to speak for all of them, "Sir, Dr. Nussbaum, we are concerned. We read some of the books that you assigned. The authors tell us different things; we become confused. Why don't you tell us how it is; we will write it down. Then we will know." They forgot one of the fundamentals of Hinduism: Truth has many faces! I did not have the last word; they were searching for the correct answer to the external examination and I did not know the questions that would confront them. The faculty claimed that they did not know but had some general ideas what would be covered.

Intermittently, Jan and I were invited to address various local, state and regional conferences on a wide range of subjects. "The Role of Women in America," "Physical Education in the U. S.," "Discipline of Children," were assigned topics. With the Indian external examination system frequent questions focussed around, "How Can U. S. Teachers Teach, Test and Grade"? Prestigious Rotary Clubs invited me to speak; the assigned topic usually was some phase of "Education in America." Indians seemed insensitive to assigning a subject impossibly broad within the time limits. Perhaps they assumed that we would be sufficiently selective in sensing what they would like to know.

Nationally, one of the most contentious issues was the prevailing official language. The constitution stipulated that Hindi, prevalent in North India, was the official language and English the associate official language. South India opposed

Hindi as their official language. Much of the University instruction was in English, although states of South India also had their official state languages. Throughout India there are innumerable languages and dialects, estimated from six to eight hundred. North India wanted Hindi to become the official language for all states; South India with languages that had a different alphabet adamantly refused. They threatened to convert all their colleges and universities to their state or regional languages rather than adopt Hindi. In this respect, their conduct was that of parochially separate princely states, not a modern nation. Today much of the business of Parliament is conducted in English; yet India now has some eighteen official languages and much of the college and university education in South India is in the state languages.

Occasionally, I was expected to address teachers' conferences with attendance of several hundred. At one conference the state minister of education was to be the key speaker. While the teachers seated in a hot hall waited impatiently, the chairman asked me to speak extemporaneously to the crowd about testing in America. Two hours late on arrival, impressed with his status, the minister did not express one word of apology! Then he spoke tiresomely for an hour as the audience suffered their compulsory attendance. To Americans, many Indian conferences would have seemed interminable.

Every few weekends except near vacation times, Jan and I rode a bus to Bangalore to visit the children. We stayed as a family at the West End Hotel. Although the children had adapted to Indian food, the school diet was monotonous, contributing greatly to their enjoyment of restaurant meals. We eagerly listened to their experiences, took long walks, attended movies, and church on Sunday morning. They had made friends and were increasingly content.

On weekends in Mysore, we usually attended Church of South India English language services where the Rev. William Karl was the pastor. This congregation had roots in the Methodist Church; we could identify with the order of service. Over time we became friends with the Karl family; he was later named a Bishop in the Church of South India. (For years we sent them honoraria from our many speeches on India.) Throughout the year, the absence of Western vocal and instrumental music pained us greatly. We especially missed the glorious music of the Christmas season. Having the family together at vacation times was very rewarding to all of us. Rarely, during holiday periods we were guests in Indian homes. We entertained Indian guests for tea but not for meals. We were not equipped to prepare elaborate meals; also our house servant was not sufficiently sophisticated to handle dinner entertainment.

One of the most rewarding times of the year was the weeklong visit of Dr. & Mrs. Harry N. Fitch, one of my favorite professors and personal role model at Ball State. At retirement they moved to San Jose State College in California where he taught for several years. Following his second retirement, on their two-year trip around the world they stayed with us. Together we enjoyed recalling the years at Ball State.

The timing of their arrival was propitious at the beginning of the six-week "Career Master's Course" (February 2, 1959) for forty senior high school teachers and vice-principals. Dr. Fitch lectured in that course on "Teacher-Student Relationships," befriended participant members, students and faculty; they referred to him as the "Guru of Gurus." The Fitches were remarkably adaptable, astute observers, penetrating questioners, and took a keen interest in University events and scenery in the Mysore area.

Preparing the syllabus and teaching the "Career Master's Course" was one of the greatest challenges of my professional career. In the West, choosing a career is a matching of the abilities, the potential and the inclination of the individual male or female, with the requirements for a particular career. In India thousands of years of tradition decreed that a young male has a very narrow range of careers allocated to the caste and within that sub-caste. Typically, the son would follow the career of his father, more by the father's assignment than the son's choice. Currently, many girls were also educated, usually in gender segregated schools through high school. In this course we had only boys available in the school attached to the Teachers College.

Now India as a new nation, whose constitution prohibits discrimination on the basis of "religion, race, caste, sex, place of birth or any of them," was determined to form a democratic society in which young people need to learn to choose a career. The burden of this transition falls heavily on the teachers and vice-principals in the high schools of India. How can this process begin? That was the focus of this experimental course assigned to me.

To begin, I had to understand as much as possible of the complexities of the caste system, tradition, and its pervasive and penetrating prescriptions on the individual. The focus was not on the individual; the individual at birth was subservient to and locked in his place in the caste system. There was no room for individual initiative, originality or decision; the system decided for him. Teachers were victims of the system. Were they interested in challenging tradition; were they open to change for the sake of their students? Whoever selected the participants believed that these individuals were.

Indian teachers and students had never taken short answer tests such as true or false, multiple choice, or completion. They were strangers to timed tests in which speed was essential and affected the score. They knew only essay tests with no limit on time. They had not experienced independent thinking; their elders decided for them whether selecting a marriage partner or a career. For example, I administered some twenty-minute editions of Otis Intelligence Tests. One item read, "The father is wiser than the son." with the answer selected from four stems: sometimes, never, always, rarely. More than 98% of the hundreds of students and teachers who took the test answered, "always." In their tradition, the elders are _always_ considered wiser. When introduced to the test, my assistant M. S. Satya Murthy, insisted that was the only correct answer. Was their intelligence to be lowered because their culture had a different answer than our culture where the test was made? Other culturally conditioned answers raised serious questions.

When among participants a descendant of low caste parents earned a higher score on the Otis test than one of the Brahmins, Satya Murthy angrily challenged the validity of the testing instrument. "This can never be, Dr. Nussbaum. We know Brahmins, the teachers and priests, are always smarter than any low caste." The focus pre-determinedly was on the caste, not on the person. We decided to release test scores only to the individual participant; each person could decide whether to share his or her score.

The principal of the nearby boys Practicing High School where college students did their practice teaching agreed to cooperate with us in the course. I assigned two boys to each participant, without regard to caste, to prepare a detailed biographical case study. This included administering preference instruments and selected tests, preparing a life history, visiting parents at home, and writing a report using the learned data to determine what might be some possible career options for each boy. Satya Murthy vigorously challenged this assignment; "Dr. Nussbaum, this will never work. No one from one caste visits in the home of another caste. Teachers never visit the homes of students." My reply, "Satya Murthy, how do you know it cannot work?" "We have never done it," was his standard assertion. This program was innovative and experimental; we did not dare limit ourselves by what had been done in the past. Participants shared case studies with each other. We did and it worked!

Satya Murthy and I along with other members of the faculty gave a series of lectures and conducted discussions with participants, in an effort to open their minds. We exposed them to a variety of Western instruments such as the Kuder Preference Record, Strong Personality Test, Otis Intelligence Test among others, explained administrative procedures and scored interpretations. We found among them a range of openness and degrees of receptivity.

I assigned to each participant the preparation of an experimental plan for use in his or her school that could be undertaken in the next semester. We commented on each plan; participants learned from each other. Then I proposed a high tea gathering at the College of all participants, with sons and parents who participated in the case studies, on the last evening of the course. Satya Murthy's reaction was predictable, "Dr. Nussbaum, that can never work. Parents do not visit the schools, much less assemble at the College. They will not come; we cannot do that."

We did. To the utter astonishment of Satya Murthy and other objectors more than three-fourths of the parents and sons came. It was a *gala* event, a smashing success! I felt greatly rewarded. Did the course make a lasting difference in the high schools? Regrettably, I had no opportunity for follow-up; I do not know. I observed that we did open some people's minds and expose them to non-traditional options; we had made a valiant effort. For me it was an overarching learning experience.

Despite Satya Murthy's frequent hesitations, he was a very valuable colleague. He properly and candidly presented the perspectives of Indian traditions and practices, he alerted me to the need for caution at many points. However, once I decided how we would proceed he was always fully cooperative. He had a good education: two baccalaureate degrees, a master's degree and a diploma in commerce. We became good friends; Jan and I were dinner guests in his home.

I gave more lectures in various classes intermingled with those of other faculty. After the Career Master's Course the rest of the academic year was rather anti-climactic. I had developed very congenial relationships with the faculty of Teachers College; several colleagues were determined to come to the United States for an advanced degree. They conferred with me as to how that could be arranged. As far as I know only one succeeded; D. N. Seetharamaia, who was awarded a Doctor of Philosophy degree at Ohio State University

The beloved and highly respected former Maharaja of Mysore was serving a four-year term as Governor of Mysore State by appointment of the President of India. The Governor in each state was mostly a "figure head" with the power to govern vested in the chief minister and the legislature. The State of Mysore was regarded as one of the most advanced; the people gave credit to the former Maharaja who surrendered his absolute power to the citizens organized after the British system. We were told that as Maharaja he once had fifty palaces and fifteen hundred servants. Eight years after the new government was established he was bereft of power; his palaces and extensive other property were being appropriated to public use by the federal government--some to research laboratories, hotels, and institutes. Even the poorest people were sorrowful at the diminished status and property of His Royal Highness, the number of servants now reduced to one-hundred fifty!

We were privileged to know him personally; periodically he sent a chauffeured Rolls Royce to take Jan and me to one of the palaces for conversation and high tea. His Highness explained that as the former monarch, he could not have a candid man-to-man conversation with any of his countrymen. Hence, he was eager to converse with foreigners about politics, philosophy, history and world wide current events. He was a great admirer of Harry Truman. He introduced Jan to the Yuvrani, his mother not his wife, who served as the official hostess at her palace. First married to a wife of royal descent who produced no son, His Highness divorced her and married a commoner who gave birth to a son.

During a visit at his mother's palace on the late afternoon before his departure for the United States to receive medical services and lecture at major universities, we observed an astonishing event. A score of palace servants fell prostrate with palms joined, foreheads in the dust, adjoining the palace veranda, declaring in their language, "Long live the Maharaja." He remained seated, joined his palms in his lap, said not a word. The servants unobtrusively departed. He and I were of the same age; he weighed over 300 pounds, having suffered glandular malfunction for many years. This was the last time that we saw him.

In late March, the Fulbright group held their spring conference at Ootacamund high in the Nilgiri hills in Madras State at an elevation of 7,500 feet, a delightful temperature change. Several of the Fulbright members gave reports of their work and together we conducted our final evaluation. Some members were experientially disillusioned while others had found intense satisfaction in the year's work. We were among those with very positive experiences.

UNESCO sponsored the second part of the conference. Indian professors joined for a discussion of traditional values in the United States and India. Indians included dignity of the individual; Americans were very dubious. Americans referred to the Declaration of Independence stating that "all men are created equal." Indians pointed curiously at our claims of racial equality in our segregated society. Both sides conceded that vast difference between the ideal and reality.

Dr. and Mrs. Robert Brisbane and daughter, a black family from Morehouse College in Atlanta, returned to Mysore with us and stayed in our home for several days. This was the beginning of an enduring friendship. Other Fulbrighters dropped in during their travels around the country; we were the only ones assigned that far in South India.

The children returned from Bishop Cotton schools as we began the preparation for the return home; they joined us in the endless valedictory functions at Teachers College, the church, neighbors and friends. We made many purchases of saris, raw silk for window curtains, carved rosewood, sandal wood, ivory and cow dung souvenirs, inlaid serving trays and small tables, brass and painted vases, bracelets, bangles and turbans. Then we prepared required listing, packing and crating in a metal foot locker and shipped. I gave most of my books to the University library, sold my Raleigh bicycle and arranged for the return of the rented furniture to the dealers.

Unexpectedly, I was invited to remain a second year as a Fulbright lecturer in American history at another university. To the astonishment of Jan and myself, the children would have favored my accepting the assignment. If we were to stay another year I would have to resign my position at the University of Dubuque, the children's educational sequence would be interrupted too much, and their friendships at home would be more difficulty to reestablish. We were curious how accurate was the statement of Dr. Olive I. Reddick, Executive Secretary of the United States Educational Foundation in India, that a stay in another country for a year tends to build a dual loyalty and one cannot avoid a backward look wherever one lives. We found her accurate.

On April 25, we felt very sentimental as we taxied from Mysore to Bangalore. As the plane circled toward Bombay, Luther and I seated together pondered how different were our feelings about India from our arrival last summer. And this flight in the pre-monsoon season was calm and uneventful.

As we reflected at dinner in the West End Hotel in Bombay, our family agreed that we had come to love India and felt substantial pain as we prepared to leave. Our stay had been a rich learning experience living among a people whose culture, living standards, need for physical comfort, life's aspirations and expectations, religions, basic values, and foods were so different from ours. For all the contrasting differences we no longer were compelled to label their culture as inferior, however disparate. We all had our horizons extended, our attitudes toward people of other nations softened, our need to render quick judgments reduced. Fragments of information can invite hasty prejudices; deeper understanding can bring empathy and open minds. Will the reentry to our own culture be difficult, we wondered?

Departing from Bombay we headed for Cairo, Egypt for our first stop at Intercontinental Savoy Hotel. For three days we visited some museums, the Nile River, the Pyramids and the Sphinx, rode camels. As we crawled into one of the Pyramids we felt like participants in ancient history. Riding a bus in the Nile Delta we watched the harvesters reaping wheat with a scythe, a loud undiplomatic Minnesota farmer asked, "Where are the combines?" Our guide remained silent.

One of our deteriorating stuffed pieces of luggage ripped open. At a leather stall, I bargained for a sturdy, much larger leather bag. Fortunately, this was Moslem culture; the quality was much better than the Hindu non-violent leather. Predictably, this large bag was soon full; for weeks after we arrived home my back ached from carrying this heavy weight! Also, camera happy, I photographed some Moslem women in purdah and was threatened by a guard with rifle in ready position! However, our stay in Cairo and environs was very pleasant and highly informative. We were impressed with the more aggressive cultural tone among Moslems than we had experienced among South Indian Hindus. As we taxied to the airport we looked forward   to   our   return   to   the   West.

Chapter 22: Orient to Occident

1959

Our remaining stops in Europe were Athens, Rome, Zürich and Paris. Most of the family had studied some Greek history; we were eager to see the enduring city of Athens. We proudly climbed the hillside of the Acropolis reminded, as we reached the Parthenon, of the meaning of the term in Greek--acro-high and polis-city. At the time we roamed freely among the ruins, the pillared maidens were standing tall. We were surprised that we had the place almost by ourselves. We connected with some municipal tours, visited several sculpture museums and galleries where we observed this ancient city in its glory days. We deplored the damage inflicted on so much of the creative artistry, much that was removed is now in the British Museum. Greek food was gentle to our spice-conditioned palates and we felt safe walking about the city. The Acropole Hotel provided good food and services from where we viewed parades to the churches celebrating Easter in the Eastern Orthodox tradition. The Greeks smoked cigarettes in profusion so that we were often in clouded atmosphere yet we were grateful to have had a very brief exposure to one of the great historic cities.

In Rome, the eternal city, we felt that our faces had turned even more westward. Each of us, for differing reasons, was eager to see the massive Coliseum. We walked the area, with no restrictions climbed to the upper levels, and were astonished at its size and the state of preservation of many of its parts. The vast catacombs were deteriorating but unguarded. Again, we felt safe to wander without hesitation. We walked to and through St. Peters, thinking we might catch a glimpse of the Pope. The Sistine Chapel Ceiling had long been neglected and appeared worn, its colors dull, in places the paint was badly peeled. We enjoyed the statuary in the city yet the sculpture and architecture lacked the refinement of the Greeks. However, we found the art galleries very appealing. Auto, motorcycle and bicycle traffic was already hazardous to pedestrians. We were ready for the next stop, Switzerland, our ancestral home.

As we flew from Rome to Zürich, the rugged peaks of the Italian and Swiss Alps were stunning with glistening snow in the spring sunshine. A hotel porter met us, helped us with the luggage, guided us to our hotel and handed us tickets for lodging, train and boat reservations for our seven-day tour of Switzerland. I had instant rapport as I spoke to the Swiss in their conversational language. All that I had requested of Hans Schönmann last October in New Delhi, India was now being fulfilled in every detail. His travel agent in Basle had relayed to Zürich all that we needed for our circular trip in Switzerland with assurance that, as a fellow Swiss, I can pay him when we reached his office near the end of our trip. I had never realized, and probably never since, the same degrees of trust involving an unwritten agreement through a third party. Hotel porters unfailingly met us at railway stations and boat docks, and escorted us to our lodging.

Switzerland, for each member of the family, was the highpoint of our trip on the way home. Money exchange rate was much in our favor; one dollar was equal to four Swiss francs. At that time we had no credit card. International transactions depended on American Express checks converted into the local currency. Accommodations were of high quality; after very active days we slept on good mattresses with open windows breathing the fresh mountain air. Each evening our shoes were placed in the corridor near our room door, then reclaimed the next morning cleaned and polished, a long tradition in Switzerland.

Swiss hospitality with abundant, quality, nourishing meals of pork, beef, veal and chicken supplemented with röshti, fresh bread, butter, jams and jellies and unsullied vegetables and fruit were served without limits topped with luscious desserts. On the way to India, the children, with sulking disappointment, faced dining room waiters when hamburgers and French fries were not on the menu. On the return trip, after eating Indian food, tastes were much more sophisticated. The children, whose palates had forgotten their parochialism, ate with relish all food that was put before them--and asked for more. Every day on the Swiss tour was "feast day."

This was early May; the melting snows many feet deep on the mountains broke into gushing streams and rivulets from crevices and gullies on every slope. In the bright spring sunshine, the carpets of grass turning deep green with fresh vitality were punctuated with bright yellow dandelions. The powerful burst of nature in its glory could not be contained as colorful, aromatic fruit trees blossomed in pink, red and white. Bees escaped their hives already busy collecting early honey. Birds migrating northward filled the air with exulting music. The ice on the lakes had melted, boat harbors had reopened. Roads, except mountain passes, were cleared inviting people to escape their long drab, winter confinement. At the upper levels, after a winter without snow we all enjoyed snowballs in the spring. Every curve in the railroad revealed an unending array of varied scenery. We included Lucern, Bern, Lausanne and historic Geneva. We have returned to Switzerland many times since that first exposure; I have never seen the landscape and mountain scenery more beautiful or more inviting.

Our Swiss circuit nearly over, we met Hans Schönmann in Basle for a brief visit; I introduced the family and thanked him profusely for his remarkable services in our behalf. Hans and I reminisced about our visit to the Taj Mahal last October. He introduced us to the accommodating creditor travel agent; after a Swiss handshake and heartfelt thanks, I paid him in full. He exemplified the prevailing attitude throughout Switzerland--to offer satisfying service to the tourist was its own reward. Regrettably, in recent years financial reward seems to have a comparatively higher priority.

After Hans showed us his home he took us on a brief tour of Basle. We bid farewell and boarded the train for the Zürich airport. We boarded Swiss Air heading for Paris where we planned to visit for three days.

Our family was not conversant in French; rapport with the French people was much more difficult. In the hotel, we found a condescending attitude toward Americans, the American dollar and especially toward us as customers that necessitated them to speak in English. After the congenial visit in Switzerland, here we felt like unwelcome guests. Hotel menus were printed only in French; waiters showed little interest in translating into English. Happily, the children had studied beginning French at Bishop Cotton Schools; however, even more significant was their growing sophistication regarding choice of food. Margaret thought she had ordered soup; she was served a slab of cold meat. She shrugged her shoulders then without complaint cleaned her plate.

We had a message from American Express telling us that there will be five available seats on a flight to New York one day earlier than we had planned. Considering our cool reception in Paris, we readily agreed to accept the change in departure date. We took tours to visit the high points in Paris, the Louvre, Napoleon's tomb, Arc de Triomphe, Champs Elysees, Eiffel Tower, Cathedral de Notrè Dame, and walked the banks of the Seine.

We were excited at the prospect of returning home as we boarded Pan American jet Boeing 707. Transatlantic jet flights had recently been introduced; this shortened the flight time from Paris to New York by several hours. Once airborne we curiously observed the flexibility of the wings, the quiet of the motors and the size of the aircraft. The jet age had arrived and we were proud to be among the early transatlantic passengers! Food and beverage service was greatly improved; stewardesses seemed proud to serve us in this new aircraft. The seats were more comfortable and more conducive to sleep.

At LaGuardia Airport we transferred to TWA for Dayton where Jan's family greeted us at the airport in Vandalia in reunion after our ten-month separation. We were weary travelers having come from Paris that same elongated day.

Jan's father had written to us frequently, always with some opinions and many questions. We had sent them copies of our monthly reports as well as personal letters. Then we had much to report about the year to supplement what we had been able to write. I had several hundred photographic exposures on films that were not yet developed. Developing and printing in India was of lower quality than at home. Immediately, I had them developed to augment what we reported in words. In the few days that we were with Jan's family, I showed one carton of slides to a local service club, the first of more than fifty presentations, with and without slides, that Jan and I offered during the first year. India, to the general public, was even more remote then than it is today.

We discovered that on our return we needed reorientation to our own culture, from temperature and weather to the clothes we wore, the available food and beverages, sanitation and auto traffic without ubiquitous auto horns and cows. In India we had no radio and the only newspapers available in Mysore were not in English, but in the local language, Kannada. We bought an occasional copy of the Asian edition of *Time* magazine. Whenever we traveled to Bangalore to visit the children we had access to the United States Information Service (USIS) where we could do some catch up, our only access to the stock market reports and most news about the United States. Back home we faced a barrage of radio, TV, newspapers and magazines.

Our next stop was in Berne, Indiana to visit my family and to pick up our new 1959 Ford to drive home to Dubuque, Iowa. We stayed only a few days and hastened toward our home. Spring weather in early June beckoned us westward, as we watched the amazingly efficient farmers busily engaged in planting and sowing in the vast breadbasket across the Middle West. We were all eager to get relocated and re-connect with our friends.

Re-entering required more conscious adaptation to our own culture than we had expected. What we had not seen or done for nearly one year had a certain quality of originality—as if we had to learn with a fresh start. We were as strangers in our own land. Our household servant did not polish my shoes each morning, do the shopping in the market, sweep the floor, peel potatoes, cut the vegetables, boil the drinking water and fill the water tank. Happily, we did not hear the cockroaches running in the kitchen. We opened the water tap for safe drinking water twenty-four hours daily. Instead of the two burner primus stove, with a turn of the switch for cooking and baking, we had uninterrupted electrical power. We prized the abundant illumination from floor and table lamps instead of the low-wattage single ceiling light. Instead of laundry pickup and delivery by the dhobi, the washing and drying machines stood ready and waiting. Our bare feet preferred soft carpeting to the smooth concrete floors. No worry with mosquito nets over our beds; screens on the windows were much more protective. Having been without one, we were startled to hear the intruding ring of the telephone. Local, national and world news was instantaneously available by radio, and increasingly by TV, and daily with the delivery of newspapers. We had to mow our own lawn, water our flowers.

Going shopping? The car was available in the unlocked garage. Fruits and vegetables were safe to eat; refrigerated pork, beef, chicken and varieties of sausages looked appetizing. All prices were fixed and clearly marked, no haggling. We had a strange feeling when we heard only one language and we understood it all. What an array of packaged cereals, canned and frozen vegetables from which we had to make choices. At the bank we did not wait in a long line then watched two or three tellers in sequence verify the money count. How simple, we had only one money system, dollars with no old and new paisa.

The cultural transition was rapid; in a few weeks we were again entrenched in the familiar ruts as we established a daily and weekly routine. We were much more conscious of the wastefulness of American society after watching our servant rescue short pieces of string and scraps of paper for his household. Salvage and recycling took on new meaning.

Each member of the family found our welcoming friends who, on our return, received us warmly. We returned to Sunday school and church. I returned to the Kiwanis Club. However, having seen the effective work of Rotary International in India and having learned of its worldwide scope, I had promised myself that at a propitious time I would become a Rotarian. Jan returned to her prior commitments and confirmed her teaching appointment for the fall.

Chapter 23: Unexpected Opportunities

1959-60

I returned to my position as dean to pick up where I had left off. It felt strange; I had to become dis-Oriented. The telephone worked, the quality of paper was upgraded, the toilets had paper instead of a water bucket, but there were no servants standing around waiting to run errands. My faithful female secretary, Mildred Schueller, (in India they were all male) was relieved to have one person to whom to report rather than the triumvirate during my absence. I had felt insulted that I heard not a word from President Couchman during my absence. Now he appeared pleased to have me return, perhaps because it simplified some of his decision-making. The faculty also received me with genuine enthusiasm. The academic year was ending; commencement was only a few days away. I had arrived just in time for me to have to notify those seniors whose cumulative average, based on the final grades, would delete them from the graduation roster. This was one of the most painful tasks within my responsibilities. Occasionally, the anxious parents of the failing son or daughter found fault with the faculty. For example, a prominent Dubuque businessman and well known to me called to complain about his son's grade in a psychology course (not my class). His son was a basketball player and on the fringe of academic eligibility; he wanted the grade raised. When the grade was not raised he called the president. The grade was not changed.

The festive commencement ceremonies were held on the campus quadrangle. The summer weather in Iowa includes sudden thunderstorms, often with no discernible warning. In the midst of students lined up to receive their diplomas from the president, vertical bolts of lightning followed by claps of thunder triggered a heavy shower. In utter disarray, the commencement crowd retreated to the nearby gymnasium that had been prepared for this kind of emergency. Gradually, the ushers realigned the graduating class and their families; the interrupted ceremonies were completed. In some respects the atmospheric disruption made the occasion much more memorable. The band, temporarily re-organized, played as the graduates with the faculty informally marched from the gymnasium onto the well-watered campus to share plaudits and farewells with families and friends. Another crop of graduates found their way into the world beyond.

The next week I returned to the office to make a more complete assessment of the priorities. The summer term would open in two weeks. I discovered a considerable list of administrative issues awaiting decisions. In succeeding weeks I completed faculty appointments, class schedules and teaching assignments for 1959-60. I assigned myself General Psychology, the introductory course, with a total registration of 52 students. Considering the size of the class, I wondered whether students had been awaiting my return. By the spring semester I was convinced that this was correct. I offered two sections; my class record shows that I had 34 and 47 students respectively, a total of 81. There was no extra pay for an overload! I was puzzled to hear some of my fellow deans' claim with satisfaction that they did not have time to teach.

That summer I devoted my energies to accumulated tasks and current affairs of the dean's office. The family took no vacation trip; I accepted the fact that President Couchman regarded the return trip from India as vacation bonus. Instead of vacation time we made the most of the Iowa summer. As a family, we planted a large garden on a very fertile college tract set aside for faculty use. Although somewhat late in the season, we planted sweet corn, cabbages, tomatoes, turnips, carrots, beans, and peas. In late summer and fall we enjoyed an abundant harvest.

Our children had reconnected with their friends and were eager for school to begin. Jan returned to her teaching and quickly was earning plaudits from students and parents. We had developed our collection of several hundred slides of the countries we visited, especially India and Switzerland. The family greatly enjoyed viewing slides and reliving our experiences abroad. Jan and I had many requests to speak to church groups, service clubs, and associations of our experiences in India. I remember an engagement I had with the students and faculty at Beloit College. Many of our speeches were gratis. However, we had agreed with our Indian pastor, the Rev. William V. Karl, (later a Bishop in the Church of South India) to send him proceeds from our speeches as a gift for the education of his children. He and his wife were most grateful. We have had periodic correspondence from them telling us that the children, now mature adults, have all done well educationally and professionally.

The fall student enrolment at Dubuque had increased some 40 students due to a new admissions team. The quality of the faculty had significantly improved during my years as dean. I felt energized by the uplifting morale; we were off to a promising academic year.

I had been a member of some visiting evaluation teams to several Presbyterian colleges led by Ted Maxon, a member of the Board of Christian Education of the United Presbyterian Church located in Philadelphia, for the purpose of improving their academic programs. We focused particularly on their program for students preparing to become Christian Educators in the churches. On these visits I discovered anew a particular interest in learning how a total college functions by evaluating the component parts.

What are the qualitative differences between a historically strong college and a weaker one? What component parts are most significant in raising the level of quality of the graduating students? How does an evaluator determine what is the quality level of the alumni? How important, in turn, are the faculty, the president, the academic dean, the dean of students, the librarian, the admissions staff, the record keepers from the registrar to the business officers? How does the governing board relate to the quality of the institution? How can an evaluator find accurate answers to these questions? I discovered a keen interest in learning how to gather and assemble comprehensive, accurate information. Understanding the large scope appealed to me much more than long-term research in a narrow specialty. However, this curiosity and quest did not diminish my pervasive attraction to teaching in the classroom.

To my surprise, in November I received a letter from Norman Burns, Secretary of the North Central Association of Colleges and Secondary Schools, Commission on Colleges and Universities, inviting me as one of fifteen academic deans in the Association to participate in a new program to prepare Consultant-Examiners. The program included an instructional meeting in Chicago, extensive reading, after which the participants, under the tutelage of an experienced leader, would conduct two evaluative visits of different colleges or universities. The program was to be conducted during the spring semester. I did not know who nominated me or why I was invited, but it seemed ideally the kind of opportunity about which I had dreamed. Jan and I talked over this invitation. Although she did not oppose my accepting the invitation, she seemed surprised at the intensity of my interest.

On reflection, I shuddered at the prospect of winning assent from President Couchman. Would I appear irresponsible in asking for approval so soon after returning from a year's leave that he had very reluctantly endorsed? Most of the proposed time away from campus was toward the weekend so that I would not miss any classes. Yet I wondered, "Would he dare not approve my request?"

In my mind I organized the rationale for my participation. Surely he will realize the benefits to the University. I must give him assurances that the quality and quantity of work in the dean's office would not be diminished. Further, I would teach two sections of Psychology during the spring semester, saving the University the need for a part-time psychology faculty member. His first question was, "What will it cost the University? What benefits do you expect from participating in this program. How will this benefit the University?" I assured him that the Commission on Colleges and Universities of the North Central Association would pay all my expenses. I explained that learning how other colleges function would broaden my perspectives. I contended that by working with other select college deans I would learn from them, and that our college would indirectly benefit by my becoming a more effective dean. Following extended cogitation, he reluctantly concurred with my request.

Some of the senior faculty, of financial necessity campus bound for years, and later by inertia and habit, were again puzzled by my unexplainable aspirations. I quietly rejoiced at what I regarded as an opportunity of far-reaching significance.

At our Chicago meeting in January, I observed that my fourteen colleagues as Consultant-Examiners in training appeared to be a select group, several from more prestigious colleges, of which I was pleased to be a member. We were given extensive reading. We heard lectures by Norman Burns and by experienced examiners. A few weeks later half our group, guided by three veteran examiners, visited Wayne State University in Detroit in an on-site experience for their ten-year re-examination. Later in the season, again half our group, after further lectures and instructions was similarly engaged in a second on-site evaluation at Indiana State Teachers College, now Indiana State University, Terra Haute, Indiana. We were then told that each of us was prepared to serve as a member of an examining team of a college or university within the nineteen state area included in the North Central Association of Colleges and Schools (NCSCS). I already felt rewarded for having participated in this program.

The school year moved along very smoothly. Mildred Schueller, my secretary and I had an easy working relationship. She was self-confident and efficient. I enjoyed teaching as always. Faculty members were quite harmonious; three-fourths of them were appointed during my tenure. Quality was noticeably improved. I had even recruited my former Dean at Huntington College as Chair of the Foreign Language department and Professor of French and Spanish. The number of students in the College had increased and overall quality was somewhat better. Relationships with the Seminary faculty were less contentious, particularly with Calvin Schnucker who was appointed Dean when Elwyn Smith departed. My Fulbright appointment brought higher respect from key members of the Board of Trustees. University finances were somewhat improved, but always inadequate. I had developed good relationships with dean colleagues in Iowa and had served as Chairman of the Annual Stillwater Conference of Deans at Oklahoma State University. I had established good relationships through various professional organizations. I had matured and was self-confident that my career was on the move. Jan and I were well known and active in the church. I served as a member on the session and periodically taught Sunday school classes. We were both involved in civic and service organizations.

President Couchman had made some very good appointments in the offices of admissions, development and public relations. Fund-raising and student admissions had much improved leadership and effectiveness. Goldthorp Science Hall was nearly complete; this was very important for the sciences and long overdue. Nevertheless, the University lacked dynamic presidential leadership, the institution lacked financial endowment; the physical plant was partly obsolete and vastly in arrears in maintenance.

In growing numbers I received inquiries about my interest in considering an appointment in another college or university. For various reasons, I had not seriously considered another position. I had declined an unsolicited offer from President John R. Emens to return to Ball State University, my alma mater, as dean of men. The University had an enrolment of more than 12,000 students. When Dr. Emens made the offer I felt honored that he regarded me professionally equipped for the position. After considering the offer for several weeks, I remained firm in my commitment to the small, private college and my academic engagement.

In December I received a letter from President John D. Moseley of Austin College, Sherman, Texas inquiring whether I was interested in considering the position as dean of the college for 1960-61. He reported that he had received my name from E. Fay Campbell, Secretary of the General Division of Higher Education of the United Presbyterian Church in Philadelphia. Jan and I talked it over; we even shared the inquiry with her parents. My first response indicated no active interest. However, John Moseley persisted. In a telephone call he tried to provoke some interest then invited me to meet him when he was in Chicago for other business. I did not know much about Austin College; but I did agree to meet with him. We had a lengthy meeting, I learned much about the College, Dr. Moseley emphasized receipt of a sizable Ford Foundation grant to conduct some innovative curricular experimentation. What I learned stirred my imagination and increased my interest in the opportunities that the position could offer.

As I traveled home I reflected comprehensively about my present position and the advisability of considering a move at that time. We were back from India only about seven months where I had had a leave supported by one half salary. If I did not complete two years after the leave I owed the University proportionate repayment of that stipend. Was it fair to President Couchman, the faculty and students further to disrupt continuity? How would the children respond to being uprooted again so soon? Was it fair to remove them from their Dubuque friends, not for a specified time, but permanently? I was involved in a Consultant-Evaluator program with the North Central Association of Colleges and Schools. Texas was in the Southern Association, a different regional accrediting organization that was reputedly of lesser strength. Was I willing to give up my participation in this challenging new program? Should the family consider a move to the South, a totally different region that was viewed by many mid-westerners as an inherently inferior section of the country? Could our family accommodate to the extreme summer heat? My limited exposure to air-conditioning at deans' meetings in Stillwater, Oklahoma left a "chilling" effect. Were the lures from Texas sufficiently overriding and the prospective answers to my questions distinctly positive to consider further the Austin College venture? In this context, reaching a sound decision was a formidable undertaking.

Dr. Moseley was very persistent; I flew to Sherman, Texas from the new O'Hare Airport in Chicago where I parked in a pasture field with no parking fee. I had an extended interview with faculty, students and a committee of the Board of Trustees. President Moseley was a lawyer, not an educator. As President for six years, this was his only collegiate experience. I was curious whether he really understood the academic institution. He was an aggressive leader, committed to fundamental change, academically and organizationally. The faculty was academically stronger than at Dubuque, although some tenured members from an earlier era needed replacement. Buildings and facilities were generally much better. Chairman of the Board, Toddy Lee Wynne of Dallas had provided funds for an elegant new chapel recently completed. The Board commanded much more wealth, personally and corporately. Board member Robert Wood had financed a large, elegant home for the president. A sizeable grant from the Ford Foundation for curricular innovation was noteworthy.

Austin was a college of the U. S. Presbyterian church with board members, administrators, faculty and students almost totally from Texas and Oklahoma. The only black faces to be seen on campus were a few custodians and kitchen workers. In 1960 racial segregation was still complete; could I subscribe to such a policy? If not, what could I contribute to change? Would I be accepted as the only "damn Yankee" on campus bringing some very non-Southern ideas? I sensed that the campus community probably did not even want seriously to discuss issues of racial segregation so deeply rooted in the South. The small city of Sherman with a rigidly segregated population of 30,000 fifty miles north of Dallas, offered little appeal when compared with Dubuque, Iowa, a prosperous industrial city on the mighty Mississippi. Racial issues had been stirring across the country. In 1954 the Supreme Court of the United States had decreed "separate but equal" education as unconstitutional and ordered integration of schools "with all deliberate speed." President Dwight Eisenhower had ordered U.S. Army troops to Little Rock, Arkansas to integrate the high school when Governor Orval Faubus declared that integration would never happen. U. S. Marshals and Army troops forced integration at universities in Mississippi and Alabama. Did Jan and I want to introduce the family into this political, social, racial and religious climate? I would be succeeding a beloved, blue-blooded Virginian retiring dean who was planning to continue part-time teaching in the College. Were my diplomatic skills adequate? Did I want to face the prospective professional and personal hazards that were ahead?

After declining the offer one time, and yet persuaded that Dubuque would not provide an adequate long-term professional opportunity, Jan and I decided to accept and take another risk. I accepted the offer with an increase in salary of nearly thirty percent. Included was an attractive, new, two-story, brick dean's residence--Windsor House rent free--across the street from the campus. Moving expenses were provided. President Moseley offered to reimburse me for occasional consulting at Austin College during spring and summer, an amount sufficient to remit to the University of Dubuque the balance due following my leave in 1958-59.

As I consulted with faculty at Austin College, I came to understand the considerable tension on campus, much of it centered on the rather drastic academic and organizational changes that John Moseley was generating. I could see the need for me to become a discreet bridge builder between him and the faculty. With his lack of previous academic experience this could become a substantial challenge for me.

When President Couchman made the announcement of my planned departure to the campus community nearly all faculty members and many students expressed great disappointment. Once more Professor Aitchison with one of her colleagues came to my office, still puzzled about why I would want to make a move to that "strange southern territory of Texas." "You came here as a very young dean, but you have grown and grown in your work with the faculty. Now I am very sorry to see you leave." I thanked her for her gracious observation. I completed the work of the dean's office. Our many friends, especially John and Jane Graves, and the children expressed their disappointment in our planned departure. John was the friendly pediatric physician for our children.

In the student newspaper, *the dubuQue*, President Couchman is quoted in part, "An unusual balance of competence and dedication has marked his contribution to the University of Dubuque. We have deep regrets at his leaving our institution after this period of eight years of imaginative and faithful service. We also wish him the best in the future which we believe is exactly what he deserves."

The *KEY* Staff dedicated the 1960 yearbook to me, as I quote in part, "In him one quickly notes the rare blend of confidence and humility, objectivity and faith, achievement and ambition, independence and concern. For bringing these rare combinations to our campus and, furthermore, for imparting them to all within his compass, we, as educated Christians, are thankfully indebted." I felt deeply honored to be so regarded by the students; I thanked the editor for so generous a tribute.

I was particularly surprised to receive letters and personal statements of generous praise for my work and regret for my departure from various members of the faculty and the Board of Trustees, especially from Elwyn Smith, former colleague as Dean of the Seminary. He had shown to me a distinctive air of superiority. His letter read, "Congratulations on a new post with all the possibilities that I am sure it will have in your hands. You have done more for the college than those who know can ever acknowledge, and I have appreciated your courage in adopting measures not always understood. I hope you will have a very happy new professional experience in Texas." From one faculty colleague, "our losing you is a great blow and one to which I shall have difficulty becoming reconciled." Another vigorous young intellectual wrote, "It wouldn't help any to look over your shoulder and find half the faculty 'deserting' with you."

Several letters from individual members of the Board were most laudatory. From Rowe Hinsey's letter I quote briefly, "The Board of Directors asked me to write in their behalf...to express their gratitude for your accomplishments. How does a group of men adequately say, 'Thank you' for academic service of such high distinction? The key to your distinguished record at Dubuque is intellectual, moral and spiritual integrity. Your educational goals were pitched high...In the reaching you scaled the faculty to higher standards, you improved the scholastic tone of the student body and set the College firmly on a loftier level. In these very significant accomplishments you earned for yourself the critical acclaim of the faculty, the deep respect of the students and the abiding appreciation of President Couchman and the Board of Directors." He concluded with a quote from Robert Browning:

Secure, your footing on the trail
A panorama proud
Of past and present greets the vale.
Above there is no cloud,

Except a 'cloud of witnesses,'
Of friends whose thoughts surround
Each day's ascending sure success
To virtue's higher ground.

In re-reading this file, I concluded that the statements contained therein clearly exceeded my accomplishments.

Chapter 24: Austin College: The Segregated South

1960-67

We departed Dubuque for Sherman, Texas about August 15, 1960. The children had very mixed feelings. Lisha was disappointed to have to attend a third high school, and she was pained in leaving a close community and very steadfast friends. Luther had experienced a difficult year in junior high school, with a thin academic climate. He was looking for more academic challenges. Margaret, at age eleven, was most disappointed in having to leave a very close friend, Susan Braun. She felt that her life was disjointed from Dubuque to India, return to Dubuque, and now moving to a totally new social climate. However, each of the children was planning to have a separate room in our new home. They could choose their individual decor to express their different personalities. One chose lavender, one red, white and blue, and one orange and brown.

Jan was very positive and eager to move. For several years she had felt strong "male chauvinism" on the part of President Couchman that was also evident in his marriage. The yearbook of 1960 shows no women faculty or students in the Theological Seminary, even though the United Presbyterian Church had approved the ordination women as ministers four years earlier in 1956. There was little support on the campus or in the larger community, with a high percentage of Roman Catholics, for the rising tide of the "women's rights" movement. Some months before Jan had had a dream of a new brick home before we had any hint of Austin College. Now, she would have an elegant home in which to entertain in a style that appealed to her.

Traveling in our non air-conditioned late model Ford, the temperature kept rising as we headed southward. Our motel in Kansas, by today's standards, had rather primitive window air-conditioning. Sleeping restlessly we vacillated between being unbearably hot or suffering chilly blasts of cold air. Air conditioning in the middle west was still in the early stages. Few cars were air-conditioned and only a small percentage of homes were so equipped.

Each of us felt some combination of eagerness and anxiety as we anticipated our arrival in Sherman. When we arrived in Sherman the temperature was about 100 degrees Fahrenheit. We had been told that our new dean's home, Windsor House, at 1925 Grand Avenue, would not be ready until October. We were temporarily lodged in an old one-story home with window air-conditioning about three blocks north. Traditional homes in Texas were one story without any basements.

What environmental contrasts from Iowa! We discovered an obsolete non-operating oil well in the back yard. Ripe paper shell pecans were falling from the trees scattered throughout the premises. Trees were of different varieties and, we were told, because of the shallow soil they appeared to be stunted rarely more than 30 feet tall. In the yards, grass was either the drought resistant very fine leafed Bermuda or broad-leafed St. Augustine that had the appearance of the despicable Iowa weed, Crab grass. We started grass by laying sod and not by planting seed. We learned to recognize new varieties of flowers, shrubs and trees.

Jan and I were again in a racially segregated community; in some respects it reminded us of our army days in Petersburg, Virginia fourteen years earlier. Our children were introduced to some of the most negative of all the social effects of racial separation. Our washing machine was not yet connected, so one day I took Lisha to a coin laundry. She came running to the car with a puzzled look, "What do I do with our colored clothing; the sign says whites only?" The children were introduced to the racially exclusive white and Negro divisions that included housing, employment, schools, restaurants, hotels, laundries, churches, drinking fountains, toilets, libraries, swimming pools, buses, trains, and many other forms of human services that were still in force to emphasize the "superiority" of the white race. In India our children had lost their awareness of skin color in having been surrounded by persons of all shades and color gradations. To go downtown in Sherman we had to drive through Negro residential sections that included the Negro school. Much of the housing was of poor quality and badly maintained. It was very depressing. Streets in these sections were also in need of repair and almost uniformly without curbs or sidewalks.

Thirty years before we arrived a Negro man had been lynched downtown. Racial tensions became so inflamed that the Grayson County Courthouse was destroyed by fire. We soon observed that Negro men and women were "properly" deferential to the whites. But in 1960, in many parts of the country--especially in parts of the South--pursuit of racial justice was very much astir. We had arrived in a time that would lead to many changes, however slowly and despite highly organized legal and vigorous resistance by the southern power structures. Our family discussed what we could do to smooth our part as "damn-yankee" new comers in the community.

Austin College was deeply entrenched in Texas and Southern racial traditions; there were no Negro students, faculty, administrators or members of the board of trustees. The only black faces visible on the campus were a few male and female custodians and cooks. Whites and Negroes did not visit each other's homes. The conditions gradually began to change when federally compulsory school integration began by moving some of the lower grades from the Negro school to one of the white schools. One Negro teacher had been teaching in the white school before integration. By 1966, no white teacher had volunteered to teach in the Negro school.

After a few weeks following our arrival, Jan and I felt that we should undertake to challenge a tradition. We began by inviting a few Negro professionals to our home for conversation, although we were well aware that this was contrary to accepted social practice.

We included Negro teachers, men and women, the principal of the Negro school and his wife, a Negro minister (who had a pervasive sense of humor) with his wife from the African Methodist Episcopal Church, and a Negro mortician. Two courageous white couples from the Austin College faculty joined us. Everyone was very gracious, cautiously trusting us in our experiment, yet the relationships were quite stiff and formal. We served beverages but no food. We talked about our careers and other non-inflammatory subjects. With an early adjournment

302

we agreed to meet monthly, rotating among the homes of the white members.

After nearly a year of such meetings one of the Negro couples felt "safe enough" to invite the Fellowship of the Concerned, as we designated our group, to their home. Slowly, we came to understand some of the human effects of the practices of centuries of segregation. Understandably, the Negro members felt more vulnerable than the white members and needed enough time to ascertain that our interracial concerns were genuine and not opportunistic. We had to show that our intentions were authentic and trustworthy. Our Negro friends understandably feared for their own safety. Negroes had no social traffic in the homes of whites, except as servants or in certain service roles. These new friends and their kin had suffered in too many ways, and many had observed lynchings. The Ku Klux Klan was alive and active in many parts of the South—there was the ever-present fear when they might assert themselves. Our friends explained that Negroes could use no public toilets, drinking fountains, eating establishments, public parks or places of lodging. This was especially burdensome when traveling for they had to be fed and lodged with friends. Or, they would have to keep driving north until they crossed the boundaries of segregation. Even if they slept in their cars, there was no safe place to park during the night without the risk of being arrested. At every turn they were imperiled with insults, threats, and embarrassments, all of which engendered fear and anxiety.

Jan and I suffered no violence, although the campus night watchman discovered a burning cross on our lawn that he extinguished and informed us the next morning. Gradually, after a year of meetings of the Fellowship of the Concerned we shared carry-in dinners, discovered that we could share humor and racial jokes, and discuss differences in racial practices. In good humor, the Rev. William McGruder introduced us to "CPT"(Colored People's Time). In the latter 19th century, one Dallas Negro family had been given a few acres of "worthless scrub land." They later built an elegant home with gold bathroom faucets in Dallas. In accounting for their home, they explained that their mineral rights yielded millions of dollars of petroleum, much to the chagrin of the donor white family.

Our Fellowship of the Concerned venture over time attracted additional persons, Negro and white, and it had some lasting effects. In 1966-67 school year, Jan, the only white face in the Negro school and the first white teacher, taught high school English. Her teaching greatly reinforced our relationships with the Negro community. When we moved to Coe College in Cedar Rapids, Iowa, Sandra Jackson, her best graduating senior student joined us. We supported her financially, and she lived with us during the fall semester and successfully completed her freshman year. Years later she wrote to us of the transforming significance of that college year at Coe. More than 25 years later I was at Eckerd College while directing a federally funded project in which Austin College was a participant. Our former black colleagues living in Sherman surprised Jan and me when they attended a reception at Austin College in our honor. We were truly flattered. But to me the most significant event was Austin College awarding an honorary doctorate in the mid-90s to the Rev. William McGruder, our friend, the jovial Methodist minister. Those cherished memories still have a special place in our hearts and minds.

Now, let me turn to other dimensions of our family's many experiences in Sherman, Texas. Our family settled into a new routine. Lisha prepared hesitantly to enter her third high school. Sherman High School was unaccustomed to credit equivalency from an Indian school, but finally accepted the courses she had completed at Bishop Cotton School in Bangalore, India. Luther was pleased to enter the new Dillingham Junior High School, looking for a challenging academic program. He also played football where he learned how it felt to be a member of a team that had no victories. Margaret, the most hesitant about another school transfer had made a friend, Sarah Spencer, daughter of a professor at the College. She found her teacher gentle and caring; that helped make the transition. Her school was only a few blocks from home. Lisha and Luther were of similar ages as President Moseley's two older children, although they did not develop close friendships. Jan had decided not to teach during these key adolescent years of the children to help them with the transition.

Jan and I with Margaret joined Grand Avenue Presbyterian Church right across the street from our house. I taught an adult Sunday school class intermittently and served as a member of the session for a three-year term. During most of our membership there Jan was director of the choir while Margaret was a choir member. In our ongoing attempt to encourage independent thought among our children, we agreed that Lisha and Luther could join Trinity United Presbyterian Church across town because that church had a stronger program for youth and fewer southern traditions. I was invited to join two service clubs--Rotary and Kiwanis. Recalling the substantial service projects Rotarians completed in India, I selected the Rotary Club. This provided me ready access to the business and professional dimensions of Sherman. That fall Rotary International introduced a new program of high school student exchange and offered to the Sherman Club an unidentified boy or girl from Belgium, the Netherlands or Scandinavia for 1961-62 academic year. When no Club member volunteered to accept this unknown student, the Club President, who was also the principal of the white high school, made an appeal to the Club. By then we had moved into our delightful, spacious two-story brick new home on a corner lot.

With only one week for our Rotary Club to accept the offer, at breakfast one morning, I asked the family whether we should volunteer. Each child had his/her room; if we volunteered Lisha or Luther would have a roommate for next school year. All agreed that after adapting to India, we would welcome the opportunity for another international relationship, male or female, from any of the prospective countries. Weeks later we learned that a female student would come from Gothenberg, Sweden. A year later, that brought to our home Annika Steen in August 1961. How fortuitous and mutually rewarding that decision turned out to be. From the beginning and continuing today, 40 years, Annika is a member of the family. Our lives have been greatly enriched as a result of that breakfast decision that we made in a few minutes.

When Annika arrived with limited attire and a travel-worn piece of luggage, we assumed that she came from a family of modest means. We arranged a family allowance for her and the local Rotary Club also provided monthly support. Jan quickly sewed some skirts and dresses. Annika's demeanor was unpretentious; during the year we were surprised to learn in a phone call from Sweden of the birth of her second younger brother, the youngest of five children. In all respects, Annika was a member of our family, one of four adolescents.

Some two years after her return home, we received a letter in which she extended an invitation in behalf of her father for Jan, Lisha and me to visit them as their guests for as long we wanted to stay. Her father's invitation included round trip airline tickets. We were astonished but politely declined. In a second letter Annika was emphatic, "When my father sends an invitation, he expects an acceptance." We accepted for the following summer. After we arrived at their home, I asked her father, Jan Steen, "Why would you do this," he replied with two reasons: "When a family takes care of my daughter for one year the way you did, I could never repay them no matter what I did." He also stated that, "Your country has been so generous in helping the needy in Europe, especially after World War II, I want to let you know that some of us have noticed." They treated us royally for two weeks with lodging, food, entertainment and travel. We learned his family was very active politically and he owned a large architectural-construction firm, a man of great wealth. Now, our family could never repay Ulla and Jan, Annika's parents, who became fast friends.

We arranged for their second daughter, Malin, who was about the age of Margaret, to join us for the next academic year. Lisha was in graduate school and Luther was away at college. During the year Ulla and Jan visited us; once more he insisted that he provide the cost for Jan, Margaret and me to take Malin for a visit to Mexico which we did the next spring. Malin and Annika, and their parents, as well as their children have visited our family at intervals during the past four decades.

As I began my work at Austin College, I quickly learned that the man who had recruited me to Texas, President John D.

306

Moseley, was in a hurry, given to compulsive change of Austin College. He strongly believed that the future of collegiate education would be reshaped to combine or integrate academic disciplines. Because of the increasing complexity of society and the rapid advances in the sciences, research, invention, and cosmic exploration results would much more often come from the work of interdisciplinary teams rather than a solitary individual. He anticipated that that should be reflected in undergraduate education. A primary exhibit at the College, funded by a grant from the Ford Foundation, was a sequence of experimental courses for selected freshmen and sophomores labeled Basic Integrated Studies (BIS). This combined courses from English, religion, philosophy, and arts with heavy emphasis on writing. The traditional faculty opposed the action. My challenge was to mediate the differences. Some of President Moseley's assumptions are recognizable in developments of the past 40 years, such as many varied teams sharing the planning and executing the space program.

To design this curriculum, he had brought to campus some academically venturesome faculty members especially for this purpose. One, Lucile Allen, a creative key figure, who was a former dean of students at Stanford University, served as a consultant. But another was Ashby Johnson, a freewheeling professor of religion and philosophy who was being lured away to the new Florida Presbyterian College in St. Petersburg, Florida. Faculty at that College were in contrast to most of the Austin College faculty members who were traditionalists, and were not given to academic experimentation in this academically solid but staid Lone Star institution. Nearly all Austin College faculty members were natives of Texas or Southern United States, the great majority having completed their education in this section. The beloved retiring dean, James Moorman, a blueblood Virginian, was a sound biologist. He combined an engaging sense of humor with notable absent-mindedness. His pleasant personality was more humanistic than scientific.

One of his favorite stories was that having agreed to meet his wife, Elizabeth, downtown, James driving by waved to her as she stood on the street corner. When she arrived home via public transportation, he claimed that he could not find her. His administrative style was simply to engage in cautious maintenance with conformance to the wishes of the president. In retirement, he continued to teach a course in biology. Memoranda and letters in my file indicate that we enjoyed a very cordial relationship without any unpleasantness.

Our good relationship is confirmed by a letter from one of the senior faculty members concerning the Honors Convocation on the retirement of Dean Moorman. In his letter the faculty member wrote, "my admiration and appreciation of your gracious and very human gesture extended to Dr. Moorman. Your coming down from the platform to clasp his hand in recognition of his long and effective service, created one of those 'high moments' of audience rapport such as we seldom experience even in our small college family. And your action, I must add, served further to convince those present that the administration acted wisely in choosing Dr. Moorman's successor. Your discerning judgment, in all campus affairs, I have come increasingly to admire."

When I arrived about mid-August, faculty committees for the academic year had not been appointed. Faculty members did not participate in committee appointments that were made exclusively by President Moseley, (John D.) and the dean. John D. was accustomed to appointing to key committees only faculty members more likely to conform to his points of view; known adversaries were sidelined where some had become campaigners and snipers against the president's policies or against him personally. I contended that adversaries should be included on committees where they can be held accountable, and further, some of their perspectives and knowledge may be of value to the committee. One of John D's strongest and vocal antagonists was a Princeton Ph.D., and Professor of English, (Phi Beta Kappa.) I believed in the collegial and parliamentary procedures that in later years were increasingly reflected in making appointments. John D. was uncomfortable with that direction. He did not trust faculty and did not understand why faculty did not trust him. Although he seemed to respect me as dean, my more independent thinking and different administrative style from my predecessor often added to his discomfort and insecurity.

Another area that commanded my attention as dean was that the College lacked a clearly defined admissions policy. I worked with the director of admissions and the admissions committee and by the end of the fall semester the faculty adopted the recommended policy. We made no significant changes from current practices but, instead, clarified standards and procedures. I was especially concerned with our all-white student body. Although there was no written statement of policy in the College catalog against admitting Negro students, (it was just understood) during this time of racial unrest and turmoil, there was no hope of a change in practices. Most of the members of the board of trustees were no more ready to admit black students than boards in Mississippi or Alabama, and John D. didn't even want the question raised. The size of the student body was increasing, curricular experimentation was continuing, and there was need for additional faculty.

President Moseley, who came from a non-academic background, felt his own insecurities, especially when surrounded by tradition-bound faculty. His administrative style was intent on keeping adversaries off-balance. He sought to engender and increase their insecurities by annually changing faculty committee assignments, redefining the duties of each committee and other forms of manipulation. To deal with stronger opponents, he sought to isolate them from the faculty mainstream; in turn they effectively calculated how to subvert President Moseley. Thus the morale of some faculty was uncommonly low.

He did not trust the democratic or collegial processes of academia. However, rather than openly deleting the use of parliamentary procedures, he preferred in practice to subvert them. He was almost fearful of direct confrontation, either with an individual or a group. Frequently, in his office in a one-on-one negotiation he would argue his case, completely oblivious to time, his own schedule commitments, and that of his adversary. His next appointee could cool his heels in the outer office for ten, twenty, or thirty minutes. In a committee or faculty meeting he sought to avoid vigorous discussion to be followed by a vote.

John D. came to a meeting with a conclusion determined to wear the opposition into conformity. When his adversaries were exhausted he then might plead the Quaker system—silence signifies unanimity.

As the new "Yankee" dean of the college, my principal duty was to serve as a negotiating buffer between the aggressive, visionary president and the calculatingly, resistant faculty. Many faculty members felt threatened, and as is usually the case, threat generates fear. A few of John D's ideas were good; however, because of his style of operation most of the faculty ignored the good ideas. I needed all the diplomatic skills of an academic Lincoln! John D. early proposed to me the elimination of all faculty academic rank. "After all," he said, "with our different talents we are all working together as a community." He was unable to comprehend why academic rank was so important to faculty. I explained that academic rank in the disciplines in which the degrees have been earned provide their only professional identity. Academic rank proclaims who they are. It is the identity that represents their life-long studies, and it gives them status on their career ladder. Rather than my being a fellow advocate, John D. found me the obstacle to his strong urge. He was doggedly persistent; I was commensurately obstinate. After many weeks of periodic consideration, I finally said, "John D., I do not wish to discuss this issue any more unless you at the same time agree to delete your title as president." He blushed, as if he had not thought of that. I regarded his proposal so inflammatory to the faculty I did not share it with any faculty member. I could just imagine what "grist for the mill' this would have been for principal adversaries. Gradually, the whole matter faded from the agenda. We moved on to other weighty matters.

As a result of John D.'s successes, Austin College was becoming noted beyond Texas borders. In the December 5, 1960 issue, *Time*, listed "50 four-year liberal arts colleges that can give a good education to the high school senior who cannot get into Amherst & Co....At Texas Austin College, a hefty Ford grant is aimed at building the school into a Southwestern Amherst or Swarthmore." That Ford grant was made before I arrived. This was a lofty ambition in which I found myself caught up having arrived only three and a half months before the article. The road to success was only dimly perceived, and the financial and other costs had not been calculated.

All trustees and more than 98% of the students were from Texas and Oklahoma, as were the vast majority of the faculty. It seemed to me that a proposed change not on John D.'s list should be to expand geographic and educational diversity of prospective faculty. Without raising this as an issue, I succeeded in bringing young faculty with Ph. D. degrees from the Ivy League and the Big Ten. They were more open to curricular experimentation. Two in the original group were given dual academic rank. Arvid John Carlson, with degrees from Michigan and Princeton, Assistant Professor of History and Basic Studies, and Charles Kennedy, with degrees from Yale, in Religion and Basic Studies. Later Lee Scott, with Yale degrees, came on a two-year leave from Denison University. Frederick Eutsler, with Berea and Yale degrees and a veteran in integrated studies, followed him. I recruited these, among many others, by telephone and mail. I did not travel for recruitment.

Basic Integrated Studies had run its original cycle under the Ford Foundation grant. These experimental courses were to be followed by broad revision of the curriculum. Many faculty members had a fixed aversion to "Integrated" in the course titles and were disinclined toward major curricular modifications. Devoid of previous academic experience, John D. may not have realized the amount of work required to prepare a new syllabus. After weeks of wrangling in the College Council, comprised of the Area Chairmen who were mostly of the traditional faculty, the Council recommended a four-course sequence titled Basic Studies I II III IV. (Students soon called it "B.S.") These courses would be designed by teams of rotating faculty from the humanities combining history, religion and philosophy. Chronologically this sequence encompassed principal features of the Judaic, Christian, and Hellenistic eras through Western ideas, institutions and cultures from the ancient era to the twentieth century. Asian cultures were added later. One lecture was followed by two periods per week of discussion in small sections. The syllabus required heavy reading and substantial writing.

Other general education courses included science, art and social sciences. Adopted by the faculty, many felt it was too far out whereas John D. had wanted more. A change in racial segregation was not on his admitted agenda. Certainly, most of the trustees were not open for any such consideration.

In the absence of any black faces among trustees, administrators, faculty or students in the early '60s and with little prospect of any changes, I pondered what I could do to make some advances on the racial front. Finally, I calculated that if I could not bring black students to the campus, I could introduce selected white Austin students to the cultures of newly independent African countries through a creative summer program, *Operation Crossroads Africa*. The program founded by Dr. James Robinson, a black Presbyterian Pastor in Harlem, proved so successful that it became the model for the *Peace Corps*.

Without any general announcement of my plans, in conferences with some of the brightest sophomores and juniors, I explained *Operation Crossroads Africa*, not as an alternative to black students on campus, but as a reliable and highly desirable international educational opportunity. In *Operation Crossroads Africa* students from the United States and Canada were carefully selected to participate in the eight-week program with African counterparts of comparable age in manual labor projects in the "bush." Groups of eight or ten students from the U. S. and Canada who were fluent in the language of the host country, English or French, were paired with an equal number of native students. One experienced adult leader competent in the skills required for the project was assigned to each group for six weeks of labor. Projects ranged from clearing the land for pathways, digging drainage ditches, to constructing a one-room brick school building. Food, lodging and tools were of the most primitive sort. After six weeks of labor, two weeks were allotted to travel that offered broader exposure to the cultures within the country. Costs were shared by funds raised by families of participants, *Operation Crossroads Africa,* and by the respective colleges and universities. Students in the first year returned with such infectious and glowing reports of their experiences that recruiting in subsequent years became much easier. Our daughter, Lisha, was one of the Austin College participants, which found her experience in Senegal very educationally rewarding and in 2001 her daughter, Nicole, a student at Syracuse University, traveled to Zimbabwe for a semester abroad. Within six years Austin College provided more participants than any other college or university in the U. S. and Canada, a total of thirty-two.

This program and my own strong convictions about intercultural education encouraged some faculty to connect with other off-campus educational opportunities, domestic and international. This led to the Washington, D. C. term with American University, Summer Institutes Abroad with Florida Presbyterian College and Junior Year Abroad with other established college and university programs. Soon after, faculty approved a few courses in history and cultures of Southeast Asian countries. With assistance from Mr. A. C. Deva Gowda in India, I brought a sequence of visiting Hindu and Moslem faculty to teach those courses. However modest, these kinds of educational opportunities opened doors beyond the rather provincial Texas atmosphere. On an annual schedule, we also brought some young faculty from Germany to enhance instruction in that foreign language and literature. Several Austin College students who majored in German were attracted to spend a semester or a year in Germany to amplify their German language mastery and two or three found careers as Foreign Service Officers.

The effects of our year in India continued to bring letters from Indians who had come to know me asking for help in bringing them to the United States for advanced study. I was able to help only a few. Two examples: Ram Kulkarni who was a capable teacher in the practicing high school was a guest in our home for a month to observe the American system of high school education. D. K Seetharamaiah on the faculty of Teachers College was able to secure a grant and completed his Ph. D. degree at Ohio State.

For my own professional development, several opportunities came my way. In the summer of 1961 Jan and I were invited to attend the Pugwash XI Nova Scotia Conference July 18-27 for academic deans. Fifteen deans were selected from the Association of American Colleges to assemble in Thinker's Lodge for a program of study, discussion and recreation funded by the Cyrus Eaton Foundation. To attend the invitational conference, we drove from Sherman, Texas via Maine and Quebec, before the Interstate System was completed, which greatly enhanced our appreciation of parts of New England and marine provinces of Canada.

We were assigned reading of several books including Plato's, *Meno* (Great Dialogues of Plato), Swift, *Gulliver's Travels;* Alexis de Tocqueville, *Democracy in America*; Walter Lippman, *The Public Philosophy;* John Dewey, The *Public and Its Problems.* President Richard Weigle of St. John's College, known for its Great Books curriculum, and Professor George Barton of Tulane University led the intellectual discussions each morning. Afternoons were free for recreational activity. One of Cyrus Eaton's chefs prepared abundant food and beverages. On Sunday we sailed to Prince Edward Island. The Pugwash Conference was a salutary intellectual and recreational event. Each August I continued to participate in the Stillwater Conference of Academic Deans at Oklahoma State University. The Conference was thematic, developed by the elected chairman from among participants, and also provided opportunities to exchange information with other deans from across the country about curricula, teaching and faculty development.

Jan and I also continued with the Danforth Associates program that included a regional conference each year. We had several students who were winners in the prestigious Danforth Fellow Program for prospective teachers. As I previously mentioned, our lives had been greatly enriched at the six annual conferences at Lake Miniwanca on the east shores of Lake Michigan. The Danforth Foundation always brought a pair of national and international scholars as lecturers including the famed Japanese pacifist, Toyohiko Kagawa, and produced lasting friendships among faculty..

One of the most rewarding conferences that I attended was the Aspen Institute of Humanistic Studies. This was a unique opportunity to share substantial readings and ideas with some fifteen upper level business executives across the nation. I was the lone academic participant within the discussion group led by the former President of Oberlin College and former Ambassador to the Philippines. Two resource persons were Bishop James Pike and an Assistant Secretary of State whose name escapes my memory. This, too, yielded some lasting friendships from a different sector of society.

Into the 1960s, programs of international studies and increased student exchanges had developed considerable national momentum. Academic leaders promoted the inclusion of Eastern religions, philosophy and cultures through conferences that included the presidents and academic deans. An example was a ten-day foundation-sponsored Bennington College Islamic Conference of Non-Western Studies led by an Islamic scholar in which President Moseley and I participated. In preparation we were assigned readings of Moslem history, the Islamic surge into Europe and the centuries-long Islamic threat to Christianity in France, Spain, eastern Europe and the Middle East.

While at the conference, President Moseley received a call from parents disturbed by the book *Lord of the Flies,* an assigned reading during the summer for Austin College freshmen. He reported this to me. "What on earth are we requiring freshmen to read?" he asked in amazement. Handing his note to me he told me to take care of it. These were protective parents fearful of what college was going to do to their son. I called the parents, who had looked at the book but not read it, and soothingly I explained the curricular context in which the book was to be used. Although not fully satisfied, their son did show up in the freshman class.

During the sixties the struggle toward racial equality was heightened and accompanied by campus student unrest, challenge to authority and defiance of traditions all were on the increase. This took many forms such as demands from student leaders to share in campus governance by attending and having rights of the floor at faculty meetings, serving on faculty and board committees. The students' challenges to authority and traditions were expressed, among other ways, by sit-ins in college and university president's offices, blocking traffic on campus streets. Campus unrest was fed by growing opposition to the Vietnam War. Demonstrations commonly took place in front of and blocking entrance to Selective Service Board Offices. Longer and unkempt hair on men, beards and mustaches, strange dress and "streaking" (meaning nude) were quite prevalent on campuses. Destruction of campus property was increasing.

Although the Austin College budget was always tight, John D. succeeded in getting several kinds of additional grants from foundations, corporations and individuals. He was fiscally venturesome, sometimes to the discomfort of the executive committee of the Board. John D. was a more effective fund-raiser than he was a fiscal manager. The chief financial officer, Ellis Lockhart, had been in small business enterprise but had no previous experience in managing the finances of a not-for-profit collegiate institution. Later, Fred Detweiler, retired CEO of a major defense corporation joined the College as director of administration in charge of the business manager, controller and plant manager.

I felt deeply troubled in having no black students or faculty at the College. The Presbyterian Church, U.S., that founded Austin College, had a long history of sending missionaries to the Belgian Congo. So in the fall of 1963, I called the head office in Nashville to talk with the Rev. George Cooley, in the Office of World Missions, about the possibility of bringing a college student from the Congo to Austin College. He visited the campus and was a guest in our home. I discovered that on the racial front, he and I were kindred souls. We agreed that he would send me an application of a Congo student whom he would recommend for admission to Austin College. Surely, not even the board of trustees would dare oppose admitting a Christian Congolese student, Pierre Shamba, the fruit of decades of Presbyterian missionary activity. He was admitted, became a friend of many students and, fortunately, was able to accommodate himself to those persons on campus and in the community who reacted negatively to his presence. One of the traditional administrators native to the south in the development office, also a Presbyterian, told me emphatically that "It's all right for this Congo mission student to come to the College for an education, but he better not get involved socially with any of our girls." Later, we brought a second Congolese student whose adaptation was much more difficult. Pierre graduated in due course and became a prominent educational leader in the Congo. The second student, whose name I cannot recall, was not as versatile and did not complete his degree program. How paradoxical, black students from Africa were admissible, but domestic black students were not. Time and diligent effort do bring changes. As of this writing scores of black native-born American students have graduated from Austin and some have been elected student body leaders. I am uncertain whether any black faculty, administrators or trustees have been appointed.

In a time like this, I felt strongly what is expressed by an anonymous author, "God give us men (and women), for a time like this demands strong minds, great hearts, true faith, ready hands; Men whom the spoils of office cannot buy, whom the lusts of office cannot kill, Men (and women), who possess opinions and a will..."

For several years I had sought John D.'s assent to my recruiting some black faculty. The answer was always firmly negative, in keeping with the College tradition. Finally, looking to the summer term of 1967, my last term there, he cautiously approved my appointing Dr. Robert Brisbane, Professor of Political Science at Morehouse College in Atlanta. Morehouse was and is a traditional black college with a high academic reputation including a Phi Beta Kappa chapter. Dr. Brisbane had been a professor in the Fulbright program to India with me; I knew him very well. He and his family had been guests in our home. However, John D. would not entertain my considering him for appointment to fill a vacancy during the academic year. I had the feeling that he probably feared the rebuke from "dyed-in-the-wool" unyielding segregationists on the board of trustees.

A new round of prospective grants from the Ford Foundation required a ten-year academic plan including a budgetary projection. Other Texas foundations were considering various kinds of grants to Austin College. The College lacked very knowledgeable and experienced staff in the area of development. Consequently, John D. was required to devote

317

substantially more time to fund-raising.

I also devoted considerable time toward "earning my spurs" as a Texan and as dean. However, my love for teaching in the classroom had not diminished. I refer to my grade book to note the difference in grading today. In the fall semester, 1960 I taught one section of General Psychology with 23 students. I gave only two students a grade of "A" and one "F." In the spring semester, I taught one section of General Psychology with 30 students; I gave four "A" or "A-" grades and no "F." Each semester I required several short research papers; my reputation spread rapidly as a professor with expectations that each student do his best. Another professor also taught sections of this course. Compared with what today is labeled "grade inflation" and attendant student complaints, surprisingly, I faced no rebuttals about grades. In 1966-67, the last semester I was at Austin College, in a General Psychology class of 35 students, student performance had improved. I gave seven grades of "A" and no "F." Although the College had raised its admission standards, this unselected sample may reflect the higher level of student ability or it may indicate that more of the brighter students selected my section.

From 1963-65 I taught freshman sections of required Basic Studies instead of Psychology in response to College policy of rotating course assignments of faculty from different disciplines. Admittedly, I did not enjoy the classroom as much with several of the 20 freshmen, some of them wallowing in intellectual doldrums. Nevertheless, I did not depart from my strong conviction that administrators in small colleges should show their mettle in the classroom. If done effectively, that tends to enhance the mutual respect with faculty and helps to bring the administrators closer to students.

During my seven years at Austin I taught 12 sections of General Psychology with a total of 344 students. Class size varied from 17 to 45 students. In each class, at the end of the course, each student completed a copy of the College Teacher Rating Scale with 14 items ranging from (1) Objectives Clarified by Instructor to (14) General Estimate of Teacher in summary, each item on a ten-point scale from 1-10. On General Estimate of

Teacher 8,9,10 were Very Superior Teacher; 4,5,6,7 were Average Teacher; 1,2,3,4 were Very Poor Teacher. The last item ranged from 75% to 100% of the students in a section who checked 8,9 or 10; the mean of the means was 90%, the median of the means was 93%. Looking back at these results I am amazed. I did not show the results to any of my colleagues or to John D. On reflection, I wonder why I didn't. I should point out that faculty members did not use a rating scale in the Basic Studies sections.

In the absence of a faculty policy manual, John D. was intent on my devoting some of my energies to preparing such a document. Understandably, as the College was striving to raise its overall quality, a few faculty members who were appointed in an earlier era, did not rise to the challenge. Also, the president was hoping that some of the more able faculty, whose respect he had difficulty in commanding, would choose to move elsewhere. Yet, in spite of his commendable move toward a policy manual, I realized that John D. was less intent on having an operational guide, per se, than to have such a document available for foundations and accrediting agencies. Every so often on a specific policy matter that might favor the faculty, his comment was "Let's fuzz it up a little." Many faculty members were suspicious of the president's honest intentions; my task was to work diplomatically with faculty without showing disloyalty to my superior—often a tough maneuver.

In developing the Faculty Policy Manual, at various stages I worked closely with the Chair of the Education Committee of the Board, Bob Jones who was the pastor of a large congregation in Fort Worth. Although conservative in his philosophy of education, he understood the need for clear academic policies related to faculty selection, appointment, promotion and tenure. In fact, he was a key advocate with the board for adopting sound academic policies and practices. Although an alumnus and a native Texan, he supported cautiously expanding the geographic base of Austin College faculty and students, domestic and international. However, he was not ready to push for interracial ventures. In 1960 international on-site programs for students and faculty were in the early stages of development. It led to rapid expansion in the 60s and 70s. Records of the graduating class of 1966 show very modest gains in geographic expansion of students. Among 173 in the graduating class only 15 domestic students resided outside of Texas with a single international member from Turkey. Proportionately, my effort at recruiting faculty with geographic and educational diversity and more terminal degrees produced more results. I was very pleased with the general upgrading that derived partly through faculty retirement and attrition. Yet, I pondered whether the deep entrenchment of Austin College in the history and culture of Texas would permit it to evolve into a national institution.

From a layman's perspective the South had two cultures denoted by race, a legacy from the days of slavery. From the perspective of the professional sociologist, the white race had completely obliterated the culture of the African slaves, including their family life, housing, language, religion, music, diet, and type of dress, even their personalities. Among the slaves a subculture of the white race gradually evolved.

From my point of view, under whatever cultural label, master and slave had developed dual personalities, or in Greek terms, two levels of persona or masks. When master dealt with his own race and his social level in society he wore one mask. This mask, depicted his personality, his language, his demeanor suited to the conditions that the wearer faced. Sometimes when dealing with the black person the mask of the white person completely beguiles his other persona. Wearing some kind of mask may also become habitual, even subconscious. I believe this applied to members of both races.

The descendant of slaves also formed a dual persona. When he spoke to the dominant race, he told them deferentially what he thought they wanted to hear. When he was with "his own kind" he spoke about how he really felt. He fully realized the perils of wearing the wrong mask in speech, conduct and manner or to venture a crossover, even a hundred years after freedom from slavery. As we became more deeply involved with Southern society, we observed that some of these characteristics were still being practiced.

This is graphically illustrated in Hamilton Jordan's book, *No Such Thing As A Bad Day,* when he writes about his father who had served during the Vietnam War on the Selective Service Board with the first black member, Dr. Thomas Jenkins, President of Albany State College. When Hattie, the Jordan's black maid, proudly announced to Hamilton's father, "Dr. & Mrs. Jenkins are at the *front* door," "My father--flabbergasted to have a black couple at our *front* door paying a social visit-- maintained enough social composure to exchange pleasantries and invite them in. He seemed surprised that they accepted his invitation....The Jenkins' visit was a landmark in my father's life."

It seemed to me that these legacies of slavery served another function. When I talked with a Southern person, black or white, it was sometimes difficult to determine behind which mask was the real person. A mask enabled one to avoid full exposure. For example, a mask could be selected to avoid candid talk about certain subjects. Some whites sought to becloud the real facts about slavery or the feelings of disdain for descendants of slaves, or to acknowledge the utter failure of so called "separate but equal education" based on the U. S. Supreme Court decision *Plessey v. Ferguson* of 1896. Following the reversal of that decision by the Court in *Brown v. Board of Education* in 1954 for decades there were layers of organized obstruction in the South to keep blacks from voting at the ballot box and authentic integration of schools. In the early 1960s, to members of both races, the relationships were still vertical; no one could imagine relationships being or becoming genuinely horizontal.

Even at the time of this writing, some black women in Florida serving as caretakers for a member of a black family enter the home only through the back door. Many sophisticated white natives of St. Petersburg candidly admit that they have never visited in a black home or invited black persons to their home for any social reason. One must wonder whether a single culture or a horizontal racial relationship is attainable in the South or the North.

This reminds me of other memorable interracial experiences in Texas. In the early 1960s I had a telephone call from Heald, Hobson & Associates of New York, an educational consulting firm, asking me to serve as their consultant at Bishop College, a traditional Negro institution, in Dallas. (Later, they also sent me to Texas College, in Tyler, that appeared to have no prospect of earning accreditation.) In recent years Bishop College had moved from a small rural area to a tract of land in Dallas, established a new campus, and constructed new buildings for its growing student enrolment. Faculty and administrators were nearly all black but the board of trustees was all white. The members were drawn significantly from Dallas leaders and prominent persons including Federal Judge Sarah Hughes and Donald Zale, president of the national firm, Zales Jewelers. My assignment was to help Bishop College to strengthen the academic program and assure its integrity working toward full regional accreditation.

At that time the Southern Association of Colleges was in transition from two distinctive levels of accreditation, one for Negro colleges and a higher one for white colleges, to a single level for all colleges and universities. Many Negro colleges did not meet the new accreditation standards but were diligently striving to remain in operation. Most received some financial assistance from the Federal Government. Deficiencies included inadequate funding, undefined standards of admission of students, inadequately prepared faculty, deteriorated physical facilities, poor academic and financial record keeping, and poorly qualified boards of trustees and administrators. Notably among these colleges, however, were many devoted faculty and administrators.

I secured John D.'s somewhat hesitant assent for me to accept an appealing invitation from Heald-Hobson. Not only did this open new experiences for me in the area of institutional accreditation, it also offered new opportunities for interracial relationships. First, I was advised by Heald-Hobson & Associates to make some assessments of the quality of academic record keeping and the level of student qualification for college studies, to be accompanied with recommendations for improvements. Second, I was to make some evaluation of the level of qualification of faculty members with recommendations for upgrading the faculty. My working relationships were to be principally with the College's academic dean and the president. I was paid a per diem stipend.

Academic record keeping in the registrar's office was in a shambles. High school transcripts were often incomplete or missing, course sequences were frequently ignored, and progress toward a degree was often not discernible. Necessary grade requirements were vague and often ignored. I began consulting during the football season. Bishop College, along with Austin College, was a member of the N.A.I.A. (National Athletic Intercollegiate Association) and committed to follow its rules. After checking the roster of football players, the registrar acknowledged that he had not reconciled that roster with registration or with required grade records of players. When I examined records of the players, I learned that some players were not registered as students. They were playing Bishop College football just for the fun of it; the coaches were unconcerned. The academic dean claimed the he was totally unaware of the violation. He appeared surprised but exhibited no great concern. The registrar evidently was unaccustomed to verifying grade eligibility of athletes.

It was quickly obvious to me that many students were woefully deficient in grammar, writing and mathematics and needed extensive remedial work that the College was not providing. Having been assured that special grant funds were available at the College to teach remedial courses during the summer term, I helped the academic dean organize such courses. I employed some bright students from colleges and graduate schools. (In different summers I included our daughter, Lisha, who taught grammar and writing, and our son, Luther, taught mathematics.) This program was continued for several summers, although not nearly all the deficient students could be included.

Some of the Bishop College Board members were justifiably uneasy about the financial management and accounting of funds. The federal grant agency called Bishop College repeatedly for overdue financial reports. Three trustees called me for personal conferences about the competence of the president and the chief financial officer, although financial affairs were not part of my assignment. The executive committee debated whether the President of Bishop College should be continued. Jan and I even entertained the president and his wife for dinner in our home hoping to build stronger working relationships. Although I felt that I was of some help in the academic program, I began to realize that the range and depth of help that the College needed was far more extensive than I could provide. In my report to Heald-Hobson and Associates I expressed my concern about the leadership and the great need for basic changes. When the term of my assignment ended I declined any further involvement. The demands on my time at Austin College did not permit me to give the range of attention that Bishop College problems required. They were too deep seated. By the end of my consultantship, some stronger faculty had been appointed, and academic records and student progression toward graduation were somewhat improved.

The interracial relationships in Texas at the time had many complex facets. I kept asking myself what steps I could take that would make a difference. I decided to take a high-risk action. In the fall of 1966, I had arranged with the athletic director for Austin to play a pre-season home football game against Bishop College. Bishop won. This greatly angered some members of the Austin Board of Trustees. The game was more interracial activity than they were ready to tolerate. John D. was pressured to end my time as dean of the college, but he did not have the courage to fire me. He probably anticipated strong disapproval from the students and majority of the faculty. In retrospect, although my intentions were altogether honorable, however, in the short term that athletic contest probably did not serve to advance interracial relationships at Austin College. Afterwards, periodic news reports emphasized repeated financial crises at Bishop College. Regrettably, in later years the College filed for bankruptcy and soon thereafter was closed as an educational institution.

I became involved with the Southern Association of Colleges as an evaluator of colleges for re-accreditation. Every ten years each college and university had to undertake an extensive self-study, followed by a visit on campus of an evaluating team that filed its report with the Association. The overarching purpose was to improve the institution's educational functions. The net result was pointing out strengths and weaknesses leading to full or conditional re-accreditation. I was also assigned as a consultant to two unaccredited struggling black colleges that were seeking candidacy aspiring to future accreditation. I did not see much in their condition that offered any hope.

Getting back to John D., he was a complex personality with a brilliant mind and a propensity for hard work—even a workaholic. He raised millions in new money for College construction from individual Texans, Presbyterian Churches and Texas foundations, over-reaching his development staff and presenting an astonishing contrast with the previous history and development of the College. From 1957 through 1965, for example, nine new buildings were added, literally transforming the campus. The list included a spacious president's home, and Windsor House, a home for the dean's family (our residence for seven years), both located across the street from the campus. Buildings for College programs included: Wynne Chapel; Louis Calder Stadium; Craig Hall for the Music and Art Departments; Arthur Hopkins Library; Caruth and William A. Dean Halls, residences for women and men respectively; and Moody Science Center. This was a remarkable achievement, even by Texas standards.

Despite his successes in raising funds for capital construction, cost overruns, combined with rapidly growing academic programs and increased personnel outpaced fund raising. The rate of spending for the College was always faster than the revenue. Consequently, the budget for current operations was continually in distress. At the same time, however, the board was not unmindful of changing growth and public reputation of the College.

Although he and I had worked closely together for years, John D. seemed totally baffled about my reasonably successful administrative style. He was apparently unable to comprehend that I could maintain very positive relationships with faculty and students without being disloyal to him. He found it very difficult to share openly what his feelings were; one had to infer his feelings based on observable behavior. Although a sensitive, southern gentleman in so many respects, conferences in his office continued without regard for anyone else's schedule.

With my phlegmatic and calm disposition and my Swiss, near fanatical adherence to schedule, interminable conferences with John D. weighed a heavy toll on me, and it became increasingly very stressful. One day in the middle years of our working together, during an endless conference that continued long after his secretary had notified him of the next visitor's arrival, I exploded at his complete disregard for other people's needs and schedules. "John D., you have absolutely no regard for anyone. You have no sensitivity for the needs and schedules of other people. None of us can ever know when a conference with you will end." He was utterly astonished, visibly shaken and didn't say a word. After a few minutes of cooling off I apologized. Then I asked him to agree that at the beginning of all future conferences we would set and adhere to the terminal time. He concurred. Thereafter, whenever I entered his office for a conference I began with the question, "What is our terminal time?" Not wanting another unexpected outburst from me, his behavior changed--at least with me.

When he faced certain difficult problems and disliked a confrontation, John D. sometimes referred them to me. For example, the Sherman police notified him that they had found one of the College male faculty members in a parked car with behavior that looked suspiciously homosexual. After my conference with the professor, he had a very successful career at the College, which concluded with a celebrated retirement.

The College had a visiting Christian minister from Korea for a week. The provincial Sherman police observed him curiously looking at automobiles on a downtown used car lot, picked him up on suspicion that he was preparing to steal hubcaps. Theft of hubcaps was then widely prevalent. The Korean minister told the police that he was a guest of Austin College. I secured his release. The next morning I called the police chief and verified the claim that he was a guest of Austin College, that he was new to this country and was astonished to

326

see the hundreds of beautiful used cars available. I explained to the chief that this is the kind of police action that confirms claims made about mistreatment of international visitors. I asked the chief to come to my office on campus and in behalf of the police department apologize to our Korean guest. In a conference among the three of us, our guest graciously accepted his apology.

The most devious faculty adversary of President Moseley continued to be the tenured Professor of English and former chairman of the department. That year he was president of the local chapter of the American Association of University Professors (AAUP). He thrived on gleeful response of faculty colleagues who shared his ridicule and demeaning of the president. He was academically, politically, religiously and economically very conservative. In some respects, John D. was much more liberal. Some faculty colleagues, however, avoided the professor while regarding many of his remarks highly inappropriate. Some students reported to me that he made very flippant remarks the day that President John Kennedy was assassinated in Dallas. One of his more discreet colleagues prodded me, "Why don't you do something to stop him?" In sympathetic reply I countered, "I am quite aware of his unprofessional and offensive comments. In his expanding cockiness, one of these days he will make a major misstep that I will then be unable to ignore." It happened! He openly disagreed with President Moseley and me concerning the granting of tenure to a colleague in his department.

The professor had agreed to teach this colleague's class while she was ill. Immediately after class several disgusted students came to my office to report that he did not teach literature. Instead, he used the class period to justify his views about the tenure decision concerning his departmental colleague and to attack the views of the president, dean and the department chairman--with attendant demeaning comments. I questioned the students in careful detail, made generous notes and thanked them for their candid report. To myself I recalled the various times that faculty members had asked me to deal with this adversary of the president. Perhaps this is it, I thought.

I called the professor to my office. I relayed what the

students had told me and asked: "Sir, is this student report correct?" He blushed deeply, restlessly moved about in his chair and finally replied, "I guess it is essentially accurate." Reflectively, I reminded him that as president of the AAUP Chapter he must understand the AAUP position concerning the inappropriateness of using a class period for that purpose. He thought for a few minutes after which he acknowledged that what he did was contrary to AAUP policies. We had an extended discussion; I decided now was the time for decisive action.

"You know this is a serious matter. You have one of two choices; it is your decision. You can bring me your resignation within two weeks from today. Your other choice is a formal hearing before a committee of your faculty colleagues as stipulated by the AAUP who will then recommend to me what is an appropriate action. Obviously, this will be an open hearing with attendant publicity."

When I told John D. of my action, he was uneasy, fearful of that professor and his supporters, wondering whether I was on firm enough ground with the terms that I had stated. The professor was obviously shocked. In due course, he brought in his resignation as a tenured professor effective at the end of the academic year. One of the professor's colleagues was reported to have said, "The dean finally got him." No one had defended him in my presence. John D. never discussed the matter further but I assumed that he felt a deep sense of relief.

This professor speaking to his supporting colleagues had ridiculed John D. on many subjects, including his curricular ideas, his large president's home instead of using those funds to raise faculty salaries, and his belonging to the Rotary Club, in part for what he regarded as intellectual vacuity. (When he left Austin College he went to a Tennessee college that had a reputation among Presbyterian colleges as small and very conservative. While there he joined the Rotary Club. At the time of his retirement he informed me by letter that he had a very fulfilling career.)

As president and dean, John D. and I lived one block apart. I sensed that he felt we were in competition at the College and between our families. However, that was not my perception

328

of our relationship. John D. and I never had open conflict, Jan and I never were dinner guests in their home and John D. and Sara Bernice were never dinner guests in our home. At the time this seemed not important to us; I guess we waited for the Moseley's initiative. He and I were both elders in the Presbyterian Church in different congregations. Jan and I were members of Grand Avenue Presbyterian Church located between our homes. The Moseleys were members of First Presbyterian Church located downtown. Mrs. Moseley, Sara Bernice, later was Moderator of the U. S. Presbyterian Church shortly before the merger (in 1983) with the United Presbyterian Church. After the merger she continued her rewarding career in Church positions of leadership.

As previously mentioned, John D. was not comfortable with a strong, independent thinking dean. After five years, he asked me whether I planned to stay much longer. Possibly, this was prompted by my detailed evaluation of him as requested by the Board of Trustees. He referred me to other positions elsewhere hoping that I would pursue one of them. I told him that I planned to stay at least two more years, until Margaret's graduation from Sherman High School. This did not please him but he chose to offer me a contract in each succeeding year, with very modest salary increases, cognizant of my bonding relationships with faculty and students.

Lisha applied for a Fulbright Graduate Student Fellowship to France. I was on the Fulbright Selection Committee for the State of Texas. On November 23, 1963 Lisha and I went to Austin, Texas for the annual meeting of the Committee. It was a beautiful, sunny late November day. During the intermission for lunch several of us were strolling on sidewalks. While passing a pub with an open door we heard a breathtaking radio announcement that President John F. Kennedy, visiting Dallas, had been shot. Our Committee completed its work as soon as possible. Lisha and I drove through Dallas passing the very spot where the dramatic assassination had occurred. On our return home that evening, the campus was in a state of shock. Grief-stricken students needed to talk and turned to whatever source of solace they could find.

Classes were suspended the next day, and during the funeral hours several days later. Faculty and staff made every effort to comfort the distraught students. (In the keen competition, regrettably, Lisha did not win a Fulbright.)

Earlier, we had a Dean of Students, Richard Bjork Ph. D., who was brilliant, clever, ambitious, aggressive and a fast mover. The organizational chart indicated that the dean of students report to the dean of the college. John D. had convinced him that he would have opportunities for advancement at the College, though without defining what that meant. At times John D. and Dick tried to circumvent me in the discharge of my responsibilities and authority. It appeared to me that John D. was considering appointing him in an invented combination of positions. Despite the circumstances my rapport with Dick was not noticeably damaged. After two years he got other opportunities in the northeast and left Austin. Within a short time he was a college president but he died very young. Following Dick, we had two other deans of students who were not very successful.

John D. chose to work directly with the student body president in 1966-67. He was determined to establish a nominally stronger student government through which he would immediately install a complete Honor System by decree. He did not understand the need for broad student cultivation and acceptance for such a plan to work successfully. As with faculty policies, he believed he could give the appearance of an effective Honor System with new organizational charts and a presidential decree. My efforts toward his gaining understanding were futile.

A very capable editor of the student newspaper, *The Kangaroo*, wrote an editorial dated May 13, 1966 titled "Are We Just Kidding Ourselves About 'Community Government'?" An excerpt stated: "But in the present euphoria surrounding the reorganization of that administrative structure, a sense of perspective requires all of us to stand back and remember that Austin College has been—and still is—a benevolent autocracy, ultimately responsible to the assemblage of businessmen and church leaders who comprise the Board of Trustees....In short, the vast organizational apparatus under the President acts basically as a group of advisors and assistants responsible to him and over whom he rules with as dictatorial or benevolent a hand as he feels necessary for institutional harmony, (only)....playing 'community government.'"

Some members of the Faculty anonymously sent a lengthy untitled, undated statement to the president and dean on March 13, 1966. I quote very briefly to convey the tone of the statement, "At Austin College over the years we have had a variety of organizational (charts) and structure, but structure itself has been largely irrelevant....There has been a pretense of sharing decision making but few have been misled....The Spring of 1966 saw the farcical 'Conversations' in which the President... pressured the Faculty to approve rather sweeping changes in many programs."

It was evident after my six years at Austin College that while the student editor focussed his management concerns on the president, the anonymous Faculty members in effect lumped together the president and dean. Significantly, I never shared with faculty my penetrating but diplomatic seven-page evaluation of the President's office submitted at his request, but never acknowledged!

To release my pent-up aggressions, I continued to play badminton regularly, with athletic coaches as my opponents. I won more than my share of the matches, and supplemented them by regular water skiing on Lake Texoma. After having diagnosed my gall bladder as non-functional, following years of intermittent gall bladder disruptions, I had it surgically removed in 1965. A small peptic ulcer attributed to the combination of a defective gall bladder and stressful work conditions then healed very quickly.

Amid the serial events at the College, how had our family adapted to Sherman and Austin College? We greatly enjoyed our home and the many associations with educationally, politically and religiously prominent visitors many of whom were guests in our home for meals that Jan so artfully and efficiently prepared. Social life was more formal and more graciously arranged than in Dubuque. Even Lisha and Annika prepared a meal for Annika's grandfather, a Senator in the Swedish Parliament, who one day arrived unannounced in his chauffeured limousine when Jan and

I were out of the city. Jan and I were much involved in the social life of Sherman. She directed the choir in Grand Avenue Church and was also an active member of the Junior League, the League of Women Voters, and the Rejebean Club engaged in book reviews. She also devoted a lot of time to the needs of four energetic adolescents in our home. We also enjoyed contract bridge with faculty couples.

The family shared breakfast seven days a week, (amazing, isn't it) and usually dinner. We were summoned to dinner punctually at 6:00 by banging the small plate-sized brass gong brought from India, located at the foot of the stairs. Sharing ideas and our experiences of the day, dinner conversations were very important and enjoyable, including especially frequent ranch pecan ice cream for dessert. Also high on the list of our conversations were: Miss Littrell's comments on Lisha's paper; Luther, as editor, working on the issue of *HiTalk*, the student newspaper, and Margaret's introduction to Bartok at her piano lesson.

Our family also enjoyed other activities together, including College football and basketball, as well as the many events at the children's schools. Lisha and Margaret seemed to derive emotional catharsis by practicing their piano lessons. From my listening I derived some of the same releases. They also sang in several vocal ensembles. Luther had grown much taller and played very good high school basketball. They won awards for their writing in state competition and locally for foreign language mastery. Luther won in a state science competition demonstrating comparative gravity on the earth and the moon.

Lake Texoma, with a circumference of about 1,200 miles, was only about ten miles from Sherman. We had learned to water ski while enjoying a picnic with friends. Each of the children and I became addicted to skiing. We bought a 14-foot boat with trailer that fit in our two car garage. Whenever we had no set obligation on Sunday afternoons, after church we ate a quick lunch, and the family with the boat in tow was off to Lake Texoma. With its vast size, we could always find a cove with calm water where we skied in turn by the hour. Jan enjoyed her book while basking on the beach. When Annika joined us in

August 1961, she reveled in sunny Texas that was in such contrast to Sweden and she quickly became a water skiing enthusiast. Soon after Annika returned to her home, Ginger, Luther's girl friend, evolved into informal family membership, as well as a shared addiction to Lake Texoma events.

Each of our three children graduated from Sherman High School as salutatorian. We offered each of the children a choice-- live at home and attend Austin College without responsibility for summer earnings, or work during the summer and attend another good, private liberal arts college of their choice. Lisha chose to attend Austin College and graduated in three years. She did work as a bank teller and taught remedial English at Bishop College. Luther and Margaret chose to graduate from Southwestern-at-Memphis (now Rhodes College.) Margaret worked as a park playground supervisor in Sherman and Memphis and served as a restaurant waitress. Luther worked at cutting weeds around Texas outdoor advertising signs, pickup and deliver for a dry cleaning establishment, a "go-fer" in a law office. He worked at a packing box manufacturing company and taught remedial mathematics at Bishop College. As they reflected on their summer work, each of the children asserted that each job offered important learning opportunities that supplemented classroom studies. Each of them graduated from college with a distinguished record. Luther and Margaret earned Phi Beta Kappa keys and Lisha's record was at the same level, but Austin College did not have a Phi Beta Kappa chapter.

For social dining, there was no quality cuisine restaurant in Sherman. So, to drive fifty miles to Dallas to entertain visitors or to celebrate a birthday or other anniversary event was not unusual. Speed limits then were no deterrent.

In recent years, I had frequent inquiries about my interest in presidencies of various colleges. I had not expressed interest in a presidency; I enjoyed teaching and academic leadership at the level of the dean. Among such inquiries, for example, Theron Maxson, President of Hastings College in Nebraska was very persistent that at least I do them the courtesy of an interview. Although I told him that I was not a candidate, he seemed to believe that if Jan and I came to the campus he could persuade us. We finally assented. We had extensive interviews for two days with trustees, faculty and students. After returning home we had a telegram with more than one hundred signatures offering me the position as executive vice president and dean. I declined the offer, feeling that Hastings College was not of the quality and stature to justify a move.

I felt that if I made a move it would have to be to one of the Associated Colleges of the Midwest (ACM), or another private college of similar stature. Sometime later, after conversations with President Joseph E. McCabe of Coe College, Cedar Rapids, Iowa, at the annual meeting of the Association of American Colleges, he invited me to Coe for an interview, which I accepted. Jan and I found the city very appealing. Margaret was going to college the next fall, and Jan was eager to resume her teaching. After an interview with the principal of Franklin Junior High School, she was promptly offered a position, even before completion of my interviews at Coe. The dean had been dismissed and there was much challenging work to be done. I thought it should be easier to succeed him than to follow a very beloved retiring dean at Austin College--which I had done seven years earlier.

When we returned home from Cedar Rapids, I was amazed to have a handwritten letter from John D. who seemed to have undergone a late change of mind. The letter stated:

"Dear Leo: I think you know how essential you are particularly at this time of installation of the program planning that you have done.

 I hope you know and realize how much you are needed and wanted.

We are not surprised but complimented that others want your services.

I hope you can see the contribution you have made and the real pay off that is just ahead. Have a good trip and a happy return with every assurance of my confidence and support.

 Sincerely yours,

 Jno. D. Moseley"

For several months the faculty at Austin had been at work, in developing and then adopting new graduation requirements and a new 4-1-4 academic calendar. This was to be effective at the beginning of the 1967-68 Academic Year. Suddenly it struck me that John D. was anxious over the prospect of losing the "refined architect of the curriculum" as he described me to the faculty. Appointments to the faculty during my tenure brought fresh, vital intellects to the campus. They were broadly representative of more geographic regions and colleges and graduate schools across the country. Austin, the little college of the South was steadily being transformed. Regrettably, during my tenure, we had not comparably broadened the geographic base of the students. However, students were more selectively admitted and their quality was notably upgraded.

I received the offer from Coe College. After seven years of very stressful engagement with a president whose insecurities and anxieties pervaded the campus, I was weary of serving as mediator between him and the faculty. (Also, there is a theory, notably by Gail Sheehy, that some persons find their self-development enhanced by changes on a seven-year cycle.)(I had been seven years at Dubuque, plus one year on leave, and seven years at Austin College).

Jan and I discussed the offer from Coe. The College had a Phi Beta Kappa chapter since 1949. Austin College was just making preliminary application. (As of this writing Austin College, in 2001, has just been granted a chapter). Jan had been offered an appealing teaching position in Cedar Rapids. Could she leave our model new home and adapt to an old, rather antique, one? We would miss the convenience of the College and the church right across the street from our home. We had friends in Sherman we would greatly miss. Our three children would be in college and graduate school. We agreed, however, that we were ready for a major change.

Jan's teaching at Fred Douglass School during 1966-67 brought many new experiences and, as a result, both of us gained a deeper understanding of the differing white and black cultures of the South. That understanding also reinforced friendships that we had begun seven years earlier in our Fellowship of the Concerned.

Furthermore, when she applied for a teaching position in the white high school in Sherman she did not get a positive response. For that reason, I visited with the Superintendent of Sherman Schools trying to understand why Jan was not promptly offered a position to teach English. He was rather hesitant "to level" with me, but I understood that because she had taught in Fred Douglass School she was "tainted" in the minds of some of her white colleagues who taught English in the white school. Two black teachers were already teaching in the white school. The system was required by federal law to broaden the cross-racial teacher and cross-student placement. This is another example of the duplicity of scores of techniques Southerners used to defy and postpone the enforcement of federal law. What was happening in Sherman was typical throughout much of the South—integration of white and black schools by grades and teachers by steps. The step-by-step process often led to abandoning the black school buildings, that was an implicit acknowledgement of the inferiority of the black school facilities.

The power structure and the power brokers in the South foresaw the sharing of education between the races as a step leading to the ultimate breakdown of the respective cultures. To envision the end result was disquieting, if not frightening, to both races. However unjust a dual system had been everyone knew his place, providing certain forms of security. However demeaning the system of segregation was to both master and servant, as Martin Luther King asserted, providing more equal educational opportunities should gradually lead to changing from the vertical racial relationship to a horizontal one depicting equality of opportunity. In many respects this was a fearful prospect to members of both races.

The already deeply entrenched system of educational segregation in the South had been reaffirmed by the U. S. Supreme Court in its 1896 *Plessy v. Ferguson* decree. It legally established the "separate but equal" doctrine as the law of the land. This interpretation remained in effect for more than half a century. The U. S. Supreme Court, composed of eight white men and one black man, changed the interpretation of the U. S. Constitution in the 1954 *Brown v. Board of Education* decree. This was based in large part on the recognition that education was separate but not equal. The Court left to the Congress and lower courts to determine how the corrective measures were to be accomplished. What we observed in the 1960s in Sherman was typical of the response of school boards in the South— vigorously oppose then delay through any devious action they could devise.

Jan and I felt that we made some white people very uncomfortable in what we did to challenge the status quo in regard to interracial relations. We tried to make some modest contributions toward the equalization of opportunities and to help open some doors for blacks. In the process, we also understood a little more about the scope and magnitude of the tasks yet to be accomplished.

I accepted the offer from Coe College with a substantial increase in salary (38% to $22,000 plus housing, utilities and expense account, a four-week vacation and a two-week study leave annually). Due to the press of time, the two-week study leave was never realized. I looked forward eagerly to a different climate of human relationships and some fresh opportunities in Iowa. Faculty members at Austin College were overwhelmingly gracious when they learned of my planned departure. Many were laudatory and some that understood the complexities of the dean's role were sympathetic.

I was totally surprised and deeply honored when I learned that the editorial staff dedicated the Austin College annual to me in the year of my departure. The students dedicated the yearbook, *Chromascope 1967,* to Dean Leo L. Nussbaum. The citation reads in part:

> "Here is a man who has dedicated his life in the
> the behalf of youth...Here is a teacher who is con-
> stantly challenging his students...Here is a leader
> of youth tirelessly giving of time...Here is a Christ-
> ian who goes the extra mile time after time...Yes,
> here is he to whom we at the College owe a lasting

debt, and of whom it will be said as we look
back over our years in College 'Dean Nussbaum'
… there was a man!"

This dedication was the finest award that I had ever received
from students.

I was astonished when I was also given a certificate at a
student leaders' banquet. "The Student Affairs Division
presented to Dr. Leo L. Nussbaum in sincere appreciation of his
service as Dean of the College 1960-67, in special recognition of
his support of student involvement in the life of the college, and
in gratitude for his friendship with each of us." July 10, 1967.
Signed by student body presidents of 1966-67 and 1967-68 and
three vice presidents.

In a further honor, the faculty presented me with a
statement that touched me deeply:

"As his Colleagues, and On Behalf of Students and
Colleagues in Other Years, We, The Faculty of Austin College,
Hereby Express Our Utmost Respect and Appreciation to Leo L.
Nussbaum For the Quality of Leadership Which he, As Dean of
the College, Has Rendered to the Faculty During These Past
Seven Years. Given This 18th Day of May in the Year of Our
Lord Nineteen Hundred and Sixty Seven In the Year of Austin
College One Hundred Seventeen. Imprinted with the Official
Seal of Austin College."

Fully realizing that I had been "a nettle in the seat" of
some Board of Trustee members in racial matters, so when they
adopted "In Tribute to Leo L. Nussbaum" at their July 13, 1967
meeting I was greatly surprised. The tribute read in part:

"It is particularly fitting that at this meeting of
the Board of Trustees of Austin College we
should honor our distinguished Dean and Professor of Education and Psychology, Dr. Leo L.
Nussbaum, a member of the College administration
for seven years. He has been a teacher among teach-

ers, and so tribute is rightly made at this place of
learning....This calls for a rare combination of
scholarly learning competence, the wisdom to know
when to speak and when to listen, firmness and flexibility, the capacity for unobtrusive counsel, com-
passionate concern for people, commitment to Christ
and His church, and graciousness to all. Leo Nussbaum is one in whom all these qualities are joined..."

Imprinted with the College Seal and signed by Toddie
Lee Wynne, Chairman of the Board of Trustees and Robert F.
Jones, Chairman Education Committee. These generous tributes
and the belated words of John D. stirred within me in a very
emotional departure.

Part of the transition from Austin College to Coe was a
foundation-sponsored conference on Non-Western Studies on
India at St. Johns College, Santa Fe, New Mexico to which Coe
College was invited in July, 1967. That required participation of
three faculty members and the dean. John D. agreed to my
participation in spite of my plans to leave Austin College. Jan
and I drove from Sherman to Santa Fe. On the return trip there
was snow on the mountain pass above Colorado Springs
followed by drenching rains and flooded rivers and streams all
the way across Colorado and Kansas. I returned to the campus
until about August 15 when we moved to Cedar Rapids.

At the Conference I joined three representative faculty
members from Coe. They were Jean Kern, English; Charles
Lindsay, Mathematics; and Frank Pennington, Chemistry. We
quickly established good rapport. My experience in India served
to provide valuable experiential background to the subjects
offered. We met on the campus of St. Johns College, widely
known for its emphasis on the Great Books series. The College
did not permit a film or slide projector on campus "lest this
technological equipment dilute the intellectual atmosphere."
Once the Conference leaders located a projector and screen off
campus, the program proceeded to incorporate visual learning.
Participants felt no diminished intellectuality!

Early in August, Luther with his old Rambler drove his

mother from Texas to Cedar Rapids to prepare the house for the move. In their absence, I stayed in the home of Edna and Fred Detweiler, Vice President for Administration, in their absence. On August 15 Ginger, our future daughter-in-law, joined me in towing our boat to Cedar Rapids. The furniture followed in a day or two. In spite of making a few inroads in race relations, we were happily leaving the segregated South and returning to the lovely state of Iowa. Margaret, just graduated from high school, accompanied Malin to Sweden as a guest of the Steen family for several weeks, another of Jan Steen's generous gestures to our family. She left our home in Sherman and returned to our home in Cedar Rapids. Felicity returned briefly to Iowa from graduate school at Indiana University.

Chapter 25: From South to North: Coe College

1967-1982

Jan and Luther found the home on 3rd Avenue S.E. in gross disarray, as if my dismissed predecessor dean was being revengeful. This eight-room house had much dated architectural character. It had been the former family home of a Jewish Coe College trustee, with the mezuzah still in place. Constructed in 1920s, this two-story house contained solid doors, wide baseboards, stair steps with railing. Living and dining rooms had generous four-foot wall paneling of solid oak. The hot water furnace was fuelled by natural gas, heated by tall radiators supplemented by a living room fireplace and cooled by window air-conditioners. The house was equipped with an old style kitchen, attic storage and a full basement. The front entrance, with several concrete steps, had side landings, a perfect place to exhibit our two sculptured lions in crouching position. The entrance to the detached two-car garage was from the alley. This home had greatly reduced conveniences from an earlier era, in sharp contrast to the home we had just vacated. That required each of us to make many adaptations.

Jan and Luther labored diligently for ten days disposing of accumulated trash from the basement to the attic and cleaning all over. Jan distressingly observed, "I have never seen such a mess in one house. At the end of each day we were utterly exhausted."

In a few days Ginger and I arrived with the family boat in tow. The furniture van arrived shortly thereafter. We had returned to the State of Iowa and our new community of Cedar Rapids. We arranged a hurried family reunion as we gathered from various directions to equip the children for their departure to continue their educational pursuits. Margaret arrived from Sweden where for several weeks she had had some new experiences as a guest of Malin's parents. The Steen family entertained Margaret lavishly at Gothenburg and at Fjälbacka. Margaret had not liked beer until Jan Steen, in his inimitable style, said, "Margaret, you try drinking our beer. You will like

341

it." After drinking it with distaste, she learned to like it. Rich foods and elaborate beverages were part of the family routine. She told us of the wonderful time she had in being so royally entertained.

Felicity came from graduate school at Indiana University where she was pursuing a doctorate in 18th century English literature. (Until graduate school she was registered as Lisha). Within a matter of days Felicity returned to graduate school, Ginger returned home to Sherman and Luther, a college senior and escort to Margaret, the freshman, were off to Southwestern-at-Memphis. (Now Rhodes College). Because of only brief stays on vacations and holidays, the children never felt that Cedar Rapids was home. It was a good place to visit their parents.

We avoided the empty-nest syndrome by bringing with us to Coe College, Sandra Jackson, a promising graduate of Fredrick Douglass School in Sherman, Texas. Jan believed that Sandra had the ability to do college work. The College provided her with financial aid. By living with us Jan could offer help with her studies. In addition, Sandra saved dormitory lodging and food costs. We discovered that there were few black students at Coe. Living off-campus, Sandra found it more difficult to break into the College social life. We thought we were quite knowledgeable about interracial living conditions, but we learned much more by having Sandra living with us.

For example, she had no interest in our kind of breakfast. She explained, "My family never ate real breakfast. Often we skipped that meal, or if we had left over pork chops or sausage. I would eat that with mustard. I'd just have a little soda to drink, if we had any. We had no dining room and our little table wasn't large enough for the whole family." She was committed to junk food for lunch. We were unsuccessful in changing her well-entrenched eating habits, and in trying perhaps unintentionally added to her own insecurities.

Jan also sewed clothes for Sandra to dress up and took her shopping for some basic college needs. She also needed heavier clothes in Iowa than in Texas. Although we lived only five blocks from campus, as a typical adolescent she struggled to walk to class on time. In the winter term we decided it would be better for her to move to the dormitory to become more involved in the social life and find more friends. As a freshman she successfully earned a "B" average. To our regret, her mother insisted that she could not return to college after her freshman year because she was needed at home. For many years we exchanged letters at Christmas; Sandra recalled how that year in college had opened new vistas and transformed her life. She finished college after she was married. Many years later when her children were grown, she entered the Divinity School at Southern Methodist University in Dallas determined to become a minister.

To establish roots in Cedar Rapids, we chose a family physician, Dr. Percy Harris, a black native of Mississippi; a broker, John Knapp; and a dentist. Our lawyer was William "Bill" Shuttleworth, a College trustee, who became a staunch friend and frequent personal and collegiate adviser. We joined First Presbyterian Church as active members. We opened accounts at Merchants National Bank. I joined the Rotary Club, and we continued our participation in international programs. Over several years, for brief intervals we housed international students from Belgium and Australia. After seven years in Texas, returning to Iowa felt as if we had come home. Jan, during adolescent years, had lived in two other Iowa communities. From 1952-60 our family had lived in Dubuque. We both felt a kinship with Iowans, a stronger educational system, the fertile soil, abundant crops, tall trees, and gently rolling landscape. We felt that Cedar Rapids was a rather ideal city. Jan was teaching at Franklin Junior High School where, in the minds of parents of her students, she quickly became the key figure in our family. In one of my first visits to the bank, the Chairman of the Board, Forbes Olberg, whose daughters attended Franklin School, happened to see me. As a newcomer, I introduced myself. "Could you be the husband of Mrs. Nussbaum, who teaches our daughters?" he warmly asked with a twinkle in his eye. That described the tone and the ready acceptance of Jan as a teacher in the community.

I found my office on the first floor of Old Main, part of which was built in 1868 in English half-basement architectural style. Thea Leslie, Secretary to the Dean, with a clean desk was awaiting my arrival. I introduced myself and inquisitively observed, "You must be all caught up with your work." "Yes, I am," she replied with a slight hint of boredom. I replied confidently, "Don't worry Thea, this may never happen again." She took me on a tour of the administrative offices in Old Main. I quickly recognized that she was a very intelligent, efficient and organized secretary, unpretentious and self-effacing.

I had learned much about Coe College before accepting the position as dean of the college. From my previous positions and my consulting experiences I had learned to ask many questions of President Joe McCabe, Board Chairman, William P. Whipple and former Chairman, Robert Armstrong. Whipple and Armstrong were devoted alumni of Coe. They introduced me to an array of historical facts and perspectives. The College had gone through a period of continuing unsettledness and instability from 1941 to 1956, having suffered a dictatorial chairman of the board. He had summarily dismissed popular President, Harry Morehouse Gage after 21 years, for reasons that I never understood. This led to faculty, student and alumni unrest and a parade of short-term presidents. After years of unproductive haggling the board of trustees finally mustered enough courage to replace the chairman with Charles Lynch, a prominent Cedar Rapids attorney. They brought back the retired former President Harry Morehouse Gage on an interim basis, from 1956 to 1958, and his return had a calming effect on the College community. Then the board cast a wide net in search of a new president. In 1958, they appointed Joseph E. McCabe, Ph. D., a popular Philadelphia pastor and part-time Professor of Homiletics at Princeton Theological Seminary. Although inexperienced as an academic leader, he entered the college presidency with confidence and vigor. After such prolonged unsteady leadership by the board of trustees, many kinds of problems required attention and he tackled them one by one.

After several accidents involving student injuries, an urgent problem was the hazardous student crossing on Avenue B, to and from the library, which cut the campus in half. After judicious negotiation with the city council Avenue B was closed and removed from the campus. Students rejoiced, for several student generations had agitated for its closure.

A series of buildings was added from 1959 to 1968: Marquis Hall for Music and Daehler-Kitchen Auditorium; Armstrong Hall, Douglas Hall, Murray Hall, all student residences; Gage Memorial Union, Peterson Science Hall and Cherry Auditorium that provided much needed facilities, classrooms, laboratories, faculty offices, and student residences. The campus and the City of Cedar Rapids had been decimated of the majestic elm trees that required much new planting and landscaping. Fund-raising was given a high priority. The quality of faculty was good but needed expansion to accompany plans for a larger student body.

Coe also had a proud and lustrous record in athletic achievement in the Midwest Intercollegiate Athletic Association (MIAA). In 1958 members of this MIAA revised its by-laws with a firm recruiting and financial aid code to emphasize that intercollegiate athletics was subordinate to the academic enterprise. All athletes were students first, and only secondarily athletic participants. This was very much in accord with my own persuasion. The MIAA then formed an academic association, the Associated Colleges of the Midwest (ACM), to share in academic pursuits, domestic and international for faculty and students. ACM wisely engaged Blair Stewart, former Academic Dean of Oberlin College, as the first president. Coe was a charter member of the Association.

What were the urgent concerns that I, as the dean, needed to address? Faculty morale was low. There were too many visiting faculty members and salaries were low in comparison with other ACM Colleges. Faculty members were displeased with student response to the weekly academic schedule. Too many faculty and administrative positions remained unfilled. Academic leadership had been very weak. My predecessor dean of the college (whom I had known for many years) was dismissed after two years in office. Some key faculty members had long tenure, a common historical pattern at Coe, and were approaching retirement. Some very promising younger faculty members were being lured to stronger or more stable colleges and universities.

.   Vacant positions were registrar, chair of the department of political science, and a professor of chemistry. Visiting faculty had been appointed in several departments. Classes were heavily scheduled on Monday, Tuesday, Thursday and Friday. Theoretically, students were expected to concentrate on study and research on Wednesday, but many faculty members felt that too many students used Wednesday as mid-week recess. Coe had the rare three ten-week term academic schedule, a total of thirty-weeks rather than the more typical thirty-four weeks. Furthermore, the dean of students was a very pleasant, intellectually turned gentleman who talked good theory but clearly lacked widespread student respect because he was not a man of vigorous, well-focussed action.

Realizing the scope and range of tasks to be undertaken, I asked President Joe for an assistant to the dean. "With the heavy overload that you have, I realize that you need an assistant but financial stringency will not permit me to provide such an appointment," Joe replied. Then he added, "Do you suppose you could direct the staff in the registrar's office for the year, so we can save on a salary there?" And then further, "I wonder whether I could persuade you with your background in social sciences to chair the department of political science; the dean just didn't get around to making that appointment?" I wondered what else Joe had on his list.

Within my short time at Coe, I had suspicions about the comprehensiveness of the records in the registrar's office. I did some quick checking. My previous consulting at colleges had revealed some remarkable deficiencies in the offices of the registrar at other institutions. The departed registrar at Coe had become a college president. "Joe, I will be registrar at least for a semester. Since we have only a very young assistant professor of political science and a professor in post-retirement I will handle that, but I will teach no course in that department." And "By the way, with all these extra titles, I will beg off teaching for the fall term that I really would enjoy. Will you settle for that?" "That's fair enough," he acknowledged. As I left his office, I pondered the negative response to my request; instead, two other loads were dumped on me. Was this to be a pattern, or was Joe testing me to find out what workload I could absorb? At least, to have prompt decisions by him and a conference within a predictable schedule was gratifying.

What I found in the registrar's office was generally sound record keeping but some policies and practices that were open to question. Students who had not fulfilled their graduation requirements by the June Commencement, but who promised to complete their deficiencies during the summer terms, participated in commencement exercises. Several dozen such students from previous years had failed to complete their degree requirements. There were no firm limitations on securing transcripts. At my request, the faculty changed the policy so that only students who had completed all graduation requirements could participate in commencement exercises. Consequently, Coe set a second commencement ceremony at the end of the summer term. The registrar's staff refined several other practices such as student class status and regular checks on students' progress toward graduation.

Coe had a remarkable variety of domestic and international off campus study programs of its own, as well as those linked with other colleges and universities, especially through the ACM. Off campus study programs across the nation increased rapidly after World War II, prompted in part by the Fulbright Program of Congress that offered opportunities abroad for graduate students and faculty.

Through ACM, domestic programs included Argonne National Laboratory semester, Summer Field Study at Basswood Lake, Minnesota, Newberry Library Seminar, in Chicago, Washington Term, The New York Term and Urban Student Teaching. For international experiences students had available Central American Field Study Program, Junior Year Abroad, Summer Institutes Abroad and Individual Research at Universities. Coe also offered Senior Air Force ROTC. The graduation honors programs with a required senior thesis appeared to be well established and soundly rooted in many departments. Phi Beta Kappa and Phi Kappa Phi chapters added to the academic distinction of the College. Incidentally, as Dean of Austin College I was listed in Marquis, *Who's Who in the South*. Soon after I arrived at Coe College, I was listed in *Who's Who in America*, a possible indication of the different status of the two Colleges.

Coe attracted students from forty-two states and seven other countries, giving it far more cosmopolitan status than any college with which I had been associated. Faculty brought degrees from strong academic institutions across the country, except for the Deep South, and from several foreign universities. The members of the board of trustees also were national except for the southern states. The ACM comprised a group of strong liberal arts colleges, academically respected nation wide. It seemed to me at the time that Coe would benefit by having more members of the faculty and administration who are alumni and more likely to know and understand the history of the College. Having a wholesome respect and admiration for, if not passionate love of, a college should bring more of its graduates as faculty and administrators who commit their careers to their alma mater. I felt that was another challenge. I was eager to increase the international dimensions with students from more countries, additional study programs abroad and with more faculty members whose roots were in other countries and cultures.

Although I knew of no formal ranking of ACM Colleges, I sensed that the ten member Colleges thought of Coe in the lowest third, especially based on Coe's internal problems during the 40s and 50s. Joe had the ambition that I strongly shared to raise the status of Coe among its counterparts. I perceived this a formidable undertaking that required upgrading administration, faculty, students, the library, physical plant, campus appearance and financial support.

One of the long student traditions was a springtime "Flunk Day," the origin of which was [1]somewhat vague. Early in the morning of a spring day when the weather forecast appeared

---

[1]Ironically, at the time I was writing this chapter, the new editor of the *Coe College Courier*, featured "Flunk Day" in the Spring 2001 issue with several articles and many photographs. Obviously, she had done much research and conferred with alumni concerning many "Flunk Day" events. She reports that "the instigators, the first students to call Flunk Day, Picknicked and canoed by the Cedar River May 3,1911." If anyone needed confirmation as to the historic significance and the entrenched status, this exhibit should serve to do it.

favorable, the president of the student body announced to students, "This is Flunk Day." With this announcement the student body president exercised the assumed authority to cancel classes and grant the students a spring fling. Without realizing the deep roots of this historic tradition, early in my time at Coe I tried to assess the most effective way to get rid of this unseemly academic intrusion. Quickly, I sensed the bemusement on the faces of senior faculty members whose support I confidently assumed. "Good luck," said one. "That will never happen during my tenure," said another. As an administrative dean I had learned that I must be very discreet in the changes I tried to bring about. In due course, after visits with faculty, staff, students and alumni and observing two "Flunk Days" myself, I reluctantly concluded that the tradition would prevail long after my tenure was over.

Despite the rare academic schedule of three ten-week terms with classes meeting mostly on four days of the week, the curriculum overall was quite traditional. In non-laboratory courses, lectures were widely prevalent. The unit of credit was the quarter hour but graduation requirements were stated in terms of courses. A total of 21 majors were offered with prescribed and some optional courses. Proficiency in speech was required. In the junior year a comprehensive oral examination was used to determine the student's degree of knowledge and attainment of a liberal education. There were no courses designed to introduce students to the liberal arts per se or to show the interrelationship of subjects. In the senior year there were no overarching courses to relate disciplines to the broad questions of life and living or to challenge students in value formation. All juniors and seniors were required to complete the advanced test of the Graduate Record Examination. Departmental faculty established the required passing scores.

It seemed to me that the quality of education that graduates had was uneven. Strong departments included history, mathematics, economics and business administration, chemistry, biology, psychology, art and music. The library, political science, English, speech and theater, physics, sociology, foreign languages, physical education, and teacher education needed vitalization.

The faculty and the curricula were departmentally organized. There was no interdepartmental structure. Departments jealously guarded their own turf; voting often reminded one of political "log-rolling." I formed the impression, without sufficient documentation, that the quality of teaching ranged clear across the pedagogical spectrum. There was no systematic evaluation of teaching either by faculty colleagues or by students. As an academic dean and professor I strongly believed that the student should participate in his or her own education by regular class participation and by frequent written exercises in all courses. Many faculty regarded the quality of student writing as the responsibility of the English department, insisting that other departments evaluate only their subject matter content. The faculty members that taught English strongly resisted such separation of subject matter from overall quality of writing. They asserted that whatever the discipline, the professor was responsible to evaluate grammar, construction, punctuation, vocabulary, spelling and style of writing. We had to face some fundamental educational issues, particularly since English faculty members agreed that entering students showed less ability to write. The lower schools were blamed.

At Austin College we had observed in the segregated south racial unrest and demands for equal opportunity for blacks in education, elections, public transportation and parks, libraries, employment, hotels, restaurants, churches among many other aspects of living. The U. S. President and Congress responded with a notable array of civil rights legislation followed by enforcement of the laws. This brought about many changes. Black students in the North demanded separate meeting facilities, more black faculty and staff, courses on Negro history and culture, more favorable financial aid, more participation in student government and revised admission policies.

The 1960s, across the nation, ushered in growing student unrest on college campuses. The numerous troublesome issues included demands for a larger share in campus governance, challenges to authority, and increasingly vigorous opposition to the Vietnam War. Students aged 18, 19 and 20 wanted full majority status. Student leaders envisioned membership on trustee and faculty committees and representative attendance, if not membership, at all trustee and faculty meetings. Their demands involved the right to vote in local, state and national elections, the privilege of legally consuming alcoholic beverages, the right to sign contracts. Students insisted that women should have no dormitory restrictions; they wanted dormitory visiting hours extended or eliminated. Some students wanted women and men living in the same residence halls, separated by room or floor. Individualized hair styles for men and more varied forms of dress for men and women were increasingly prevalent.

The agitation across the country developed its own momentum. When deliberative trustees, administrators and faculty did not respond promptly and positively, students became more obstructive and aggressive. Across the nation, they engaged in prolonged sit-ins in administrative offices, obstructed street traffic within and around campuses, fostered campus and public demonstrations and frequently resisted officers of the law. Student actions damaged campus buildings and facilities at many universities, though we had no such damages at Coe.

The issues in question covered a wide spectrum of challenges to the existing order. Appropriate response posed special difficulties for the church related liberal arts colleges with their traditional administrative paternalism. Parents of students thought of these colleges "in loco parentis." To respond to the student agitation by supporting the status quo was not a solution but an invitation for intensified demands. Gradual deliberative response required more time than compulsive students would tolerate. That often generated mounting demands and a wider gulf between the parties rather than cooperative solutions.

To compound the complex issues, the Vietnam War had been accelerating; college students, reinforced by Martin Luther King's zealous opposition to the war, were among the first to demand that the war was unjust and must be ended. With nearly half a million American troops in Vietnam and daily "body counts" reported on TV and other news media, this became a major issue not only on college campuses but increasingly with the electorate, including some members of Congress.

Expressing opposition to the war took many forms.

351

Across the nation students marched in front of Selective Service offices with placards, burned draft cards in public, refused to register for the draft, and sent masses of protest letters to members of Congress. At Coe, a group of students paraded in front of the Selective Service Office in shifts around the clock. Jan and I took blankets, food and beverages to the protesters as a form of lending support--at various hours of day and night. I called a special convocation in behalf of concerned faculty and students to provide a forum for venting their opposition to the "unjust war."

The toll was heavy among exhausted college and university presidents who were unable to deal with the revolutionary issues that confronted them. There were no precedents; conditions required flexibility, creativity, and diplomacy to an extent not in the purview of the styles of many administrators, trustees or regents. These volatile campus conditions significantly affected my career at Coe.

In contrast to my years at Austin College, President Joe McCabe and I had a congenial working relationship. He had five earned degrees including a Ph. D. from the University of Edinburgh, Scotland where his ancestors were rooted. He enjoyed fund-raising and his dealings with trustees and the public; he was a popular public speaker and preacher. At the end of my first year at Coe, Joe had completed ten years. His management style was paternalistic but with a forthright delegation of responsibility. He understood the role of the faculty. He was very well regarded in the Cedar Rapids community and across the area. In operations, the dean of students reported to me. Joe made clear that I was the academic leader. At the beginning of my second year I felt that I had won the respect of the great majority of the faculty, with steady hard work, an open door and operating with integrity.

How did we respond to the wide range of student demands at Coe? Student Senate leaders insisted, "We want action now." They insisted on faculty meetings being open to student leaders. They demanded membership on faculty committees and board of trustee committees and attendance at board meetings. Some of the senior trustees favored taking a firm stand for maintaining the status quo. They did not grasp the depth and momentum in these demands for change in the existing order. On the other hand, trustees with adolescent children or grandchildren more readily realized the need for understanding, mediation and compromise. When Congress responded to nation-wide agitation by granting majority status to 18, 19 and 20 year olds, that greatly changed the framework for student negotiations on campus.

Discussions for organizational changes were intense, many faceted and extended for months. In the end, to summarize the most notable changes, two students with vote were named to most of the faculty committees. No students were named to trustees committees; however, Student Senate representatives were invited to attend certain trustee committees when issues pertinent to students were being discussed. Student Senate leaders were invited to semi-annual meetings of the board of trustees to present their concerns. A member of the faculty with vote was named to those trustee committees that dealt with faculty matters, such as the Education Committee. Coe College no longer served "in loco parentis." Students with majority status were treated as adults in all matters pertaining to the law. Greater residence hall visitation rights were granted; beer was served in the Pub. Other student personnel rules were changed appropriately. In practice, the composite of these changes greatly altered campus administration. Life for college administrators was different, but not easier.

We made some strong faculty appointments—in the Departments of Chemistry, English, Philosophy and Religion, Mathematics, Music, Biology, and a chairman of the Department of Political Science. Computers had invaded the academic community and for the first time we appointed a faculty member with computer skills to the Mathematics Department. A year later his appointment as registrar forecast the use of computers for academic record keeping.

In my second year, the need for reform of the academic calendar and curricula had become evident. At Austin College we had adopted an increasingly popular 4-1-4 academic calendar that originated at Florida Presbyterian (now Eckerd College), St.

Petersburg, Florida. The fall term began in early September and ended before Christmas vacation. Each full-time student registered for four courses in the fall and spring terms. The course was the academic unit. The month of January constituted the winter term when each student registered for only one course. The winter term was variously defined at different colleges but always distinctive from fall and spring terms. Variations included individualized research, non-catalog courses taught on or off-campus in this country or abroad wherever the subject could be taught most effectively. Honors students could do research and write their honors thesis. Spring term of 14 weeks began in February, typically with a week's recess at Easter or mid-term and ended in May. This academic calendar claimed to make more efficient use of the academic year and the winter term was regarded as a very desirable variant at each college.

During the summer of 1969, Coe College was very fortunate to receive a grant from the Danforth Foundation to engage a faculty committee at a two-week workshop at Colorado College, Colorado Springs, Colorado. I joined three faculty leaders in proposing a curricular plan and academic calendar that became the Summer Study of 1969. The resulting proposal suggested two required interdisciplinary courses in Introduction to Liberal Arts. The syllabus was to be prepared by a team of five faculty members, each from a different discipline. Principally, the proposal was that instead of a list of specific course requirements for graduation, the faculty adviser and the student would devise an individualized graduation list of courses. The faculty adviser was <u>responsible</u> for guiding the student to ascertain that the student earned a broad liberal education in addition to the courses essential for the major or majors. The faculty, by a strong majority, voted for the plan that included the 4-1-4 academic calendar. Even some tradition minded faculty members were pleased.

In my role as College dean, I appointed the faculty syllabus team chaired by Fred Eutsler whom I had brought from Austin College where he had similar experience. After each use, the syllabi for Introduction to Liberal Arts were reviewed and revised by a team combining continuing and new members after each academic year. The themes for each term were periodically changed. I appointed team chairs that also served as course chair for that year. All full-time faculty of the College (except a few obstinate old-timers) rotated to teach sections of the course. Each section was limited to 20 students. The courses had no lectures but occasional films. Sections met three times weekly. The syllabus provided for extensive reading and substantial writing. The primary instructional mode was discussion. The teacher of each section, whatever his or her discipline, graded the papers for quality including subject matter, grammar, spelling, punctuation, sentence structure, style, etc. With those guidelines, some faculty feared having to grade student papers. Obviously, many faculty members teaching in this course learned much about subjects that they had not previously studied. The calendar change also necessitated substantial syllabus revisions in their departments that for some faculty were very burdensome.

Then I proposed to the syllabus team that we add one more experimental component. At that time, coming to know the community, I discovered that there were many well-educated spouses of professional men who were eager for some kind of intellectual engagement. Some of them were broadly read although not all of them had degrees commensurate to their intellectual development. I suggested to the team that, experimentally, we invite carefully selected persons to serve as "Assistants in Liberal Arts." The assistants needed to be well read, intellectually alert, interested in educating college age youth, show ability to share in class discussion and agree to read all student assignments. They needed to agree to serve for a term. They would be selected by faculty members that choose to participate in this experiment.

Why did I propose this addition? Professors are educated as specialists. In leading discussions in a course as broad as "Introduction to Liberal Arts" the professors would have to deal with many subjects beyond their specialties. Each professor, therefore, would need to become a generalist. For some faculty members this was an alien concept, let alone experience. I believed that pairing another well read generalist, preferably very different in education and life experiences to share in leading

355

class discussions would broaden and enhance the questions and interpretations of the students' reading topics. The team discussed the proposal in my absence. The members concluded that they were too busy to add this questionable venture, although they did not object to the basic idea. I was convinced that this addition had sufficient educational merit that it should be tried. Some time later I approached the team again. "Will you give your support to this experiment if my office handles the whole procedure including the defining, propagating, recruiting and selecting the number of persons to be paired with faculty members who choose to participate?" They soon responded, "Yes, if you do it."

Indeed, I agreed to undertake this venture. Six faculty members, including me, among seventeen who were teaching sections of "Introduction to Liberal Arts" wanted assistants. So, I called a few friends and acquaintances that found this venture exciting. In a meeting with them I explained the plan more fully and they readily committed themselves to it. They even suggested other persons whom they knew and who might be interested and qualified to engage in the role. With minimum effort all six assistants' places were filled. Under the plan "Assistants in Liberal Arts" varied greatly in levels of formal education. Some were high school graduates, and others had earned bachelors and masters degrees. Some assistants enjoyed their role so much that they continued for as long as seven consecutive years. The "Introduction to Liberal Arts" courses, with the assistants, lasted for thirteen years. After the first year additional faculty joined until nearly all that taught in the course regularly drew on these "living library resources." Faculty acknowledged that the assistants' knowledge and experiences usually supplemented that of the professors and thus broadened and enriched the discussion. This became an important aspect of enhanced teaching and learning. Faculty, assistants and students evaluated this program very positively.

The initiating team chose the theme for the fall term, "The Nature of Man;" for the spring term, "The Nature of Knowledge." The new academic calendar and academic program were initiated in the fall term, 1970-71, representing drastic change accomplished in so short a time, since the idea was introduced in the summer of 1969. Many of the new faculty appointees with strong academic and leadership credentials moved into this program with confidence and excitement. Some senior faculty members given to more traditional approaches reluctantly entered the new era. I found myself very pleased with the overall faculty response; morale was substantially improved, and Coe College had new educational momentum. We had engaged a new director of admissions with recent alumni added to the staff; student enrolment was on the increase. We also had a new dean of students.

Then I experienced a very unexpected turn of events. President Joe McCabe was so excessively weary that in December, 1969 he proposed to me that I be named president, and with his deep commitment to Coe, that he remain as chancellor with responsibilities in fund-raising, legislative and church relationships. As a paternalistic president, he was very uncomfortable in facing student agitation and demands when they were not content to accept his decisions in which they did not participate. When I agreed to come to Coe, I never dreamed of such a prospect, and I had brought no such ambition. He proposed a novel definition of the offices of president and chancellor that so far as we knew had no precedent. Joe had observed the trend of very positive results from adoption of the new academic program, and he acknowledged that I had won the respect of faculty, students, and trustees. Jan was notably successful in her Franklin Junior High School teaching, and together we had earned our way in the Cedar Rapids educational, business, social and church communities. Student unrest with demands challenged patriarchal or traditional styles of management; signs pointed to more participatory governance. This raised the levels of administrative discomfort with no foreseeable ready solutions. Beyond the campus Joe's wife, Peggy, was experiencing declining health and he felt strongly that he wanted no more wear and tear with administrative burdens on him and his family.

I was soberly flattered and challenged. Jan and I talked over the prospects of such a change. She had a notable talent as hostess and had done much social entertainment of faculty and students. Could she do equally well with trustees and donors? She felt venturesome and was assured by the chairman of the board that she could continue her teaching. "I will do whatever is needed; we are not averse to taking risks," she offered.

Professionally, I had returned to consulting and evaluation of Colleges with the North Central Association of Colleges and Schools (NCA). Each year I was actively involved in serving on college evaluating teams and in consulting. I served as chairman of some teams. For many years I attended the annual Stillwater Conference of Academic Deans at Oklahoma State University; in 1966 I served as chairman. I was deeply engaged with the Iowa Association of Academic Deans and the ACM Deans as well as some of the Presbyterian Colleges. I had earned my spurs in those associations. Yet, I was burdened with this question: after 18 years as a respected academic dean, should I engage in the hazardous risk of becoming president during an unparalleled time of college student turbulence?

In several earlier instances when I was invited to become a candidate for the presidency of a college or university I had declined consideration. I enjoyed the classroom and had earned high marks from students in their evaluations. As president, could I continue to teach a course? I found the intellectual challenge of the academic dimensions and working directly with students very rewarding. As a dean I had much responsibility, but the ultimate fall guy was always there if I needed him. Did I want to fall to the cliche that "a dean is a mouse in the process of becoming a rat?" Would I have to do much fund-raising with which I had little experience? Joe assured me, "Fund-raising has for a long time been one of my main suits and I want to continue to do that. Of course, you will have to make some calls on donors that only the president can do."

As I weighed in the balances the risk of dealing with an unknown president or filling that office myself I leaned toward the latter. Finally, I said to the Chairman of the Board, Mr. James Coquillette, President of Merchants National Bank, "If you will confer with the faculty of the College and with the elected student leaders and find that my assuming the presidency is essentially unanimous, I will accept your offer. However, if you find significant hesitation or negative responses I must decline." He agreed to do so and in a matter of days he returned to report, "The Executive Committee of the Board and I have conferred with both groups and the results are altogether positive." We hadn't even discussed salary. He met my terms, including salary, moving to the president's home, auto travel expense, country club membership, household help and entertainment expense. So, after conferring with Jan I accepted. Together, we took another risk! I told Thea, who while I was dean was my secretary, that I want her to move with me. She, in her quietly subdued manner, agreed.

Meanwhile our children were engaged in their respective pursuits toward careers. We funded the rising tuition bills for their undergraduate studies; we supplemented their graduate fellowships and their earnings as needed. Lisha completed her doctoral studies earning the Ph. D. in English with specialties in 18th Century Literature and Women's Studies in 1970. She began her teaching career at Indiana University South Bend. That summer we took delivery of a Volvo in Munich, Germany and traveled a month, accompanied by Margaret and Malin Steen in Germany, Switzerland, Austria, and Denmark. In Sweden we were guests of the Steen family. Just before our departure we shipped the Volvo home from Sweden for Lisha.

Luther graduated from Southwestern at Memphis in 1968, Phi Beta Kappa, with a major in economics. He applied for admission to several graduate schools for a Masters degree in Business Administration (MBA), with his eye cocked toward Stanford. He was admitted to Indiana University and the University of Virginia, and was waitlisted at Harvard. Stanford advised him to work for two or three years and then to reapply; their policy was to admit almost no students without full-time work experience. Draft Boards in the Selective Service System were calling many young men during the Vietnam War. Luther was registered in the draft. Because of the response from Stanford, Luther accepted a position at Memphis University School to teach mathematics and Bible. He and Ginger were married in Fort Worth, Texas in August. They promptly moved to Memphis where Ginger could complete her senior year at Memphis State University. She graduated in 1969 and accepted a teaching position in a Memphis elementary school. In 1970 Luther reapplied at Stanford and was promptly admitted. In late summer they moved to Palo Alto, California where Ginger secured a teaching position; they managed frugally to cover the cost of Luther's tuition, fees and books. In 1971-72 Luther campaigned and was elected President of the MBA student body. In the summer of 1971 Luther accepted a summer position at Cummins Engine Co., Columbus, Indiana, a prelude to an administrative post on graduation in 1972. His first position at Cummins was assistant to the chairman of the board. He rose rapidly in the Company, was rotated among several departments and soon was earning a higher salary than his father! By 1975 Luther was named manager of the Mexican operation of Cummins Engine Co. involving sales and service. Luther, Ginger and Kari lived for two years in Mexico City where Kristin was born.

Margaret graduated from Southwestern at Memphis in 1971, Phi Beta Kappa, with a major in psychology. She was admitted to graduate school at the University of Chicago to pursue a degree Master of Arts in psychiatric social work. Guy Cooley, graduate of Southwestern at Memphis, 1969, completed two years of Civilian Public Service as a conscientious objector to war, began a program at Chicago toward a Masters in Social Work. After graduation from Chicago in 1973, Margaret and Guy were married at our home in Cedar Rapids on my birthday. They promptly moved to St. Petersburg, Florida to undertake their respective careers.

Jan and I enjoyed Cedar Rapids; it had become the favorite city of all in which we had lived, with its gentle rolling terrain, the scenic Cedar River running through the heart of the city, and appealing residential areas. I was elected an elder at First Presbyterian Church. We had found new friends in the Church, at the College and in the Rotary Club where I was also much involved and later served as president. In the annual Cedar Rapids inter-club competition for several years I won the badminton championship. We found other couples that enjoyed bridge as much as we did. Several of the Coe Board members befriended us. Armstrongs, Killians, and Smulekoffs retail stores provided shoppers with every need for the home. Although we missed the sophisticated cuisine of Dallas, the Cedar Rapids Country Club membership that accompanied the Coe presidency offered excellent dining service that met our entertainment needs. Dr. Percy Harris, our family physician and one of several black residents, and his wife, Leleah, became close friends. Our broker, John Knapp, was a resourceful adviser and good friend. Merchants National Bank treated us as preferred customers. The residents of the city were a compatible blend of national, ethnic and racial families including Czechs, Lebanese, Christians, Jews and Muslims with whom Jan and I developed close friendships. Cedar Rapids had the oldest mosque west of the Mississippi. The Rotary Club included male members of each religious group, among them a Jewish rabbi. Cedar Rapids had the highest per capita export business of any city in the United States. The school system was generally of high educational quality as was historically true of the State of Iowa.

With regionally and nationally respected Coe College located in this prosperous city of 110,000 residents, I faced both a remarkable opportunity and a substantial challenge. One historic distinction of Coe was its men's athletic teams, particularly football, basketball and track. Coe and neighboring Cornell had the longest continual football rivalry west of the Mississippi. Among Coe's many alumni athletic coaches, probably the best known today is Marvin Levy, Phi Beta Kappa, and Masters degree in history from Harvard. He had coached at Coe, at other colleges and universities then had a long career with several professional teams of the National Football League. (Incidentally, he recently retired after many years with the Buffalo Bills that he took to the super bowls in 1991, 1992, 1993 and 1994, but never earned a championship.)

Joe McCabe was eager for me to take over the presidency as early as possible. Because of the change over to the new academic calendar and revised curriculum, in order to have everything in readiness for the fall term, I felt that I should devote full time to the dean's responsibilities until September 1,

1970. He and the board agreed. In late winter, 1969-70, the board gave Joe and Peggy a trustee financed sixty-day leave for an extensive world trip. Prior to my installation, I named a faculty search committee to find a successor to me as dean. We chose Dr. Carson Veach who began September 1, 1970. Jan and I moved into the president's home on Country Club Parkway in late May. The Veach family occupied the dean's residence on Third Avenue SE in August.

Al McIvor, Director of Admissions, with bagpipes accompanied me up the creaky stairs of Old Main into the president's office on the second floor. On September 1, 1970 I was ensconced at the president's desk. Joe, as chancellor, chose to move into an office in the adjunct to Moray L. Eby Fieldhouse. Al McIvor and his staff had done a good job in recruiting students. Coe was off to a promising year despite the growing national momentum of student unrest. The new curriculum was introduced without significant obstacles.

Personally, I continued a well-disciplined singles game of badminton in the gym early in the morning; usually my opponent was Glen Drahn, Athletic Director, Head Football coach, and Chair of the Physical Education Department or Jerry Owen of the Music Department. I still found this very beneficial as a release of my aggressions rather than venting them on my wife, faculty or students.

The apparent September placidity of the president's office was soon interrupted when the athletic director and four male coaches came to my office. They reminded me that during the two previous years a growing number of student athletes showed up for practice with deviant hair styles, unaccustomed mustaches, long side burns, disordered hair over the collar, even a rare scraggly beard. The coaches with spare crew cuts acknowledged that they had not issued a clearly articulated hair code for athletes. Following World War II until recently, crew cuts were widely fashionable. As the coaches anticipated, when student athletes returned from summer vacation the coaches noticed more pronounced "rebellious" hair styles.

The athletic director was the spokesman. He stated: "We want all of our players to wear short hair for the sake of cleanliness and neat appearance. Last year we talked to our players individually; some of them blatantly refused. We observed that some other Midwest Intercollegiate Athletic Conference (MIAC) college teams last year were very shaggy. We decided to nip this in the bud before it gets worse. This summer we drew up a hair code that is unmistakably clear: No facial hair of any kind, even if well trimmed. No long side burns below the ear lobe. No unkempt hair and never over the collar in the back. Together, we coaches made a blood covenant; none of us will relent or compromise. We recognize that to enforce this code and to get full conformance in all sports we need your full support. Dr. Nussbaum, we ask that you give this your stamp of endorsement to be put into effect immediately." The instigator of this code was reported to be a recent Coe appointee with a militaristic demeanor, Robert Thurness. The two women coaches and part-time male coaches were not involved.

"Why do you want to be so rigid and uncompromising?" I asked. "That is the only way to make it effective," they asserted. "Have you discussed it with any students?" I wondered. "No, of course not. We coaches have the authority; we want to make sure they understand." What a clash with the student trend of rebellion, was my instant thought.

The coaches and I discussed their proposal at some length. They emphatically conveyed to me that they would not consider any modification or compromise. I summarized my response, "I agree that if you tried to put this code into effect, you would invite mass rebellion from athletes and from student government leaders. With your rigidity at a time when your proposed code runs strongly against national trends in high schools and colleges, even my endorsement will not make it effective. As president, I am your head coach. In my view, either with my endorsement or without it you are inviting major disruptions of our athletic program. I cannot support it as now written," I concluded, "think this over, and bring me a code that is more flexible."

They left my office, apparently surprised and disgruntled. Their neat solution had run into trouble. I was convinced that the coaches did not understand the momentum and profundity of the forces for change that are at work in our society, especially on college campuses. Some of the coaches had confronted individual players with small mustaches, telling them they had to shave these before they could try out for a team. One coach was quoted as claiming that unwillingness to conform to the code "was a form of national disloyalty." These students complained to the Student Senate that they were being discriminated against although their hair condition would in no way impair their team participation. Other players signed petitions stating that they fully supported the coaches. There were no easy answers.

At that time Coe had an active and aggressive Student Senate as was characteristic of the period, with a stern, single-minded young woman as president. Senate officers arranged meetings with the coaches trying valiantly to reach some compromise agreement. In repeated efforts over several weeks, they were unsuccessful. All these attempts at resolution of an issue that was not basic to the education of students consumed an incalculable amount of time and energy on the part of scores of faculty, students and administrators.

In other respects, Coe College was very fortunate in the new Air Force ROTC commandant, Major Ernest Dean, who had just arrived. He immediately showed adaptability and willingness to change. As he and I talked about social issues and racial stresses, I felt that he was just the man for the times. He dealt with cadets with tolerance, reason, understanding, and sound judgment. With cadets, the hair issue was unobtrusively handled. Major Dean and his wife were native North Carolinians. To exemplify their openness, with two biological children, they adopted four more who were interracial. He handled with aplomb young men who were conscientious objectors to military service. He openly explained, "Let it be understood that if one of my sons chooses that route, I will fully support him."

In several additional conferences with the coaches concerning the proposed hair code they were implacable. I appointed a faculty-student committee, including Major Dean, to try to reason with them. The coaches stonewalled every attempt. They did not try to put their code into effect, as if they expected me to relent. If they had final authority, as they claimed, why did they not put it into effect? Meanwhile, Glen Drahn, Athletic Director and I continued our badminton competition; I won more than my share of the matches. While the proposed hair code was in suspense, college classes and activities were not interrupted.

On Saturday morning, October 24, 1970 in Sinclair Memorial Chapel, I was formally inaugurated as President of Coe College. The Chancellor, Joseph E. McCabe, offered the invocation, two members of the English Department, Professors Signi Falk and Neal Woodruff, spoke in behalf of the Faculty, the President of the Student Senate, Karen Johnson, spoke in behalf of the Students. The Chairman of the Board of Trustees, William G. Murray, '24, who spoke for the Trustees and Alumni, offered the charge and invested me with the President's Medallion. I chose to give a brief response rather than the more typical Inaugural Address. Scores of Colleges and Universities were represented in the Inaugural Procession. Many of the Presidents in the geographic region attended the ceremony. The Coe Brass Choir performed for the Processional and Recessional, and the Coe Concert Choir presented two anthems. Most of the members of our immediate families were present. To my astonishment, during the ceremony I observed the abrupt departure of the representatives of the Black Student Organization (BSO). As president I worked diligently to hear their concerns and demands and to mend the relationships engendered in previous years. (I cherish some letters of apology from certain members of the BSO that arrived years after those fractious times.)

At the Inaugural luncheon in Gage Union, I had invited John D. Moseley, President of Austin College, with whom I had worked for seven years, to address the guests. Jan and I entertained family members at dinner at the Amana Colonies. The Inauguration could be described as unpretentiously formal and not disruptive to the ongoing educational process. By the following Monday morning the College was back on schedule.

Discussions of the proposed hair code continued with no prospective resolution. Early in December the coaches made an appointment to see me. They were obviously tense. "Mr. President, we have to make plans for the spring term. We had hoped that it would not come to this, but unless you support our code in the spring term, we will all resign." Again, I tried to reason with them, but to no avail. Faculty and students knew of the proposed hair code; it was evident to me that my position represented an accurate reading of the times. I discussed the matter with the chairman of the board of trustees. I conferred with some presidents of the MIAC colleges, about how their coaches were dealing with changing male athlete hairstyles.

In my eighteen years as a dean, with my wide range of experiences in India, the years in the segregated South and my work with the Coe faculty I had developed confidence that my diplomatic skills were considerable. With the complexity of this problem, however, I was utterly baffled and I was more frustrated than with any other college-related issue of my career. Some persons are so tied to the past that they rigidly want to retain recent human practices as if they were ordained of God. They do not understand that society is not static. Facial hair was not in vogue during the recent World War II. However, in the Civil War era throughout World War I, many generals and lower rank officers wore long hair and full beards, often with mustaches. Hairstyles reflect personal preferences as well as social practices.

Where does one look for reliable solutions to problems in a period of turbulent national social change? Social change generates and accentuates sharp differences of opinion. Beyond the issue of hair was the matter of lines of authority and autonomy. With their implacable rigidity these coaches combined a lack of understanding of lines of authority. They accorded themselves, right or wrong, the power to have the last word. I faced a decision not only of exercising my authority but also cushioning the effect on Coe College from the reactions of its various constituencies. All my life I have been a praying person; in this particular situation my prayers were greatly intensified as I sought the "wisdom of Solomon." I believed that I had the support of most of the faculty, students and members of the executive committee of the board of trustees. I anticipated that the reaction of alumni athletes and some sports writers could be shocking when I announce the acceptance of the resignation of the coaches.

The press had already been involved for some weeks. At the *Cedar Rapids Gazette,* Gus Schrader, the chief sports writer, without ever conferring with me, wrote repetitive articles accusing me of being a pawn to the whims of students by refusing to support the coaches in their proposed rigid hair code. In contrast he extolled my predecessor, Joe McCabe, and his contrasting paternalistic administrative style. Gus would have given unqualified support to the coaches. From a broader perspective and with a different interpretation of events, *The Des Moines Register* sent a photographer showing Glen Drahn, the Athletic Director, and me with my mustache, playing badminton. With the photograph they humorously observed that "the President of Coe College would not even qualify to try out for Drahn's athletic teams!"

[At my retirement, 12 years later in a letter addressed to me, Gus Schrader wrote "I envisioned Coe forever losing its athletic reputation as a result....I have told you in person since, of course, that it turned out you were right and I was wrong, as the Kohawks came back stronger than ever with an almost entirely new staff....I want to tell you how much you will be missed as president of Coe, as past president of the Cedar Rapids Rotary Club, and as a good friend."]

[Another alumnus from Cedar Rapids, Reg Watters, an executive in the leading department store and elder in the largest Presbyterian congregation in the city, had expressed vigorous public opposition to my action. He even withheld his annual College gift for a time. Later, after observing two years of notable athletic successes, he mellowed considerably. Quoting from a handwritten letter ten years later following a Presbyterian Synod meeting on campus, that he sent to me, "I want you to know that you would have been <u>VERY </u>proud of Coe and would have taken much satisfaction from the many complements which were paid to the host College....we Coe people were proud to say to the many delegates 'I'm a Coe alumnus.' My two years with the Coe board was one of the finest experiences of my life."] He offered me another form of deferred satisfaction!

I called a meeting of the executive committee of the board of trustees to explain the events of the fall, my countless efforts to resolve the matter peaceably and reasonably, and the many discussions with the coaches and their implacability. In view of their defiance of me, regrettable as it was, I had to accept their resignations. Two of the lawyers on the committee who were very senior members, felt that I was responding too much to student whims. The rest of the committee fully supported my proposed action. In striking contrast one insightful trustee, mother of adolescent children asserted, "Fire them, don't let them resign."

As soon as the students left for Christmas vacation, on December 18, I summoned the coaches to my office. "You have put me in the position that I have no choice but to accept your resignations. The athletic director ends his service as of December 31, 1970; the resignations of the four other coaches will be effective at the end of the contract year. It is my plan to have a new athletic director in office by February 1, 1971. He will work with you in writing an appropriate hair code adapted to the times." Our public relations department sent out a press release, then all hell broke loose.

Everyday I received letters that accused me of being too weak-kneed to support the coaches, of my having collapsed under student pressure. I had some nasty telephone calls. From Coe alumni jocks, the principal charge was that I was using this method as a ruse to diminish the significance of intercollegiate athletics at Coe, if not to eliminate athletics altogether. Key alumni, including top executives of major corporations, from many parts of the country read the interpretations of the press and abruptly announced that their financial support of the College was being withdrawn—some even cancelling current pledges. High school administrators claimed that my failing to support the code would make their task more difficult in the high schools. Although this came early in my presidency, once I had made the decision I never doubted the correctness of my action.

Here are a few quotes from the scores of letters that came from all parts of the country. A Wisconsin superintendent of schools: "Being an alumnus of Coe College, I have, in the past, been proud of the institution. Your stupid handling of your relations with the athletic department has demolished what pride

I had left. How can you be so naive?" Another head coach from a high school wrote: "The UPI story indicates that you as president of Coe "urged the department of athletics to bring its requirements for hair and dress 'more in line with the changing times.' It is inconceivable to me that you would undermine the authority of a department that thrives on discipline, sacrifice and dedication." Another: "You have decided to bow to the wishes of the dirtest (sic) group of young people in our Country."

Far fewer letters came from supporters as varied as a major at U. S. Military Academy, West Point, New York, some parents of student athletes, an assistant professor of political science at New York University, and one of my former students. It was heart warming to me that, editorially, both *The Des Moines Register* and the *Cedar Rapids Gazette* supported my accepting the resignations of the coaches. Gus Schrader of the *Gazette*, however, kept up his periodic diatribes for weeks in his sports column, though he did not know me personally and never asked me for my interpretation.

I had a good number of candidates for the position as athletic director. After interviewing several candidates, in February 1971, I appointed Barron Bremner of nearby Cornell College, a well-known and popular wrestling coach in the conference as well as in other parts of the country. He was on the job before the end of the month. One of Bremner's early public relations acts was to hold a conference with Gus. They had known each other for years. Gus finally gave up.

I announced the other coaching vacancies to be filled. Barron and I agreed that we would appoint only three to replace the four who resigned. We had many applicants and in a few weeks we selected a black basketball coach, Marcus Jackson; a popular alumnus, Wayne Phillips, as football coach and Roger Schlegel as track coach for the next academic year. Other positions were filled with part-time coaches. [As a student Wayne Phillips and his family lived next door to us in Dubuque while he was a student athlete at Coe.]

From the beginning, the new coaches were very successful. Neither discipline nor hairstyle became issues. The athletes respected the coaches and these coaches respected the authority of their head coach, the College president! During my twelve years as president, the male and female coaches and their successors, assisted by part-time personnel, produced the most MIAC championship teams, for a similar time period, in the history of Coe College. Within two years most of the critics during the "hair fuss" rejoined as enthusiastic supporters of the teams, apparently fully persuaded that I was not intent on destroying the athletic reputation of Coe College.

The next year, 1971-72 continued to be stressful with continuing student unrest, and the usual fund-raising requirements. In the fall semester, I taught one class. Moreover, I seemed to do more traveling than usual. During the winter months there was more flu than usual. Whenever I was on a plane trip more than half the people seemed to be coughing and sneezing. Southwestern at Memphis, where Luther and Margaret received their bachelor degrees, was searching for a president. The chairman of the board of trustees who knew me when I was dean at Austin College, and as a parent, called several times to invite me to become a candidate. I thanked him but declined. Southwestern was a high quality college but I had much work to be accomplished at Coe. About mid-January, the chairman called me again from Hawaii confronting me with the challenge, "At least do me the courtesy of visiting our campus to meet trustees, faculty and students." I sensed that he envisioned my presidency as a step toward membership for Southwestern at Memphis in the ACM. I was flattered. In late January Jan and I did visit the campus for two days and were royally entertained. Had I been available for a position, this one would have had great appeal but I reiterated that I was not a candidate.

Again, on the plane trip home from Memphis it seemed that most passengers were coughing and sneezing. When we reached home I was obviously ill. Dr. Harris, our family physician, took me to the hospital, where I was diagnosed as having pneumonia with a very high fever. In the following days, instead of improving my condition worsened. One evening Dr. Harris brought one of his specialist colleagues then told Jan that in my delirious condition I might not live through the night. However, I did survive, and then started to improve. After ten days in the hospital, as I was discharged I was extremely weak. Dr. Harris recommended a trip to the arid climate of Arizona for a few days of recuperation. Jan and I went to Phoenix for several days; my condition continued to improve. Full recovery required more time but in a few more days I was back at work. From that time on until now I have never failed to take my daily dose of vitamin C, vitamin E and Zinc.

As president of Coe, I was delighted to be able to address issues other than male athletes' hairstyles! Plans for the campus included a new building for the art and theater departments. The art department was housed in historic Old Main on First Avenue N E. The theater department was housed in a dilapidated wooden structure across Thirteenth Street. Among the gifts to the College, Joe had received a pledge of $1,125,000 from the Sutherland Dows family. Mr. Dows was for many years a Coe trustee and Chairman and CEO of Iowa Electric Light & Power Co. (i.e.) with headquarters in Cedar Rapids. Henrietta Arnold, his daughter, was also a very active Coe trustee. Her husband, Duane, was President of i.e. Following Mr. Dows' death Duane succeeded him as Chairman, President and CEO.

A difficult question that faced the trustees was where to locate the Dows Fine Arts Center. Old Main was an attractive landmark, with a flaky red brick exterior part of which was constructed in 1868. It was an antique architectural structure with hazardously tinder-dry wood frame, floors, stairs, window frames, laths under the plaster, and doors. Also fronting on 1st Avenue NE was the four-story Carnegie Science Hall that, except for the fourth floor, had been recently vacated when Peterson Science Hall was completed. The board engaged an engineering firm to do a comprehensive evaluation of both structures. The engineering firm recommended the demolition of Old Main and renovation of Carnegie Hall.

After extended discussion the board approved the demolition of Old Main, and the construction of the Dows Fine Arts Center on that location. Suddenly, intense although not wide spread, alumni sentiment for Old Main burst open. This was most notable among graduates of the 20s, 30s and 40s who remembered Old Main in its better condition as the "flagship" of

371

the campus. Among the most outspoken was William L. Shirer, class of '25, whose name was known across the world as the author of *Berlin Diary, The Third Reich* and *The Third Republic* and as a very popular radio commentator from Germany. I visited him at his home in Massachusetts to explain the fire hazard of the wooden core of the building, the flaking soft brick exterior, its antique heating system, and its obsolete electrical wiring and plumbing. I explained that to salvage Old Main would require its demolition and rebuilding at a prohibitive cost. With obvious pain, his objections diminished. Trustees, Chancellor Joe McCabe, and the development staff made similar explanations to concerned alumni. Slowly the alumni resistance subsided. Yet, because Old Main was the original building with so much alumni sentiment, I was pained to see Old Main demolished during my watch. In the transition, during construction administrative offices were scattered among several buildings. The president's office was moved to Eby Fieldhouse. How convenient this location was for my early morning badminton one floor below, with showers two floors down! And I couldn't help but note the irony that the president, previously accused of wanting to destroy the athletic program of the College, should be officed in the fieldhouse!

Carnegie Science Hall was renovated to house classrooms, faculty and administrative offices. Flora and fauna collections on the top floor were left intact. Even the name change to Stuart Hall, prompted by a major gift from the Stuart family, produced no significant alumni or faculty resistance. On its completion, I was delighted to move into the new third floor president's office.

The renovation of the physical plant was continued. Old Main was demolished. The Dows Fine Arts Center, with its distinctive angular architecture, was erected in its place to house the art and theater departments. Housing for married students was built across Center Point Road. An admissions office was added to Gage Memorial Union. Eby Fieldhouse was substantially renovated, deteriorated north side windows removed and the spaces bricked in. Retracting bleachers were installed. Later, an Olympic size swimming pool was added.

Greene Residence Hall for men and Hickok Hall, for classrooms and faculty offices, were totally renovated. Coe College was on the way to having an updated physical plant that more nearly met its needs.

Our trips abroad, especially to European countries, had made me aware that urban landscape in northern U. S. was almost devoid of outdoor sculpture. The campus had none. Funded by a generous alumnus, Ed Whiting, formerly on the art faculty, offered to build an angular copper sculpture in harmony with the angular architecture of Dows Center. Later, in cooperation with the art department, I secured a grant for a regional competition to create a sculpture located in the court formed by Stuart Hall, Cherry Auditorium, and Sinclair Chapel. A third sculpture was placed next to the main entrance of Gage Memorial Union. The campus was also upgraded with additional landscaping of trees, bushes and flowers.

As to fiscal plans, in September, 1970 I was determined to double the endowment of $8,043, 603 during my presidency. K. Raymond Clark, class of '33, Chicago attorney, and trustee had established an irrevocable trust totaling $182,000. He and I had established good rapport when we visited during my three years as dean. Joe and Raymond seemed unable to establish a mutually comfortable relationship. One of the trustees had negotiated with a donor for an Endowed Faculty Chair in Music for $250,000. The trustees set a minimum of $500,000 for a named future endowed chair. But they refused to be really venturesome and set the minimum at $1,000,000, though that was my conviction. I then defined an endowed chair as requiring a gift or legal pledge of $500,000 to $1,000,000 with a plan to secure nine additional chairs during my time as president. In writing the description, I determined that the assigned chair should be renewable or rotational after a term of five years. The earned income from the endowed sum should be large enough to provide the designated faculty member's salary plus some funds for professional development. At the end of my term I had a total of nine such commitments, seven of which were fully in effect. Since my retirement it has become obvious that even an endowment of one million, with falling interest rates, is not nearly adequate.

In 1970, faculty salaries at Coe were near the bottom among ACM Colleges; I was determined to raise them into the upper half. Several women faculty had contracts that paid well below the contracts for men at the same rank, quality and years of experience notwithstanding. In response to national demands of equal pay for equal work I took the initiative in corrective action before the issue was raised on the Coe campus. My predecessor took the historically vertical position: "These women have husbands with good earnings" or "they have no dependents; they don't have so much need." In the same vein, he often spoke of middle aged women on the staff as "the girls." He was content with the traditional stance that male superiority justified issuing contracts to women at lesser salaries.

I realized increasingly that for a dean or president to have the respect of and solid rapport with faculty would enable one to establish remarkable forward-looking policies, that with less favorable rapport, could never be accomplished. Based on this fact, I made several unusual but desirable recommendations. In studying academic rank and the ages of faculty members it became obvious that in the decade ahead Coe would have a disproportionate percentage of faculty at the tenured upper ranks. I regarded as desirable to have a reasonable balance of academic ranks within departments and in the College as a whole. The faculty adopted my recommendation that up to 10% of new faculty appointments could be on non-tenure track. These positions could be shifted to other departments as faculty members retired or left Coe. At the same time the faculty approved the rule that one of the requirements leading to tenure was a faculty member's ten-year plan for professional development. This individual plan was to be revised and extended at the end of every five years. Faculty members who were already tenured would also prepare their individual ten-year plan in a sequential arrangement. Each ten-year plan would be evaluated after each five-year revision. This was to help countermand the objections to tenure appointments as a one-sided contract of "job security without a compensating requirement for professional vitality and advancement." I knew of no other college that had adopted such a rigorous and innovative plan.

Policy issues concerning the board of trustees and the president also needed to be scrutinized. The board had members from many parts of the country; however, when I became president the power structure of the board was entirely in the hands of trustees from the Cedar Rapids area. The officers of the board, members of the executive committee, and the chairs of each committee were from the Cedar Rapids area. Other members who attended the semi-annual board meetings often felt more like observers than active, responsible participants. Without making this a contentious, conspicuous issue, I was determined to move gradually and discreetly to engage all board members with more participation. Some trustees had felt that they had no vested interest, that they were mere spectators. In my latter years in office, the board chairman was from Chicago, the treasurer from Minneapolis, and the chairs of other committees from various parts of the country. Except from the South, board membership had become national in scope.

When I took office, there was no systematic evaluation of trustees by the nominating committee, either when proposed for initial election or when re-nominated for another three-year term. There was no limit to the number of successive three-year terms that a board member could serve. Some board members served consecutively for 35 years. I recommended the adoption of a policy to require the nominating committee systematically to define qualifications for trusteeship and to evaluate prospective trustees on the basis of their commitment of time, energy and resources to Coe. In a similar vein, all members to be considered for re-nomination must be evaluated on the basis of their records of service on the board. Further, I proposed that after having completed three consecutive three-year terms each trustee should be required to rotate off the board for at least one year before being eligible for re-nomination. In each of the first two years the board failed to take positive action. When I submitted these proposed policies for the third consecutive year, the board adopted them to be required of all new trustee candidates. It was also agreed that each new trustee would participate in a comprehensive orientation about board of trustee policies and operations. Either the board gradually understood and accepted the merits of such policy or they simply wearied of my repetitiveness.

It used to be said, perhaps jokingly, that the first question to be voted on at each meeting of the board of trustees should be, "Shall we fire the president?" This approach to the presidency implies that there was no regular, systematic evaluation of the president's performance. In practice nationally, any formal evaluation occurred only when the president's performance had become a major issue and a matter of open contention. In such a climate, a balanced assessment was impossible because many people were already firmly committed for or against retention. An evaluation at such a time is not likely to be highly objective or to persuade the advocates of either position to change their minds.

Having voted policy changes for themselves, I was persuaded that the board should conduct a formal, systematic evaluation of the president's performance once every three years. Participants in the evaluation should include board members, faculty, student leaders, officers of administration, and perhaps officers of the alumni association. If as a result of these evaluations the board decided to terminate the relationship, the president should be so notified with a one-year terminal contract. If the results led to a vote of affirmation, the president should be given another three-year contract. The evaluation, it was agreed, should occur in the latter part of the middle year of the three-year term. The board voted approval of that policy to be put into effect immediately. I was so evaluated for the rest of my twelve years as president; the results always brought a strongly positive vote of the board. After my successor took office, this practice was not followed. I never did learn why.

I also made some other changes. For more than 25 years, I had listened to commencement speakers, some stimulating, others dull. Feedback from many graduates and some parents asserted that they did not long remember the name of the commencement speaker, his subject or what he said. Perhaps traditional commencement speakers were obsolete. During the years of student unrest many colleges experienced disruptive behavior and demonstrations at commencement exercises. I had watched the restless, often inattentive, graduates dressed in their unaccustomed-fitting caps and gowns impatiently waiting for the climactic event of crossing the platform to receive their diplomas. This should be the central focus of the graduation ceremony. Increasingly, I became convinced that commencement should be brief, a celebration for the graduating class, their families and friends. So, I implemented that conviction in the following ways. Formal procession of students, faculty and administration, accompanied by the band, was followed by an invocation. Instead of the commencement speaker, I addressed the graduating seniors with a seven to ten minute parting word. Then followed the reading of citations and awarding of honorary degrees. I conferred the degrees, the dean read the names, as members of the graduating class, guided by the marshals, marched across the platform as I shook hands with my right hand and gave the diploma with my left. When the last graduate had received his diploma, the audience gave them hearty applause. Led by the band everyone stood and sang the Alma Mater. The band played the recessional as participants marched out of the gymnasium in reverse order of entry. There were few complaints, and many favorable comments, on the revised commencement ceremony.

In 1972, by administrative action, I formed a President's Advisory Council consisting of nine alumni and three parents of students. Each member was appointed for a single three-year term. The purpose of the advisory council was to advise and consult with the president on the continuous improvement of the quality of Coe College. A secondary purpose, not formally announced, was to identify capable, very committed participants who might be considered for future membership on the board of trustees. Once in each academic year, the advisory council was sent pertinent informational materials on some designated facet of College policies and operation. The advisory council met for two days for on-site evaluation, by observation, interviewing of key personnel, observe workers, and to formulate comments and recommendations. This proved to be a valuable resource for the president. The advisory council has been continued by my successors.

Student unrest prevailed from the mid '60s through much of the '70s. As students succeeded in some of their demands or wearied from repeated efforts, they would raise new issues. Another disturbing issue on many campuses was the objection to college involvement with the military. Military recruiters were literally driven from a number of campuses. Other actions were taken against ROTC units. At nearby Grinnell College students, joined by some faculty, succeeded in having ROTC abolished. Some students at Coe, aided by the chaplain and a few pacifist faculty members, were similarly determined to have the ROTC unit banished. Students did not know that I was reared as a conscientious objector, and although I served in the army, I shared some degree of empathy with them. With complete candor, I discussed my personal feelings with the open-minded ROTC commandant. Then I announced to the campus that I would give no consideration to terminating ROTC. There was room enough at a liberal arts college for militant or pacific objectors to war as well as a military unit. In my view, neither group should be permitted to drive from the campus those with opposite convictions. Again, I reminded the chaplain that he was chaplain to all students. It was his responsibility to accommodate diversity within community and not to foster divisiveness. To emphasize my determination, when teaching Introduction to Liberal Arts, I invited the Commandant, Major Ernest Dean, to be my assistant in liberal arts. He succeeded admirably and was well accepted by most faculty members and students.

The student newspaper was named the *Cosmos* from the Greek Kosmos, meaning harmony and order as opposed to chaos. Editors apparently forgot the meaning of that name as they joined in many forms of demands and rebellion. Their use of ill-chosen non-traditional language was especially offensive to the oldest generation. One unhappy senior trustee, wintering cozily in Florida, called to respond with his own counter demands. He said, "I'm awfully mad. Something must be done about the *Cosmos*. Some days I'm sorry that my two granddaughters are freshmen at Coe." Many days I struggled mightily trying to decide the wisest action for a president caught in this crossfire. If I chose the middle ground neither side would be satisfied. In moments such as these I was thankful for younger trustees with college age children who better understood the complexities of what was transpiring. I also had to remind myself that as a college president, I could not expect to be loved by everyone; however, I strove to be respected.

A younger trustee with adolescent children was Chairman of the Board, Jim Coquillette, President of Merchants National Bank in Cedar Rapids. In a letter to me only a few days later he wrote, "Our Instruction Committee meeting last Friday accomplished much, in my opinion. However, there are two more hurdles, and I think it not only important, but absolutely vital that adequate groundwork be laid. The amendments to the Comprehensive Living proposal added strength, but I do not believe you can be too careful or comprehensive in apprising first the executive committee and then the full board of trustees about the student-inspired willingness to install safeguards."

"You also expressed doubt about the effectiveness of the present *Cosmos* governing board. We should be working toward a strengthening of some kind of external influence which could act as a restraint upon the editorial policies." By those comments, he impressed me as being appropriately sensitive to the differences between his generation and the oldest generation of trustees. Those comments also illustrate clearly why I was resolute in required rotation of trustees. Policies, procedures and edicts of the '40s and '50s were no longer effective in the '70s. The rigid positions of some members of the oldest generation were bewilderingly obsolete.

In the fall semester during each of my first seven years as president, I taught a section of Introduction to Liberal Arts. I greatly enjoyed teaching that course with several different assistants in successive years. I shared my student evaluations each term with the faculty chair of the course. These evaluations were always very high. I instructed the course chairman that whenever there was any doubt about the quality of my teaching, he should relieve me of my assignment.

In the last five years of my tenure as president, with my

increased intensity of fund-raising for endowed chairs as well as for the annual fund and my broader external responsibilities, I could no longer devote the necessary time to teaching. So I painfully gave up that responsibility. I served as member of the Board of ACM, for two years as chairman. As a member of the Iowa Association of Independent Colleges for one year as chairman I had increased involvement with the Iowa State Legislature. Locally, I served on the board of the Cedar Rapids Chamber of Commerce, United Way and the Cedar Rapids Symphony Orchestra. Jan and I were active in First Presbyterian Church, I as an elder and I chaired the long-range planning committee. We were engaged in many social, cultural activities and as spectators at Coe athletic events at home and when Coe played at other conference colleges. We had cultivated a few close friends with whom we also enjoyed occasional bridge and formed many casual friendships. All these responsibilities and activities required much energy and time.

In the Rotary International year 1975-76, I served as President of the Cedar Rapids Rotary Club that had about 275 members. Each year, at Club expense, the incoming president attended the Rotary International Convention held that year in Montreal, Canada. Accordingly, Jan and I drove to Montreal with selected stops enroute. We greatly enjoyed the trip and our visit to the city of Montreal. Convention programs were very informative, colorful, dramatic, and time consuming.

The only leave-time that I had had during 23 years as a dean or president was as a Fulbright lecturer in India in 1958-59. With the compelling demands on my time for three years as dean of the college at Coe, I had never been able to take the two-week annual study time provided in my contract. The stresses and strains of office during the 60s and 70s nationally had reduced the average presidential tenure to about four years.

My stress was increased by having to dismiss the dean of the college at the end of 1974-75. Dean Carson Veach acted as if he had a compulsive need, under the guise of humor, to demean and intimidate certain faculty members. This generated insecurity and mistrust. He had difficulty dealing with all faculty even-handedly, showing favoritism to those with whom he developed close personal friendships in contrast to those whom he disliked. At times he failed to follow through on promises made to some individuals.

Charles Lindsay, Professor of Mathematics, a highly respected member of the faculty and a very good teacher, was recommended by several faculty members to succeed Veach. Charles was uncertain as to whether he was interested. So, I appointed Charles Lindsay Interim Dean for a year inn order to determine his long-term interest. In many ways, for me to take leave was untimely. Yet as I looked ahead I could not foresee a better time. With some reluctance the executive committee of the board granted me a leave of two months, December 1975 and January 1976.

In December Jan and I revisited India seventeen years after our year as residents in the Fulbright program. We investigated changes that had occurred in India during that interval, at Mysore University, and in the pre-college educational system. We observed the advances in agriculture, industry, business, and transportation. Several of our friends had died during the interval, however, we had good visits with those who were still living. As a Rotarian, I attended several Rotary Club meetings and was asked to address several Clubs. Indians received us graciously and generously. Our visits to cities included Bombay, Mysore, Bangalore, Jaipur, New Delhi, Agra, Calcutta, Varanasi, and Katmandu, Nepal. On our return to the United States, the most frequent question we were asked, "How much has India changed?" Our stock answer was, "For India, probably more changes occurred during these seveenteen years than in any previous century. However, compared with the rate of change in this country, only minor changes were evident."

In January 1976, we stayed in St. Petersburg, Florida where I spent most of the time in the libraries of Eckerd College and the University of South Florida in Tampa. I found the time in the libraries very rewarding. I was able to read current literature and periodicals dealing with educational policies and practices for which there was not time in a president's schedule at Coe. Our pace during January was more relaxed, in such contrast to the pressures of the president's office. Jan and I were able to visit with Margaret and Guy. Later in that month Annika, coming from Sweden, joined us.

We returned to Cedar Rapids at the end of the month. Thea and her husband, Roger, had moved into the president's home. She even kept some records related to the construction of our lake house at North Coralville Reservoir near Cedar Rapids. This became our occasional weekend hide-away without a telephone, and it was known only to a few of our closest friends.

I accepted an appointment as a member of a nine-person Advisory Panel to the Secretary of the Air Force. On a three-year term, I represented the colleges with Air Force R.O.T.C. units who were members of the Association of American Colleges. We met annually at the Pentagon to be briefed by Air Force generals about policies that affected R.O.T.C. A lieutenant colonel was assigned as my aide for the day.

After a year's experience as Interim Dean, Charles Lindsay decided to continue his position as Professor of Mathematics. As a result of a national search, J. Preston Cole was appointed Dean of the College. During the student unrest and the legal changes granting majority status to all persons who attained age eighteen, the dean of students' position posed great challenges for the incumbent and his staff. The functions of that officer had to be redefined. Consequently, several individuals occupied that position during my twelve years as president. I never found the ideal person. Al McIvor, Director of Admissions, also served briefly as dean of students but soon departed for a position in Hawaii. Van Snow, Business Manager, and Jack Laugen, Director of Development, continued faithfully in their offices throughout my tenure.

Because I found no current record of certain traditions and operational modes of the College, I periodically asked staff members to dig into the archives and other historic records to search for specific information. We made some unexpected discoveries. Although college colors being used were crimson and gold, there was no record that these had ever been officially adopted by the Coe College Board of Trustees or by the Alumni Association. At times other colors were used. Also, there was no record of official adoption of a President's Medallion. So in connection with the celebration of the 125th Year of the founding of Coe College, definitive crimson and gold colors and a new President's Medallion bearing the Seal of the College were officially adopted by the board of trustees.

Historically, scores of honorary degrees had been conferred as the highest award accorded by Coe College for many purposes and to persons with widely different levels of achievement. The board had not adopted policies covering the qualities or characteristics of persons to be so honored. I discussed with trustees whether the practice of awarding honorary degrees should be continued. After extended discussion, the executive committee voted that the practice be continued but with systematic evaluation of persons proposed for such an honor. Faculty members were invited to propose names of distinguished persons for consideration, however, trustees emphasized that honorary degrees were awarded by vote of the board of trustees only.

Through the years Coe had conferred honorary doctorates on a few nationally and internationally distinguished alumni. The College had no higher honor to confer for even more notable achievements. On my recommendation, the board of trustees, authorized a capstone honor designated as the "Founder's Medal." The medal was designed by Richard Braley and executed by the Hamilton Mint. "The Founder's Medal is given by the Trustees of Coe College to persons of rare and exceptional distinction. Persons so honored should be distinguished nationally or internationally in their fields of accomplishment, in service to Coe College, or persons who exemplify in extraordinary degree those qualities of a liberally educated person."

One of the medals was conferred on William L. Shirer, '25, internationally renowned journalist, author and radio commentator. The other awarded to Paul Engle, '31, Rhodes Scholar, founder of The Writers Workshop at the University of Iowa and prolific author and poet on Founder's Day, December 5, 1976, celebrating the 125th Anniversary of the founding of Coe College. Dr. Jerry M. Owen composed "Music for a Gleeful Rite" played by the Concert Band for this celebratory event. I felt deeply moved on this very special occasion for the privilege to serve as president who placed a capstone on a century and a quarter in the undulating life of this fine collegiate institution whose alumni were spread across the world. Their achievements in scores of professions and careers had really made a difference.

In my professional life two other events had recently occurred to bring me distinctive honor. I was completely surprised to learn that Ball State University, on the occasion of Homecoming, October 16, 1976, named me one of three recipients of its annual Distinguished Alumnus Awards. Jan and I attended the celebratory events with great pleasure. I enjoyed being back on campus and seeing a few professors who remained from my student days.

Reflectively, after the event I said to Jan, "I really am flattered to be so honored; however, when I consider the comparative status of Ball State and Northwestern my ego would really be inflated if I had a similar award from that Big Ten University. Of course, that will never happen." I must confess that I aspired to rank high enough on the list of Northwestern University alumni for such an honor, but was fully convinced that this would not happen.

One day the next spring, Jan after opening the mail, called me immediately at my office. She said, "I have in my hands a very important letter from your alma mater, Northwestern University. Are you sitting down?" Incredibly curious, I sat down and she read "Each year the Northwestern University Alumni Association names one alumnus from each of the Colleges to receive the Alumni Award of Merit. You have been selected to receive the Alumni Award of Merit for the College of Education on April 30, 1977." I was stunned speechless! Jan laughed, "My husband who thought he never could."

The inscription of the Alumni Award of Merit read: "In recognition of worthy achievement which has reflected credit on Northwestern University and each of her Alumni." The significance of the award really hit me when I saw who were some of my fellow awardees. That they included the Publisher of the *Chicago Tribune*, the President of Continental Illinois

National Bank, and the Judge of the United States Court of Appeals for the Seventh Circuit suggests the league in which Jan and I were counted. As I reflected on my very humble beginnings, all the sacrifices that Jan made in our behalf during the demanding months and years in my pursuit of the doctorate, I uttered prayers of thanksgiving for blessings that I received beyond my fondest dreams. I recalled the unconditional vote of confidence that the Chairman of my Doctoral Committee, Professor Shirley Hamrin (now deceased) had projected for me when my doctorate was conferred. Now, I envisioned that in the spirit realm he must surely feel gratified.

On April 30, 1977, Jan and I attended the celebratory event. A Northwestern University professor was our host about the campus and at the formal dinner in the adjoining Orrington Hotel. [Jan had served as an evening waitress in the Huddle, a student hangout, while I was writing my dissertation. Now she had her own record as an exceptional teacher of English.] The President of the Northwestern Alumni Association presided and the President J. Roscoe Miller University congratulated each of the recipients.

Jan and I toured the additions to the campus, the acres of sand-filled water front planted with new buildings, and we reminiscently walked the Lake front, a favorite place for the children to walk and swim in Lake Michigan. We reviewed the heart of Evanston and went shopping in downtown Chicago. I even indulged myself by buying an upscale brand of navy blue suit for the then extravagant sum of $400. Late Sunday afternoon we drove back to Cedar Rapids reflectively discussing our family's living at 1925 Orrington Avenue in the 1950s and our surprise return to Northwestern twenty four years later for this celebration. I wondered, "Is this the apex of my professional career at age fifty-eight? What surprises are still ahead?" On Monday morning we descended to the "realities" of mid-life responsibilities.

I continued to serve as a consultant-evaluator for the Commission on Colleges of the North Central Association of Colleges and Schools. I dealt with a wide range of colleges and universities including such struggling institutions as Fort Wayne

Bible College, and the Detroit campus of Shaw University of Raleigh, North Carolina principally for black students. It was located in the section of Detroit that was burned out during the 1968 racial riots, only about a mile from the world headquarters of General Motors Corporation. The Shaw institution was tragically under funded. Both colleges were aspiring to candidacy for accreditation. The president of the Bible College firmly prohibited the teaching of evolution or any laboratory science lest it dilute their literal interpretation of the biblical story of creation.

On a very different assignment, I served as chair of a 25-person committee representing four regional accrediting associations to investigate historically highly respected Antioch College, Yellow Springs, Ohio. Antioch College had established centers in Maryland, Texas, Minnesota and a law school in Washington, D. C. Most of the centers, especially the one in Columbia, Maryland, were highly experimental. These ventures were generated by a very aggressive, experimental dean. The faculty members at the Yellow Springs campus had filed an official complaint that funds drawn for these centers were endangering the financial soundness and reputation of the long-established operation of the Yellow Springs campus. Our committee worked for a full week and issued a report of eighty-five pages that supported the concerns of the faculty and admonished the president who was administratively lethargic. This was the most extensive evaluation that I ever undertook. Some weeks after our report was filed, the Antioch College faculty urged me to become a candidate for the deanship of the Yellow Springs campus. I declined. Several years after the visit Antioch College filed for bankruptcy.

A different type of reaccreditation visit was Notre Dame College of Ohio for women, in Cleveland. Other assignments ranged from colleges in Kansas, Wisconsin, Michigan, and Ohio in the mid-west to New Mexico.

Each visit offered a range of educational experiences in observing the policies and practices of such vastly different institutions. I learned practices that deserved emulation, but I also observed practices that were ineffective, inefficient and even counterproductive. There were notably few institutions that were

386

systematically innovative. Practically all were very tradition bound. There were none in my visits that had devised intensive studies that measured teaching and learning effectiveness. Yet I found twenty-five years of consulting-evaluation on college campuses were far more instructive than many professional meetings and national conferences.

Periodically, the Ford Foundation offered grants to private colleges for various designated purposes. In the mid seventies the Foundation invited select liberal arts colleges, including Coe, that had established innovative programs or academic experiments to apply for a Venture Grant. We filed an application which led to a campus visit by a Foundation representative. Coe received a Venture Grant of $150,000, one of twenty-five awarded in the whole country.

The grant was used for faculty to gain practical experience in some work in other parts of society that would supplement their academic pursuits. A chaplain, who was an associate professor of religion, worked anonymously on a manufacturing assembly line mingling with a segment of society to which he would otherwise be unexposed. A professor of music was engaged as manager in a Seven-Eleven convenience store for a four-week January term. A professor of political science worked with an elected member of the State Legislature to observe government operations. These assignments were based on the assumption that liberal arts faculty members in their academic pursuits by associating only with their own kind tend to be persons removed from the practical world. Teaching liberal arts requires breadth of perspective that can be enriched and broadened by practical experience beyond their specialties.

Faculty policies in research universities require research and publication within narrower and narrower specialties, with rare, if any, reference to liberal arts. My conviction was that faculty in liberal arts colleges should also include the extension of their own liberal education as models for their undergraduate students. Applied experience should be one of those dimensions. Accordingly, I invited a few business corporations to furnish executives to develop and teach courses in the January term, to offer students fresh perspectives from business.

For students the grant provided funds for internships and community service opportunities that would help them to decide in or out of a prospective career direction. For those who found their niche, this often led to a job offer after graduation. For others it served to move in a different career direction. I regarded the grant program in general as successful but regretted that the lack of funds prevented us from continuing all of the innovations that emerged from it.

Meanwhile, changing conditions in the medical field, particularly in nursing, prompted curricular modifications at Coe. For several decades the College and adjacent St. Luke's Hospital shared a program in nurses training that led to a three-year diploma. The basic academic courses were taught at Coe; nursing theory and practice was taught at St. Luke's. Professional nursing associations were campaigning vigorously for all nursing students to earn the four-year degree, Bachelor of Science in Nursing. In negotiations with St. Luke's Hospital, the three-year diploma program was closed and Coe College added the degree Bachelor of Science in Nursing. Coe added a nursing department with an appropriately credentialed nursing faculty. In the minimum time, the degree program was fully accredited.

When we added the Dows Fine Arts Center in 1974, regrettably, this was too late for the distinguished Professor of Art, Marvin Cone, who was a good friend and colleague of renowned artist Grant Wood in nearby Iowa City. The art and drama faculty now faced a formidable challenge to render quality productions proportionally commensurate with the new building facilities.

The admissions office had lost its space with the demolition of Old Main. In 1975 we built an addition to Gage Memorial Union for admissions that was readily accessible from Center Point Road. This upgraded facility, with a very competent staff, led to larger entering classes. In 1980, we attached to Moray Eby Fieldhouse an eight-lane natatorium, an indoor swimming pool and diving area with 400 spectator seats. The hilarious photo showing student leaders dunking Jan and me in the pool appeared in several publications. It was also included in photo exhibits by George Henry, College photographer for more than fifty years. The natatorium was immediately popular not only for swimming classes and recreation but also for intercollegiate competition. Needing more housing for a growing student body, we built two two-story apartment buildings across Center Point Road.

Other buildings required long delayed maintenance and major upgrading. Moray Eby Fieldhouse had been built in 1930. It was then one of the finest fieldhouses on a small college campus in the country. Its large wooden windows on the north side, now literally falling apart, were removed and the openings permanently bricked in. rollback bleachers were installed; offices were refitted.

Hickok Hall, built in 1950, was basically renovated with central air-conditioning, and thoroughly remodeled faculty offices and classrooms. Greene Residence Hall for men built in 1938 had suffered decades of roughhousing and fraternity parties. In 1977, every room, floor, wall and ceiling was thoroughly renewed and the outside brick walls tuck-pointed.

Carnegie Science Hall built in 1910, was now the oldest building on campus. Except for the museum on the fourth floor, Carnegie was essentially vacated in 1968 on the opening of Peterson Science Hall, connected by corridor, and had been largely unused. Structural engineers evaluated the building and declared it an edifice with sound foundation, concrete floors, and brick walls that could endure indefinitely. But it needed a new roof, windows, doors, inside walls and ceilings, modern plumbing, heating and cooling plus an elevator. In 1976 total renovation produced offices for the president, dean of the college, vice president for development and staff, director of alumni affairs, public relations on the third floor. On the ground level and second floor attractive faculty offices, classrooms and computer laboratories served a growing student body and faculty. Carnegie Hall was renamed Stuart Hall for benefactors John and R. Douglas Stuart, honorary alumni. It attracted some of the heaviest campus traffic. These renovations surrounded by new landscaping and out-door sculptures served to make the campus more attractive.

One of the rewards and satisfactions of the presidency is

to learn of the successes of many graduates to whom I had handed diplomas. At alumni meetings across the country and from the quarterly issues of the *Coe Courier*, I gleaned such information. Many graduates attended graduate and professional schools to prepare them for careers in many different specialties. Graduates of the '70s as a group seemed to have among them an unusual share of high achievers. Daryl Banks, '72, physics major, an Afro-American student, was the first Rhodes Scholar since Paul Engle, class of 1930. Others were on the climb to notable careers in medicine, business, scientific research, law, investments, teaching, manufacturing, computer industry, the military, social work and the ministry. Today graduates of the '70s have a disproportionate number of positions on the Coe Board of Trustees. Several have joined major donors, including the endowment of faculty chairs.

In an historic perspective, College trustees, over more than a century, had badly misjudged the future needs of the College. Daniel Coe, a New York farmer, the original major donor had made a gift of $1,500 to the Rev. Williston Jones, founder of the College, to purchase an 80 acre farm. Mr. Coe stipulated that he wanted the prospective ministers to engage in work while they studied. This forward-looking farmer also stipulated that he wanted the College open to young men *and women*. That mandate was years ahead of his fellow citizens. To relieve their ubiquitous financial distress the trustees, less visionary than Daniel Coe and assuming that the farm contained far more acreage than the College would ever need, periodically sold parts of the farm. Over many decades this farmland became individual city lots; ultimately a home was built on each lot. By mid-twentieth century the College was outgrowing its small campus acreage. At that point the trustees, still suffering financial stress, realized that they had to begin to buy back the land so confidently sold in an earlier era. These purchase prices were hundreds of times the price trustees had realized from the land at the time of sales.

When I became president in 1970, trustees were developing plans for use of the land east of Center Point Road, and they realized that each time a property came on the market the College would have to buy it. Most sellers realized that they had one assured bid; it seemed that they prodded other bidders to increase the seller's market price. As a result, hundreds of thousands of dollars that were needed for more direct educational purposes were appropriated to buy overpriced homes leading to their demolition. Hindsight was of no consequence, the College had to have the real estate for future expansion. I often was deeply sorrowful at the plight which the board of trustees and I inherited.

The distressingly low stock market prices throughout the 70s exacerbated my frustration. We could not draw significantly on market gains to help balance current operating costs. [In retrospect, the irony was that within weeks following my retirement the stock market began an ascent that lasted through most of the 80's and again in the 90's. The College then appropriated large sums to balance current income and expenditures and too little to increase the endowment.]

During the latter 60's, the 70's, and thereafter, many private colleges merged or closed because of severe financial distress. A growing percentage of students attended public universities. Historically, private colleges did not seek or receive funds from public sources. Their income came from tuition and gifts from private sources. On the other hand, public colleges and universities did not receive a significant percentage of their income from private sources. Tax supported institutions kept the tuition costs very low, alike for the rich and the poor. The Iowa State Legislature appropriated the necessary balance from tax revenues. This results in the poor paying taxes to educate the children of the rich. With effective public relations and development staffs public sector colleges secured increasing gifts from private individuals, corporations, foundations and the federal government. What appeared to private colleges an intrusion in the private sector by public institutions, the private colleges advocated a commensurate response.

Therefore, the Iowa Association of Independent Colleges decided to lobby the Iowa State Legislature to make public funds available as grants to students of needy families who chose to attend private colleges. The legislature began to appropriate modest funds but with inflation above ten percent during the latter 70's the grants quickly became inadequate. Befriending and lobbying legislators became another chore for private college presidents. Accordingly, I had an additional assignment the next year. I really found that perpetual necessity increasingly burdensome.

In 1978-79 I served as Chair of the Association. At a dinner meeting of the Association we invited key members of the Iowa Legislature as guests. As chairman I addressed my colleague presidents and legislative guests offering recommendations for policy actions that would provide a framework for future annual increased tuition grants to needy students who chose to attend private colleges. One of my senior presidential colleagues wrote, "I thought that Leo's words Monday evening were an admirable, tough, succinct statement of our policy and rationale." The legislature responded positively but with less support than we felt would have been fair and equitable.

Despite all these demands, and my unfilled longing for the classroom, some of my financial goals were being realized through increased private fund-raising, both current and long term. Jack Laugen, Vice-President for Development, and Joe McCabe, Chancellor, whose time was principally devoted to fund-raising, provided excellent help. Their maturing years at Coe became increasingly productive. I devoted more time to the annual fund and cultivating donors for endowed chairs. Some major deferred gifts in estates, trusts and annuities matured, exemplifying a college presidents' motto, "Where there's death there's hope." Among ACM colleges in the latter 70's, Coe's faculty salaries were above the median for several years.

K. Raymond Clark, Coe's principal donor, in the 1970's was setting up a series of irrevocable uni-trusts, one of which was to fund an endowed chair in physical education for $1,000,000. Moreover, as an avid admirer of flowers and trees, he envisioned the establishment of an arboretum of several acres as a laboratory to teach botany. I did some investigation and found that such an arboretum would require a great variety of plants and several kinds of professional caretakers. That alone would make it thoroughly impractical at a liberal arts college. For many months I tried to disabuse him of his plan without success. Finally, a letter from an entomologist at the agricultural college of Iowa State University convinced Ray Clark why an arboretum would be impractical. As a life-long tennis player, his alternate project was the construction of a racquet center on campus. For several years over very modest priced meals in Chicago German restaurants, such as Berghoff Gardens, I persisted in raising his sights of the cost for the quality of racquet center in his mind's eye. As his financial resources increased his plans for a greatly enlarged, esthetically enhanced building grew accordingly.

He was doggedly determined that the racquet center should be built with money from other sources to be off-set by maturing uni-trusts after his demise. The elegant K. Raymond Clark Racquet Center with indoor track, Clark East Campus and football field and outdoor track with stadium and six out-door tennis courts and Clark Alumni Center, were completed by my successors during Ray's lifetime. (Jan and I were especially delighted to be housed in the Alumni Center for three nights when we returned to campus for Homecoming at the 150th Anniversary Celebrations in October, 2000. At age 82, in the 5K run with students and alumni, I was the last one to cross the finish line!)

In securing commitments for endowed chairs, Henrietta Arnold with the Endowed Chair in History was a pacesetter with a final pledge of $1,000,000. Amazingly, George Baker '51, Executive Vice-President of Continental Illinois National Bank, grimly disillusioned at the time of the "hair fuss" with coaches, in due time became a Coe trustee, and agreed to secure $1,000,000 for the George Baker Endowed Chair in Business Administration. He also set up funding for the Richter Honors Scholarships for economics students. He and I became friends. For several years he employed at the bank top economics graduates of Coe, some of whom are now Coe trustees. His daughter became a Coe alumna. During the athletic "hair fuss" in 1970, he had cancelled his pledge to the annual fund—what a transformation!

I had set the policy that a public announcement of

naming a professor to an endowed chair would be done only when a least one-half of the pledge was paid. At the time of my retirement we had secured pledges of $500,000 to $1,000,000 each from donors to endow eight chairs. Regretfully, the ninth and tenth chair that I had promised myself eluded me.

In 1970 when I became president the College budget was $4,039, 978, market value of the endowment was $8,225,603 of which $182,000 consisted of K. Raymond Clark uni-trusts. When I retired August 31, 1982 the budget for 1982-83 was $9,834,918. At the end of that fiscal year the market value of the endowment was $19,809,447. Of this $3,562,838 consisted of the K. Raymond Clark uni-trusts. My goals of doubling the College budget and doubling the endowment were successfully accomplished. Although Ray Clark's trusts would not mature until his death, I was especially delighted with the dramatic increase of his commitments to the College. Of course, by the standards of today, these figures are remarkably modest.

In our personal lives, Jan and I found ourselves increasingly absorbed with events that attend the college presidency. We entertained and in turn were guests at numerous dinners and social events. We attended official events at the College, including lectures, musical performances, football and basketball games at home and sometimes away. We entertained students, faculty and trustees as well as friends in our home, with an occasional evening of bridge. Rarely were we able to spend even part of a weekend at our hide-away Lake House. I jealously guarded my four weeks of summer vacation. At least two weeks of that time we greatly enjoyed spending at the Lake of the Ozarks in Missouri, a sequel to Lake Texoma while we lived in Texas. We towed our boat, and carried an ample supply of books. We combined adequate sleep with hours of reading that I daily alternated with my addiction to water skiing. During the other two vacation weeks, we sometimes visited family and often made another trip to European countries.

In 1972, our son, Luther, President of the Student Body, School of Business at Stanford University earned his MBA. Upon graduation he was named assistant to the chairman, Cummins Engine Company. His wife, Ginger, was enjoying her success as an elementary school teacher. In 1973 Luther and Ginger joined us on a trip to Switzerland, Germany and Austria that we greatly enjoyed. Lisha had moved from Indiana University-South Bend to Syracuse University and was thriving in her profession. Lisha and Rene Wilett were married in a private ceremony on August 12, 1975. Marc Charles was born to them on October 2, 1976 and his sister, Nicole Ann followed him on May 17, 1978.

After twelve years of stressful teaching of English literature and writing to eighth and ninth graders at Franklin Junior High School, Jan decided that she had too many demands on her time. With the endless responsibilities as official hostess and wife of the college president, she decided to retire from teaching in 1979. In 1980, at home in Cedar Rapids, watching TV one morning Jan saw a catastrophic event. In a windstorm a loaded oil tanker crashed into structural supports of the Sunshine Skyway Bridge and knocked out a section of the Bridge. Several cars and a Greyhound bus dropped into Tampa Bay. Jan was overcome with anxiety as she realized that at the moment of the crash Margaret usually would be crossing the bridge on her way to work at the clinic in Bradenton. She frantically tried to call to learn whether Margaret had crashed but all she got was a repetitive busy signal. When she finally got through, Jan learned that Margaret was safe at home suffering from morning sickness, in her early pregnancy state. This probably saved her life! Jan promptly called me; together we said a prayer of thanksgiving for her safety and prayers for hopeful rescue of those who fell in the vehicles that dropped into the water. What a catastrophe!

There were other events on the humorous side both at Franklin School and at Coe. Frequently students responded with Jan as the subject of poetic creations. For Halloween they gave her a witches' hat and a broom. One morning we found a large alligator on our front lawn. When it remained stationary for too long, we realized that it was lifeless. When the biology department sent an SOS "one lost alligator" we saw the connection. At another time, a pair of crouching lions disappeared from our front porch. I fully expected them to be conspicuous on stage at commencement! Regrettably, we never saw them again.

[2]I had passed age sixty and occasionally Jan and I conversed about when and where we should plan to retire. In contrast to President Emeritus Joseph E. McCabe who remained in Cedar Rapids, my constitution would not enable me to retire near the College to watch my successor succeed eminently or fail miserably. In either event, as unavoidable observer and listener to comparisons with my predecessor I would be quite uncomfortable. To add momentum toward retirement, Jan was approaching the time for her 30-year post-polio syndrome. She was advised by her physicians to locate in a year round sunny climate and to practice a regimen of daily exercise. We added two more conditions. As lovers of travel for education and pleasure we wanted to be near a good international airport. Ubiquitously committed to life-long learning, we wanted to be near a good liberal arts college. Our eyes turned south, prospects included Texas, New Mexico, and Florida. Having lived in Sherman, Texas we found the Dallas area appealing but both Texas and New Mexico have long periods of dry, dusty weather. Jan and I both were allergic to dust. Given the choice, we preferred the persistent humidity of Florida.

Margaret and Guy were married on my birthday June 27, 1973 in our garden and promptly moved to St. Petersburg, Florida. In 1980 with our eyes blind to the future, we chose St. Petersburg, Florida, that met all our specifications plus the bonus of our childrens' families living in the eastern third of the country. The St. Petersburg area is known for almost daily year round sunshine, the home of Eckerd College, and Tampa International Airport.

We visited Margaret and Guy for a few days each Christmas. As I jogged in the area of their home in the balmy temperatures and floral fragrances of late December, I yearned for this alternative to the frigid Iowa ice and snow. I asked myself, "Why not now?" During our visit in 1980, Jan and I bought a home, to become our residence two years later, at 5819

---

[2] While revising this chapter I received a call from the Coe president's office that Joe McCabe died April 9, 2001.

Third Street South in Bahama Shores for $72,000. We chose that one from among several that Guy and Margaret had sorted out to facilitate our search. With no retirement date set at that time, we decided to lease the home, with them serving as our agents. We sold our Lake House. Price-wise the two transactions almost balanced out.

In 1980 I was elected to the Board of Directors of Iowa Electric Light and Power Co. (i.e.) where I served for ten years until the compulsory retirement age applied. I regarded that as a privilege especially in serving with James Van Allen, the world renowned Professor of Physics and Astronomy at the University of Iowa whose name is on the Van Allen Radiation Belt. Another prominent Board colleague was Robert Ray, the former fourteen-year Governor of Iowa. I also served on the Board of Directors of the active Cedar Rapids Chamber of Commerce. Robert Faxon, President of the Chamber, and his wife, Ruth, were good friends with whom we enjoyed playing bridge. They were planning to retire to south Texas. Another public service assignment was as a member of the Board of Iowa Public Programs for the Humanities. Congress established a similar board in each state in an effort to establish the Humanities components, especially history and literature, as of critical importance in the formation of public policy.

The presidency of a college demands extraordinary versatility and ability, with aplomb, to shift instant focus from one subject to another. The office required a personal inner security that made it unnecessary to dump my problems on my subordinates. My duties included a monthly meeting of the College faculty and also the faculty executive committee. I scheduled a one-hour executive weekly staff meeting, each of which I chaired. The executive committee of the Coe College Board of Trustees met monthly and the full board twice a year, each of which required extensive preparation. In addition, there were regular meetings of the various associations of ACM Board, the Iowa College Board, the North Central Association of Colleges and Schools, Consulting and Evaluation Committees, National Association of Independent Colleges and Universities. Then there were the calls for speeches at various kinds of organizations.

Time in the office brought a daily stream of appointments and unscheduled drop-ins by students, faculty, parents, trustees, alumni, and donors in response to my open door policy, intermingled with telephone calls. At various seasons correspondence was profuse, all of which required background knowledge with calculated discretion and at times high diplomacy. Thankfully, Thea Leslie, my assistant, always demonstrated her high level of intelligence and sound judgment in sensitively handling whatever situation confronted her.

Did I become weary? Yes, certainly. I had a high level of tolerance but tensions accumulated. I needed regular release of my aggressions for which an hour of badminton with one of the coaches served me very well. I never took naps, but I needed seven to eight hours of sleep on a regular basis to maintain my equilibrium and on occasional week ends quiet time in my study with classical music, time for reflection and prayer. Unhurried time in solitude and with Jan, in front of a glowing fireplace was very helpful to me. I felt considerable satisfaction with the progress at the College. Gradual but continuing increase in student enrolment, higher average in SAT and ACT scores and a rising class rank at high school graduation were gratifying. A larger percentage of faculty members had terminal degrees with more having had experiences as students or teachers at good liberal arts colleges All departments had two or more faculty members with almost no interim appointments. More faculty and administration members were Coe alumni. However, I realized that there were also many more kinds of upgrading essential to the future of the College. Nevertheless, it seemed timely for a change in the presidency.

Even the Iowa weather offered inducements for a change. The Iowa winter of 1980-81 was exceptionally severe with temperatures as low as 20 degrees below zero, Fahrenheit, for several days. In typically depressing mid-west weather, heavy clouds obscured the sun. As late as April 10, Cedar Rapids was submerged by thirteen inches of snow. Enroute to a meeting of ACM in Minneapolis, I was snowbound in a country motel in northern Iowa for thirty-six hours. I missed the meeting.

In this context, Jan suffered seasonal depression, pained with polio-deadened and damaged muscles with the onset of thirty-year post polio syndrome. We discussed several times at length whether I should retire at age 64, a year earlier than planned on August 31, 1982. On one memorable frigid winter evening while relaxed in our Lake House, we decided to do so and to announce our plans in the spring. This would offer the board of trustees some eighteen months to conduct a deliberate national search for my successor.

Joe McCabe advised me not to make the announcement so long in advance of my departure lest I be viewed as a "lame duck" and, thereby, lose my effectiveness as chief administrator. I silently disagreed for I felt sufficiently secure and confident that the respect for me within the community would enable me to conduct the business of the College until the very last day. (My conviction proved to be correct.)

In the spring of 1981, I informed the Chairman of the Board, Paul Scheele, and the Executive Committee and then the full Board of our plans. I told the faculty in a meeting. There was obvious surprise. Many faculty members shared their regret over my plans for retirement and expressed their apprehension about the choice of my successor. Some sent letters of approbation. Several trustees and faculty gallantly tried to persuade me to continue past retirement age of 65, even if less than fulltime. I quote from a letter by Robert Drexler, Associate Professor of English, who was on leave in Japan, referring to his youthful memories when his father was Professor of Biology. I quote in part...

> "While I am sure that you are looking forward to retirement, Coe will miss you and I, personally, will miss you. Especially this year when I have a chance to talk with professors at many other colleges, I have come to realize how fortunate Coe has been to have your stable and wise leadership. As you know I grew up knowing a College that was plagued by bad leadership. I realize now that because of your tenure as President, Coe has

399

become so used to good leadership that we take it for granted."

(Thea, my assistant attached a note, "Let's require every professor to teach abroad for a semester)." I was flattered with such approbation; however, Jan and I tenaciously clung to our plan. Feeling that for me a total of thirty years as a dean and president was long enough, I steadfastly asserted that *"It is good to leave when I'm still wanted."*

Joe McCabe had retired as Chancellor and was named President Emeritus but he continued to do part-time fundraising. Paul Scheele, Chairman of the Board, appointed a committee that included trustees, faculty, alumni and students to conduct a national search for my successor. The committee planned to have my successor in place by August 1, 1982 to permit us one month of overlap, with my official retirement on August 31, 1982.

Chairman Scheele, had become a good friend. An alumnus, and a retired top business executive of a multi-national firm, he came to the board by way of the President's Advisory Council. He was also the first chairman not from the Cedar Rapids area. I endorsed Joe's retirement from his position as chancellor and his being named president emeritus.

The board of trustees proposed to me that, Joe and I, each be given an honorary degree. With this proposal I faced a delicate decision. First, I had been a severe critic of granting an honorary degree too casually. Historically, an honorary degree, Doctor of Divinity, sometimes jokingly labeled "donated dignity," was often conferred on a minister. Each of the three presidents with whom I worked before coming to Coe, (two of whom were ministers and one was a lawyer), had only honorary doctorates. Each of them clutched and used his degree as if it were earned. I found this academically indiscreet and distasteful. As president, I never awarded an honorary degree, Doctor of Divinity, but declined to do so several times when such proposals were submitted. Joe who had an earned doctorate was not given an honorary degree when he was named president emeritus.

I understood why the board proposed to me giving both

400

Joe and me honorary degrees. Joe had served Coe much longer than I had. I was retiring from the presidency, Joe had retired from the presidency twelve years ago. If a degree was to be awarded to Joe McCabe it should be done at another occasion. I reflected thoughtfully on Chairman Scheele's offer on behalf of the board and thanked him for the generous proposal. I chose not to discuss this issue with Joe lest I create offense but declined the offer. I had discussed this proposal only with Jan. Chairman Paul Scheele was obviously very disappointed.

I continued to travel widely, throughout the mid-west, from California to Boston and New York, from Minneapolis to Chicago to meet alumni, donors and prospective donors, to meet parents of students and to encourage student recruitment. My goal of getting commitments to fund ten endowed faculty chairs at $500,000 to $1,000,000 was still elusive although I was making progress. Frequent lunch or dinner meetings with K. Raymond Clark, previously mentioned, were designed to raise his sights, to keep him challenged and enthused as plans evolved for the racquet center-track combination to bear his name. His family had a history of remarkable longevity; his uni-trusts were not likely to mature during my watch. Henrietta Arnold continued to contribute significantly in the name of her family.

As I reflected on my tenure as president, I saw more clearly that the presidency of a college is in many respects an awesome responsibility. The president is, at once, the educational leader and head of the institution, a member of the board of trustees to whom he is accountable, a member of and chairman of the faculty. He is the chief administrator, the one who is accountable for good or ill. His constituencies include not only the trustees and the faculty, but also the alumni, students, parents of students, donors and, to some extent, news media and the public.

Among the president's goals in running the college must be the cultivation of each of these constituencies, to earn their respect and earn, and keep, their support. When matters run smoothly his successes are scarcely noticed. When disruptions or conflict break into public attention the institution is suddenly newsworthy and the focus is frequently on the president. One of the greatest challenges that a president faces, especially during times of unrest, social turmoil and change, is to deal evenhandedly with all constituencies to maintain their respect— and all this while maintaining his personal integrity.

Change amid continuity appear to me to be the nature of the universe. People tend to regard change as an imposition, and the more so, if it interferes with what they have for a long time been accustomed. To promote change does not make one popular, especially when one proposes change on one's superiors, such as a board of trustees. It took me three years of repetitive proposal to bring about required rotation of trustees following three consecutive three-year terms. On October 26, 1973, the board of trustees finally adopted it as part of its self-discipline. This action on my part led to a cooling relationship with some of the most senior members, who had served consecutively for thirty-five years or more. However, overall I maintained a very cordial relationship with the board throughout my fifteen years at Coe. Evaluations of me as president in the middle year of each three-year contract by the board of trustees, administrators, faculty and student leaders were consistently very positive.

When I became president, ironically, the Coe Board of Trustees, whose average age was 65 was the legal entity overseeing the operation of an institution whose customers were the 18 to 22 year-old students. Traditionally board members and students never met. Maintaining such distance tends more often to generate mutual suspicion or mistrust. It does not build mutual regard. In an era of dynamic social change could this board understand the youth two generations younger? Could the students understand and accept the decisions of these senior persons whom they never met and who wanted to adhere to some policies similar to ones in effect during their own college days of half a century ago? By instituting required rotation off the board after serving three consecutive three-year terms, and adding five trustees below age 35, the average age of 65 in 1970 dropped to 58 in 1982,. The chair was elected each year to guard against inappropriate continuity as Coe had experienced in the 40s and 50s.

The new trend was clear; it helped to bring fresh vitality and new perspectives. These policies and procedures facilitated the combination of continuity and change. In reflecting on my twelve years as president, I regarded these as some of the most important long-term changes that I accomplished for the future of the College. Related to these concerns, I introduced the practice of having the executive staff give reports in person at each meeting of the board. I also secured board approval to name a faculty representative to each board committee that dealt with faculty matters. To establish closer relationships with students, the board invited student officers to present their concerns at each board meeting. These changes were part of the transition from the paternalistic attitude toward increased participatory government.

Approaching the end of the school year and the commencement season always brought much strenuous activity involving the whole campus community. For many students the tendency is to postpone the completion of large tasks, such as research papers, to near the end of the semester, then to combine their completion with preparation for final examinations. Other students devote last minute energy focussed toward a certain grade in a less favored course or feeling desperate to reach a certain cumulative grade point average, whether a minimum for graduation or achieving a particular level of honors. Anxiety, frustration, and mental and physical exhaustion from prolonged lack of sleep, are pervasive in those closing days, often compounded with colds or other derivative ailments. Residence hall rooms are mostly in gross disarray as the occupants plan their prompt departure after graduation. These tensions often reach their families, perhaps the more so if they are distant from the campus, as they make their plans for the climactic commencement day.

The faculty members are often victims of student delay, as they are engrossed in grading term and research papers, conducting examinations, and calculating final grades, trying to be honest and fair. They too suffer mental and physical exhaustion, sometimes caught in rugged debate with marginal students about what they regard as unjust grades, especially when faculty already feel that they have been too lenient. The faculty is hounded by the registrar who has to decide which students to delete from the graduation roster that is in the hands of the anxious printer. The faculty marshal always suffers last minute adjustments in his reorganizing the procession that includes students, faculty, administration, trustees and honored guests.

The dean of students and residence hall supervisors deal with the hasty departure of students, final settlement of all bills and room reservations and deposits for those who will return. Not the least of concerns is the last minute assessment of room or furniture damage and ascertaining that it has been paid at the business office.

Campus grounds workers have the unenviable task of obtaining and arranging the seating and decorating to accommodate the hundreds or thousands of attendees at commencement ceremonies. These workers must also be prepared for parking hundreds of visitors' cars. To avoid the hazard of sudden summer thunderstorms Coe Commencements were held in air-conditioned Moray Eby Fieldhouse.

Food and beverage services face heavy demands for the various special lunches, dinners and receptions and hospitality to the hundreds of visitors. If these services are adroitly provided they are mostly unnoticed; however, no campus service is more unfavorably remembered when individual tastes or decorum are not satisfied.

Commencement time for me, as president, was especially hectic because too many events were piled layers deep in such a short time. From Thursday through Sunday, we faced the following events: meeting of the board of trustees; greeting alumni class reunions, individually welcoming the 50-year class members; greeting graduating seniors and families in a receiving line, and by entertaining honorary degree recipients at lunch. Further, I presided at baccalaureate service, conducted the commencement service, which included presenting a six to ten minute farewell homily to the graduating class, conferring degrees, shaking hands and presenting the diploma to each graduate. Still further, after the ceremony, I posed for photographs, mingled with graduates, their families and friends as they concluded their emotional academic celebration. Jan shared in nearly all these events. After enduring this interminable series of activities for some twelve years, I pondered the wisdom of having deleted the traditional commencement speaker, realizing that this is one speech preparation I could have shifted to someone else.

Through thirty years [half of them at Coe] as a dean or president marching to commencement to the music of the band, such as Elgar's *Pomp and Circumstance* or Purcell's *Trumpet Tune,* was always an exciting and deeply moving experience, repeated annually. However, for members of the graduating class and their families it was a distinctive if not unique celebration of having reached another milestone. To the parents, remembering hopes and dreams realized following years of joys and sorrows along the way,commencement was also a celebration of the last tuition paid. What a collage of collective mental and emotional reflections! While celebrating with graduates and anticipating many more deferred satisfactions, the faculty members were thrilled that another academic year had ended.

Typically, when the commencement crowd had drifted away, the food and beverage servers were tiringly engaged in clean up. Jan and I would amble toward the parking lot reflecting on the profusion of activities during the last four days, yet exhilarated by the knowledge that we had shared in another climactic ceremony that was also a prelude to great achievements in the lives of the graduates. As with each commencement, it was a joining of the past and the future. We were still too emotionally engrossed to feel the weariness of our minds and bodies.

The commencement season in May 1982 was, of course, different. Although I would not officially retire until August 31, the May commencement season signaled the end of my career. I was then assuming that after retirement I would not be further employed full-time. For months our family, children and spouses, had been planning a reunion as a celebration at Coe during commencement season that included Annika, one of our Swedish daughters, and her husband, Peter Ekman, who came from London. We missed our other Swedish daughter, Malin, and her husband, Melchior, who lived in Sweden. Jan and I needed to vacate the president's home by June 30 because it had been sold, to serve the housing preference of my successor.

The Coe Board of Trustees held a dinner at the Cedar Rapids Country Club, a gala occasion at which time they gave us a generous retirement gift for a two-week trip to Greece. Thea, my administrative assistant, and Nancy, secretary, and other staff had cleverly maneuvered, without any suspicion on my part, to assemble a bound volume of more than one hundred fifty commendatory and congratulatory letters. These came from faculty, trustees, student leaders, alumni, and friends of the College, colleagues from the Iowa Association of Independent Colleges and the Associated Colleges of the Midwest. Some were addressed to Jan and me. The letters were professionally bound in a hard cover volume, in the official colors of Coe College, Crimson and Gold. The inscription read, "Presented With Appreciation to Leo and Jan Nussbaum for Service to Coe College, May, 1982." Many of the letters, while flattering to Jan and me, can be ego inflating; one of the hazards in reading them is that I might begin to believe the words of praise. Except for a letter from Gus Schrader to which I earlier referred, I decided not to quote any letters or portions thereof in this *Memoir.*

The Chairman of the Coe Board of Trustees prepared a citation read at Commencement naming me President Emeritus. It reads:

> "Leo L. Nussbaum, having faithfully performed the duties and responsibilities as President of Coe College, and having decided to retire from this office, by the authority of the Board of Trustees, I now have the honor to present to you the diploma which signifies that you have attained for life the rank of President Emeritus. Congratulations and with every good wish to you."

Presented by Paul D. Scheele
Coe B.A. '44, M.B.A.
Chairman, Board of Trustees
23 May 1982

The children and spouses were all present at commencement. This was a truly memorable family reunion. When all the ceremonies were over we lounged around our home on this joyous occasion and relived many family events of the past. The children surprised us with a generous gift of patio-pool furniture for our new home at 5819 3rd Street South, St. Petersburg, Florida. We were planning to construct a swimming pool 11x38 as soon as we were moved in.

Early in the next week the children, and Annika and Peter, departed for their respective domiciles. As always there were many loose ends to be attended to following commencement. And our eyes were veering southward while assessing all that was awaiting us between then and moving day near the end of June. There were many more social events, mostly farewell dinners and parties with friends, even to the stage of utter weariness. Yet, having lived in Cedar Rapids twice as long as we had lived in any other place, we had developed many friendships on campus, among trustees, at church and in the community at large. We had to bid a sad farewell to a few friends to whom we were very close.

In my latter days at Coe, I had to take another disquieting and painful action. We had celebrated disproportionately large numbers of athletic conference championships. Somehow, my long-term relationships with coaches undulated between mutually warm and esteemed connections, contrasted with occasional coaching actions that led to fractured relationships. As described earlier, the athletic director and four other male coaches resigned because I found their proposed "blood covenant" athletic hair code untenable. The coaches whom I appointed to replace them developed harmonious relationships and the record numbers of championships.

Each year I required each coach, full-time or part-time, male and female, to sign a statement that "failure to conform in every respect with Coe College, Midwest Inter-collegiate Athletic Conference, and the National Collegiate Athletic Association could lead to dismissal." During the first eleven years of my presidency at Coe, I did not learn of any violations.

In the spring 1982 outdoor track competition, the head football and head track coach for several years had been highly successful in both sports. He was intent on winning the eleventh consecutive Midwest Intercollegiate Athletic Conference outdoor track championship. As the season ended, he reported another victory. However, some time later the Coe Faculty Athletic Committee informed me that he had permitted an ineligible track team member to compete. Either, he did not confirm the runner's eligibility or he knowingly let him run in spite of it.

In joint conferences with the track coach, the director of athletics, the chairman of the faculty athletic committee, the coach refused to admit that whichever action he took, he had violated the rules by permitting him to run. After several further conferences with the coach, he firmly refused to apologize or to admit error while I was fully persuaded that he had failed to do his duty. I told him that he that he had violated the terms of his contract, and regrettably, I dismissed him. Because he had two remaining years of his three-year contract, he sued the College for reimbursement of the balance. After my departure, the College made an out of court settlement. The Midwest Intercollegiate Athletic Conference conducted its own investigation and cancelled the Coe championship. The coach could not find a coaching position; regrettably, his career was in ruins. Instead of firing him, I could have taken no action. I chose not to leave the matter to my successor, convinced that this kind of violation with refusal to admit and apologize could well lead to further and even more serious violations. If I had not reported the violation of conference rules, the conference would also have penalized Coe College. Blemished coaching integrity, if left unattended, could not help but damage the College reputation and lead to institutional penalties. However, I was greatly saddened that in closing my career at Coe this action was necessary.

On campus during June I made a few remaining appointments, dealt with donors, began preparation for the transition of Coe's leadership to John E. Brown, selected as my successor. We were scheduled to work together during the month of August to provide an orderly transition. I introduced him to campus colleagues, the board of trustees, some key community leaders, and a few of the major donors. At the end of summer term, I presided at the small commencement for those students who completed their studies since May. On August 31, 1982 I abdicated and turned over full responsibility to my successor.

Chapter 26: At Home in Florida Multiple Retirements

1982-

In Cedar Rapids, Jan and I found that our eyes had turned southward. We continued to discard hundreds of books and sort furniture in preparation to move into our smaller home at 5819 3rd Street South, St. Petersburg. In late June, the movers loaded our furniture. Jan and I departed Cedar Rapids on June 30 towing our fifteen-foot ski boat, planning to meet the moving van in St. Petersburg. We drove unhurried to Columbus, Indiana, to visit with Luther, Ginger, Kari and Kristin. They seemed contentedly settled in that small city, nationally and internationally known for its unique architectural distinctiveness. Luther had advanced rapidly at Cummins Engine Co., and from all appearances he was being groomed for the long term.

Then we angled southeastward from the rolling plains of Indiana toward the hills and mountains of Kentucky and Tennessee. I recalled that as a sophomore in college I had greatly enjoyed a field trip through the Smoky Mountains, but Jan and I had never driven the hills, mountains and valleys of these states. The verdant trees and bushes of spring and summer were at their best in late June. Sumac was one of the few plants that we recognized. We greatly enjoyed the mountain scenery. The cruise control in the V-6 Oldsmobile could not effectively handle pulling the boat through the mountains; intermittently, it failed to function. I relearned the tediousness of sitting for hours in one position while holding my right foot on the accelerator.

In Georgia the peach season was beginning. We paused to taste the widely reputed, delectable, tree ripened peaches. We were easily persuaded that the Georgia peach reputation was fully deserved. Remembering our former home canning of Michigan peaches in September, we wished we could carry a bushel of Georgia peaches to St. Petersburg. Then we realized that we no longer had any Mason jars.

At the Florida border we were happily welcomed to the

citrus state with samples of orange and grapefruit juice. The high humidity and essentially flat Florida terrain were in such contrast to the preceding three states. When we reached 7143 10th St. South, St. Petersburg, Margaret, Guy and Bryan, not yet two years old, warmly welcomed us to their home. We stayed with them for a few days until our furniture was moved in and the beds had been assembled.

Guy and I celebrated the early morning of July 4, by removing all the carpeting in our new home except in my study. We were surprised to uncover the attractive terrazzo floor throughout the house. Jan and I, bunking at Margaret's, bought carpeting and had it promptly laid so that when the furniture arrived we were ready for it.

The house suffered from much neglected maintenance. Window cranks were missing and many screens needed replacement. Palmetto bugs had taken possession of the garage; dung was literally piled inches high in corners. Gutters needed to be added and the lawn was a total disaster. Orange and grapefruit trees needed trimming and fertilizing. Dead branches by the score had piled up under the eleven-trunk Reclanata palm tree, a haven for palmetto bugs. Dead limbs needed to be removed from the tree. Rows of infectious five-inch spikes were harbored two feet from the base of each Reclanata branch. Ignorantly, I defied them as they pricked my arms and elbows with the result the injury developed into an inflamed staph infection that lingered for months. After we removed some of the excess trees about 25 remained, including palms, mahogany, grapefruit, orange, pin oak, various live oaks, royal poinciana, ash, evergreen, Cuban laurel, sweet gum, magnolia, and frangipani, among others. I devoted much of my energy to basic trimming and cleaning up the yard. Later we would tend to the miserable condition of the lawn and the strange new St. Augustine grass that looked very much like Iowa or Indiana Crab grass, where it was regarded as a despicably invasive weed. Most exciting was having our very own swimming pool under construction. The obsolete sprinkler system needed many repairs, if not total replacement. To make it much worse, as the pool builders dug they demolished the underground piping in that area. They worked rapidly. We were delighted to see our swimming pool take shape according to plan as the pool deck became integrated with the covered back patio.

I felt like a strangely divided self, returning to Coe for six weeks after having moved the furniture into our Florida home. In the ensuing weeks Jan diligently scrubbed walls and ceilings, cleaned windows, hung drapes polished furniture, painted walls and ceilings. She rapidly turned the house into a home. She critically viewed the pool construction, building of the screened cage, the filling of the pool and necessary water treatment. We had already invested great energy in the home and the trees

In the middle of July, I drove back to Cedar Rapids to finish my commitments to Coe by the end of August. Joe and Peggy McCabe, who lived in a Coe College home, were in Montana for the summer. They had graciously offered me their home during my stay at Coe.

Jan joined me in Cedar Rapids the last few days of August and on September 1 we departed for Florida. We paused in Macomb, Illinois, for a brief visit with Gary and Jo Schwartz. Gary was my first cousin and my roommate throughout college. Jan and I were eager to return to our new home and another venture into a geographic area that was new to us.

Entering retirement was an undertaking with which we had no experience. What were the risks that attended this phase of life? How long would it take me to shed the burden of heavy responsibilities, consciously and subconsciously, that I had carried as dean or president of a college for 30 years? How would retirement be different from vacation? Could one enjoy long term doing what is so gratifying during a vacation of two to four weeks? Would the repetitiveness of leisure- time activity become dull and boring? I read of other people's answers but would their answers be the same for me? Some people emphasized that doing something different during vacation, in contrast to the monotony of daily work, is what made it so precious. After a few months, play in whatever form also became monotonous. At that stage in my life, I did not envision returning to fulltime work.

I had made a few plans to make the transition from work to retirement less abrupt. I had agreed with my successor, Coe

412

President John E. Brown, that a few days each month I would do some fund-raising among Coe alumni. Historically, Florida had only a small number of Coe alumni. High school graduates in Florida had not been attracted to college in cold northern states. With the exploding Florida population, a growing number of Coe alumni joined the inward migration. I had also agreed to do a few days of periodic consulting. Mary Holmes College in West Point, Mississippi, a Presbyterian mission junior college was designed for black students from rural areas that could benefit from remedial work before entering the more competitive four-year colleges. These tasks appreciably eased my transition.

As always, when moving to a new community, Jan and I had to establish our connections with a church, a physician, dentist, lawyer, broker, plumber, sprinkler and lawn service, and a Rotary Club. With the automatic devices, Jan, as the regular swimmer and principal user, opted to take care of the swimming pool rather than have a commercial contract.

Serving on the Board of Directors of Iowa Electric Light & Power Co. based in Cedar Rapids was to continue in retirement. The board held five regular meetings each year, plus an occasional special meeting. Having devoted my whole career to the not-for-profit sector, I found service on the corporate utility board highly informative, stimulating and remunerative. Five annual trips from St. Petersburg to Cedar Rapids also enabled me to visit the Coe campus and some close friends.

Jan and I needed to attend to the remaining neglected maintenance of our home including windows, screens, doors, and tree trimming. We now addressed the sizable and monotonous task of developing a new lawn. The palmetto bugs (similar to cockroaches in the North) pretended ownership of the house and garage. After trying for many months to dislodge them, we conceded defeat and called professional exterminators.

The lawn soil consisted of sand and shells with very low fertility; the lawn was a spectacle of disaster. Since the previous owner had regularly washed his boat and trailer on the lawn, desalinization along with fertilization was a major task before sod could be productively cultured into a good turf. We bought rectangles of St. Augustine sod that we laid in checkerboard

413

pattern; then we fertilized and watered with a renovated sprinkler system. It took us three years to develop a respectable turf. I had pruned and fertilized the orange and grapefruit trees. We began to enjoy the harvest of bushels of Duncan grapefruit and two varieties of oranges, Pineapple and Temple. That success inspired me to grow a papaya tree. The soil was unsuitable for a vegetable garden.

We installed a new overhead garage door. After a long search I finally found a dealer that provided the obsolete cranks for the windows. After six months we finally had the 23-year-old residence appearing respectable. It was time to explore new horizons.

Recreationally, we loved to luxuriate in and around our new cage-screened swimming pool. What a delight to eat meals in the bug-free environment of the pool deck and to enjoy an occasional nap in mid-afternoon, lounging on the furniture our family gave us. We readily adapted to the more casual dress and disposed of our Iowa winter wardrobe. We thrived on the fresh citrus fruit and enjoyed more frequent restaurant dining. Watching the glorious sunsets across the Gulf of Mexico was a rare treat. The scenery had changed to water, water everywhere!

After visiting several Presbyterian Churches, we joined First Church, with its strong music program. I had naively envisioned joining a large congregation where I, no longer a college president, could become if not "invisible" at least inconspicuous. Somehow that did not occur. Then I began to wonder whether I really wanted such "invisibility" and whether I could handle it if it happened. I was soon elected an elder, the fifth congregation that I served in this way. I joined the Rotary Club, and Jan joined a book discussion group at Eckerd College. We found a temporary broker while keeping our stocks principally in Cedar Rapids. We connected with a lawyer, Joseph Fleece, and recorded our wills in Florida. We found a female physician. A male dentist was located in a strip mall about half a mile from home. Jan mastered the new tri-cycle and said that she felt more independent than she ever had during our marriage of forty years. I paid a visit to Eckerd College that had recently established a Program for Experienced Learners (PEL). The

College employed adjunct faculty to teach courses for commuters in the evenings. The Director of PEL invited me to submit my curriculum vitae so the faculty could consider me for an adjunct position. Despite my having continually taught one or two courses in my 18 years as an academic dean and at least one course per year up to the last five years, I was rejected "for having been too long an administrator." My ego deflation was one of the first psychological casualties in retirement.

Between 1982 and 1985, I made calls on a number of Coe alumni in central Florida who had been quite successful in their professions and careers. Some of them had been regular financial contributors while others had not similarly supported Coe. I enjoyed visits with them and was able to persuade some of them to make significant increases in their annual support. One alumnus, a prominent attorney, Paul Raymond, '28, who resided in Daytona Beach, had positive memories of his student days. He was especially fond of mathematician Professor Yothers and, after several visits, responded to my suggestion that he establish an endowed chair in his memory. This struck a responsive chord; a few years later he designated the John F. Yothers Endowed Chair in Mathematics with principal funding of one million dollars.

In 1983, Jan and I also began our consulting visits to Mary Holmes College. Jan assisted the staff in writing some of the College bulletins. I made a valiant effort to open doors for new relationships between the College and the business and professional community in the city of 10,000 people. The College never had any organized fund-raising endeavor in the community. Historically, the racial climate did not permit such an undertaking. I called on presidents of the banks, manufacturing firms, the head of the chamber of commerce, the mayor, and the police chief. I reminded them of the economic value of Mary Holmes College to the city. At that time federal support for the College was being sharply reduced; businesses and individuals in West Point would have to assist in replacing federal funds. Surprisingly, most of the community leaders seemed not to have considered the College an important economic citizen worthy of note. In the next year the College

415

conducted its first fund raising effort. Although only modestly successful, this was a beginning. I found much satisfaction in seeking to help Mary Holmes College in its desperate financial struggle to serve the underprivileged black students. Though twenty years later the College is still desperately struggling, I think it continues to fill an important educational niche.

One of the reasons we had chosen St. Petersburg for our retirement location was about to be erased. When we moved to Florida each of the children lived east of the Mississippi River. Soon after we were well settled, however, Luther, Ginger and daughters, after ten years with Cummins Engine Co., left Columbus, Indiana. He had wearied of diesel engines (having been vice-president for parts worldwide) yearned for the excitement of the computer industry. He became a vice-president of a new company, Business Land, based in Silicon Valley near San Jose, California. The family promptly moved to Fremont, where Luther entered a new career.

Having retired in late summer 1982 and now having essentially completed the maintenance tasks of our home, I realized that I might be open to consider some new endeavor. The transition from the consistently heavy burdens of office for so many years to none at all, at times left me depressed. In April 1983, Peter Armacost, President of Eckerd College, made a well-timed appointment to visit in our home. He explained that he had just fired George Schurr, Director of the new Academy of Senior Professionals at Eckerd College (ASPEC). Its purpose, he explained, was to elect to membership men and women who had been high achievers in their respective professions and careers, and had been leaders in and contributors to their communities. He went on to explain that ASPEC was to offer members intellectual and social intercourse, to stimulate them mentally, and to contribute to intergenerational education for the students of the College.

Formally inaugurated on October 31, 1982 with fourteen charter members, ASPEC now had twenty-eight members. Peter had sought one hundred members by Christmas, 1982. During this academic year 1982-83 the College had invested several hundred thousand dollars bringing a number of nationally renowned persons to the campus as speakers, some remained in residence for many weeks. ASPEC did not yet have by-laws. There was debate among the steering committee, consisting of members and non-members, whether ASPEC should become a freestanding corporation related to Eckerd College or a unit of Eckerd College.

On that day in April, Peter was very frustrated. He had previously engaged high level consultants who brought diverse opinions. A previous director, Lloyd Averill, stayed only one year during which he conducted various surveys in the St. Petersburg area and collected substantial data. George Schurr followed him; in his second year he started an organization. However, at this time, no programming beyond June 1983 had been planned. Peter's challenge to me was to become director immediately and to promise him at least three years in that office. He wanted ASPEC to become known, regionally and nationally without delay, as a highly visible and functional organization. During 1982-83 ASPEC had five staff positions: a director, an assistant director and three other full-time staff. Peter said that the budget and staff would be drastically cut for the next year; there will be no assistant director. With all the uncertainties, without model or precedent as an organization, I felt that I should commit myself for no more than one year. After a year each of us should take stock as to whether we want to continue the relationship. I told Peter about some consulting commitments and membership on the utility board in Cedar Rapids. He assured me that those obligations need not interfere with my accepting his offer.

There were a number of issues and difficulties to consider. I explained to him that Jan and I had scheduled a two-week trip to Greece within the month of April, which was a retirement gift from the Coe College Trustees. I had other commitments that would occupy me until late June. Further, he acknowledged that the purposes and functions of ASPEC were not well defined, and it was not yet a functional organization. I believed that he was ill advised to promise me three years.

Peter and I had known each other when he was president of Ottawa University in Kansas while I was at Coe College; we had shared in panel discussions at educational meetings. He had been on an evaluation team at Antioch College that I chaired. Peter had invited me to become director of ASPEC several years earlier, before I retired, while the idea of such an organization was still gestating. Although I was intrigued by the vision of such an organization I had too much unfinished work at Coe. Ironically, now the offer came a second time when I was more ready to consider it.

I thanked Peter for his vote of confidence and informed him that Jan and I would have to consider carefully this prospective diversion from our retirement. Peter was eager, even anxious, for a prompt and positive response.

Jan and I recognized that, if I accepted, it would be another risky venture. After a rather successful academic career of thirty-five years, what if I capped it with a failure? When I asked him how he planned to execute the intergenerational education involving three generations, students, faculty, and high achieving retired men and women of ASPEC, he said that he had no formulated plan and concluded with a snicker, "That will be your job!" Peter had a reputation for institutional innovation combined with notable single-mindedness. As director, I wondered whether he wanted a pawn that could be easily manipulated or a strong director determined to inject some principles and practices of his own?

Peter began his college career as a dean of students; he had never been a teaching member of a faculty. Never having been one, I wondered if he really understand the culture of college faculty? How would his perspectives and experiences affect our working relationship? If successful, what might ASPEC be ten years later?[*] These are the kinds of questions with which I struggled.

In a few days I met with Peter and told him that I accepted his offer with two conditions: first, I would accept the appointment only for one year. (Based on his experience with my two predecessors.) At that time each of us should take stock whether a further contract is advisable. Second, I could not begin

---

[*] As of this writing in 2001, ASPEC is a thriving organization at nineteen years of age.

until July 1. He instantly accepted the conditions, and we agreed on a modest salary. He also told me that Shirley Nadzak was available to continue as secretary to the director. Three orders of business would be urgently addressed in July. First, design a program for the next year; second, engage in vigorous recruiting of new members; and third, work with the by-laws committee and the senate to complete that large task of the organizational process.

When I visited the campus in the next few days, there was a news item posted on the bulletin boards that stated, "EXTRA EXTRA EXTRA. Dr. Leo Nussbaum is appointed as the Director of the Academy of Senior Professionals at Eckerd College." I was amazed at the importance given to this announcement, which was followed by a full-page listing my credentials. Apparently the announcement was intended to raise the morale and expectations of the senate and ASPEC members. I sensed that the challenge for me was even more formidable than I had expected!

In mid April 1983, Jan and I were off to Greece, one week on land beginning in Athens, and the second week by ship cruising among the islands as far as Istanbul and Ephesus, Turkey. Our trip was planned by American Express and we were very fortunate to have a small group; our tour leader was a graduate of the University of Athens and had been engaged in archeological digs. Our experience was a rich study and review of Greek history. Jan and I wished we could have had this kind of on-site visit during our college days and had the benefit of the expanded horizons during the intervening decades. In addition to Athens, we visited a number of cities by land. The Parthenon and other ancient monuments showed further deterioration from pollution in the air compared with their condition that we observed in 1959 on our return from India. Several nights we returned to our hotel in Athens. We also toured to Olympia, Delphi, Delos, Corinth, Colossus and Thessalonica. As a history major in college with a full quarter of Greek history, I deeply appreciated the chance to expand my understanding as well as bring back many memories.

Sadness interrupted our trip. When we were at Olympus,

we received a cablegram reporting the sudden death of our good friend, Duane Arnold, Chairman and CEO of Iowa Electric Light and Power Co (i.e.). Jan and I were greatly shocked and saddened. We were torn between continuing the trip and trying to return to Cedar Rapids in time for the funeral. After considering that we were near the beginning of the trip and that we no longer lived in Cedar Rapids, we decided to continue the tour. Duane had had heart by-pass surgery some months ago. He had told us that he had no interest in additional surgery. As a member of the board I pondered selecting his successor.

The cruise among the islands revealed the distinctiveness of each one and yet an important dimension of the remarkable ancient Greek civilization. Except for a few lunches, the ship was our hotel and dining room. We saw Mykonos, Santorini, Crete, Knossis, and Rhodes. Our visit to Istanbul was brief including visits of only a few shops on the Asian side. In Ephesus we spent several hours. The city was and continues to be restored in a program that will continue for decades, supported by a number of European countries. The structures include temples to several Greek gods, the main street, the baths, the library, the markets, the shops of silversmiths and the huge arena among many others.

Seeing the historic durability and current vulnerability of ancient ruins brought sadness mixed with delight. Well-preserved museums brought new meaning to many facets of Greek civilization, including: the variety of sculpture; the distinctive architecture; sensitivity to form and style; the town meeting in the polis; the roots of the male democracy; and the pervasive importance of Greek gods. We concluded this tour convinced that our education in Greece had been deeply enriched and broadly expanded.

As we returned home at the end of April, we reflected on the commitments that were unfinished and needed to be completed before my date with the Academy of Senior Professionals at Eckerd College. I was curious where this new adventure would lead. Would it be a new career or a short-term diversion?

On July 1, I found my office in the Administration Building. Shirley Nadzak, who had assisted my predecessor, was ready to go to work. Another staff member was also present. The boardroom across from the entry way was the only space for meetings of the Academy. I found piles of completed questionnaires and survey material of the area to offer data that might help to give form to the goals and programs of ASPEC. However, I found little that clearly indicated what the objectives were and, even less, how they were to be achieved. In general, one purpose was to provide intellectual and social intercourse among members who were to be recruited from a wide range of professions and careers in which they had been notably successful. The membership was to include retired professors, lawyers, physicians, dentists, business executives, ministers, musicians, artists, therapists, accountants, engineers, architects, bankers, brokers, military officers, and government officials among others. The other facet, vague and undefined, was to develop a program of intergenerational education. In theory, this was to engage ASPEC members to enhance the education of Eckerd students, a lofty and noble objective. Everyone seemed to agree readily, in principle. How was this to be accomplished? This was the burning question.

In anticipation of how ASPEC might affect the educational program at Eckerd, some faculty were very apprehensive, others were anxious, and a few quite fearful in their mistrust of Peter's real intentions. High achieving professional ASPEC members might become intrusive; could they be safely ensconced on campus without impinging on faculty responsibilities and prerogatives? As I sampled the faculty, their attitudes were far from positive or even neutral. On a scale of 1 to10 attitudes seemed more like a –6. Ironically, unease was not only with the faculty. Some ASPEC members harbored encrusted feelings from their collegiate years that would make it difficult for them to establish easy working relationships with (what they remembered as) faculty elitism. Such mutual apprehensions raised imagined barriers to a ready formation of meaningful intergenerational education. As director of ASPEC, could I build mutual trust within and between each of these groups sufficient to enable them to work cooperatively? First, I had to win their trust in me as the new leader.

After considerable debate in the senate, and my consultation with Peter, we agreed that ASPEC would become a unit of Eckerd College, not a separate corporation. The ASPEC Senate, staff and I had to proceed simultaneously on several fronts. We had to set policies and practices such as membership requirements, fees, and expected or required rules of participation. Without a demonstrable record of ASPEC's achievements, but a high-flying false start the year before, I had to begin a vigorous recruiting program. Accordingly, the by-laws committee proceeded to draft the necessary terms and conditions. This was an onerous task. Peter was concerned that ASPEC might in future by-law changes, shift direction away from the College. When the senate and I proposed that the Eckerd College President and Board of Trustees approve the original and all future changes of ASPEC by-laws, Peter was satisfied.

In my mind I was shaping a unique experiment in intergenerational education. We developed programs for ASPEC for summer 1983, and the academic year 1983-84 consisting of forums, discussions, lectures as well as an occasional social event at the home of a member. Most programs were presented or led by members. For example, one member had been a Quaker conscientious objector to military service during World War II. He chose to participate in a government sponsored hunger program, conducted at the University of Minnesota, with greatly diminished nutrition that almost simulated starvation. Then diets were gradually restored until the participants regained their normal weight. This served as a model to nourish war victims who were on the verge of starvation. Another member presented results of a range of experiments with persons housed in an institution for the blind. We found great diversity of life experiences on which we could draw.

In a new organization routine matters required precedent-setting actions. With the great range of degrees earned, professional titles, kinds of organizations, and positions held how should members address each other? Were we to be formal or informal? Such issues generated vigorous debate. One woman physician, a member of the senate protested, "If I can't be addressed as doctor, I will have lost my identity." Another member of the senate, an internationally renowned rug merchant, never attended college. To emphasize horizontal rather than vertical relationships, all members would be addressed by first name. [Though objecting vigorously to the decision, our woman physician survived in good condition.]

To reduce faculty resistance to ASPEC, I worked individually with faculty members, never in faculty meetings. I had the full support of the Board of Trustees, President Peter Armacost, and Dean of Faculty, Lloyd Chapin. Other administrators curiously observed the evolving organization. While devoting much of my time to recruiting ASPEC members, with no record of accomplishments to point to, the task was dauntingly uphill.

The curricular design of Eckerd College required every freshman to take two courses titled *Western Heritage,* and every full time faculty member rotationally was required to teach a section of twenty students. One day a week the whole freshman class heard a lecture. Two days a week each section, led by the assigned professor, discussed the substantive readings and related lectures. I observed that faculty members in specialties not directly related to the generalist *Western Heritage* courses often were terrified by this assignment. It was this observation that largely led me to ask, "Why not offer them some relief by pairing them with an ASPEC colleague from a career and life experiences as different as possible to share in leading the discussions? Students would benefit by different kinds of questions and perspectives that such a colleague could bring. This should also help to enliven discussion. When properly instructed, the ASPEC colleague would in no way impinge upon the authority or responsibility of the professor. He or she would agree to read all subject matter assigned to the students and attend classes regularly.

In theory, the president, the dean, and associate dean for general education all endorsed the idea. The novice associate dean chose to try the introduction of the proposal with some younger faculty members who were teaching a section. She did not find even one instructor willing to try the experiment. In December 1983 she agreed to let me proceed directly with some faculty members.

I met separately in the offices of each of three veteran faculty members to explain my plan. I employed my best powers of persuasion. Each of them responded positively to engage in an experiment in the spring semester. Accordingly, each interviewed an ASPEC prospect that I had nominated. An avid pacifist, professor of sociology was paired with a retired Major General of the U. S. Army. A professor of literature was paired with a business man with a Ph. D. in psychology who was mostly a career business consultant, and a professor of Asian studies and religion was paired with an ASPEC member with a degree in aeronautical engineer. Within a week, students from one section rushed to my office to report how much more exciting the discussions were with the addition of the ASPEC colleague. The colleagues worked with faculty for the whole spring semester. At the end of the semester all participants reported varying degrees of positive experiences and all agreed to repeat another semester paired with a different ASPEC colleague. This experiment, labeled the Faculty/ASPEC Discussant Colleague program, became one of the models of the intergenerational education program.

Positive reports and discussions of the experiment infected a few other professors. With my discreet individual encouragement of several ASPEC members, in the fall semester I arranged seven pairings with faculty members. Faculty discovered that an ASPEC colleague can help generate lively discussion. From the colleague's career he or she brought different experiences and perspectives to which students responded.

I also set up additional models. We began to think of ASPEC members as "Living Library Resources," an extensive untapped, living reservoir of information. With that model in mind, I arranged for an ASPEC member whose career was kindred to the professor's specialty course to bring his/her special knowledge and experience through lecture and discussion. For example, an ASPEC specialist in pension funds, designated a Resource Colleague, could address a class in Human Resources. With practice, this program developed into several variations using ASPEC panel presentations, ASPEC coaches for teams of students, and ASPEC members assisting students with research projects. Once a professor had broken away from the solitary traditional model, creativity and variations of all kinds evolved. I greatly enjoyed brainstorming with individual professors to develop new options and the Colleague program became the most distinctive aspect of the Academy programs. I was able to persuade individual faculty members by showing them an ASPEC member's record of life experiences pertinent to the course that would supplement the professor's resources. Contributing to the education of students offered ASPEC members intellectual engagement, new forms of retirement and inner satisfaction. To some students these ASPEC Colleagues became surrogate grandparents.

By April 1984, ASPEC had fifty members. Academy morale was flourishing and members were enthusiastic; they wanted to celebrate. One of the members provided for a celebratory dinner at which they presented me with a sterling silver bowl inscribed, "Leo L. NUSSBAUM WITH ADMIRATION AND AFFECTION OF THE MEMBERS OF ASPEC APRIL 1984." Members correctly observed that the director's job was very demanding. However, I reflected that compared with the college presidency this was a soft touch. I was deeply grateful for the honor ascribed to me. Debating what the membership limit should be, we pressed on to one hundred members.

We had more program activity, some for ASPEC intellectual and educational benefit, in others ASPEC members were engaged, with faculty teaching, as Discussant or Resource Colleagues. Some ASPEC members were involved in both. Peter envisioned that the Academy should have at least seven hundred fifty members. I saw that number as grossly unmanageable considering our limited facilities and current program activities. I believed that two hundred fifty paying members would make the Academy financially fully self-supporting. By March 1986 the membership reached one hundred and members held another dinner celebration at the Yacht Club. I even told them a few Swiss jokes at the celebration. Morale was high and enthusiasm contagious.

I continued to devote much time to recruiting. I had the greatest success by visiting with individual prospects, either on their turf or over lunch, where I could hold their undivided attention. I explained to them where and how they could fit into a specific kind of opportunity within the ASPEC program activities. With more committees functioning effectively, we expanded program activity. We introduced interest groups that were formed with ASPEC Senate approval such as current events, philosophy, and opera and some groups quickly prospered. As interest in a group waned, that group was deleted. New ones were frequently formed; some flourished and others soon died for want of continuing participation.

A very important step in the Academy's life was the move to Lewis House on the Boca Ciega Bay in September 1984. Personally, I found this thrilling, sitting in my office with a glass wall about one hundred feet from Bay I watched the dolphins play. Frequently a young blue heron walked nearby on the shore. Mine was probably the choicest office location on campus.

Lewis House provided the much-needed space for the growing membership. Having been occupied for several years by the lower grades of Canterbury school Lewis House showed need for substantial maintenance and repair. Arthur Gregorian, our international rug merchant member, contributed several attractive oriental rugs. With some publicity in national media we were visited by an increasing number of representatives of colleges and social service agencies that imagined emulating ASPEC. The only productive result that we knew was Hope College in Holland, Michigan.

I had great difficulty persuading Peter Armacost to accept my retirement as director. Finally, in February 1987 I wrote the letter of resignation, to be effective June 30 of that year, and took it to Peter for his signature. While I watched he signed two copies, one for me and one for him. I felt that I already had more approbation than was merited; I wanted to withdraw unobtrusively. But the ASPEC members insisted on a retirement dinner. At that time the membership was one hundred nineteen. The Senate presented me with a brass plaque that reads:

DISTINGUISHED DIRECTOR
1983-1987
Leo L. Nussbaum
During four crucial years of
impeccable leadership, he shaped
and stabilized the
Academy of Senior Professionals
at Eckerd College.
The Members acclaim his
imagination and insight,
his grace and objectivity,
his vision and counsel.
His influence will reverberate
in the future
he secured for ASPEC.

I was astonished. I had never felt that accolades ascribed to me were more exaggerated. Nevertheless, I was gratified with genuine hope that the future of ASPEC will prove to be durable.

Jim Deegan, Dean of Special Programs, was responsible for vigorous development of the Program for Experienced Learners (PEL). He observed the growing effectiveness of the Faculty/ASPEC Colleague programs for residential students and faculty. Speculating about adapting the program to PEL, he suggested that we apply for a grant to the Fund for the Improvement of Post-Secondary Education (FIPSE) in the Department of Education, Washington, D. C. Eckerd College received a two-year grant of $200,000, effective in September 1988. I had agreed that if we were successful I would serve as director, part-time. Once more I was engaged in an untried venture, another form of post retirement. I had a new part-time secretary; and understandably, in my absence for more than six weeks, there was some delay in beginning the grant program.

Our schedule became over committed. Beginning in early September, Jan and I had committed ourselves to a 17-day trip through Yugoslavia, Bulgaria, Romania and Hungary, followed by a one-month Home Exchange via Rotary International with a couple in Muri, Switzerland (a suburb of Bern). This exchange was especially appealing. My father's mother was born in Canton Bern. We planned to visit the small town of her birth.

Stir and unrest in Yugoslavia was evident; after Tito's death the units of the country such as Serbia, and Kosovo showed prospects of breaking apart. In 1988, the Soviet Union was on the verge of disintegration. But Bulgaria and Romania were still in the Soviet clutches. However, we were warmly received in Bulgaria. We observed Bulgaria's national celebration from an earlier tyrant before the Soviet Union.

To cross the border from Bulgaria into Romania required more than two hours as if we were entering enemy territory. Romania was tense; farm workers on the thousand-acre communist tracts were glumly harvesting the early fall crops. Clerks in hotels and shops looked grim and unhappy. Hungary seemed much more open and Budapest was a delight. After three days in this pleasant and friendly city, our travel group rode a hovercraft on the Danube from Budapest to Vienna. We found that bouncing craft was more descriptive than hovercraft. And I was appalled that this was not the *legendary Blue Danube* but a dirty gray river heavily polluted by eroded agricultural soil. The heavily clouded sky and chilly, rainy weather conditions did not bring any cheer. In Vienna we visited art galleries and shopped for two days until Jan and I left the tour group, headed by train for Bern via Zürich, Switzerland while they were homeward bound.

In Bern, an adult son and daughter of the couple, Werner and Mathilde Martignoni, met us at the railway terminal and took us to the Exchange Home. The Swiss home was a spacious edifice with full basement, two floors and a partially finished attic. I was introduced to their old model gearshift BMW, the vehicle for our stay from September 19 to October 17, 1988. Their parents were already enroute to St. Petersburg where our daughter, Margaret, and Guy would introduce them and their related couple to our home.

We traveled to many towns and lakes including several from which my ancestors had migrated. From the town of Aeschi, above Lake Thun, from which Grandma Lengacher

Mazelin's ancestors emigrated, is now a minor ski resort. We went to the Gemeinde Schreiber (Recorder) office. I wanted to verify some names and dates that I carried from the family record *The Lengacher-Steury Family History* by Joseph Stoll, an Amish man living in Aylmer, Ontario, Canada. He had collected so much data that I was curious how he accomplished it with all the restrictions imposed on Amish travel. I found every item to be completely conforming to the meticulous detail of Swiss records.[3] That work completed, Jan and I went across the street for lunch. In low tourist season, the owner was his own chef. Having prepared our meal, he joined us at the table. He and I talked in conversational Swiss, a hybrid language almost impossible to learn as an adult. Immediately he asked, "Where were you born?" I replied, "Berne, Indiana, U. S. A." He looked at me curiously, never having heard of that Swiss community. In a few minutes he asked me a second time. With my same answer he was no more convinced. As we were leaving, he asked me a third time in English, "Now tell me honestly, where were you born?" With my same reply he abruptly dismissed me, "You are just another one of those damn Swiss who won't admit that you were born here." What he intended as a harsh condemnation, I could accept as the highest form of compliment—I spoke the native language so well that he was convinced I was native Swiss. [4]

Wherever we drove we always found paths to walk whether around a lake, across farmer's fields, through the woods or in towns. In Muri we were just above the Aar River that had concrete and gravel walks next to the rapidly flowing water. The paths led to a zoo, playgrounds and in a few kilometers to the heart of the city of Bern. In the other direction varied paths led to

---

[3] Later, Jan and I visited Joseph Stoll in his home in Aylmer, Ontario. He completed three years of high school, is a very talented writer, has published several other books and a full curriculum for grades one through eight that is widely used in the U. S. and Canada. He conducted the research for this book while living in Honduras where the bishop was lenient in permitting foreign travel by air. After persisting for seven years to establish an Amish settlement in Honduras it was not successful, they returned to Ontario.

[4] This was one of several similar experiences challenging my native roots.

farmers' fields and woods. Where we walked or drove, there were always new and different scenes. A tram passed only a few hundred feet from the house. The autumn weather was very pleasant; rarely did we have chilly or rainy days.

Our daughter, Felicity, Professor of English and Women's Studies was teaching that semester in the Syracuse-in-London Program. For several days she, with Marc and Nicole accompanied by Zan, Marc's favorite caretaker, came to visit us.[56] One day we drove to Lucerne, hoping to see the peak of Mt. Pilatus. However, the day was misty with dense local fog. But Marc was intent on riding the cable cab into the fog with Zan, probably more excited than if it had been a day of bright sunshine. The fog did not encompass Muri or Bern, otherwise the weather was pleasant. Their visit was a very memorable time.

So that we could meet, our exchange family remained in St. Petersburg until we returned. They joyously greeted us, "Every day we felt that we were in paradise. We swam in the pool, we walked on the beach, and visited the art galleries. Every day was sunny." Because the home and auto exchange worked out very well, we felt that we wanted to try another home exchange.

Within the flexible schedule of retirement, we arranged another three-week exchange with a former Lord Mayor of Birmingham who retired in Breeden, England, a small village about forty miles south of Birmingham. He was eager to attend the Rotary International Convention in Orlando, Florida. We met them at the Orlando Airport; they lived in our home and used our car while we visited family in California. Later, for our visit there he met us at the airport in London and took us to their home. While we resided in their home, they cruised in their boat on the Avon River. This was a delightful, scenic location on the banks of the Avon overlooking a fifty-acre pastureland with a large herd of Holstein cattle. This Cotswald region offered an endless variety of hiking paths. There was history under every rock. Quaintness of the towns added much to our stay. For the first time I drove a car on the left side of the road and learned to

---

[5] Nicole loved the cowbells and the Bernese Swiss Mountain dogs.

manage round-abouts and laybys. At the end of the visit, our host drove us to a town near London where we boarded a train to the airport. This was another very successful exchange.

During our stay in Breeden, we enjoyed two bonuses. One was a two-day visit with my nephew Stan and Lorri Nussbaum, and their children Anji, and Adam, who were living in Birmingham, the longest time we ever had with them. The other bonus was the arrival for a one-day visit of Ulla and Jan Steen, with Annika and Peter Ekman. We greatly enjoyed their visit and dinner together at the Fox and Hounds pub in Breeden. On the visit Jan and Ulla agreed to bring Annika and Malin to visit us in Florida next year.

Our third Home Exchange, in 1994, was again in Switzerland, in the small town of Allenwinden. It is located three kilometers above the small, up-scale city of Zug, with the adjoining Lake of the same name. This couple met us at the Zürich Airport and introduced us to their residence. Later that day they left their car for our use and their son drove them to the Zürich Airport, enroute to St. Petersburg. Another advantage of retirement in facilitating home exchanges is the adaptability of our schedule with theirs.

One of our goals was to walk one hundred miles during the three weeks of our stay, across fields, hills and valleys, around lakes, in towns and cities, and on mountain hikes. As best we could calculate we reached that goal. We drove to many locations, parked the car and walked. Our neighbors were very friendly; the roaming cat in our home was an irritant. Their son and wife, with an infant child, who lived in a nearby town, befriended us. We were dinner guests in their home. Allenwinden was a lovely community with a small chapel and a well decorated cemetery, located on a very steep hill. In nearby towns we found many Nussbaumer families among tradesmen and professional people, but no family named Nussbaum. One writer from St. Gallen, who was intent on validating our distant relationship, came to visit us. I was not convinced.

Ironically, we were in Switzerland when a new law went into effect granting conscientious objectors to military service an option to serve in alternate civilian public service. My Mennonite ancestors were among the thousands who over many generations emigrated from Switzerland to the United States because of compulsory military training.

Our fourth home exchange was in the small community of Ruidoso, New Mexico for ten days. This was the shortest exchange and we never met our counterparts, Mr. and Mrs. Fred Trailer; in this regard our experience was very different. We exchanged car keys through the mail and described where each of the cars would be parked at the respective airports. On departure we parked them in the same area. The Ruidoso residence was a vacation resort home, next to a golf course, at an elevation of 9,000 feet. The large single panel living room window revealed a mountain peak at more than 10,000 feet. Although we are not horseracing enthusiasts, we enjoyed watching the sulky races at the track.

Each of our Home Exchanges through Rotary International worked out according to plan. For $50 any Rotarian in the world could register by providing a 70-word description of his home and area to the Home Exchange Committee. He or she also needs to specify the country or countries in which he wants an exchange, length of stay, and other stipulations. Irrespective of significant differences in the value of homes or autos, no money was exchanged. Although we strongly recommended this program to our Rotary Club in St. Petersburg, we know of only one other couple in our Club who arranged an exchange.

We return now from our Home Exchanges back to the work at Eckerd College in 1988. After what was our longest stay in Europe, for more than six weeks, it was time to settle in to work. The grant money applied to PEL (Program for Experienced Learners); and I began individual visits with PEL faculty members. PEL was different from the residential program. Introduced in 1979, this was designed for commuting students age 25 or older, with four of the five teaching locations twenty miles or more from Eckerd campus. Classes met five hours one evening per week in a term of eight weeks. Nearly all PEL faculty members were part-time adjuncts, teaching one course per term. During my meeting with each, I explained ASPEC members' participation. Some immediately thought the program appealing. ASPEC members were drawn to PEL largely because of the intense motivation of the older students. The FIPSE Grant provided reimbursement to ASPEC Colleagues for transportation costs plus a token stipend. PEL faculty and students easily identified with ASPEC Colleagues. Both the Discussant Colleague and Resource Colleague models were used. With rare incompatibility or otherwise defective combinations, nearly all the pairings worked satisfactorily. Overall the project yielded positive results. When the two-year grant ended, the venture was regarded as successful by most of the participants and each external evaluator.

In September 1990, the FIPSE/PEL Project having been successful, Jim Deegan, Dean of Special Programs, wanted me to continue with the Faculty/ASPEC Colleague Program. The large number of faculty rotations in each of the five eight-week terms greatly increased the time that I devoted to the program. Some ASPEC members found such satisfaction working with older students in PEL that they wanted to withdraw from the residential program. Others did not like the long five-hour evening classes or were hesitant to drive at night to the outlying teaching stations. Another group wanted variety and chose to continue to participate in both residential and PEL classes. I continued to work with faculty members and ASPEC Colleagues in both programs. Some faculty working with me became innovative in their use of ASPEC members. The programs flourished. I shall list only two examples of this notable success. In a course in anthropology the professor brought two ASPEC members as Resource Colleagues. One, a young U. S. Army captain, now a Major General, shared in the rescue of prisoners in the Nazi Concentration Camp. He was joined by a former Jewish prisoner of the Concentration camp, now a retired physician, each reported their contrasting experiences. At the time of rescue the prisoner was fearful of his extermination. The professor reported that students were spell bound.

In a senior capstone course in International Business, the professor divided the class into teams of five members each. He assigned a Harvard Graduate School case study to each team, and top-level former executive in a multi-national corporation as an

ASPEC Resource Colleague. With the prodding of the ASPEC Colleague for six weeks each team searched for answers to key questions about the corporation depicted in the case study. The assignments ended with a formal report of the teams' findings and recommendations to the hypothetical board of directors consisting of professors and other ASPEC retired business executives. What could be more realistic preparation for international business?

On a part time assignment I continued, each semester in the residential program and each term in PEL, to arrange in many varied ways to enable faculty members to draw on the "Living Library Resources" of ASPEC members. A sense of win-win-win developed among students, faculty and ASPEC Colleagues. New combinations were formed nearly every term and the program had greatly expanded. In each of my last three years conducting the Faculty/ASPEC Colleague Program on a part-time basis, a total of more than one hundred seventy-five classes in PEL and the residential program had from one to as many as ten participating ASPEC members in one class.

In March 1995, I received a letter from FIPSE informing me of a new venture to determine whether successful innovative programs on one campus could be replicated on other campuses. They invited me to apply through Eckerd College for a two-year grant to work with six other colleges whose presidents signed an application stating their intent to replicate the Faculty/ASPEC Colleague program on their campuses. I secured such requests from six college presidents scattered from Vermont to Texas. The Eckerd College application was submitted, and we received a two-year grant for the project. I was assigned as director to work with the six colleges, as follows: Green Mountain College, Poultney, Vermont; Hope College, Holland, Michigan; University of Dubuque, Dubuque, Iowa; Spelman College, Atlanta, Georgia; Austin College, Sherman, Texas; and Okaloosa-Walton Community College, Niceville, Florida. The first five were four-year private colleges; the last one was a two-year public college.

In my position, defined as part-time, I directed this six-college project and also continued the Faculty/ASPEC Colleague program. I visited each campus two or three times annually; each college sent a team responsible for their project a total of three times to Eckerd College campus to observe how this program worked and to share the respective experiences in developing their own. In the end it seemed that two or three colleges had a potentially durable program. The others lacked vitality, clear direction, and adequate financial support by the institution.

By and large, the teams had discovered that establishing the Eckerd program model was far more complex than first met the eye. The project showed the reluctance of presidents to invest the necessary funds to put such a program on a solid footing and the lack of requisite understanding of and commitment to, the program by some directors. In some colleges the necessary diplomacy was missing and the lack of talents was evident among directors to persuade disparate faculty and senior retirees to develop and utilize the "Living Library Resource".

I enjoyed trying to start such a program on other campuses and learned the many complications that showed up. It confirmed my belief that the participation of all faculty members in shared teaching of general education at Eckerd College made starting such a program somewhat less difficult. From developing Faculty-ASPEC Colleague Program, I became convinced that high achieving retired persons are an authentic "Living Library Resource" that should not be wasted. A distinct advantage contrasted with a book is that a "Living Library Resource" can ask and answer questions that grow out of the discussion, and often relate it to their work experience. The "Living Library Resource" in related or similar fields can supplement the professor. Traditional undergraduate faculty members have not had this as part of their educational conditioning and, until they have tried this plan, they often are understandably hestitant to augment their teaching with such selective human resources.

In the early 90s I retired from the Board of Directors of Iowa Electric Light & Power Co. (i.e.) in Cedar Rapids due to the company's maximum age requirement. But the (i.e.) board was my only for-profit experience and provided me with applied economics, customer service, nuclear plant operations, state and federal government regulations, weather related operational hazards, personnel policies and practices, stock market and stockholder factors. Each month as I receive my deferred board stipend from i.e., I am reminded of the monetary reward, obviously different from not-for-profit sectors.

St. Petersburg had an established program of Habitat for Humanity. From our early days as residents, every month we supported the program financially. We strongly believe in Habitat; we could see exciting benefits for new owners every week. Until I was age 80, whenever I could spare half a day, I enjoyed reviving my meager carpentry skills at Habitat, practiced during college days when I worked with my father.

From time to time in St. Petersburg, I declined to join additional not-for-profit boards, such as retirement centers, a theological seminary. Serving on too many boards with their varying meeting dates and times can impair retirement schedule flexibility. A board member of the theological seminary more than once tried to persuade me to accept the presidency of the seminary. I firmly expressed no interest in this position.

For several years, in St. Petersburg Rotary Club, I was chair of the Rotary Foundation Committee. The duties involved recruiting Club members to contribute $1,000 in support of Rotary Foundation Programs who are named Paul Harris Fellows. In one year our Committee added thirty-seven Paul Harris Fellows assisted with a partial subsidy by two Rotarians within the district. Annually, the Committee selected Rotary Ambassadorial Scholars, the best of the best, applicants from Eckerd and other colleges that were recommended to the Rotary District. Each year our Club had at least one successful applicant who was awarded more than $20,000 to study at a university abroad for one year. I enjoyed working with the Eckerd College faculty advisor in preliminary selection of promising applicants to be interviewed by our Club Committee. Another of the not-for-profit boards me was Presbyterian Homes and Housing, Inc. (PHH) that included seventeen subsidized retirement housing units scattered in west central Florida. I was a member of the Investment Committee, the Audit Committee, Treasurer and on the Administrative Council for John Knox Apartments, a unit of

PHH.

I continued to carry various responsibilities in the Presbyterian Church. In 1983, the U. S. Presbyterian Church (South) and the Presbyterian Church (North) divided over Negro slavery in the Civil War in the 1860s, finally reunited after almost a century and a quarter. In 1988, I was elected a Commissioner to General Assembly held in Biloxi, Mississippi, and served as Chair of the Committee on Pensions. That was a few years before the invasion of casinos. In 1989, the final year of Southwest Florida Presbytery consisting of 110 congregations, I was elected moderator to preside during the bifurcation into Presbytery of Tampa Bay and Presbytery of Peace River. Each of these positions came as a complete surprise. From 1990 through 1995, I served as a member of the Presbytery Committee on Ministry. One of my strengths as an administrator was finding common ground to bring reconciliation between differing or opposing groups. That involved frequent meetings and much work with congregations and sessions. The Committee also dealt with ministerial discipline including sexual deviancy. Several times I declined the nomination as chair of that Committee. Meanwhile, Jan served on Presbytery Committee on Preparation for Ministry. She had also served several years with abiding enthusiasm on the Committee on Peacemaking. Immediately thereafter I served at our church on the Committee on Finance and Investment followed by two terms on the Committee on Personnel. In 1995, while I served on the Committee on Pastor Nomination. Jan and I visited candidates in South Carolina and Texas, neither of whom was nominated.

I had earlier served on the Nominating Committee for an Associate Pastor. In 1997 I served as two terms as Chair of the Presbytery Committee on Representation and served as a member for a second term. This committee was responsible to encourage and foster interracial and intercultural church membership. At First Presbyterian Church we established a close working relationship with Trinity Presbyterian Church, a predominantly black congregation. Several members of each congregation signed on as associate members in the other congregation with a commitment to periodic participation.

During these years I was repeatedly asked to serve on our church session again, but feeling that younger church members should gain experience, I declined. I was originally elected at age 31, First Presbyterian Church in Huntington, Indiana and served on the session in five congregations. In the mid 80s I served one year as teacher of the Covenanter Sunday School Class and for many years I taught that class for an occasional month at a time. For nearly a decade I was one of "The Twelve" laypersons, originated by Harleigh Rosenberger, pastoral associate, who regularly called on the ailing and homebound. "The Twelve" grew in number as the need increased. Harleigh's diligent successor was Jim Neader, a layperson who had also been an agent for professional athletes.

Eckerd College sponsored Elder Hostel programs, at peak nearly fifty weeks a year. This international organization was designed for retired persons who wanted to continue to study subjects that were new to them. Jan and I together taught various Elder Hostel courses over several years, such as *An Overview of India; India: 50 Years a Nation, 5,500 Years a Culture;* and *India: Land of Extraordinary Paradoxes.* We also taught a course on the Amish people. Participants in Elder Hostel[7] were very curious about the Amish who, incidentally, want to be known as a "peculiar" people whose testimony is evident in their good works. (Titus 2:13-15). Course titles were *The Puzzles of Amish Life*, and *The Amish: In the World But Not of It.*

The course had its roots in the 16th Century Anabaptist Reformation. That began concurrently with the Brethren in Switzerland and in Holland with Menno Simons, Dutch leader who was a former Catholic priest, after whom the Mennonites are named. In various steps, this course led into the current closed Amish society, its peculiarities of faith, dress, social, religious and economic practices. Sometimes Jan and I appeared in Amish attire. She was in full Amish dress that she made from Amish patterns. Her attire included the dress, an apron, a white cap and a purchased black bonnet. According to Amish rules, she removed all her make-up and jewelry. Some people in the class

---

[7] Classes met for 90 minutes five days per week; students registered for three classes.

accepted her as Amish until I introduced her as my wife. On the last day of classes on two occasions, we brought an Amish husband and wife to answer questions for class members. These visits were a notable success.

Jan and I also taught courses separately. She taught one on the history and varieties of mystery literature. I taught one on _The Life, Philosophy and Leadership of Mahatma Gandhi_, underscoring his years in South Africa and his dynamic pacifist marches that reached a pinnacle in the independence of India from Great Britain.

We continued our travels, domestic and international. We visited Lisha and Luther's families in California two or three times each year. In most years we held a family reunion usually in June or July. Jan and I tried to attend all college graduations and weddings of grandchildren. We usually included at least one, sometimes two, international trips. When I reached 75, we no longer rented a car in Europe. After that most of our trips were with Grand Circle Travel. We luxuriated in having them make all the travel arrangements and handling our luggage. In 2001 we discovered that [8]Monaco, the four square-mile nation, was 49th on the list of countries that we have visited outside the U. S. We still loved travel, and the Grand Circle catalogs listed many tantalizing destinations.

As I reached age 75, Jan was approaching 70. Each of us began to weary of taking care of the house, the pool, trees, flowers and bushes. Also, as we aged we did not want to become a burden to our children. What was our best next move? Many of our friends and acquaintances either lived in or were planning to move into a condominium. Was that the right move for us? We visited several condos in South St. Petersburg and weighed the merits of taking that step. While some of the newer ones were very appealing, bright and airy with outside entrances and patios.

---

[8] Canada, Mexico, Venezuela, Chile, Argentina, Uruguay, Netherlands, Luxemburg, Belgium, Denmark, Norway, Sweden, German, Switzerland, Liechtenstein, Austria, Yugoslavia, Bulgaria, Romania, Italy, Greece, France, Spain, Portugal, Turkey, Egypt, India, Nepal, Pakistan, Thailand, Malaysia, Philippines, Hong Kong, Singapore, Brunei, Australia, New Zealand, Tahiti, Fiji, Finland, Estonia, Latvia, Lithuania, Russia, Poland, Czech Republic, Slovakia, Hungary.

Older models with hallways that reminded us of dormitories were gluts on the market. Yet, neither of us looked forward to carting everything up and down in an elevator. Jan was repulsed because none of the condos was located so that she would have ready access to a supermarket, a library, hair salon, manicurist, drug store with her tri-cycle via low traffic streets. We looked at senior living communities such as Westminster Shores, Suncoast Manor, and College Harbor. We finally decided that Suncoast Manor met all of our requirements—attractive campus, gated security, quality library, heated swimming pool, garden area, and a location with ready access to the services Jan and I routinely required. We purchased a two-bedroom unit in January 1994 for $87,500 and paid a $1,000 deposit. Our names were placed on the short waiting list, assuming a delay of one or two years.

When we told our children, they responded, "O, Mom and Dad, you are not old enough for that. Why don't you get more help to care for your house and lawn?" We replied, "Your mom's post polio syndrome makes her especially tired. She no longer enjoys preparing all the meals. And at our ages even though we think we are in good health any day could bring a heart attack, a stroke or cancer or other serious limitation. If we move in now our contract calls for assisted living and life care as needed. Your dad is having increasing back trouble from using the long-handled saw on the palm trees, and his level of energy is diminishing. We considered moving to a condo but we decided to skip that step. You will get used to seeing us here with many other old people in various kinds of deteriorating conditions."

We prepared our list of specifications for the future remodeling of our unit. In January 1995 two adjoining singles became available. We listed our home for sale with an agent. Twice we thought it was sold, but the prospective buyers could not secure the mortgage finances needed.

By May 1995, having had two near sales that turned out to be false, we became quite concerned, in fact, Jan became anxious. Luther was very encouraging with the comment, "The right buyer will come in due time. Take a trip and don't be anxious." He and Ginger invited us to visit them at their Utah home. We accepted their invitation and had a very pleasant visit in June, walking the surrounding hills, conversing, drinking good wine, and eating at upscale restaurants. When they returned to California I insisted that Jan and I visit her birthplace. We drove to her birthplace, Bliss, Idaho, that she had no memory of seeing. Her parents were waiting for her birth to make the move to another church where her father had a new pastorate. She greatly enjoyed returning to her place of birth for the first time at age 71. Bliss now is a declining crossroad town of a few hundred people. Jan purchased a short history at the post office.

When we returned to St. Petersburg in July, with greatly lessened anxiety, our house was quickly sold to a male couple for $121,500, and we moved to Suncoast Manor at 6909 9th Street South, unit N 36/37 on August 4, 1995. With optional items, the total cost of our double unit was about $93,500. When we left Bahama Shores we had lived in that home 13 years, longer than we had lived in any other home.

Although we moved only about one mile, living at Suncoast Manor prompted a new life style. We signed a contract to eat the evening meal in the common dining room; Jan was relieved of planning, and cooking. We shared our simple breakfast at home while reading the *St. Petersburg Times.* I was still working part-time with lunchtime away from home.

Within a few months, the chair of the Manor Advisory Council appointed Jan as co-librarian, with a lawyer colleague, of the 8,000 volume Suncoast Manor Library. The books were still catalogued by the Dewey decimal system; many residents were not computer literate and chose not to learn. Jan knew library work and addressed herself seriously to organizing and operating it. Jan greatly enjoyed her library work as a volunteer. That included purchasing new books with endowment fund income and special gifts from residents, often as memorials. She thrives on reading books of all sorts, as avidly as a child eats chocolate. Typically, she reads five to seven books a week. She named other part-time volunteers and developed a talent to select books that appeal to individual residents who regularly asked for help. In return they complimented her and expressed gratitude in many forms. One person gave her a prized Oriental rug.

I was elected to a three-year term on the Suncoast Manor

Advisory Council beginning in 1998. In 1999 I was elected chair and reelected in 2000. In 2001, I was reelected to the Council for another three-year term and re-nominated as chair. I asked that I not be elected; I believed that rotation was desirable. Furthermore, with the growing financial problems of Suncoast Manor, as interpreted by the Florida State Insurance Department amid the board's indifference to its legal responsibilities, I anticipated a very difficult year.

When we arrived at Suncoast Manor, the record showed reserves between five and six million dollars. For the next five years the board casually approved annual budgets with deficits from seven hundred thousand to a million dollars. Despite the alarm expressed by Joe Creaven, the residents' representative to board, in his monthly reports to the board they showed no evidence of taking corrective action. As chair of the Advisory Council, I talked with board members and wrote sharp letters emphasizing the peril to Suncoast Manor. These actions were to no avail. That is when the Florida Department of Insurance finally flashed the red light! Even under these circumstances, it was often impossible for the president of the board to assemble a quorum.

At a special meeting of residents on September 26, 2001, the Suncoast Manor Board of Directors finally announced that, after considering several options, it approved a consolidation with the Presbyterian Retirement Communities. The transfer was completed by April 1, 2002. Presbyterian Retirement Communities would take five years to adjust all residents' amended contracts to pay their fair share of the monthly dues. We expected that rates would be increased for all residents but differing widely in amount because of the diverse contracts that were in effect.

Jan and I have been very fortunate financially since my first retirement in 1982. My College Retirement Equities Fund (CREF) contract with Teacher Insurance and Annuities Association and the general upward trend of the stock market yielded much better returns than we had expected. In April 2001, CREF annual reevaluation in a sharp downward trend shocked us with a substantial reduction of income. As of this writing in

September 2002 prospects for an upward turn are not promising.

(Unexpectedly, our lives were jarringly interrupted by a national tragedy that would affect all of our lives. On the morning of September 11, 2001 while I was in the physician's office for my annual physical examination, stunning, world shattering news descended on us. What we saw on TV was totally incredible, even unimaginable. Two American and two United airliners were highjacked by four or five men in each. They took control of the planes by using razor blades, and carpet and box knives as weapons. Two of the planes, one into each, horrendously crashed into the 110-story World Trade Center towers! They instantly exploded into massive, torrid flames. After burning a few minutes on the high-octane plane fuel each tower collapsed and crumpled to the ground. Shortly thereafter an American airliner crashed into the Pentagon with another massive explosion. It tore a gaping hole in one section of the building. Occupants of buildings made gallant efforts to escape but many hundreds were hurt and undetermined thousands lost their lives. Within an hour a United airliner crashed in a field in western Pennsylvania. Passengers using cell phones informed family members that three intrepid male passengers attempted, unsuccessfully, to wrest control of the plane from the highjackers. It was assumed that this plane was directed either against the White House or the U. S. Capitol, but that three male passengers' efforts in tussling with the four or five highjackers got it off course before the crash. To clean up the debris, to determine which nearby buildings were so structurally damaged that they would have to be demolished will take many months. The cumulative effect of these dastardly acts on the economic, political, social, and religious life cannot now be determined. In response to the deep anger and call for revenge, President George W. Bush denounced the terrorist acts as war. In his early statements he was very bellicose. "We will rid the world of terrorism," he promised. On a wide defensive front, our nation prepared to respond. It may well be basically life changing for the United States and for other countries of the world.)

(With so short a time lapse following the attack, to evaluate the long-term effects of this event either domestically or internationally, will be exceedingly difficult. Many people seem totally mystified at this surprise attack and ask the question, "Why would anyone hate us so much to bring this kind of destruction of life and property, without direct provocation?" While partial answers seem fairly obvious to some of us, there have been various attempts to answer the question in the news media. One of the insightful answers that has come to my attention, basically supported by *The Christian Science Monitor*, is in a three-page exposition titled, "A Voice of Reason In A World Out of Touch With Itself: Where the Violence Comes From" by Rabbi Michael Lerner, editor, *Tikkun Magazine*. Pertinent quotations follow:

"We may tell ourselves that the current violence has 'nothing to do' with the way that we've learned to close our ears when told that one our of every three people on this planet does not have enough food, and that one billion are literally starving. We may reassure ourselves that the hoarding of the world's resources by the richest society in world history, and our frantic attempts to accelerate globalization with its attendant inequalities of wealth, has nothing to do with the resentment that others feel toward us. We may tell ourselves that the suffering of refugees and the oppressed have nothing to do with us—that that's a different story that is going on somewhere else. But we live in one world, increasingly interconnected with everyone, and the forces that lead people to feel outrage, anger and desperation eventually impact on our own daily lives."

My view is that while there are no simple answers, among other actions of the United States that have cumulatively angered the Arab and Muslim nations has been the unconditional support of Israel. With annual billions in military aid the U.S has turned a blind eye to the United Nations resolutions, irrespective of what they regard as Israel's unjust actions against the Palestinians. These issues, I believe, have helped to trigger the violent actions against the United States. The future may reveal dimensions not now known. We are warned that there may be many more to come. We have greatly increased our internal security.)

Returning to my theme, to remain in good physical condition Jan walked three miles each morning seven days per week, every month of the year. In the afternoons, in the Suncoast Manor heated pool she frequently swam for a half-hour. My routine included fifty pushups each morning, as soon as I was out of bed. In the mid-1990s I had to give up my strenuous badminton game because of a painful right hip. After X-rays in January 1999 the orthopedic surgeon advised me to quit running and return in one year. I could not quit running; my body demanded the exercise. But I reduced it from four miles every other day to three miles Monday, Wednesday and Friday.

At age 33 my eye, nose, and throat specialist in Huntington, Indiana had recommended that I have surgery to straighten my left deviated nasal septum. At that time the surgery left the patient's face black and blue for a week. I deferred the surgery until age 70 when condition of the septum interfered with my breathing, especially while running. The surgery had been considerably refined. It was followed by two nights and days of much discomfort but with far less externally visible effects. Although the surgery was not a total correction, my breathing was much improved.

Each of us consumed food and drink in well-disciplined measure. In September 2001 we bought a costly Tempurpedic mattress and pillows. We both felt that for aging joints and muscles these provided extra sleeping comfort. Overall, we enjoyed good health.

After almost twenty years since leaving my principal career, what to me constitutes a satisfying and meaningful retirement? First, if appropriate employment opportunities beckon, try them. Second, set a goal to remain in as good a condition of health as possible to remain mobile. Third, find a variety of activities, within one's financial resources, that are meaningful, especially rendering service to others. Fourth, engage in regular recreation that keeps one physically active and observe appropriate food and beverage intake. Fifth, find means of keeping one intellectually stimulated through reading, studying new subjects or traveling. Sixth, remain socially active. Seventh, plan systematically for life's final years with attendant unpredictability including one's religious and spiritual growth.

Planning for life's final months or years is a highly

individual matter. Just as in life, some people go through life with highly developed plans, short and long-term goals. Others just let life happen without much thought for the future. What we all share is life's uncertainties that are wholly unpredictable.

Chapter 27: Behind the Plow

As I think back to the days of my youth, walking hour by tedious hour behind the plow pulled by a team of tired horses, turning over the cool earth, I pondered why the divine timetable was so much different than mine. Also, early in life, I was thrust into adult responsibilities, such as, in community grain threshing, way ahead of my size and strength. My most strenuous efforts at age twelve in competing with full-grown men was interpreted by them as my father, in sending me, was failing to do his part. Despite my best efforts, the effect on me was embarrassment and humiliation. These experiences left indelible marks on me.

I was not a natural born leader. As a child and youth I was timid, shy and socially inept. My mother and father also were not public persons. I never saw either father or mother speak in front of any group or stand up and take a position in a discussion. In fact, they were rarely engaged in discussion of ideas at home or elsewhere.

On either side of my family, so far as I can determine from the available records, I do not find any direct ancestors who were strong or assertive leaders in any enterprise or venture. I had no family model of venturesome organization, management or leadership. In his middle years, my father, having enjoyed carpentry from his youth, practiced his trade and gradually employed five or six men. Mother, with an eighth grade education, had secretly aspired to be a teacher. Her shyness and retiring personality were always an obstacle. However, in her later years, she found pleasure in teaching a Sunday school class using German language Bibles.

When I visited the home of my father's parents, I do not recall seeing any books other than two or three German Bibles. My father occasionally read brief passages in the Bible but I do not recall that I ever saw him read any other book. I am confident that no member of his family ever visited a library. Except for enjoying arithmetic, Father did not speak enthusiastically about his school days that ended with the seventh grade. He had saved none of his report cards and offered no claims about having earned good grades. In contrast, my mother greatly enjoyed school through the eighth grade and earned high grades. She talked fondly about her school days, about vocabulary, spelling, and Bible stories. She systematically read the whole Bible in German and English several times. As time permitted in her later life she cherished books that she regarded as spiritually uplifting or faith confirming. Art in any form, oil paintings, watercolor, lithographs, etchings and sculpture were not found in our home or in the homes of either of my nearby grandparents. Consequently, my youth was bereft of things intellectual, artistic or broadly educational. In the home of my mother's family the only wall hangings that I can recall were one or two large local advertising calendars and a map of the State of Indiana. I do not remember any books on shelves.

Throughout my childhood and youth the Amish Christian Church encircled me as well as all my relatives. Though it was not verbally articulated, I sensed my first real experience with perceived different levels of status or social acceptance. Blood relatives of the dominant Bishop, especially those who accorded him observable deference of whom there were many, had the most favorable social standing in the church. That seemed to spill over into the church operated school directed by members of his larger family. There was a perceived lesser social standing of the Mazelin (my mother's family) relatives and Nussbaum families as well as others not related to the Bishop.

In the small Amish Christian Parochial Grade School (70 pupils) I showed little talent on the playground. Although I enjoyed the games, in choosing sides for a game I was often the last one chosen. I was unable to feel victorious on the playground. Only in the classroom, where I easily excelled, did I attract favorable notice. It was there that I gradually began to discover my love of learning, and soon dreamed that devoting my life to learning and teaching would be ideal. I relished tests of every kind. I loved every subject studied in grade school, and earning excellent grades caused me eagerly to anticipate the semester examinations that were county wide. As I later learned, the school did not have state approval and the teachers were not certified. Nonetheless, at the time of the Adams County Eighth Grade Commencement I felt that I knew more than I ever did in further studies. In retrospect, it was a peculiar blend of pride and self-doubt. I was graduated from a small, rural public high school (22 in the class) that was approved by the State of Indiana but not accredited by the regional association. I kept wondering whether I could compete successfully if I ever had the opportunity to go to college.

Attending a college was beyond my imagining; however, it was the avenue to a teaching job. Strictures of the exclusive Amish Christian Church constituted my world order and the limits of my horizon. The preachers, with perhaps no more than a third grade education, taught us to accept the Bible as literally God's word that was never to be questioned. In Sunday school I learned the Jewish concept of creation in Genesis, chapters one and two, all in the German language. In that version, God accomplished the whole creation in six days then needed rest on the seventh day. That served as the model for our seven-day week. Some of the Bibles had marginal notations indicating that creation occurred about 4,000 years ago. The composite restrictions of this closed community, prescribed by the Bishop, inhibited questions, condemned doubt, and trained for and prescribed total conformity. The church taught the biblical versions of the universe, the earth as the center, and even questioned whether the earth is spherical and that it rotated. The consequences for me were stunted intellectual development accompanied by inferiority feelings that hindered positive shaping of personality. This was the scope of my universe. I suffered from multi-dimensional educational chasms. I was not introduced to other creation stories, evolution or scientific investigation in either grade school or high school. Nonetheless, I was deeply curious what lay beyond. On reflection, the religious indoctrination was probably as severe, and even more parochial, than that of the Roman Catholic, Southern Baptist or Missouri Synod Lutheran Churches. Increased enforcement of The State of Indiana school attendance laws, coupled with the complete disintegration of the Amish Christian Church opened doors of educational opportunity for me. I was required to attend the public high school beginning in September 1931. After three years of required attendance, the great financial depression resulted in the postponement of my high school graduation to 1936 followed by an unavoidable delay on the farm of two more years. Consequently, I had to delay becoming a college student until age twenty.

The church disintegrated and gradually disappeared as I entered college. That momentous change left the spiritual condition of my life in a vacuous condition. How to fill that void was one of my life's greatest challenges and struggles. This endeavor took several forms. During my college years, I investigated many Christian denominations. I detoured into indifference, deliberated on and rejected atheism and explored other religions. After a protracted detour and search, I concluded that the community of faith in Jesus Christ, in the form of the church, despite all its historic and current defects, was the best choice for me. Thus, I began a new journey. Along the way, I learned to love different versions of the church and to relate to the Bible differently. I learned that Presbyterians required an educated ministry and laypersons had an equal vote with ministers in church polity. I began to interpret the Bible as a combination of historic fact, poetry, prophecy, living standards, theology, and mythology. Each of these characteristics has its own form of truth or distinctive place in the search for truth. With its endlessly varying interpretations, the Bible continues to be a textbook for Christianity. The church as a worshipping community has grown to be very important to me.

In my continuing intellectual growth and spiritual development I continue to strive toward understanding a universe in which all the major components fit together, including religion and science. I seek language that is inclusive to express this unity. I continue to pursue scientific investigation and explanation as well as in continuing religious revelation and interpretation. Ancient theologians did not know science and current scientific methods. Scientific knowledge accrued and exploded, especially in the twentieth century. In contrast, religious knowledge and terminology remained essentially constant. For centuries, many scientists and theologians functioned as if they were in unconnected, separate realms of the universe. Humankind had to choose in which of two realms they constructed their worldview, and I felt the strain of this division in college.

I believe in a God, Providence, and a Creator that commands both religion and science. With the twentieth century development of science much religious terminology and language used at other times and in other contexts is now obsolete to young people. It seems to me that instead of bringing increased understanding it often leads to obfuscation. Jesus, born a Jew, proclaimed the inclusiveness of his gospel open to all humanity. Special messenger of God in human person, he serves as the reconciler for humankind. Jesus' first and second commandments are: "Love the lord your God with all your heart, soul, mind and strength and your neighbor as yourself."

Are God and Nature the same or dichotomous? Do we have a static or evolving universe? I believe that mankind faces a combination of changes and predictable stability. Tornadoes strike a given path unpredictably; the sun rising and setting (obsolete terms based on appearance) is predictable to the minute. Daily weather conditions change, while spring predictably follows winter. I question the claims of some scientists that mankind has nearly reached ultimate laws of the universe. As a non-scientist, I believe that there may be realms of universal laws that we do not even know exist. But why do religion and theology often ignore the realms of nature and science that we have discovered in the realm of God? Are they separate from God or the source of energy, if one believes in a creative power by whatever name? I believe God challenges us to search his laws as part of the religious and scientific quest. I commend John Templeton, known for his astuteness in financial investments, who has in retirement provided many millions of funding in foundations to engage some of the best minds to explore and develop common ground between science and theology.

In my youth I learned life-guiding principles, some of which had to be discarded and others proved continuingly durable. New principles were added that arose out of fresh needs in maturing and assumption of increasing responsibilities. From my parents I learned the fundamental need for honesty, truth telling and truth living. A promise is never casual; it is a commitment. To earn trust I regularly had to show myself reliable and dependable. These qualities can produce integrity and win respect. They are basic components of character.

Of necessity in years of financial depression, my parents taught me frugality and thrift. So valuable in principle, it also inhibited my ease of expenditure during prosperous times. Based on impressions more than experience, my father firmly admonished me, "Never invest in the stock market." Although I never forgot the principle of judicious investing, on this admonition I totally disregarded my father. Thus far the stock market has been very generous to us. Out of their experience, my parents could not have foreseen the more favorable financial circumstances of our retirement years that were greatly enhanced from stock market investments. Totally beyond their imagination would be the affluence of many of their grandchildren as well as the financial abundance in which some of their great grandchildren are reared. Jan and I believe in sharing our abundance with the needy as a dominant principle of living.

I have practiced regularity and moderation in exercising, sleeping, eating, and drinking. I believe exercising discipline of mind, body and spirit. Having been reared in accord with Swiss ancestry, my family consumed wine and beer in moderation available even to growing children. By instruction and example there was no drunkenness. In contrast during my college years, I did not understand the thrill many students found in weekend alcoholic binges.

My parents taught us the harm that can result from rumors and gossip. My father, especially, warned against judging other people on the basis of fragmentary information. In the culture of my boyhood, humility was taught as never advocating or promoting oneself, rather self-diminution if not negation. This lesson was practiced to the utmost extreme by my uncle, D. D. Mazelin. In his book *The Mazelins in America: 1840 to 1940*, his identification of himself consists of only one line with no photograph.

When Jan and I were married in 1942, we agreed on many basic life values, intellectual and religious pursuits. We firmly believe that strong families are the essence of an enduring society. We came from families that were structured and cohesive, and actively engaged in their churches. However, the differences in the families were also significant. As the child of a Presbyterian minister she was upper middle class. In contrast, I was of a family of low status in the church and in a working class farming community. In addition, we had contrasting family constellations. Jan had an older and a younger sister but no brothers. I had six younger brothers and no sisters. She was reared in parsonages having moved often in a number of states from the northwest to eastern mid-west. I lived on one Indiana farm until I entered college at age twenty. As a family, we always spoke conversational Swiss-German, never English.

Jan's parents displayed affection and love openly with hugs and kisses. In my family hugs and kisses were for infants. I never saw my mother and father express endearment for each other or their sons, after infancy. Jan taught me what endearment and love means in words and actions freely expressed, although I was a slow learner. I was less expressive to her and our children than I wish I had been. With my deep love for Jan and the children, I still strive to overcome the inhibitions acquired in my youth.

Another principle that we added was gratitude for what we have in life, in opportunities, in friends, in resources and in talents. Both of us believed that an attitude of thanksgiving opens the door to increased spiritual growth and increases the flow of energy. By sharing with those in need we do not diminish what we have. Sharing one's abundance is somewhat like love; the more we give the more we feel that we have.

In college as I began to emerge from my parochialism, I came to believe that all persons deserve to be accorded dignity and respect. I also became aware that we can learn much from persons of different religious faiths, races, social and economic status, vocations, cultures, languages, and ethnic heritage. Having visited a total of forty-nine countries over my life span, I learned that through travel, (although much more by living in them,) cultural understanding can be greatly enhanced. Living in India was a transforming experience for all of us. As a member of

Rotary International for more than 40 years, its programs have meant so much to our family. Students from other countries lived in our home and traffic with their families became life-long. Rotary home exchanges in New Mexico, England and twice in Switzerland were culturally enriching. Felicity's participation in Operation Crossroads Africa, in French speaking Senegal, Africa, added greatly to her understanding of cultural diversity. After Luther's marriage their two-year residence in Mexico City was a meaningful sequel to his youthful year in India.

Our closely-knit family, including our children, their spouses and grandchildren, were always very important to Jan, the children and me. With our children we shared fun in picnicking, boating, water skiing and table games. We shared meals, had family discussions, and entertained a wide range of visitors. An unabridged dictionary was always on a stand in the dining room. We traveled widely in this country and abroad. The children were baptized, taught and confirmed in the Presbyterian Church. As adults they pursued their individual faith journeys.

Educationally, each was salutatorian of her or his respective Sherman high school class. Jan and I insisted on a good liberal arts college for the children's undergraduate degrees and helped them make the choices. In turn, each chose a very high quality graduate school appropriate to his or her prospective career. Jan and I gave them encouragement and support.

In behavior standards Jan and I strove to be consistent. We taught the children that actions have consequences and, accordingly, strove to let them realize the rewards and penalties. We emphasized the need for integrity, reliability, and trustworthiness.

As parents, we are immensely proud of their individual career choices and their respective achievements. Felicity is Professor of English and Women's Studies at UCLA, Luther in business consulting and as a CEO and Chairman of the Board, First Consulting Group, and Margaret in counseling and executive career development at Eckerd College, Management Development Institute. The grandchildren, of whom we are all very proud, are in educational pursuits or in their early stages of careers. We give them encouragement in their respective ventures.

Our seven-year residence in Sherman, Texas, where I was professor and dean at Austin College during the segregated and turbulent 1960's, helped us build lasting relationships with members of the black community. Jan, the only white face in Frederick Douglass School, taught in the early days of graded racial integration. Later, at home in Florida, we became deeply involved in building relationships between the mostly black Trinity Presbyterian Church and the mostly white First Presbyterian Church. At Suncoast Manor we promoted racial integration in retirement. As a nation we profess providing equal opportunities for people of all races, faiths, genders and ethnic backgrounds; our family believes in its practice.

My life plans in my youth bore no resemblance to the accumulated experiences that, by the grace of God, life has provided. Ideally, my plans were to become a teacher though I could not envision the pathway. Along the way, doors opened that I had never imagined. Opportunities, for which I am very grateful, far exceeded my fondest expectations. Although the approbations along the way often seemed exaggerated, following my position at the University of Dubuque I never again applied for a job. Each position that I accepted, and a number of others that I declined, sought me. I was not aggressive. I sometimes wonder whether larger options would have opened had I been more enterprising. Overall, I found great meaning and fulfillment in my career in higher education and I never wavered from my general direction. Jan, while fashioning her very successful career in teaching, always gave me the fullest support and encouragement. In retirement years, she has a supplemental career as volunteer Suncoast Manor librarian that brings her accolades and personal satisfaction in abundance.

Dreams of becoming a teacher, in due course, became real, and much more. Professionally, I was never more fulfilled than when teaching in the classroom, especially with bright young minds that stretched the elasticity of mine. In the sacrosanct halls of learning my innermost being was bestirred. When I saw the gleam of understanding in a student's eyes my very soul was uplifted.

As I reflectively strode back to my office as dean or president, I pondered the fathomless satisfaction that I had just realized. I could not help but wonder whether I had abandoned my real self when I left the full-time classroom. Later, as I read a mind-stretching research paper written by a very promising student, I rejoiced, feeling that perhaps I had a small share in her achievement. In the handshake, as I relayed that eagerly awaited diploma to one of the honor students who had been in my class, I felt that special relationship which is reached only between student and teacher.

On the other hand, as the administrator whose work facilitates relationships between scores of professors and hundreds of students, one shapes the destiny of a whole institution. To be privileged to serve as teacher and administrator was to have performed two aspects of the same profession. In my ultimate youthful dreams I never remotely imagined that this could happen.

My principal goals in life continue to be to give love and devotion to my family, to earn the respect of those people with whom I associate, and to improve the conditions of humankind in my niche. After this life I aspire to become a partner with the Eternal Spirit. Jesus said, "In my father's house are many rooms; I go to prepare a place for you."

As I awaken to each new day, I begin my morning devotions: "Eternal God, Creator and Redeemer, may your love, grace, mercy and peace which were in Jesus the Christ be with Jan and me this day, and with each member of our family, sufficient unto the needs of each hour. I give thanks for life and health this new day."

Chapter 1 Leo on porch of family home 1921

A.C. Parochial School 1930-'31

Chapter 8 Leo in the 8th grade at A.C. Parochial School

Chapter 9 Grandparents David C. and Marianna Nussbaum 1925

Chapter 9 Samual, Menno, Philip, David C. Nussbaum 1936

Chapter 9 Leo at high school graduation 1936

Chapter 10 Mazelin family- standing: Martha, Jacob, Leona, David, Noah, Barbara, Benjamin, Margaret, John Seated: Daniel and Katherina circa 1926

Chapter 12 Uncle Dave in wheel chair with Leo 1962

Chapter 15 Dad with Leo at Ball State Father's Day 1942

Chapter 15 Mom with Leo at Ball State Mother's
Day 1942

Chapter 15 Dad, Alvin, Leo, Reuben, Elmer, Milo, Carl, Mom Chrismas
1941

Chapter 16 Wedding, November 25, 1942 Cousin
Gerhart, Maxine, Alvin's Wife, Janet, Leo

Chapter 19 Felicity, Luther, Margaret in Evanston Christmas 1951

Chapter 20 Janet's graduation, Margaret, Luther, Janet, Felicity
May 1955

Chapter 20 Margaret, Leo, Luther, Janet, Flelicity Christmas
1955

Chapter 21 Mahatma Gandhi Sculpture, Bangalore "Brewing Monsoon Storm"

Chapter 25 Janet, the teacher
1967